THEY DREW AS THEY PLEASED

The Hidden Art of Disney's Early Renaissance

THE 1970S AND 1980S

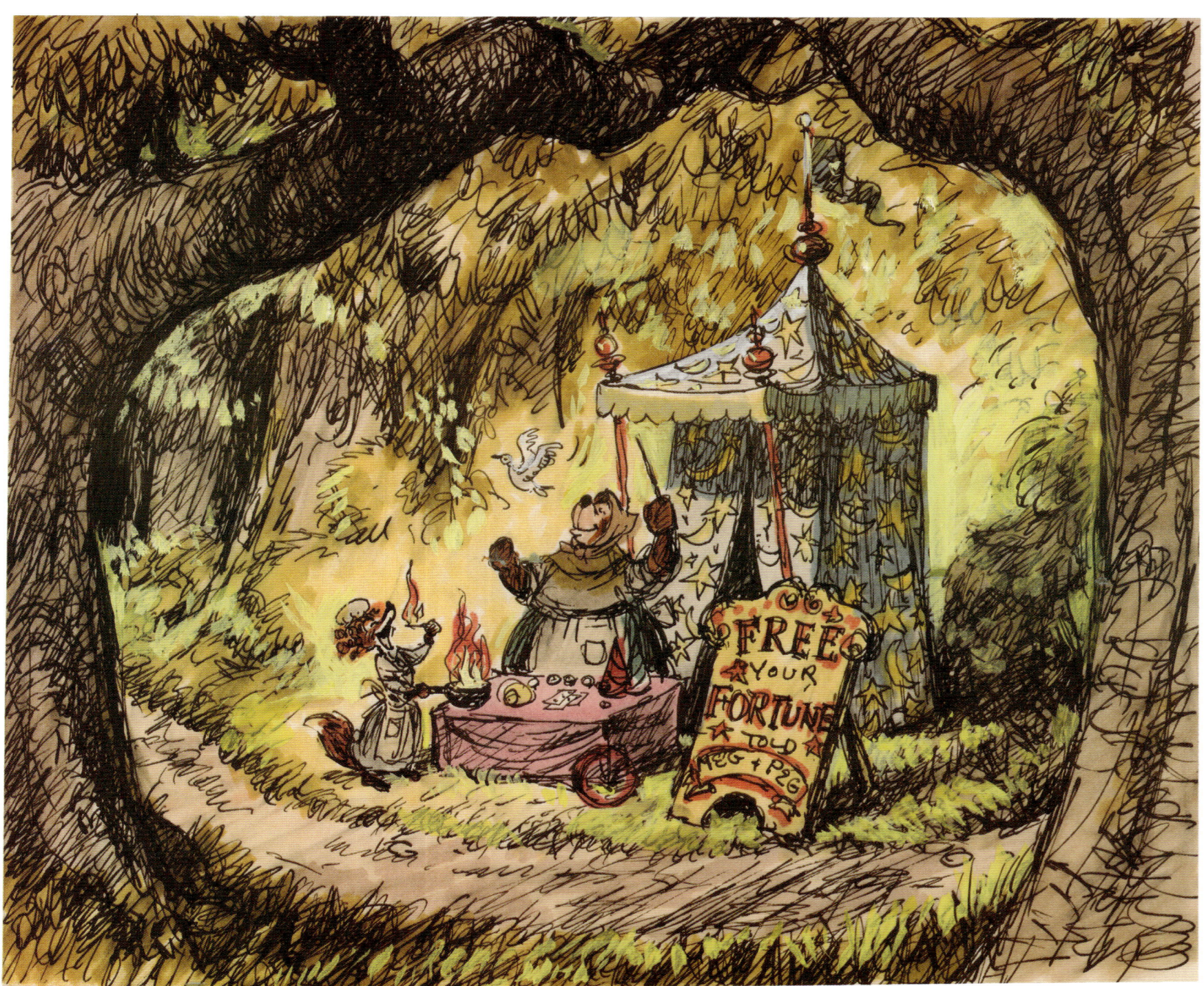

THEY DREW AS THEY PLEASED

The Hidden Art of Disney's Early Renaissance
THE 1970S AND 1980S

BY Didier Ghez
FOREWORD BY Don Hahn

CHRONICLE BOOKS
SAN FRANCISCO

Copyright © 2019 by Disney Enterprises, Inc.
All rights reserved. No part of this book may be reproduced in any form without written permission from the publisher.

Library of Congress Cataloging-in-Publication Data

Names: Ghez, Didier, author. | Hahn, Don, writer of foreword.
Title: The hidden art of Disney's early renaissance the 1970s and 1980s / by Didier Ghez ; foreword by Don Hahn.
Description: San Francisco : Chronicle Books, [2019] | Series: They drew as they pleased ; volume 5 | Includes bibliographical references and index.
Identifiers: LCCN 2018051217 | ISBN 9781452178707 (alk. paper)
Subjects: LCSH: Walt Disney Productions—History—20th century. | Animated films—United States—History and criticism. | Animators—United States—Biography.
Classification: LCC NC1766.U52 D54129 2019 | DDC 741.5/80922 [B]—dc23
LC record available at https://lccn.loc.gov/2018051217

Manufactured in China.

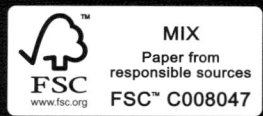

Written by Didier Ghez.
Design by Cat Grishaver.

10 9 8 7 6 5 4 3

Chronicle Books LLC
680 Second Street
San Francisco, California 94107
www.chroniclebooks.com

PAGE 2: Concept sketch for *Robin Hood* by Ken Anderson.

OPPOSITE: Character studies for Thumper in *Bambi* by Mel Shaw. Courtesy: Rick Shaw and Melissa Couch-Deranleau.

PAGE 6: Concept sketch for *The Aristocats* by Ken Anderson. Courtesy: Van Eaton Galleries.

All of the artwork featured in this volume comes from the Walt Disney Animation Research Library or the Walt Disney Archives, unless specified otherwise in the captions.

*To David R. Smith and Michael Barrier,
without whose pioneering preservation efforts no one today
would be able to write reliably about Disney history*

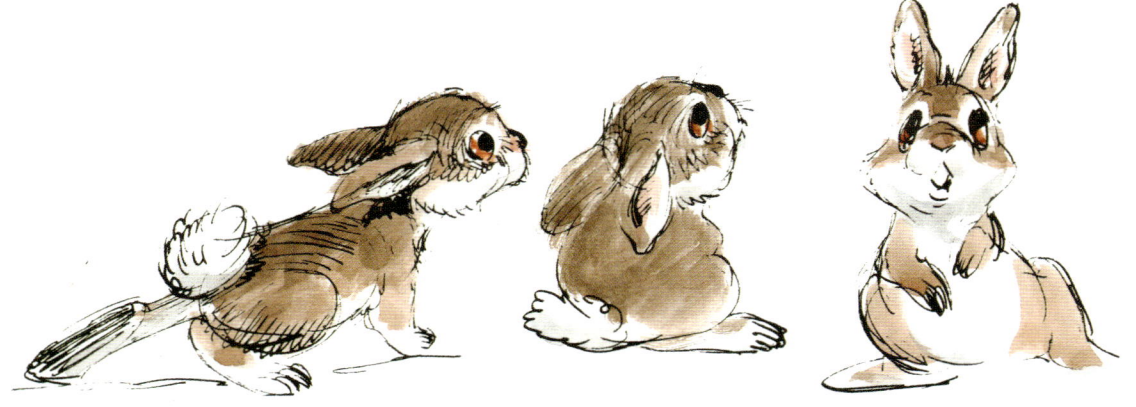

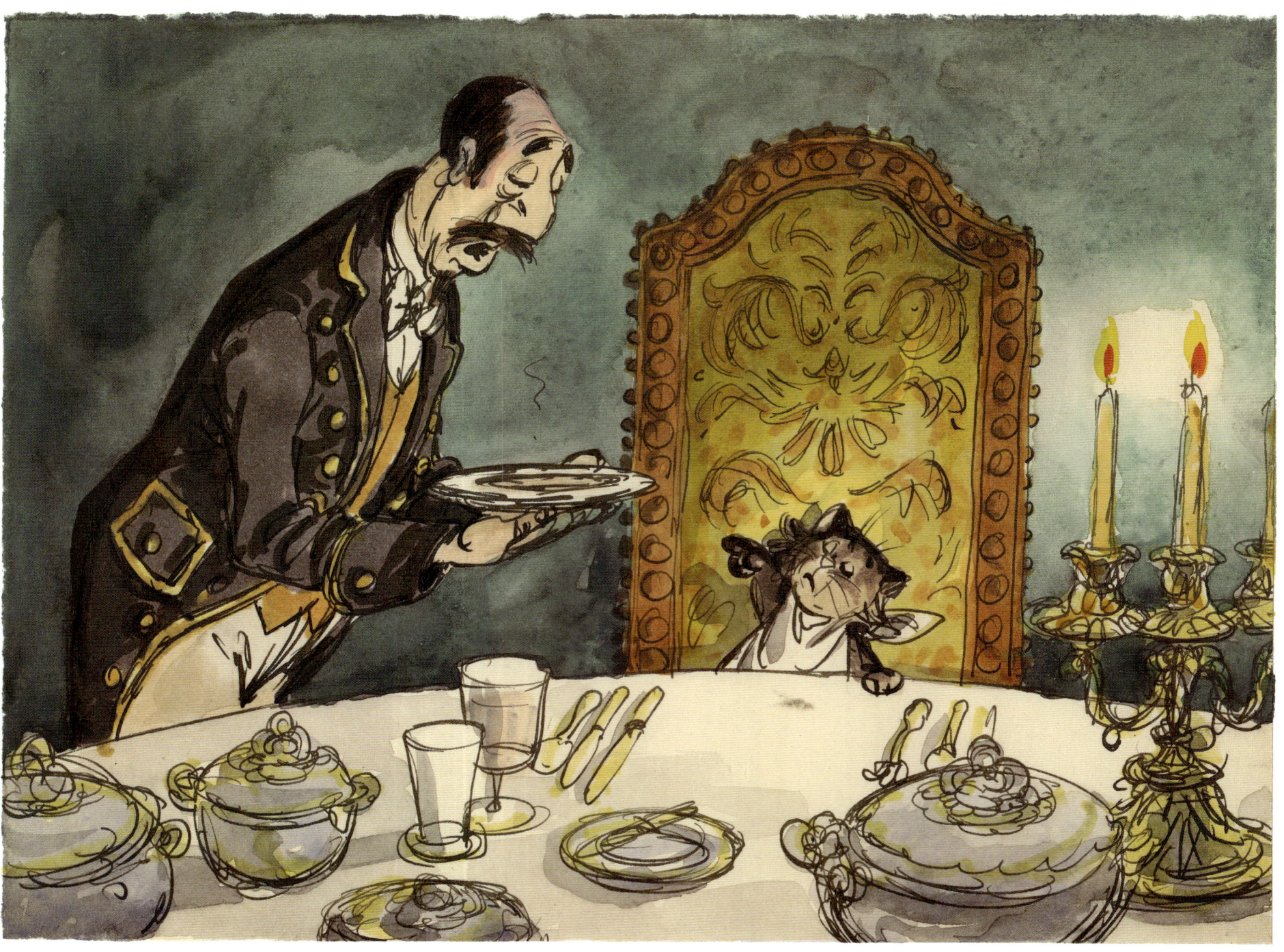

CONTENTS

Foreword by Don Hahn **8**

Preface **10**

After Walt **12**

1. *Ken Anderson* **22**

2. *Mel Shaw* **124**

Acknowledgments **201**

Notes **202**

Index **206**

FOREWORD

Great artists go through seasons in their creative lives, sometimes producing brilliant masterworks and other times languishing through hard times of growth and transition. The Disney animators once soared with films like Snow White and the Seven Dwarfs, Pinocchio, *and* Fantasia, *but by the 1970s the world had changed and these brilliant artists were struggling. Walt was gone, as were many of the artists who worked on the classics of his era. Back then, a new animated feature premiered once every four years and was met with a warm reception, and yet there was an unspoken understanding that the era of Walt Disney was over. The remaining artists realized that the art of animation would slip away if they didn't reach out to find fresh new ideas and the talent that would reinvigorate the art form.*

THE ANIMATION GROUP WAS LED BY producer/director Woolie Reitherman, who was passionate about keeping the team of veteran Disney animators together to keep the art form alive. There was plenty of reason for hope. Woolie, along with studio head and Walt's son-in-law Ron Miller, also knew they had to move confidently and quickly to find new talent, and even more importantly, to develop new film ideas that would attract and keep that talent. The two artists most often tasked with incubating new projects from blank canvases were Ken Anderson and Mel Shaw.

Ken began at Disney in the mid-1930s and soon distinguished himself as a jack of all trades. He was a master draftsman with a gift for creating characters in every shape and size with that magic component that was the hallmark of Disney animation: personality. Mel also started in the 1930s, but after a couple of years he left Disney, and after a stint in the Army he founded his own design firm. When Mel returned to Disney in the 1970s, Woolie leaned on him to generate visionary concept drawings and pastel chalk and watercolor works that would not only flesh out story ideas but

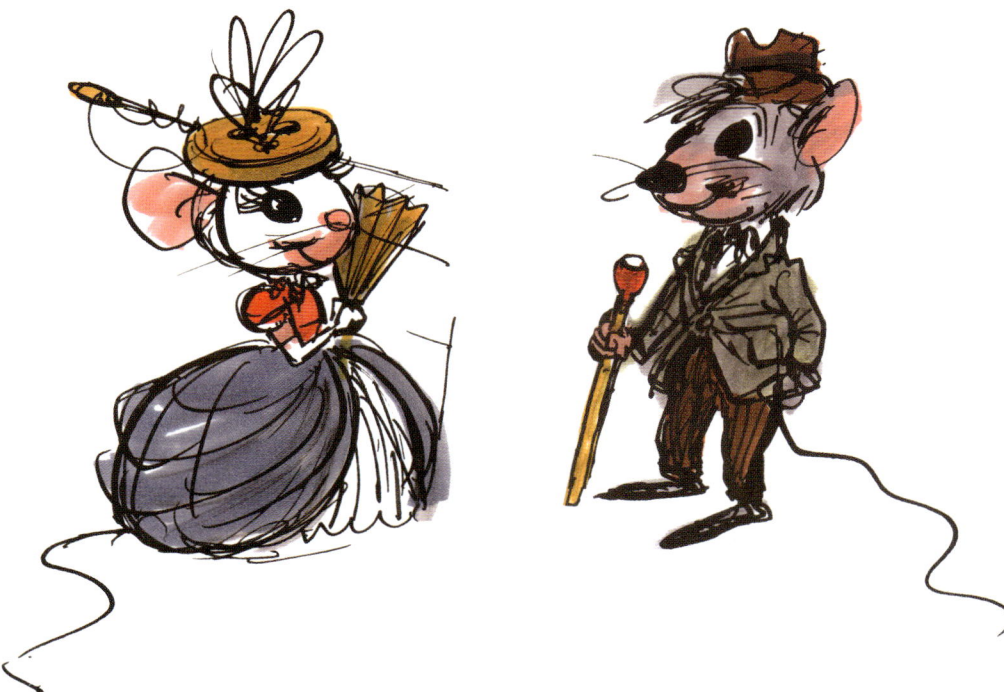

ABOVE: Character designs for Bianca and Bernard in *The Rescuers* by Ken Anderson. Courtesy: Wendy Greer.

also get the crew incredibly excited about a project. Mel was a one-stop shop. He would give you characters, setting, atmosphere, and mood all in one piece and create a vision for a new project years before the film would hit the silver screen.

These two men literally set the stage and designed the characters for every film during this crucial transition period that kept animation alive after Walt and led to a renaissance of the art form.

They were first and foremost storytellers. Both were brilliant draftsmen who could draw in clear, communicative ways, and who lived expansive lives of adventure and travel, with a joie de vivre that showed in their work. Both, along with Reitherman, saw the need to train and inspire new artists, and, by example, they taught a new generation of artists that includes present-day animation visionaries like Brad Bird, Henry Selick, John Musker, Ron Clements, Lisa Keene, and Tim Burton.

I was lucky enough to know and work with Woolie, Ken, Mel, and others like them who generously shared their time and talent with rookies like me. I learned so much about storytelling and the art of animation from them. More importantly, I learned from their ability to approach their work with fresh enthusiasm for ideas and the entertainment possibilities they held. Their attitudes about quality and storytelling were as important as the ideas they put on paper.

Historian Didier Ghez brings these artists back to life in the pages of this book by virtue of his passionate and exhaustive research into their body of work. As you enjoy this volume of *They Drew as They Pleased*, remember that these artists created work that has entertained generations and even changed popular culture, an accomplishment that only a handful of artists can claim. As you will see in their work, they were inspiring and dynamic personalities who reveled in bringing their creative ideas to life in a way that excited everyone from Walt Disney to their fellow artists, to audiences everywhere.

—**DON HAHN**
PRODUCER/DIRECTOR

PREFACE

The 1970s were a time of upheaval in the United States and an uneasy time for the artists at the Disney studio. Walt had passed away in 1966. No longer could they rely on him to lead the studio and shape its vision. They had to reinvent themselves, picture-by-picture, project-by-project, producing a rebirth of sorts. A renaissance.

I WAS BORN IN 1973, the year *Robin Hood* was released, and have always had a soft spot for the animated features of this decade, from *The Aristocats* (1970) to *The Rescuers* (1977). This might also explain why, thirty years ago, the first two Disney concept artists who caught my attention were Ken Anderson and Mel Shaw—men who largely defined the style of Disney's cartoons in the 1970s and early 1980s. When I discovered Ken Anderson's character designs for *Robin Hood* in the first edition of the book *The Art of Walt Disney* by Christopher Finch (Harry N. Abrams, 1973) I sensed that one of my life goals would be to see all the art that Ken had created for that movie. And when I first saw Mel Shaw's concept sketches for *The Black Cauldron*, my interest in the film, not yet released, immediately doubled.

In the mid-1990s, I started collecting artwork by Ken Anderson. In 2008, thanks to the generosity of Walt Disney's daughter, Diane Disney Miller, my wife, Rita, and I had the pleasure of having lunch at Diane's home with Mel Shaw, Mel's daughter-in-law, Andrea Gessell (daughter of Disney artist John Lounsbery), Diane's husband, Ron Miller, and Disney historian Don Peri. The lunch was followed by a visit to Mel's workshop. Needless to say I was on cloud nine. A few years later, I had the pleasure of helping Andrea Gessell edit Mel's autobiography, *Animator on Horseback* (Theme Park Press, 2016), for publication.*

By this point in my life, I have assembled five volumes in this series focused on Disney concept artists, as well as a number of other books. But for me, the research required to create

---

* It is worth noting, as I learned during the editing of the book, that Mel was dyslexic, which explains the small spelling mistakes you will encounter in some of his drawings reproduced in this book.

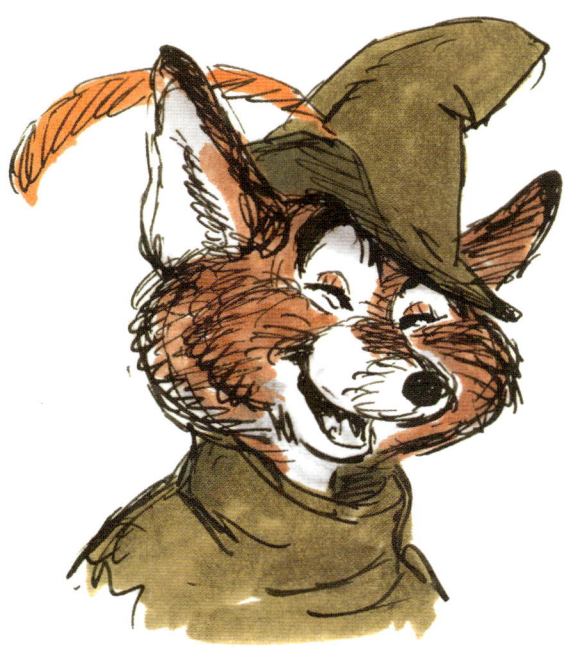

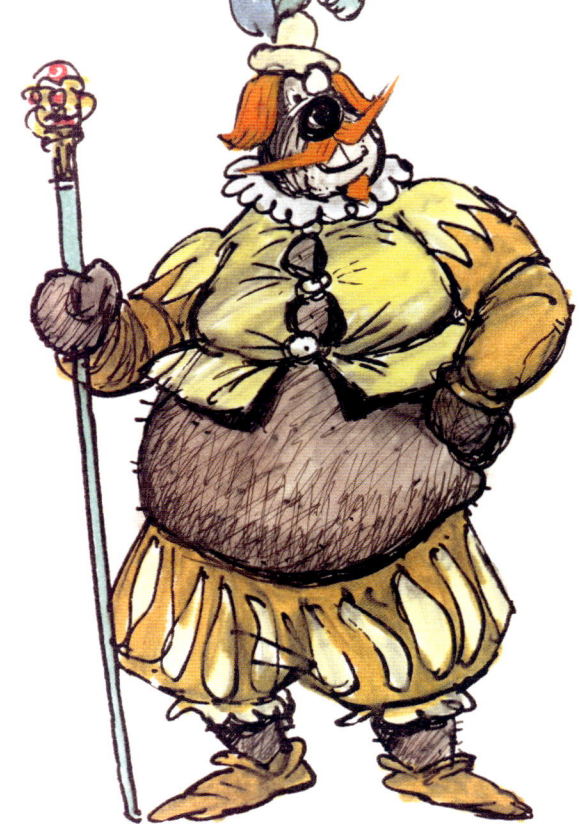

this volume was a highly personal and emotional journey. Most Disney history books tend to gloss over the animated features of the 1970s and early 1980s, as if nothing of significance happened between *The Jungle Book* (1967) and *The Little Mermaid* (1989). I was entering almost virgin territory, which was exciting. The story of those "lost decades of renaissance" was a story I had wanted to tell for years, one that is even richer than I anticipated.

Two years ago, when I opened the boxes of artwork that Ken Anderson created for *Robin Hood*, I was so overwhelmed by the experience that, unexpectedly, I started to cry. A thirty-year-old goal had been reached. The character designs in those boxes soared beyond my wildest expectations. I selected the most beautiful ones for this book. In the pages that follow, I hope you will share my enthusiasm.

ABOVE: Character designs for *Robin Hood* by Ken Anderson.

AFTER WALT

WALT DISNEY PASSED AWAY on December 15, 1966. For forty-three years he had been the visionary leader who guided the Disney studio through both good and trying times. For forty-three years all the stories within the Animation Department had been shaped, refined, and approved by him before moving to production. For forty-three years he was the ultimate guiding light, the final authority. His absence was felt dearly by all at the studio.

The Jungle Book was in the final phase of production and would be released ten months after his death. Work on subsequent animated features, however, had only just begun. For the first time, Walt's top animation artists had to chart their own path.

Former animator Wolfgang "Woolie" Reitherman, who had become a feature director in the late 1950s on *One Hundred and One Dalmatians*, became the de facto Animation Department leader. Animator Ollie Johnston recalled:

When Walt died, we got together and voted to leave things as they [were]. Woolie is the director, Don Griffith is the layout man, Larry Clemmons is story . . . and we'll make the decisions as best we can. Woolie said, "Golly, guys, I don't know whether I can do it." We said, "We'll help you." He said, "We're all going to be leaning against each other to stand up. Any one of us by ourselves would fall down. Let's try it and see if it works."[1]

Woolie Reitherman had been a skilled pilot during World War II and was a born leader. He knew when to listen and when to make decisions. He was also aware that the artists that he was now leading—Ken Anderson and Larry Clemmons in Story, Don Griffith in Layout, John Lounsbery, Eric Larson, Frank Thomas, Ollie Johnston, and Milt Kahl in Animation—were all at the top of their game. A few years after taking charge, Woolie explained:

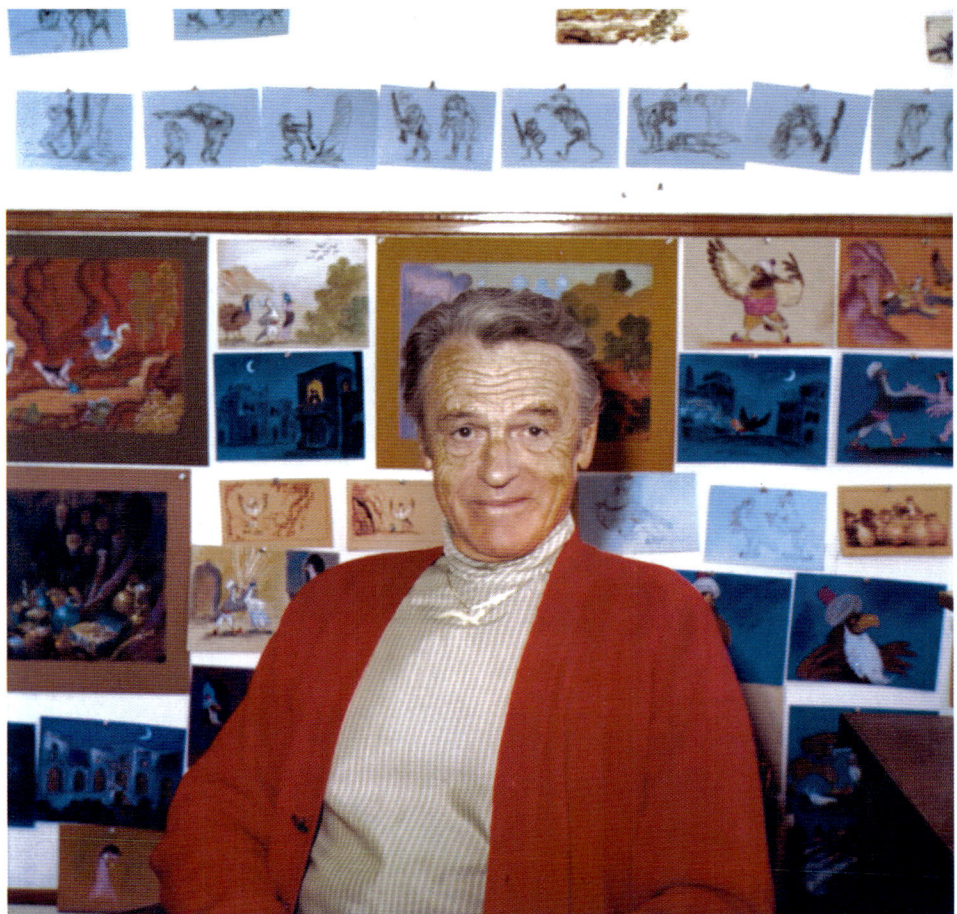

ABOVE: Director Woolie Reitherman. In the background are storyboards by Mel Shaw for the abandoned project *Musicana*. Courtesy: Bruce Reitherman.

Fortunately, the real giants of animation were willing to pull together. [To lead them] you had to respect and listen to everybody because we were equals. And [you had to] try and make decisions when they occurred without getting all involved. You can spend more money and more time vacillating than if you decide on one thing and do it as well as you can. And I think that approach was very, very fruitful... Also, I was darn lucky that I didn't stir conflict. I tried to cool it if I could... Then I always had little meetings, so that those animators who were the key to producing any picture were in on the decisions...[2]

The first challenge that Woolie faced was helping shape the animated feature that had been selected by Walt to follow *The Jungle Book*. *The Aristocats* had evolved from a live-action script, and by December 1966, it was nowhere near ready to move to production. Less than two weeks after Walt's death, on December 28, 1966, Reitherman was already involved in a story meeting to get things on track.[3] He plowed right in, as animator Frank Thomas remembered:

Woolie was doing the best he could... You know, it's a big job pulling off an animated feature film. God, the long hours he put in. Danny Alguire [Reitherman's assistant director] used to say, "Woolie can come back from flying around the world and stay there for ten hours and be ready for more, and the rest of us are all dead from an eight-hour day." Boundless energy. The one thing he held fast to was entertainment: You've got to have entertainment on the screen, you've got to have something new. Otherwise, he was willing to work with anybody and compromise. But there were an awful lot of areas he simply did not understand, which I think is true of any of us... Over those first three pictures [*The Aristocats*, *Robin Hood*, and *The Rescuers*], he grew tremendously, in stature and [in] handling people and his ideas, his judgment.[4]

THE TALENT DEVELOPMENT PROGRAM

Even with a new leader, the Animation Department was facing some daunting challenges. In the 1950s, when the studio was producing *Sleeping Beauty*, Walt Disney began to feel constrained by the rising costs of animation. By the late 1960s, things had only gotten worse, and Woolie had to find ways to address this pressing issue. In addition, the core group of artists on which he was relying was no longer young: even the youngest of Disney's "Nine Old Men" was now over fifty-five years old. It was high time to start thinking about bringing in "new blood" to pass on the mantle.

On September 9, 1970, just a few months before the release of *The Aristocats*, Woolie drafted a document titled *Ideas and Thoughts Concerning the Future of Animation in the Disney Tradition*, which tried to offer solutions to those pressing concerns.

To solve the issue of rising costs while training a new generation of artists, he recommended aiming for great characters instead of great technical achievements:

> We need to set our goals on what we can pass on to the younger generation without trying to squeeze them into our mold . . . I think we can pass on the Disney process of creativity and evolution, but maybe with much less emphasis on our expensive and extremely well-analyzed animation. By de-emphasizing this kind of animation somewhat and fortifying the new approach with stronger personality, showmanship, and story, perhaps there is a way to go which we have always thought was impossible. I know that Walt was looking for something like this for years—an easier way.[5]

To build those stories and to design those strong characters, throughout the 1970s Woolie relied chiefly on two "old timers": Ken Anderson and Mel Shaw. To lead the animation team, at least for a little while, he knew he could rely on Frank Thomas, Ollie Johnston, Milt Kahl, Eric Larson, and John Lounsbery. But from where would the *new* artists come?

> The heart of the problem is to find real talent, basically in story and animation, and put together some kind of a plan, and to provide for this talent an exciting climate in which they can develop—[with] the excitement and discovery of the old days, when our form of animation was developed . . . It seems to me that the first step, without any fanfare, should be a search for talent. Good talent. Not craftsmanship, but talent.[6]

A month later, on October 23, Woolie submitted a final version of his plan for the future of Disney animation to Disney's executive vice president Card Walker, and to producers Bill Anderson and Ron Miller (Walt Disney's son-in-law). They liked what Woolie suggested, and three days later art director and character designer Ken Anderson was able to start a training program in the Story Department. Ken mentored three young artists: Bob Foster, Allan Gonzales, and Pete Young, who were asked to develop storyboards based on the short story *The Pelican That Hated to Dive* by author Don Tracy.[7]

By December 1970, Disney's Talent Development Program was truly under way and encompassed animation and background art in addition to story.[8]

Some of the artists who were enrolled in the program in its early years had been at the Disney Studios for some time, like Burny Mattinson, Fred Hellmich, and Dave Michener. Some were new recruits, like Dale Baer, Don Bluth, and Gary Goldman.[9] And with *Robin Hood* in full production, there was ample opportunity for the aspiring animators and story men to show their mettle.

OPPOSITE LEFT: Story sketches for *The Aristocats* by Ken Anderson. Collection of the author.

OPPOSITE RIGHT: Courtesy: Andreas Deja

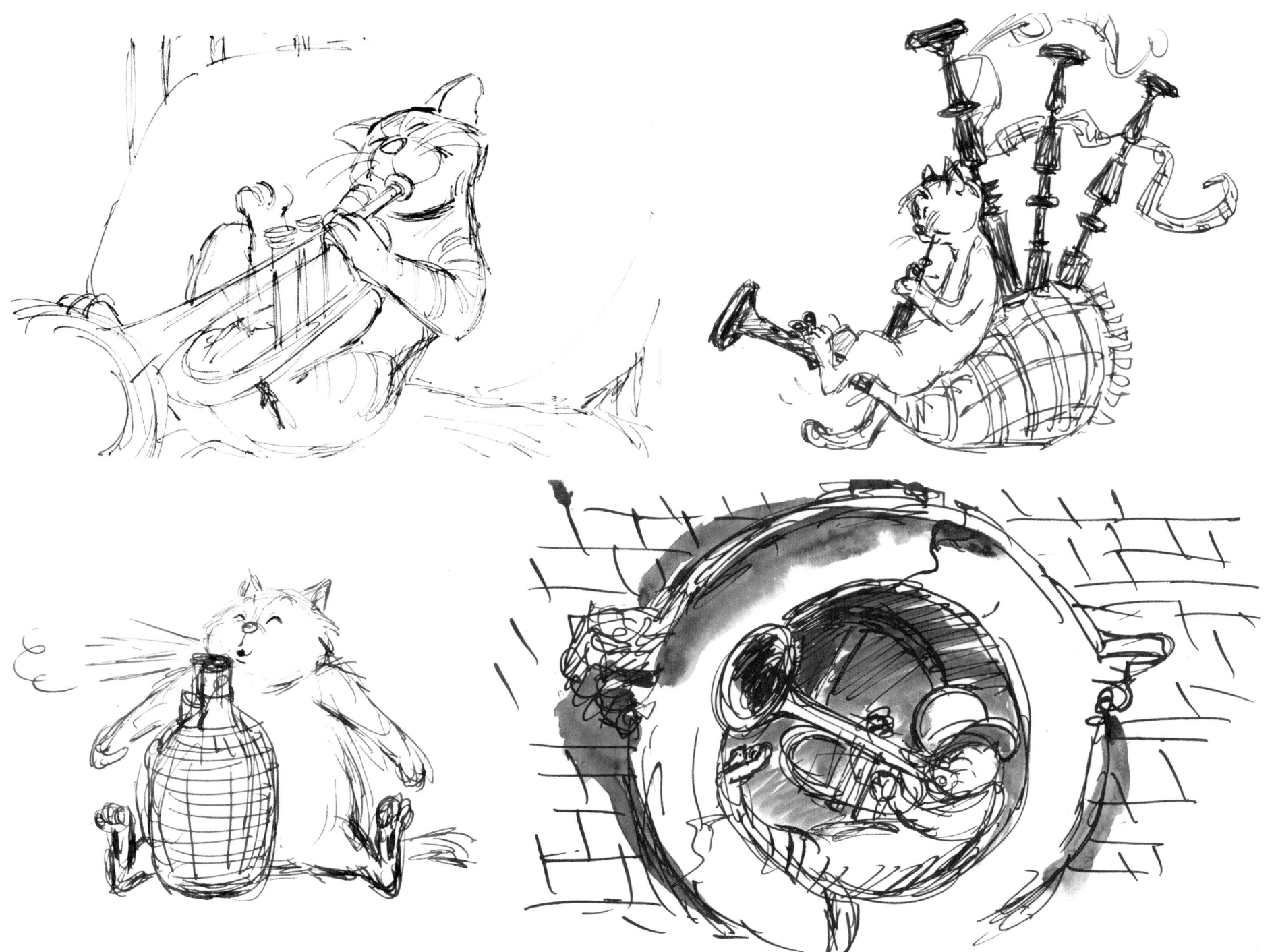

AFTER WALT

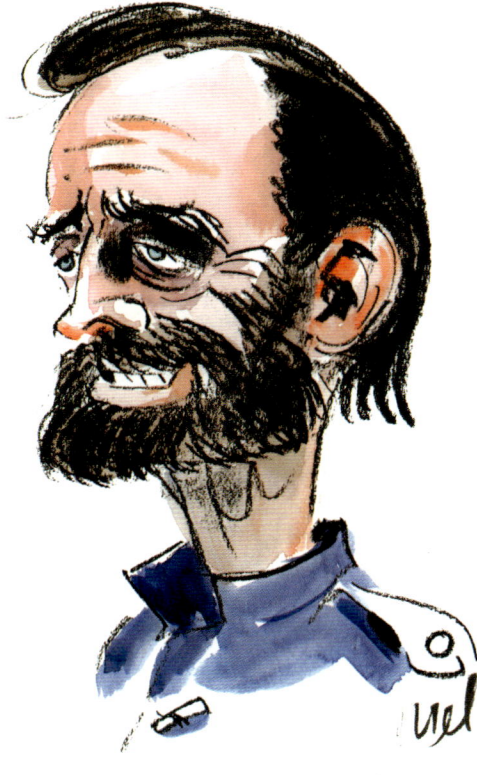

ABOVE: Caricature of Ken Anderson by Mel Shaw. Courtesy: Rick Shaw and Melissa Couch-Deranleau.

THE CHARACTER ANIMATION PROGRAM

By 1973, the studio started to realize that it would take too much time for the Talent Development Program to help train an adequate number of new animators to replace Disney's veterans by the end of the decade. Another system was needed in parallel to speed things up. Disney decided to look in the direction of California Institute of the Arts (CalArts) for help.

In 1962, Walt Disney had helped establish and finance CalArts through the merger of Chouinard Art Institute and the Los Angeles Conservatory of Music. But when the new school opened its doors in 1970, four years after Walt's death, the only type of animation it taught was experimental animation—under the tutelage of animator Jules Engel—not traditional character animation of the Disney mold.

On July 10, 1974, Disney artists Ken Anderson, Marc Davis, and Eric Larson discussed the establishment of a Character Animation Program with Mel Powell, chairman of the Curriculum Committee at CalArts, and with Alexander "Sandy" Mackendrick, dean of the Film School.[10] Two weeks later, on July 29, Ken Anderson called his former colleague, Art Babbitt, to ask him if he would be interested in heading up the program.[11] Babbitt seemed cautiously interested. However, he had been at the epicenter of the 1941 Disney strike and was therefore a controversial choice. In November, the studio dropped the Babbitt option and approached Disney veteran Jack Hannah, who reacted with enthusiasm to the offer, as he explained a few years later:

> I got a surprise call from out of the blue asking if I would be interested in heading a school of animation at the California Institute of the Arts. It was Ken Anderson. I asked him why they were calling me and he said, "It's because you are a fighter!" . . . At first, I was speechless, but I finally agreed to come to the studio and have several meetings with some of the old timers who had some ideas about developing a character-animation program . . . The more I talked with people at the studio, the more the idea sounded inviting, so I accepted.[12]

There was still one key hurdle, however—convincing members of the CalArts faculty who looked down on character animation. Robert Fitzpatrick, who served as president of CalArts, remembered:

I was hired in 1974 and I took the job at the beginning of January 1975. There had been talks, always, on the part of the studio about [building] a strong animation program. But the faculty at CalArts did not want character animation. They wanted the Jules Engel program that was the more avant-garde, abstract animation. It was a perfectly valid type of animation, but it did nothing to help the studio get the kind of animators that they needed to be successful . . . And so within weeks of my being there, I had detailed conversations with [members of the Disney family and Disney's senior management] and it became very clear that if CalArts did not have a character animation program the Disney company was going to go elsewhere, probably to one of the other art schools like Art Center in Pasadena . . . So I told the faculty . . . "If we don't have a character animation program, we are committing hara-kiri. I want to start a character animation program." It was a tough thing to do, because the character animation students came like boy scouts into an art institution that was bohemian.[13]

The new Character Animation Program debuted in September 1975. Among the students who were selected to attend its first year were Nancy Beiman, Brad Bird, John Lasseter, John Musker, Jerry Rees, and Darrell Van Citters, all of whom would soon join Disney, and all of whom would later become luminaries in the animation field.

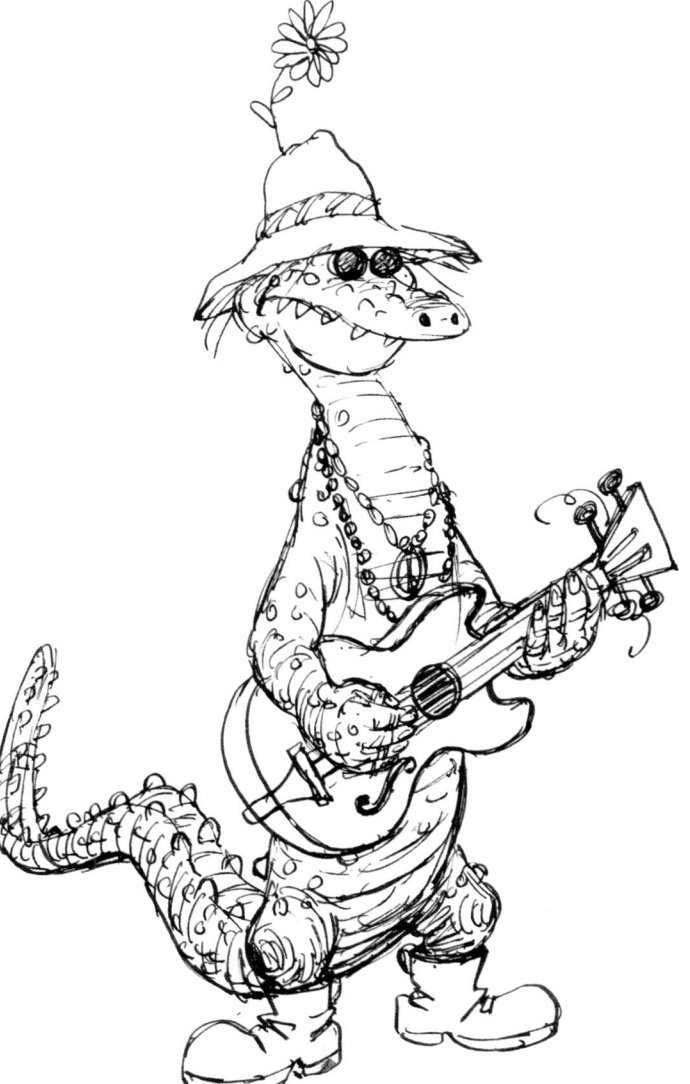

ABOVE: This character sketch created by Ken Anderson in 1970 for the *Wonderful World of Disney* magazine captures some of the spirit of the opening decade.

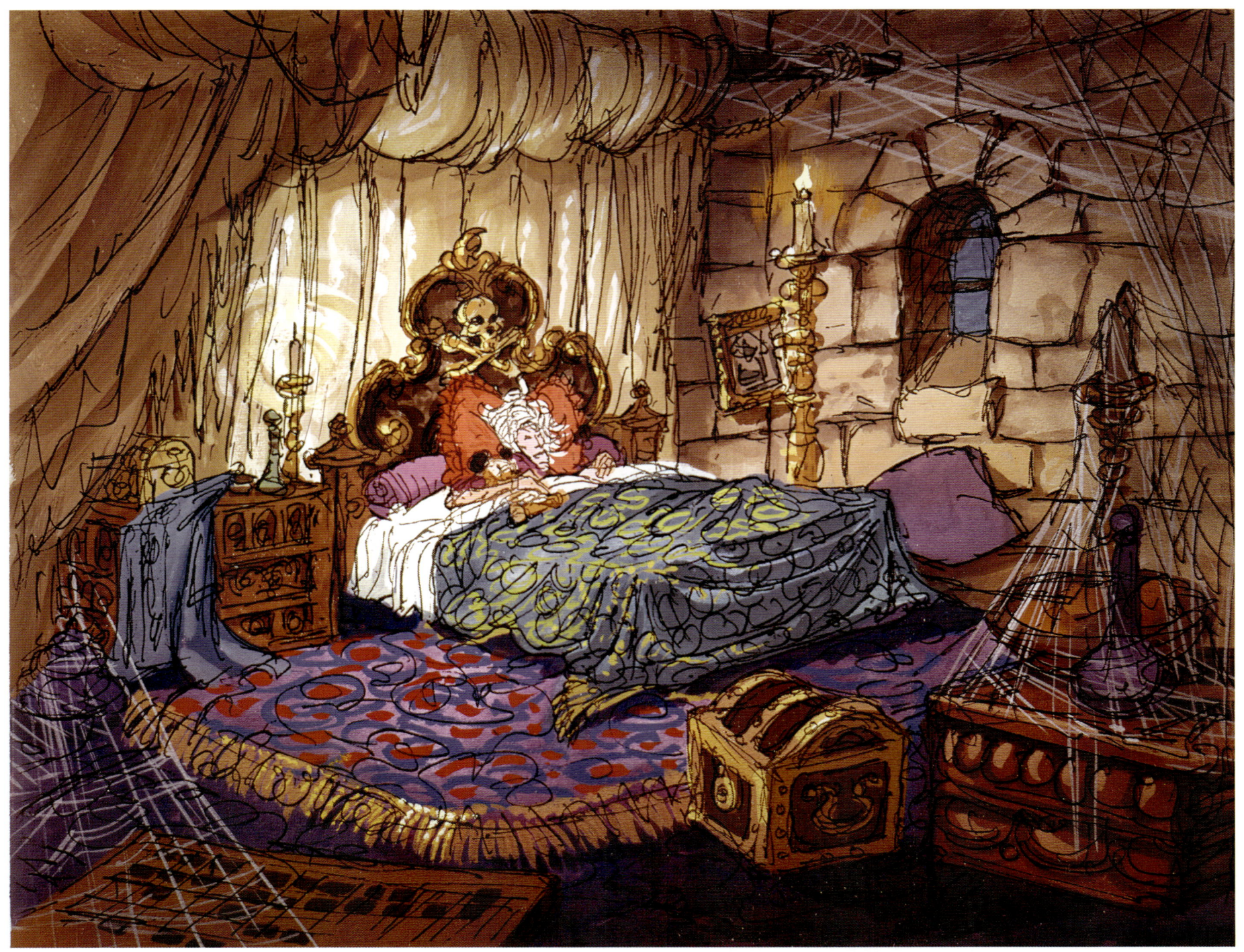

THE REBELLION

Back at the studio, production had begun on *The Rescuers*, and some of the new artists were feeling more and more restless. Woolie Reitherman had understood early that controlling costs was critically important if animation was to survive. On all the movies he directed in the 1960s and 1970s, he therefore shifted the emphasis from technological perfection to great characters. This was anathema to many, especially to the studio's rising star Don Bluth. His friend Gary Goldman explained:

> [In 1977] Don was directing the animation of Elliott the dragon in *Pete's Dragon*, adding some of the old techniques to enhance the animation with more special effects, contact, and cast shadows under the characters, color changes when the character went from full sun to the shade of the trees, and adding reflections of the characters in the river. Details that we felt were abandoned during the '60s . . . We were afraid that the loss of the details of . . . special effects animation . . . used in the early films would eventually begin to lose audience attendance.[14]

In other words, by 1977, after a period of personal dissatisfaction at Disney, where CalArts-educated animators were sometimes at odds with their artistic styles and sensibilities, Don Bluth, Gary Goldman, and their colleagues wanted change.

Gary Goldman recalled:

> In early 1979, I got a call directly into my office. It was Jim Stewart, an ex-executive vice president [at Disney] . . . Jim had left Disney with two other executives to found Aurora Productions to produce live-action films. He told me that he had heard that Don, John [Pomeroy], and I were unhappy at Disney . . . He then asked, "If we could raise the money for a feature film, would you guys form a corporation and leave Disney to produce your own movies?" . . . I immediately went to Don's office and brought John in to tell them about the call. Both of them said, "Yes! Call him back." I made the call and let him know that we would agree that if he could raise the financing for a feature-length film we would leave. Jim asked, "Do you guys have a story you want to make for the first film?" I said yes. It's a book recommended to us by Ken Anderson [the 1972 Newbery Award–winning children's novel, *Mrs. Frisby and the Rats of NIMH*].[15]

OPPOSITE: Concept sketch for *The Rescuers* by Ken Anderson.

TOP: Eric Larson in 1978 teaching some of the new artists from the Talent Development Program. In the foreground Bill Kroyer, and from left to right: Heidi Guedel, Lorna Pomeroy Cook, Eric Larson, Dan Haskett, Emily Juliano, Henry Selick, and Myrt Canfield behind Henry Selick.

BOTTOM: Don Bluth (right) and, from left to right, Gary Goldman, Glen Keane, Andy Gaskill, Ron Clements, Randy Cartwright, Ed Gombert, and John Pomeroy working on *The Black Cauldron* in 1978. The storyboards that surround them were created by Mel Shaw.

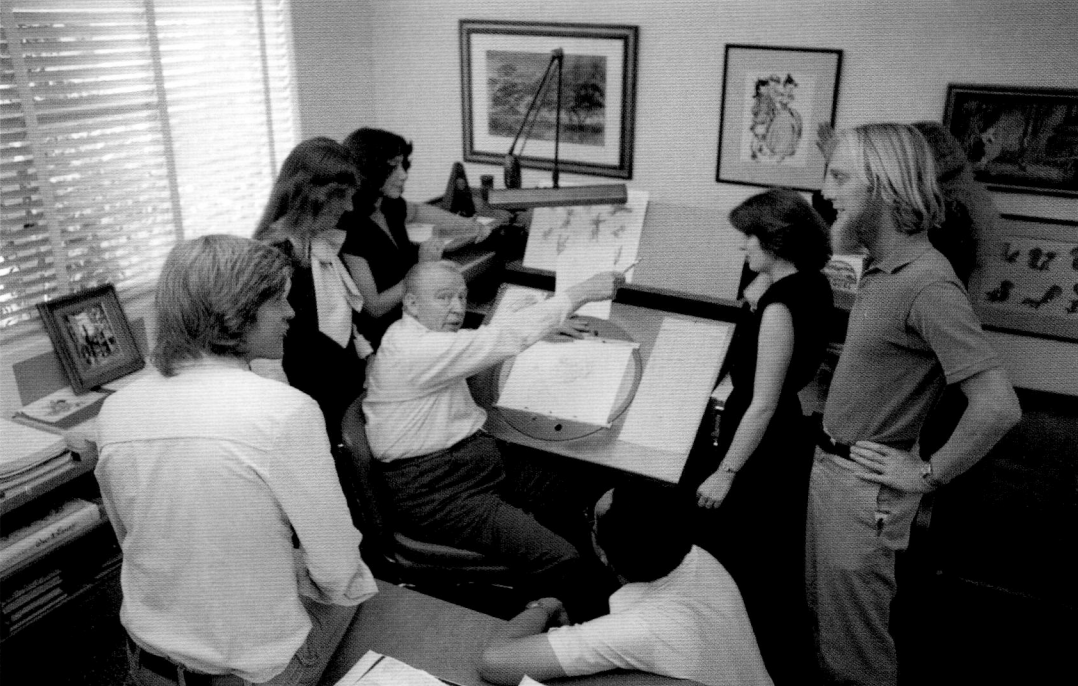

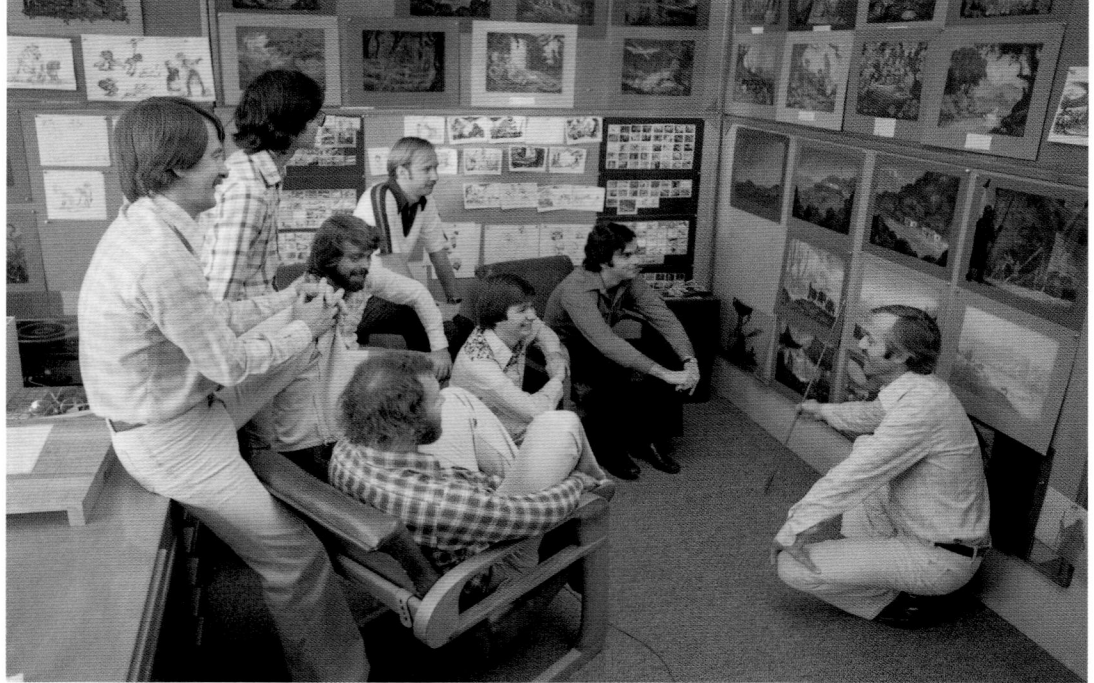

On September 13, 1979—Don Bluth's birthday—with the studio focusing all its productions efforts on *The Fox and the Hound* for a Christmas 1980 release, Gary, John, and Don resigned. The next day, eight more artists followed.[16]

Studio executives were shocked, and the launch of *The Fox and the Hound* was delayed by six months—to the summer of 1981.[17] But the exodus cleared the air: the conflict between the followers of Don Bluth and the alumni from CalArts that had plagued the studio for months was finally a thing of the past.

Frank Thomas and Ollie Johnston retired in January 1978, and in 1981, the year of *The Fox and the Hound*'s release, Woolie Reitherman, the last of Disney's Nine Old Men, did too. A new generation of Disney artists, trained by Disney's "masters," was now in charge. And when a new management team led by Michael Eisner, Frank Wells, and Jeffrey Katzenberg took over the leadership of The Walt Disney Studios in 1984, they were ready to shine. The releases of the late 1980s marked the beginning of Disney's New Golden Age. The age of renewal, initiated by Woolie Reitherman, had come to its logical and successful conclusion.

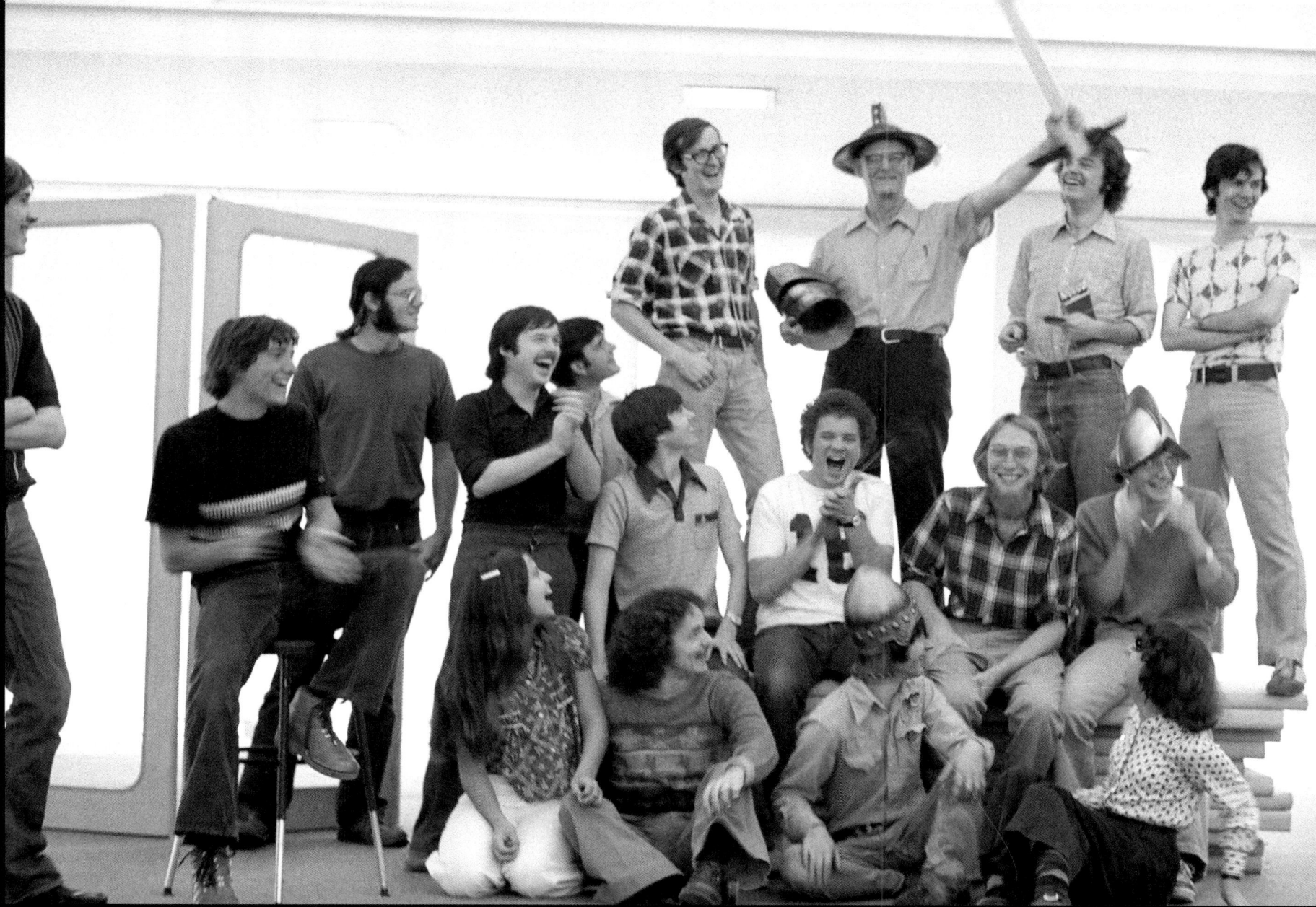

ABOVE: Some of the students from the Character Animation Program at CalArts in 1976, attending a class taught by Disney Legend Ken O'Connor. From left to right, standing: John Musker, Ken O'Connor, Harry Sabin, and Doug Lefler; next row: Mike Cedeno, Tim Barker, Brad Bird, Brett Thompson, Darrell Van Citters, Joe Lanzisero, Henry Selick, and John Lasseter; on the floor: Terry Rees, Jerry Rees, Bruce Morris, and Nancy Beiman. Photograph by Harry Sabin.

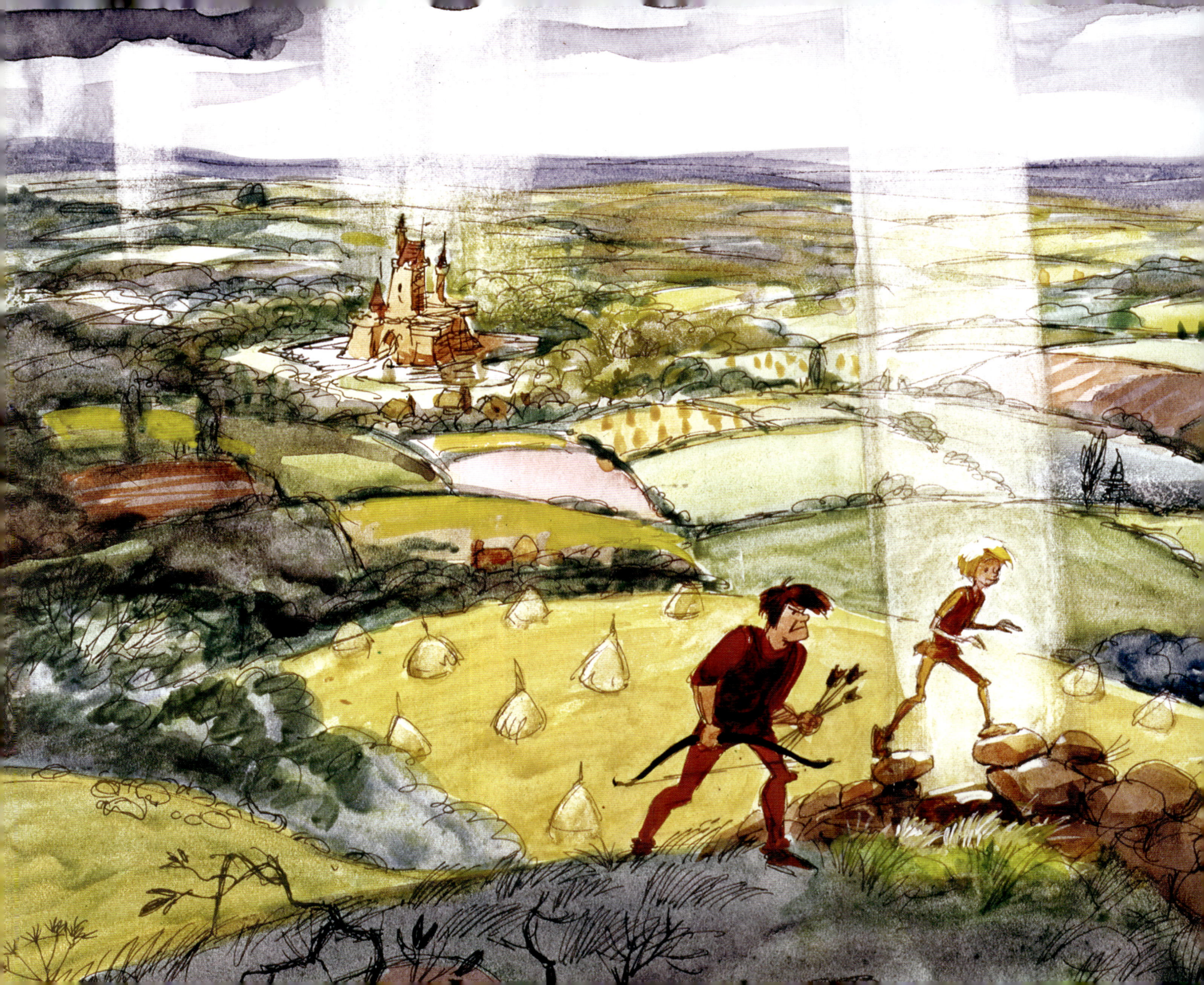

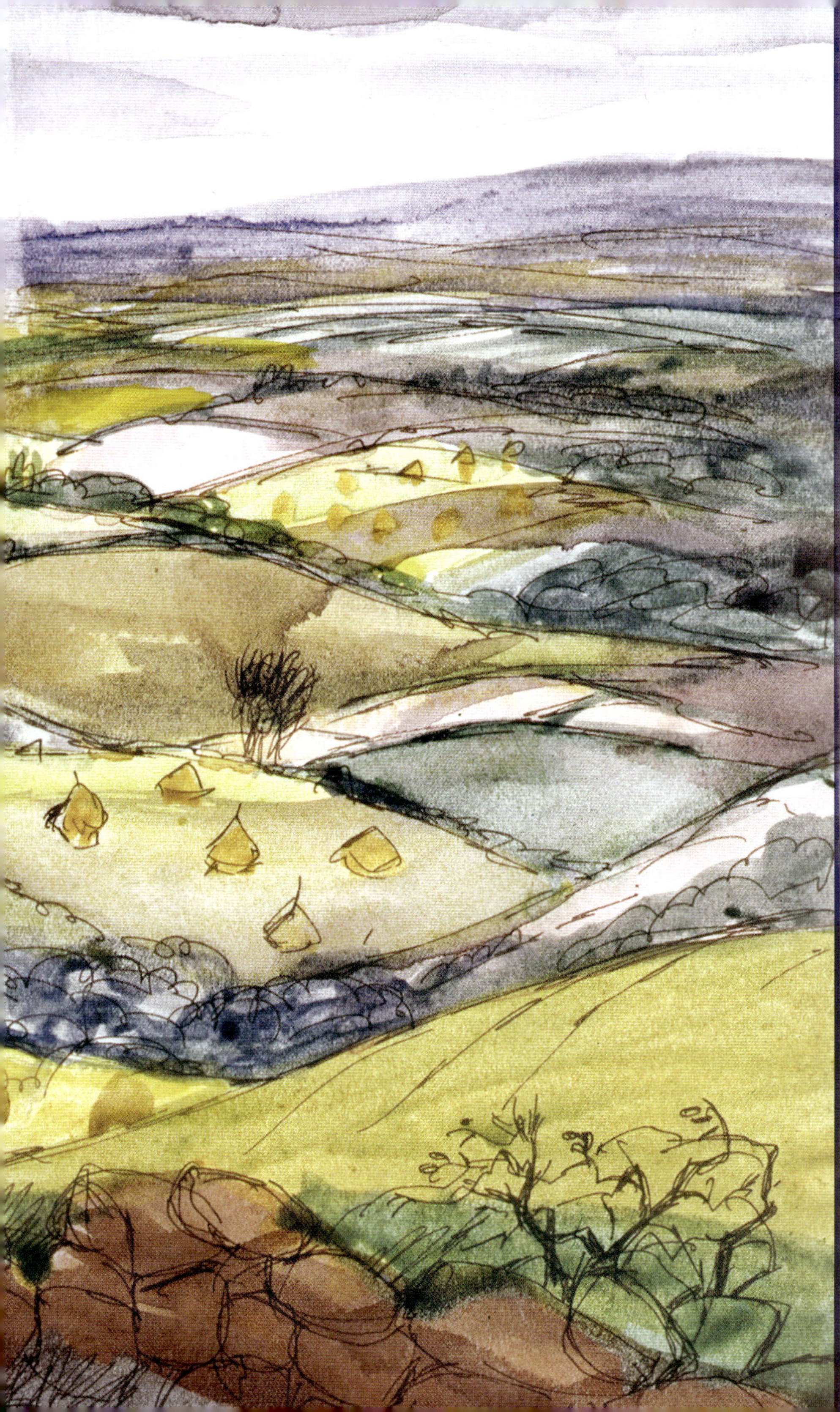

1
KEN ANDERSON

"Ken Anderson was a fantastic artist who had the ability in one drawing to suggest a whole sequence for a picture."
—STORY ARTIST VANCE GERRY

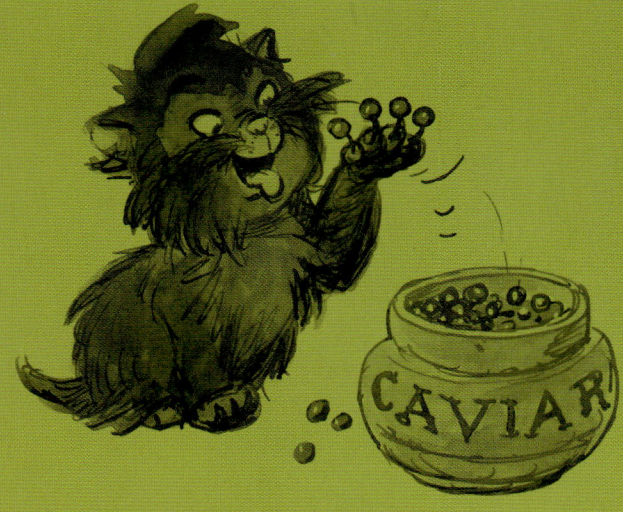

In December 1958, a few weeks before the release of *Sleeping Beauty*, Walt Disney was invited to attend a gathering of the Bohemian Club, one of the most prestigious private clubs in the world. Writer Jack London had once been a member, as had former presidents Theodore Roosevelt and Herbert Hoover. To entertain his guests with drawings and stories of studio life, Walt brought with him Ken Anderson, a blue-eyed artist who had joined the Disney studio in 1934. The audience was curious to understand what Ken's exact role was at the studio. Anderson remembered that day a few decades later:

> Walt had to introduce me to everybody, because I was making drawings for them of *Sleeping Beauty*. Whatever they asked for, I'd do . . . [Walt] said, "This is Ken Anderson who's my jack of all trades. He does everything. He's a jack of *all* trades. He's a very unusual man."[18]

This was no overstatement on Walt's part. Many of the Disney artists were versatile. Ken was a true one-man-band. During his forty-plus-year career at the studio, Ken Anderson worked on animation, layout, background, model making, art direction, story, imagineering, and character design. And he loved every moment of it. In the late 1960s and 1970s, from *The Jungle Book* to *The Rescuers*, Ken became the Animation Department's chief character designer and idea man. His colleague in the Story Department, Vance Gerry, explained:

> Ken Anderson was a fantastic artist who had the ability in one drawing to suggest a whole sequence for a picture, by not only making it a drawing that was tremendously appealing, but it would have an idea or a piece of humor that would make you want to expand the story. And that's what he did so well for us, getting the story started by leading the way with these sort of "setups," they were called, or "atmosphere drawings." Usually on every picture, he would start out by making these setups of the characters and then situations that were suggested either by an outline or by the book we were taking it from, or by something in Ken's head. There might be fifteen or twenty of them, and then we'd get together and talk about the story and what was going to happen and these things that he would suggest ideas for.[19]

Ken's childhood was not an easy one, according to an unpublished biography written by his daughters in the 1980s:

> Kenneth Bliss Anderson was born in Seattle on March 17, 1909 . . . [His] mother, Ethel Way, descended from a long line of Sains and Bains, who can be traced back to Sarah Bain, wife of John Quincy Adams, sixth president of the United States. [Ken's father, Luther,] after a rather peripatetic career as a lumber merchant, which took him and his family to such distant places as the Philippines, died when his son Ken was only seven years old and his daughter Ruth was five. A younger daughter, Ken's sister Roberta, then three, also died about the same time.
>
> These were terribly hard times for Ethel . . . Indeed, she had to place her children in others' homes so she could learn an occupation that would allow her to support her family alone. Ken was sent to live with an uncle, whose utter lack of understanding for little boys made him terribly brutal. Several times Ken ran away from his uncle's wrath, building himself a shelter in the woods, and surviving on wild roots and berries. As soon as Ethel finished her training as a schoolteacher [and] found a teaching job in Seattle . . . she brought her children back to live with her, thus putting a blessed end to this very traumatic period in our father's life.[20]

PAGE 23: Character study for *The Aristocats*.

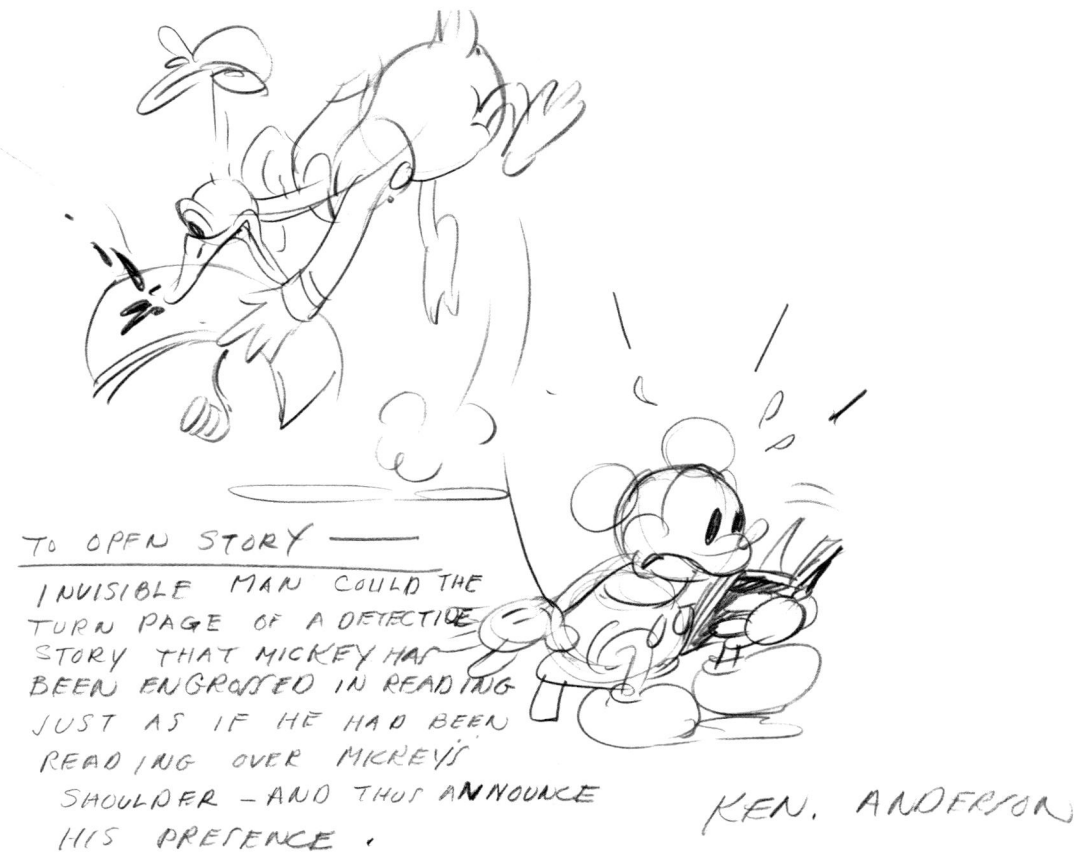

ABOVE: Gag drawing for the abandoned short *The Invisible Man*.

THE ARCHITECT

As a young man, Ken studied architecture at the University of Washington in Seattle, and then won a scholarship that allowed him to attend the École des Beaux-Arts in Fontainebleau (France) and the American Academy of Rome (Italy). When he returned to the United States in 1934, the country was in the midst of the Great Depression. He recalled many years later:

> I was an architect. There wasn't any architecture [jobs at the time]. None. One architect who was busy offered me a job if I paid him thirty-five dollars a month. I had to pay him to work for him, but he was the only one in town that seemed to have any business at all. I did work briefly at MGM . . . as an architectural set designer on films like *The Painted Veil* with Greta Garbo. They ran out of work. They were going to close up for two or three months and told me they'd like me to stay by the phone, but they never called. When I worked at MGM, I was making good money so I didn't need any extra work. When I lost that work, I had nothing else.
>
> At this time, I got married. [My wife Polly] came down from Seattle and had this beautiful car. I loved her car. We practically lived out of it. We lived on the beach, eating canned beans and such things. I was so happy. One time we drove by the Disney studio and she said, "Hey, go in there and get a job!" I replied, "I don't know how to cartoon. I'm an architect. I can draw buildings and people but not cartoons." My wife said, "Yes, you can," and that was the end of that discussion.[21]

Armed with the huge paintings that he had done in Europe, which amazed everyone (Walt Disney included), Ken managed to be accepted in a two-week tryout in the Inbetween Department:

> [The head of the department] George [Drake] escorted me into a tryout room . . . It was a big room, with about thirty or forty guys in it . . . At the end of each day, there would have been one or two guys called by George Drake to come up to him . . . I was surrounded by very well-known illustrators and commercial artists, men whom [I] loved, like John La Gatta, who was a great name in the illustrative world. One by one they were let go. [He] said, "No, we don't need you," and none of these guys were taken. We came down to where I was the last guy sitting there and it was Saturday and Saturday was going to be the last day of work and I was called. "Anderson!" I went stomping up there scared to death . . . and he said, "I think you'll do." Nothing could have been a greater thing to hear than that. It didn't matter what the pay was. The main thing was that I got a job.[22]

The following Monday, September 3, 1934, Ken Anderson officially became an inbetweener at the Disney studio. Some of the first projects he remembered handling include the shorts *The Goddess of Spring*, *Three Little Wolves*, and *Mickey's Polo Team*.[23] Ken may have been glad to get a job, but inbetweening was a thankless task. To make things worse, the boss of the Inbetweening Department, George Drake, had come up with a point system, with 10 marking the highest level of difficulty. This highly subjective system was far from flawless.

There would be five of us in a row. There were five desks and then five more desks . . . I would pick up a scene of animation from George Drake and it would be listed as a certain difficulty. There was a certain number which would mean that it was a 4 [or] a 3, which is how difficult George had assumed it would be . . . He was never too generous with the points.

On *Mickey's Polo Team*, we had a scene that was just a killer because the animator didn't know how to draw. He didn't know how to animate, make circles and things that move. Here we had these characters to draw—horses with horse faces and caricatures of people that were riding. Each character in the picture was a caricature of somebody big in the movies and they had to look like these people. We weren't getting any credit for that at all. I think we got a 6 on the difficulty of the thing and it was at least a 10 or 11. There were five of us in this cabal and we had this one big, thick scene. Jeez, it must have been four hundred pages or so . . . It was a backbreaker.[24]

Thankfully, Ken's talent was soon recognized. Along with his colleagues Milt Kahl, Frank Thomas, Ollie Johnston, and Jack Hannah, he moved into another room. They were now junior animators.[25]

Walt had a knack for using all of his artists' talents. In 1935, he decided to put Ken's architectural schooling to use on the Silly Symphony cartoon *Three Orphan Kittens*.

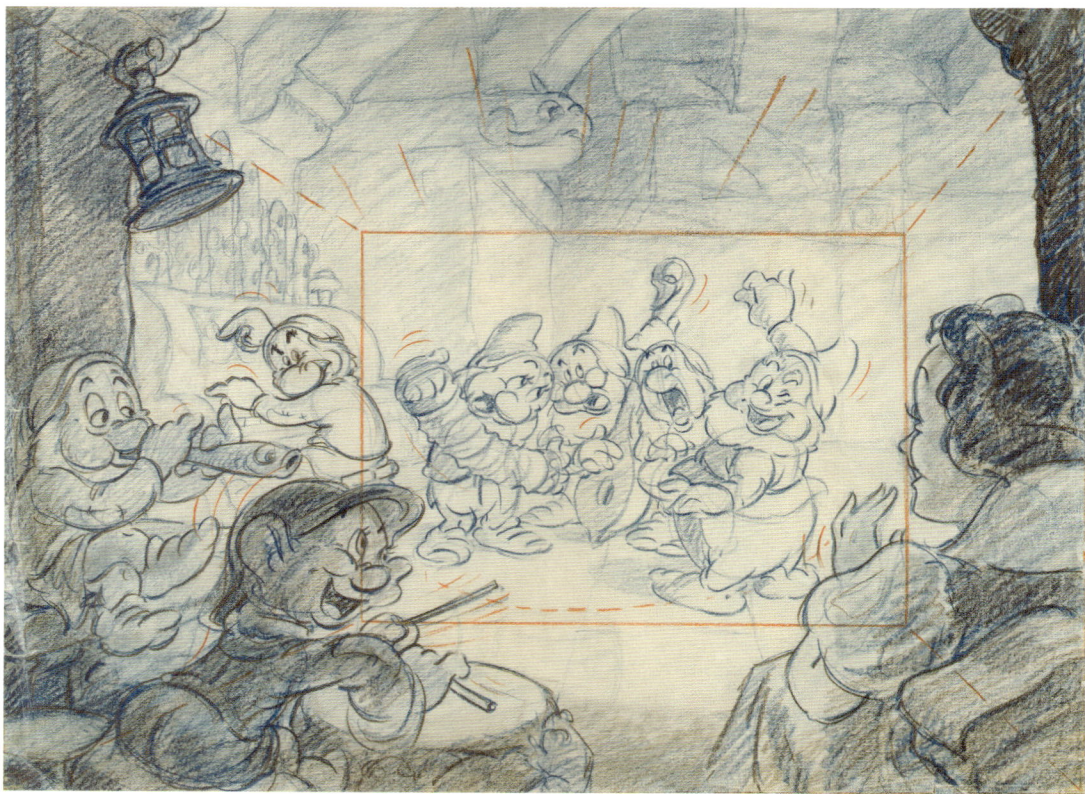

He said, "I understand you know perspective." I said "Yes, I've had training in perspective." He wanted to know if it would be practical to animate backgrounds with moving vanishing points, thus animating the complete scene, background as well as the characters. He gave me several scenes in *Three Orphan Kittens*, in which I animated the kittens and the backgrounds. The camera traveled along with the kittens at their eye level to show the surroundings as they saw it. In order to make it more difficult, he asked me to change the level of the floor during the scenes . . . He tried to animate the backgrounds to give the appearance of a moving camera before considering the invention of a camera to do the job. So I animated a tile floor, a kitchen, an icebox, a sink, and a kitchen table, with three little kittens romping across the room, jumping up a

ABOVE: Layout drawing for *Snow White and the Seven Dwarfs* in the style of Ken Anderson.

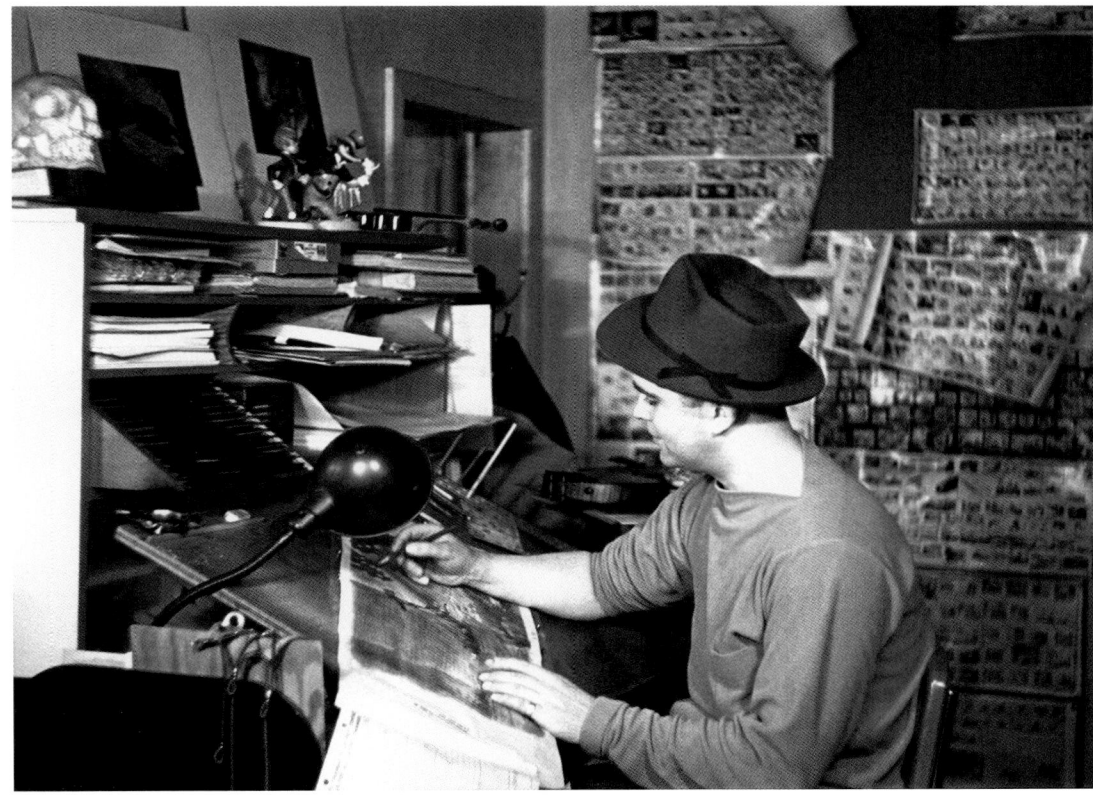

ABOVE: A young Ken Anderson working on *Pinocchio*.

step into the dining room, and under the dining room table. To me it was a rather disappointing result; it seemed to jitter . . . and there was nothing I could do in timing it to get rid of the strobe effect. But Walt seemed pleased with it.[26]

The success of this groundbreaking effort gave Walt a sense of Ken's versatility. But a strange episode would take Ken in an unexpected direction at the studio. In the summer of 1935, he was pushing his body to the limit, waking up at five in the morning each day to play tennis with his wife, and then going to work until late at night. One day, while at the studio, he collapsed from exhaustion. An unscrupulous "doctor" diagnosed him with an imaginary disease, "galloping European tuberculosis," and told Ken that he would soon die.

After the deception was revealed, Walt's brother Roy heard about it. He had himself suffered from TB at the end of World War I, and he decided to help Ken get a special assignment when he returned rested at the studio. Walt was starting to experiment with new technologies that he believed would be useful for the production of his first animated feature, *Snow White and the Seven Dwarfs*, and Roy was convinced that Ken could help his brother with those exciting experiments. Among those was the first attempt at building a multiplane camera, albeit a horizontal one![27]

Walt was trying for three dimensions. He put Jimmy Algar to modeling a foreground of trees in clay. He also had me draw three additional levels of trees—each one farther away than the preceding one. Jim modeled one plane—of the multiplane—and I painted three others on glass planes . . . Bill Garity was the mastermind of this procedure. He was both the [studio] business manager and [an] engineer. Cy Young was the effects animator. He did the animation. It was a scene from *Snow White* of the witch going through the forest. Our planes were of glass—six or seven feet long. They were mounted to slide on horizontal carriages, which were supported by sawhorses. The longest panes of glass were closest to the camera, because they moved faster and traveled farther than the more distant ones. When the three-dimensional clay trees in the foreground moved past the camera it was very real, because it was apparent that they turned, showing three sides of each tree . . . [But] it wiggled. It wasn't stable. You had to have something absolutely solid. So, Walt had the ground tested against earthquakes and rumbles and rattles and all that sort of thing and we set a *huge* block of concrete.[28]

Even this setup was still too unstable, however, and the studio eventually decided to build a vertical multiplane camera instead of a horizontal one.

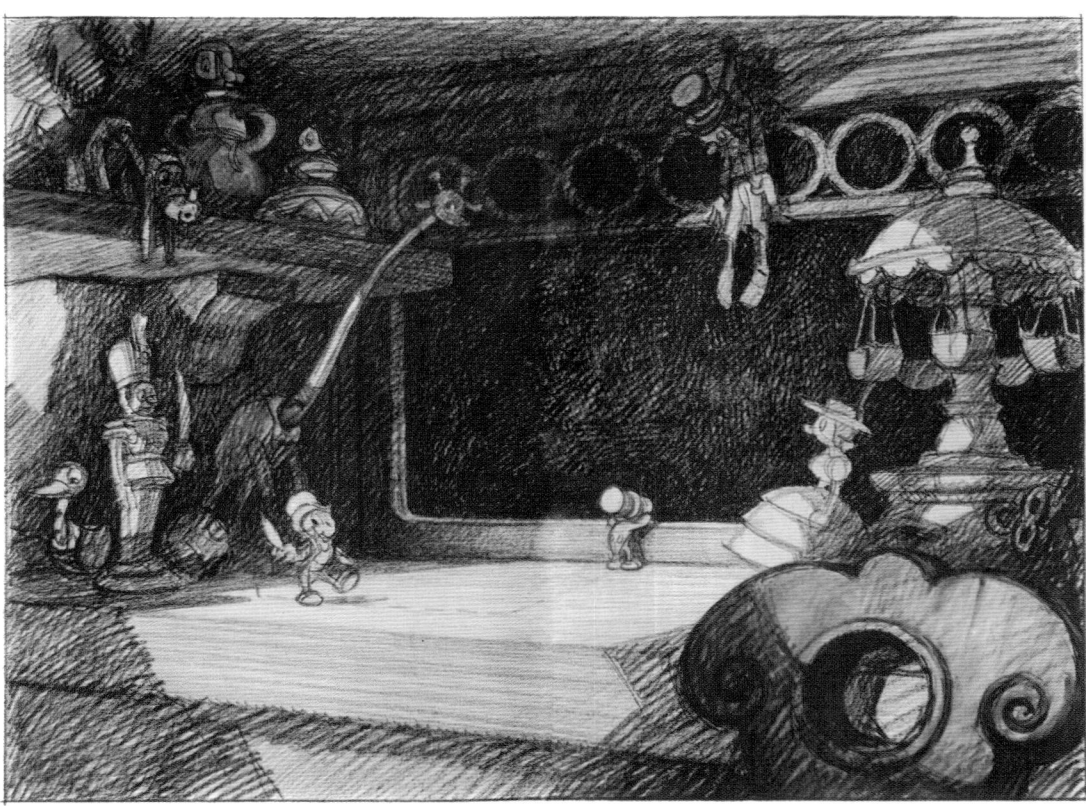 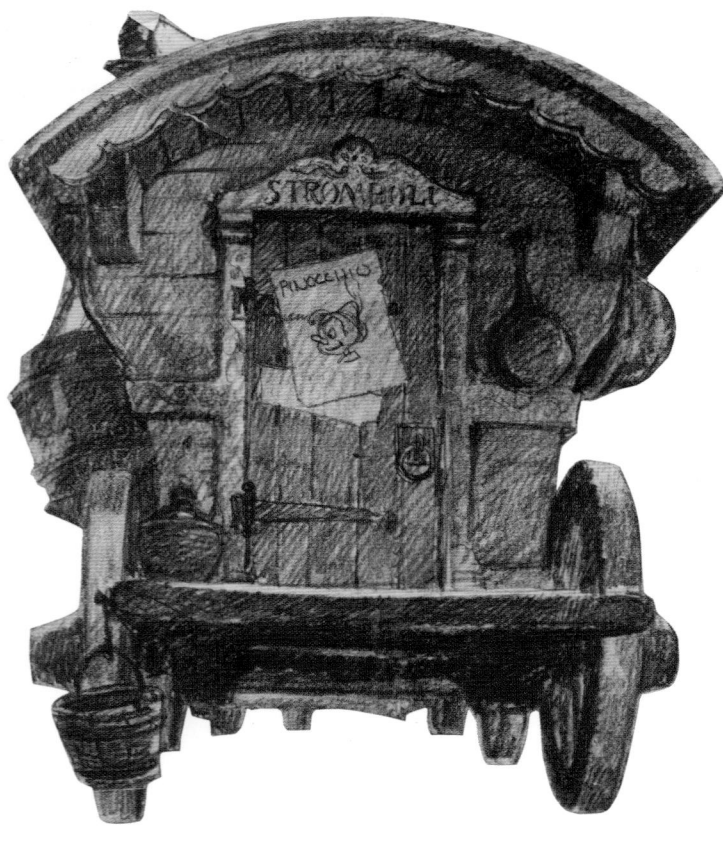

PUPPETS, DWARFS, AND CENTAURS

Ken's work on *Three Orphan Kittens* and *Snow White* had put him squarely on Walt's radar. He was determined not to lose Walt's attention. In October 1935, he submitted an idea to the Story Department:

> Mickey and Minnie conduct a puppet show. Goofy and Donald also work backstage and get into a fight which the puppets imitate.[29]

Walt did not react enthusiastically, but it did remind him of Ken's potential. He wrote Ted Sears, head of the Story Department:

> This marionette idea might work in somewhere with Mickey and Minnie entertaining little orphans. It does not sound like a lot of good gag possibilities as it now stands, but maybe it can be tied in with something . . . Ken Anderson might be a good man to keep in mind for handling the gag files, story ideas, etc., if we can get him away from George Drake.[30]

Three months later, Ken insisted that his puppet concept might be a good one for a short. Still unconvinced, Walt tried to stir the idea in a different direction. He wrote Ken on January 15, 1936:

> After reading over your note regarding puppets, what I told you regarding the making of a puppet short still stands. The thought struck me that maybe as a hobby some of the fellows here would like to work with you on the making of some little puppet act that we might put on some night when we have a shindig or something of the kind. We might work up some little skit, burlesquing some incident that happened around

ABOVE AND OPPOSITE: Story sketches for *Pinocchio*.

ABOVE RIGHT AND OPPOSITE: Courtesy: Wendy Greer.

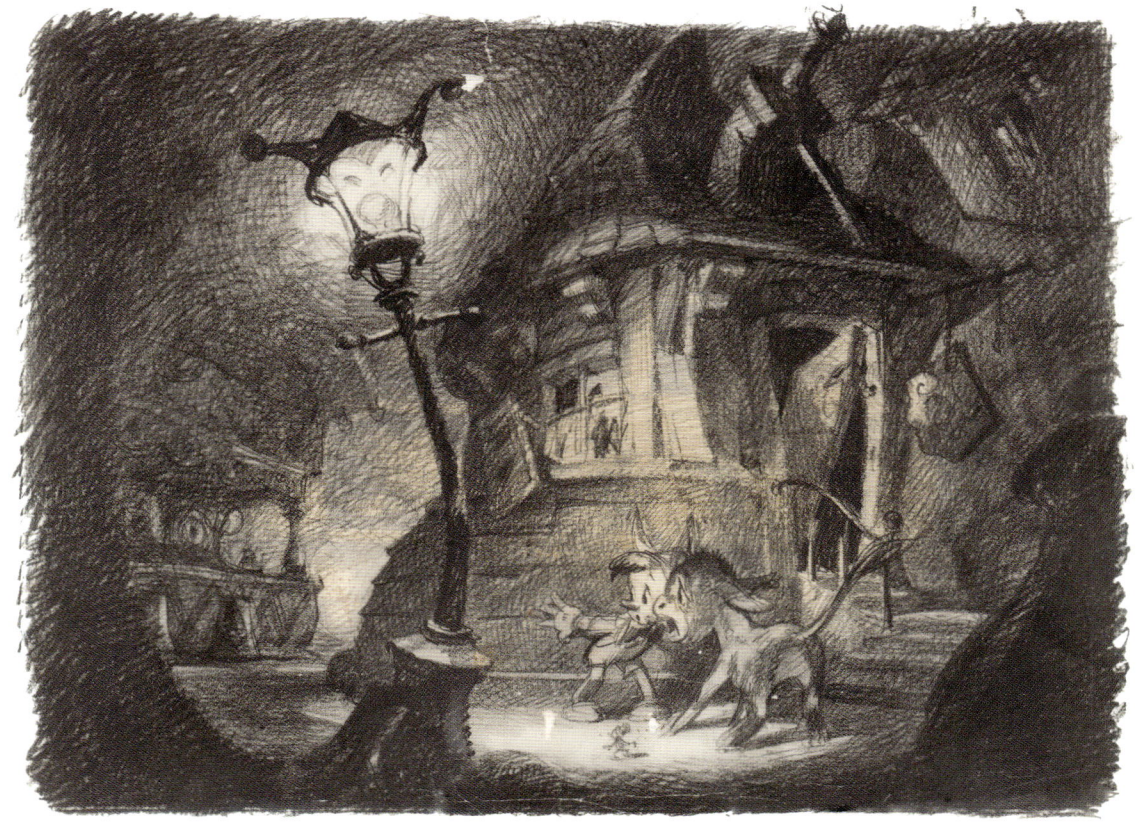

the studio. Possibly Joe Grant would like to work with you making caricatures of the fellows in the studio, or something of that order. Then we might also use this as a study some night in the Action Analysis Classes to see what can be done with action accents. I have thought of having some puppeteers come out to show us what they do to give action accents and create illusions for whatever good we might get out of it toward creating better illusions in our animation.[31]

As a rule, Walt loved being stimulated creatively by his artists. By 1936 he decided to move Ken to the Layout Department and once again was impressed by Ken's passion and inventiveness. Ken explained:

I kept notebooks of all these fancy camera moves. I had one from *Anthony Adverse* and the camera started in a long shot and I just made drawings of what . . . went on. The camera went into a close-up and then turned, looking at the ground, and went up the tree trunk and the sky. Then the sky went into a musical . . . So I made that kind of drawing of that kind of shot and from all these different movies . . . great scenes and anything else I could get that was well written or whatever was good. Finally, Walt got on to me doing that. And he liked it! . . . He would want to see them, so I would show him my book and he was impressed.[32]

Ken was an overachiever. Walt often loved it, but not always. On *Snow White*, Ken realized that he might have been too ambitious without being aware of it:

[Director Wilfred] Jackson and I considered ourselves a team. Walt gave us the Entertainment Sequence to do [the sequence in which the Dwarfs are dancing with Snow White]. So we figured [out] the best way to do an entertainment sequence. We had to figure out what it was, get the music, and had to get everything together. Walt kind of left us alone for some reason. We decided the best way to do it was for me to go through as a story sketch [and] layout man, and design all the scenes and all the dances. I was going to make a [film] with the music. We were going to have a miniature sequence, all done and photographed, and show it to Walt.

I didn't know what a layout man did. Nobody ever told me . . . So I did far more work than was wanted or was necessary or was even good . . . I just thought that a layout man should prepare everything and put the characters where they're supposed to be and have them doing what they're supposed to be doing . . . So I did the whole sequence that way and timed it. And we shot it. Jackson was happy as a tick, got this whole sequence all done, showed it to Walt, and Walt said, "What . . . are you doing? You are supposed to be in layout, not in animation!"[33]

Despite the small mishaps, Ken adored his job:

I never looked at the clock. I'd quit and I was still working. I'd come home and I was thinking about what I was doing . . . over and over, thinking about all this *Snow White* stuff. [I was] carried off into a different world. I'd grab some sleep and wake up and go to work again . . . We didn't have any clock, no punching a clock at the beginning of *Snow White* . . . You made your own hours. You came when you wanted to and there were always these guys that were there . . . I just loved it![34]

For *Pinocchio*, Ken again handled layout for some of the key scenes in the movie, including those where the Blue Fairy gives life to Pinocchio, the sequences in which Jiminy Cricket finds Pinocchio in a cage—and in which the Blue Fairy frees him—and the sequence where Pinocchio becomes a real boy.[35] His colleague Ken O'Connor recalled, "It was Ken Anderson's idea to show Geppetto's shop from the cricket's point of view, having Jiminy hop up to the window and look inside [which was] very imaginative stuff."[36]

Ken Anderson, however, was frustrated by the limited creative scope that layout offered him. "I couldn't understand what layout men were good for," he explained years later. "What do you need a layout man for? So I worked to bridge the gap between story and animation. In fact, I was the visualizer."[37] In other words, Ken was finally finding his lifelong vocation. On *Fantasia*, for the first time, he officially became an art director.

This section which I inherited along with Ham Luske, who directed it, was Beethoven['s "Pastoral Symphony"]. All the other movements had already been recorded and most all animated . . . We had to do what we were doing very fast so that economically the thing would be able to be put together and come out at one time. I think we produced the Beethoven [section] more rapidly than any other section . . . Walt said, "Read up on Beethoven and get some style." So I read up on the ribald and the classical . . . I studied the man who designed the [Parisian] metro [Hector Guimard]. I was also inspired by [Arnold] Böcklin's [painting] *Isle of the Dead* and the Isola Bella in Italy.

Within the Beethoven [sequence] . . . where you had the opening business with the centaurs and the centaurettes, I wanted to get an early Greek Elysian Fields characteristic, sort of an art nouveau, which was very popular in France at one period. It was an idealistic setting, where I felt that the centaurs and the centaurettes would have a better chance to operate. There was a man at the time . . . named [William P.] Welsh, who had done some magazine covers for *Variety* of [the Roman goddess] Diana shooting an arrow in a very stylistic way. And the only places I could find any inspiration for this style were from the things that Welsh had done, but also things that had been . . . done in France. So I looked at those things and saw how the bushes were so clean, clear, stylized . . . They just were idealized. There wasn't a rotten leaf or a rotten flower or any extra roots or anything else. Everything was very much like a well-pruned garden.[38]

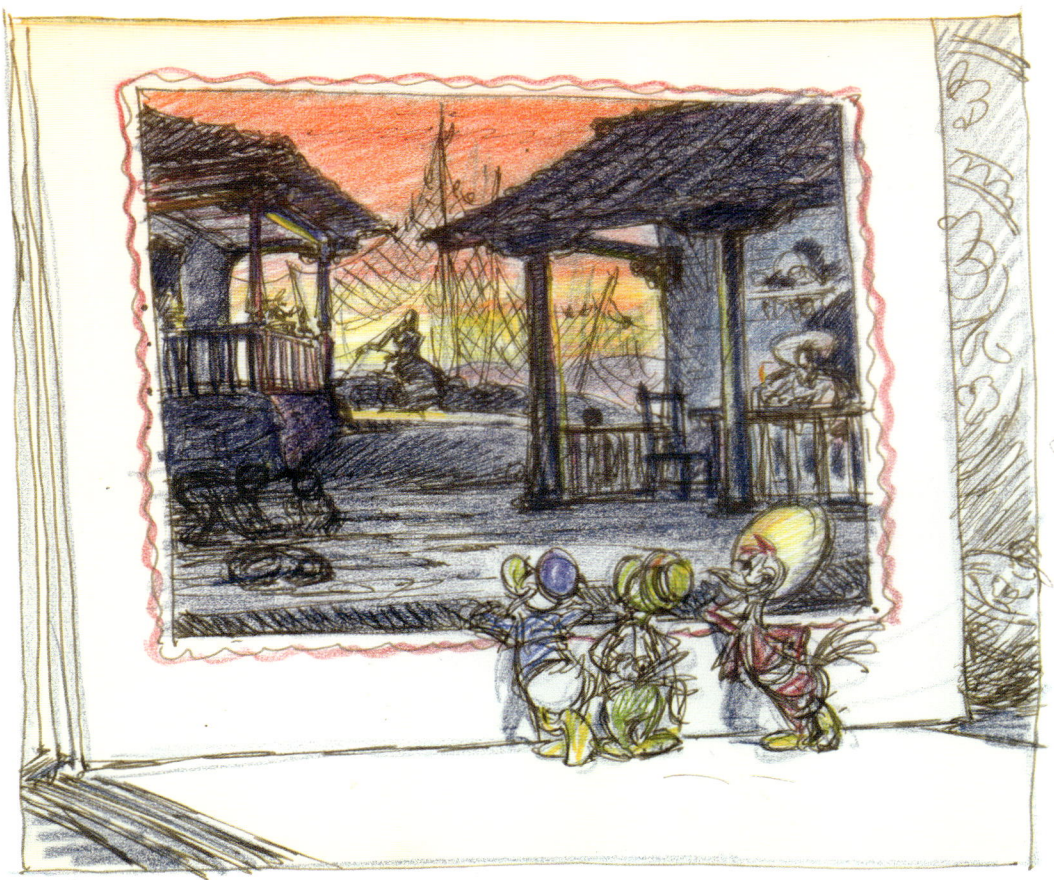

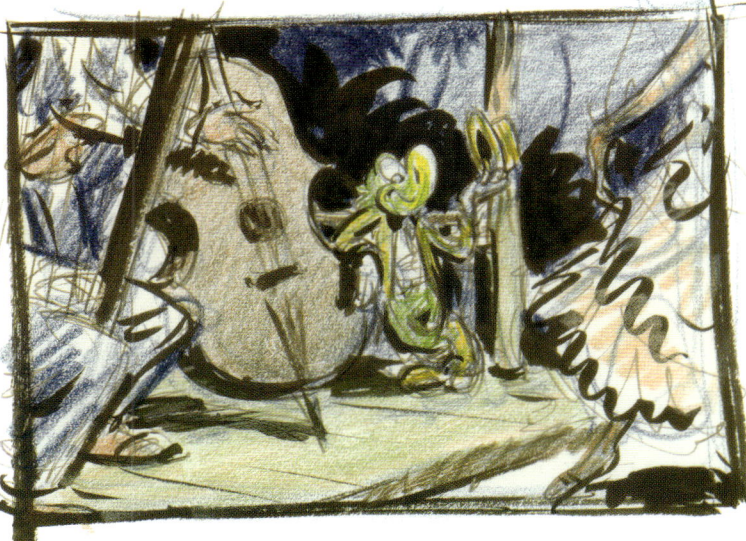

ABOVE: Concept sketches for *The Three Caballeros*. Courtesy: Walt Disney Family Foundation.

A MEXICAN ADVENTURE

When Walt traveled to South America in 1941, after the release of *Fantasia*, Ken was not part of the trip, although he was subsequently asked to handle layouts for the "Pedro" sequence in *Saludos Amigos*.[39]

Not surprisingly Ken joined the follow-up trip to Mexico, from October 9 to October 23, 1942. True to his nature, he decided to take a rather risky initiative:

> I [was] wondering what we were [in Mexico] for. We were just sitting around the hotel all the time and we'd seen everything around here. I wanted to see the rest of Mexico. Jack Cutting was the business manager and I failed to clear it with him . . . [With my colleague, artist] Ernie Terrazas, who was Mexican and part of the group, we just took off in a big limousine, went all over Mexico and I made sketches. I'd sketch back in the limousine as we went along, sketchbook after sketchbook.
>
> It was Christmas time . . . Ernie was a very devout Catholic and I talked to the Sisters in [an orphanage]. The little children in that Catholic orphanage were not going to have any Christmas. The Sisters said there wasn't any money and how desperately the children needed shoes and lodgings and clothes and things like that. So I made a magnanimous . . . move . . . I mentioned that we would be glad to supply some piñatas full of stuff . . . We didn't want to get involved with the actual breaking of the piñata . . . so the nuns hid us on the balcony [to] watch the thing. It was very rewarding and it made us feel good. Walt felt very good about it when we told him what we'd done.[40]

Witnessing the breaking of the piñata became the basis for part of the "Las Posadas" sequence in *The Three Caballeros*. And this was only the beginning of Ken's adventures. When he and Ernie came back from their unauthorized excursion, Walt loved what he saw:

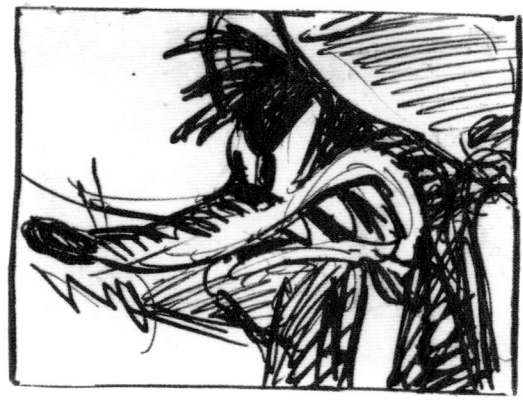 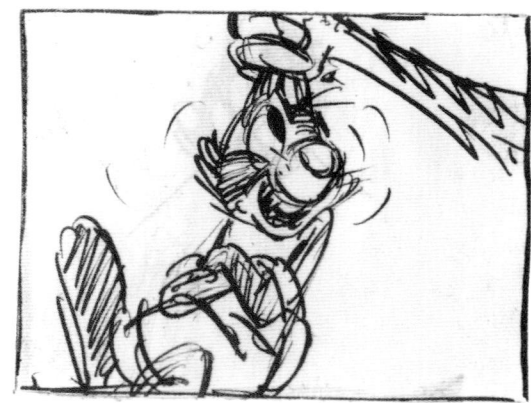 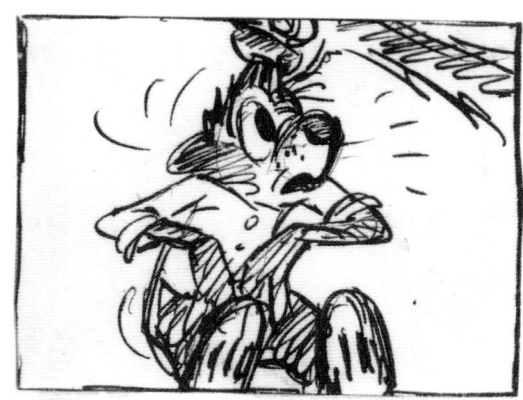

[Walt] pored over the sketches I did in Mexico . . . It was really a good idea that I knew what it was I was drawing, because he wanted to know, in detail, why I had made that drawing, and what it meant, and so on and so forth. As a result, when it came to planning [*The Three Caballeros*], I had to make all kinds of drawings, which he, again, saw, which would relate to our trip, what we had done, only adding the Disney characters, the duck and so on.[41]

The most fascinating project that followed *The Three Caballeros* was one that Ken would remember for years to come as one of his favorites in terms of technical challenges: the combination of live action and animation known as *Song of the South*, for which he was acting as cartoon director.

Walt wanted to achieve the illusion that Uncle Remus walked on the same ground with Brer Rabbit, Fox, and Bear. This called for a set which would look like a painted cartoon background. We built the set at United Artists Studio Stage 3. It was from a small color painting by Mary Blair, and when it was completed it was a huge set. The lighting by cameraman Gregg Toland was masterful in its imitation of Mary's original painting. The balance of the cartoon scenes without live characters was painstakingly matched to the live-set background. A cartoon world that Uncle Remus worked in was thus created . . . There was no rear-projection screen used whatsoever—it was all sets, or it was animation scenes directly over live-action scenes. And the final scene in the picture was a process-screen–cartoon sky—it was of such magnitude that we couldn't build it on the stage, so we went to Arizona and shot it.[42]

Coordinating the shooting of the live action with the needs of the top animators was no simple task. To make certain that everyone was on the same page before the live action was shot, Ken decided to plan all the combination sequences via a set of thumbnails.

I went through the whole picture working with [director Wilfred] Jackson . . . I made book after book of miniature scenes and who did what . . . Jackson would OK that or say, "Why don't you do it this way, Ken?" And we'd work it over, and I'd redo it . . . We had thirty or forty of these books. And they went down to the animators. "Here's a section you're going to work on. Would you like to go over it in thumbnail form? Because Ken's going to go over and shoot this stuff. Before he shoots it and you're hog-tied with the result, let's see if . . ." The different animators would say, "Yeah, I like it just the way it is," or they would come up with suggestions for changes and we'd hash it out. Jackson, myself, and the animator would come to a makeable agreement so that when I went over to shoot this material with Jackson to United Artists we had a feeling of security that we were doing something that the animators agreed upon and would like. And they loved it: they loved that way of working.[43]

ABOVE: Thumbnail sketches for *Song of the South*. Courtesy: Paul F. Anderson.

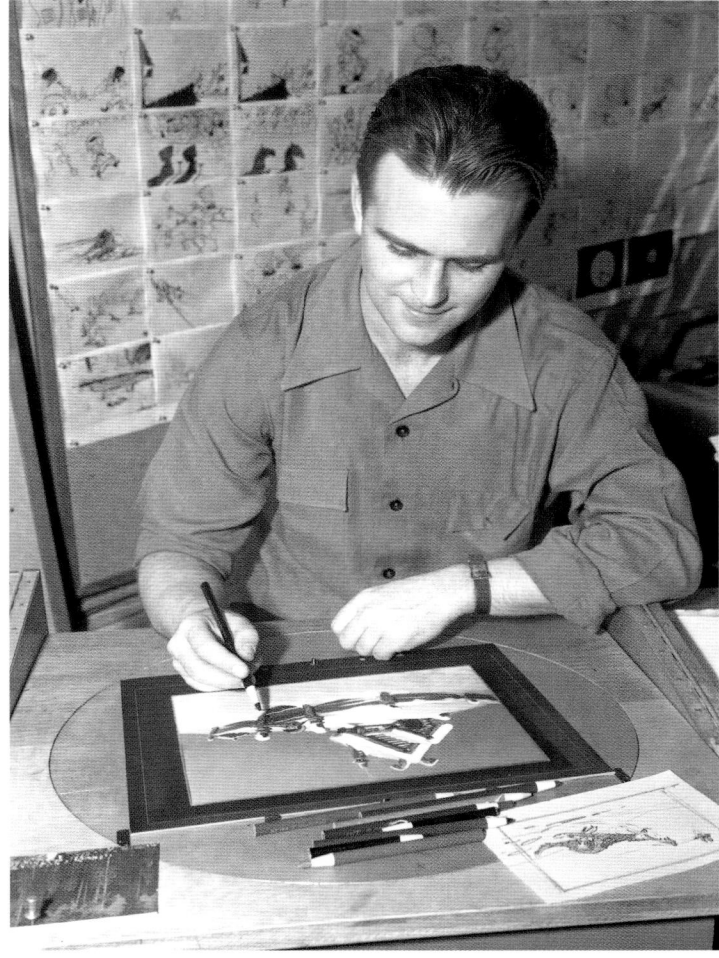

ABOVE: Ken Anderson in the mid-1940s working on the "Peter and the Wolf" sequence from *Make Mine Music*.

A PRINCESS AND A MAGIC KINGDOM

Song of the South was released in 1946, a year after the end of World War II. The war years had weakened the Disney studio financially, but by the late 1940s it was regaining its health, and Walt decided that it was ready to tackle its first full-fledged animated feature since the release of *Bambi* in 1942. The story of *Cinderella* was chosen to kick off this renaissance. For Ken the project involved one key challenge: he had been paired up on story with Bill Peet and the relationship teetered between friendship and jealousy.

Bill Peet was both a help and hard to work with. He became a pal, a buddy, but we never were really as close as we would like to have been. Because everything he did, or I would do, in a story way, was very similar, but usually it would be his drawings or mine that took the precedence in the scenes and made the reality come true. Bill was probably stronger or closer to the development of the characters in *Cinderella*. He felt the cat. And I was mixed up with trying to make the character of the buildings and the atmosphere of everything follow what I was doing with the animated characters and the business in the scene. I designed all the buildings including the round room, the tower room . . . The round room that Cinderella lived in was round because it was the best-looking background for a little girl dressed up in a fancy gown done by mice, standing in the middle of it. She was enclosed, like an egg. It wasn't a great big roomy spacious area, it was a little room, high up in the air, and it had one door that led to the wooden stairs.[44]

A few months after the release of *Cinderella* on February 15, 1950, Ken got involved in a new project that would again take him in a totally different creative direction. Walt had been thinking of a collection of animated Americana miniature displays which would tour the country aboard a train. Ken was one of the artists recruited to give life to the new idea. While the Disneylandia project was eventually abandoned, Walt soon recruited Ken for another, even more ambitious task: the creation of a new form of amusement center, which would open on July 17, 1955, under the name Disneyland. During the 1950s, Ken spent many months working for Walt personally on Disneyland, but he still directed the lion's share of his efforts toward animation-related projects.

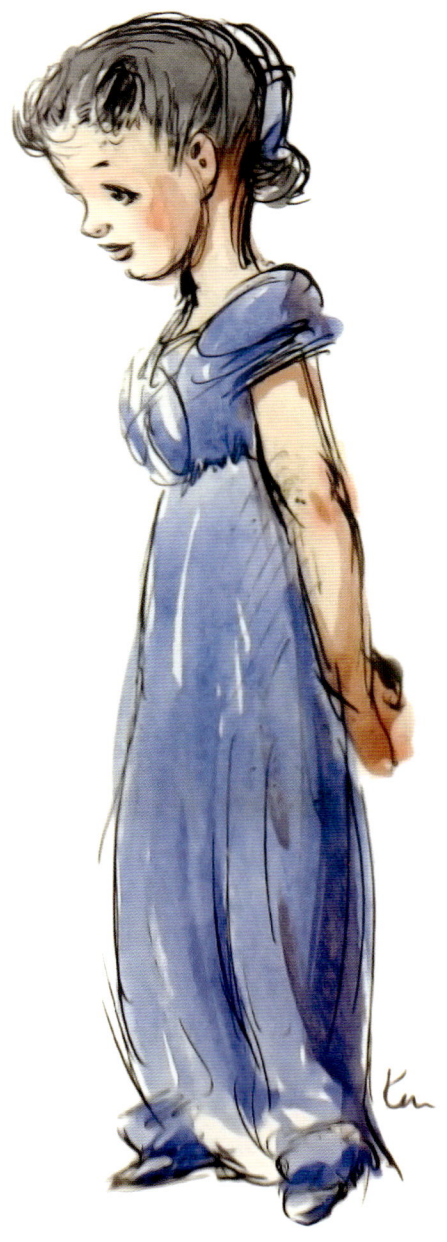

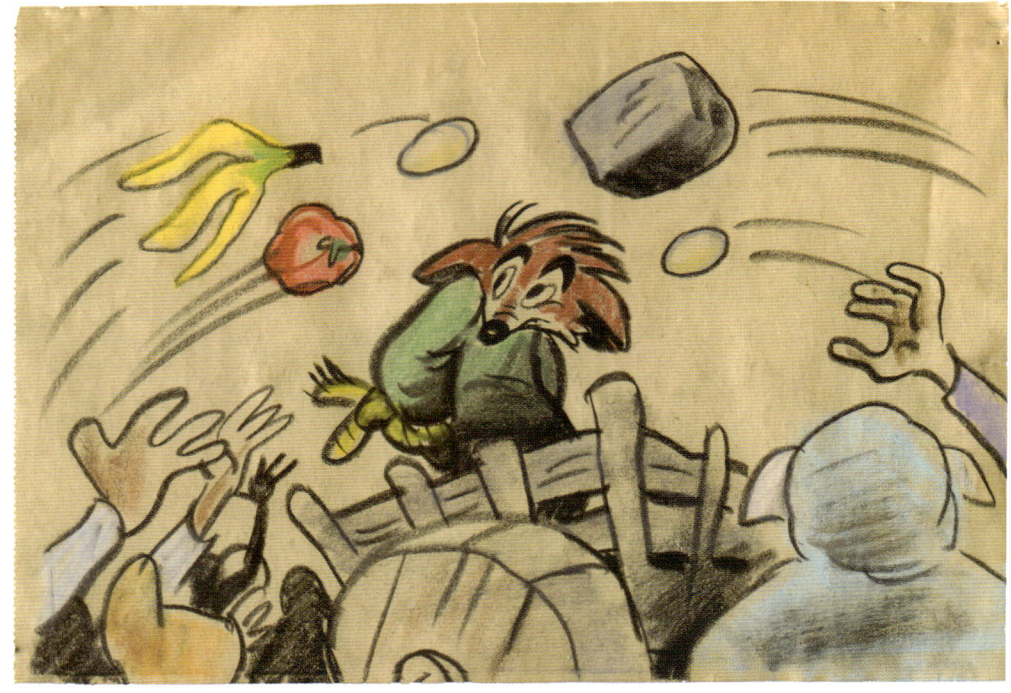

A FOX AND ANOTHER PRINCESS

In the first half of 1956, Ken developed a series of story sketches based on the story of *Reynard the Fox*, an anthropomorphic red fox and trickster figure, hero of many European folk tales from the Middle Ages.[45] Walt's story artists, including Bianca Majolie, Dorothy Ann Blank, Otto Englander, and Joe Grant, had toyed with the project as early as 1938 but stumbled upon the fact that Reynard was not a sympathetic character.[46] Jack Kinney and Norman Ferguson tried to revive the idea in the mid-1940s as short animated sequences patterned on the model of the animated sequences in *Song of the South*, which could have lightened up the mood of the live-action movie *Treasure Island*.[47] The 1956 boards were Ken's first attempt to resurrect the story of *Reynard*. It would not be his only one.

By the mid-1950s, Ken was also hard at work on Disney's next animated feature, *Sleeping Beauty*. This time he was mostly paired up with story artist Don DaGradi.[48] Layout artist Ray Aragon remembered:

LEFT: Character sketch of Wendy for *Peter Pan*.

ABOVE: Story sketch for *Reynard the Fox*. Courtesy: Paul F. Anderson.

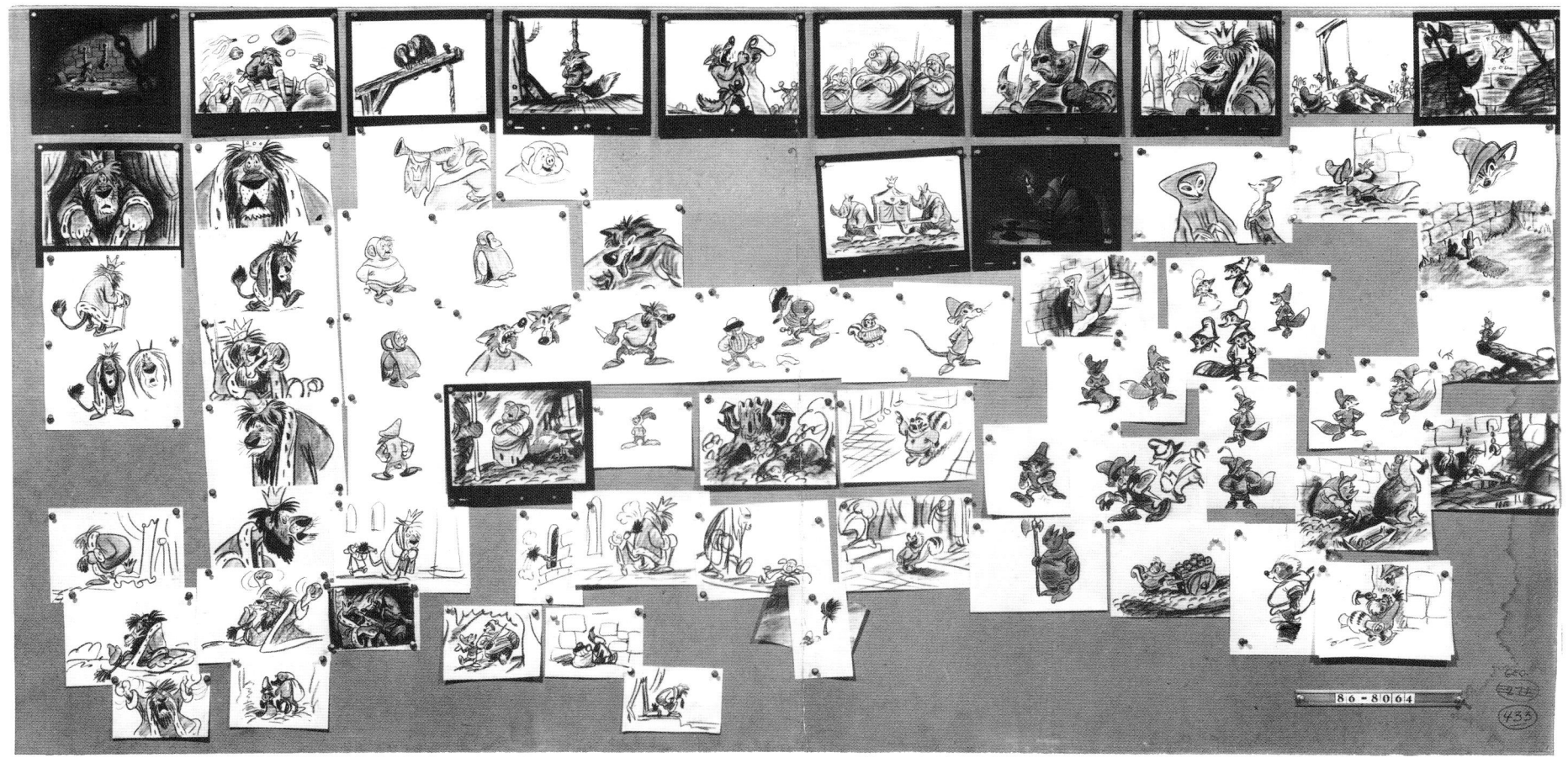

ABOVE: Storyboards for the abandoned project *Reynard the Fox*. Courtesy: Wendy Greer.

When I went to Disney on my very first day they were both on vacation. They didn't find a room for me, so they put me in the room where Ken Anderson and Don DaGradi would normally work ... I would look at their storyboards ... And these guys were masters. They were styling the picture. They were doing the compositions mainly in charcoal. Ken Anderson and Don DaGradi were top artists.[49]

Among the most memorable sequences that Ken boarded for the movie was the fight between Prince Phillip and Maleficent as she transforms into the dragon.[50] As was his custom, Ken was passionate about his work and wanted all around him to know about it. Story artist Floyd Norman remained fascinated many years later by the first presentation by Ken that he witnessed:

> One evening when we were working overtime on *Sleeping Beauty*, a bunch of us kids wandered upstairs to the Story Department. As we walked down the hallway, we noticed a guy working alone in a room filled with storyboards. I didn't realize it at the time, but this was our first meeting with Ken Anderson. Since we were a bunch of young kids, we didn't want to disturb this very important Disney artist at work. But suddenly Ken looked up from his drawing table and invited us into his office. He was working on the climactic dragon

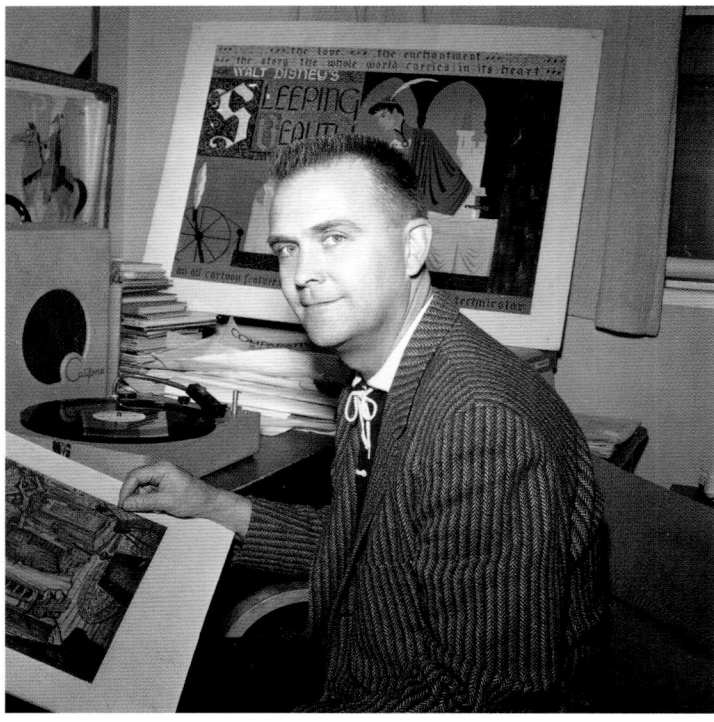

fight at the end of *Sleeping Beauty*. Ken seemed eager to show us what he had done, so he put a record on the turntable and dramatic Tchaikovsky music filled the room. As he pitched the storyboard to the music, Ken Anderson was literally jumping on the chairs, tables, and couches as he waved his story pointer like a sword. Ken was not only pitching his storyboard, he was slaying the dragon as well. Finally, the music came to an end, the dragon lay dead, and the exhausted story man flopped down onto the couch.[51]

This enthusiasm did not always please everyone, though, as animator Ollie Johnston once explained:

> I can see why Bill Peet used to maybe get a little miffed, because Ken would go through everything he did with such excitement and enthusiasm that you'd think it was the first time it had ever been thought of. He gets so carried away with what he does.[52]

THE STORY MAN

In parallel to his work on the animated features and on Disneyland, Ken was also always toying with new story ideas. On February 16, 1959, he submitted a "proposed outline for [an] *Oz* feature cartoon,"[53] and created various story sketches for the project. Walt Disney Archives founder David R. Smith explained:

> It was back in 1937, before MGM had begun production on their film, that Walt Disney first inquired about the copyright status of the *Oz* stories . . . Nothing came of the original inquiry . . . [After World War II] on November 16, 1954, Disney purchased the rights to eleven [*Oz*] books by L. Frank Baum from Baum's son . . . In 1954 . . . the *Oz* stories were considered as the basis for a two-part television show on the "Disneyland" series, starring Mouseketeers Annette and Darlene . . . [In 1957] as Walt Disney began discussing plans for his *Oz* film, he realized that it had become too large, and too expensive a project for TV. So, on July 24, newspapers reported that Walt Disney had announced a multimillion dollar live-action musical feature . . . [But] in February 1958, newspapers reported that rumors were circulating that Walt Disney had dropped the *Oz* picture.[54]

It is in this context that a year later Ken wrote his proposed outline. But despite his attempt and despite a rough treatment for *Return to Oz* written by Joe Rinaldi and Otto Englander on October 4, 1962,[55] the *Oz* project was shelved once again.

A year after his aborted attempt at reviving the *Oz* concept, Ken started working with Marc Davis on a proposed adaptation of the French play by Edmond Rostand, *Chanticleer*.[56] This was another property which had been considered by the Disney

ABOVE: Ken Anderson working on *Sleeping Beauty* around 1957.

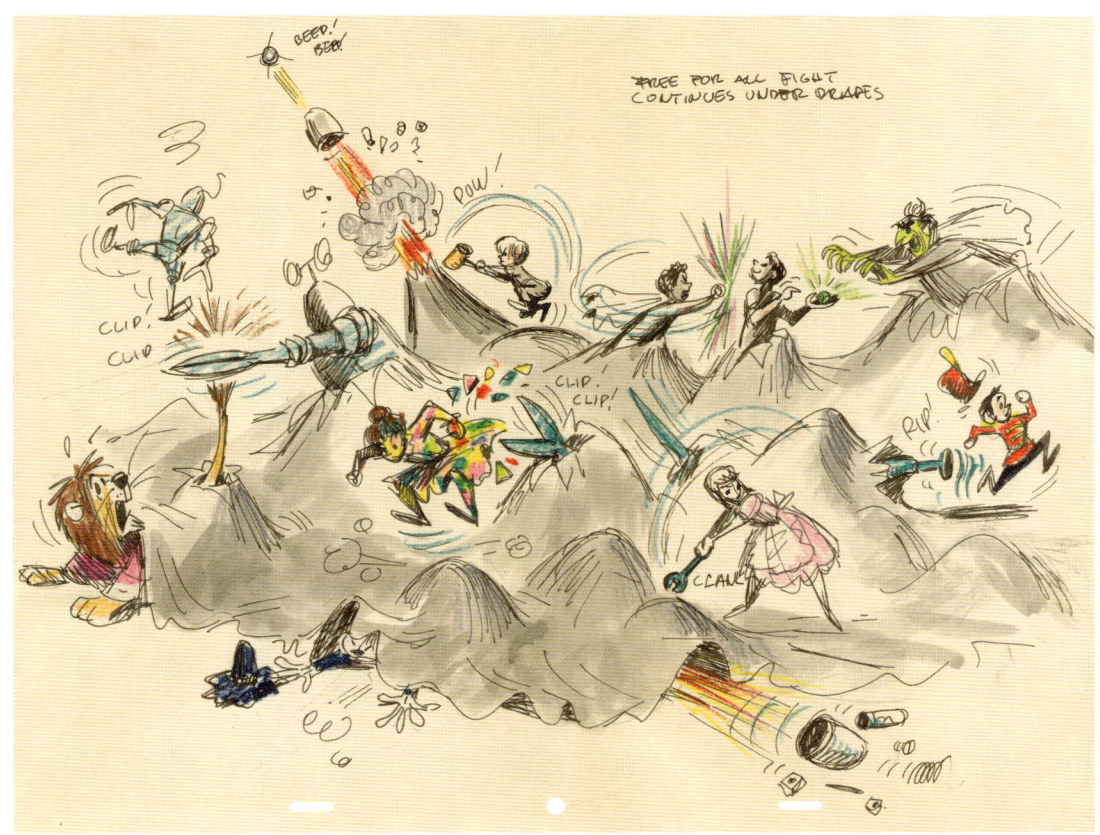

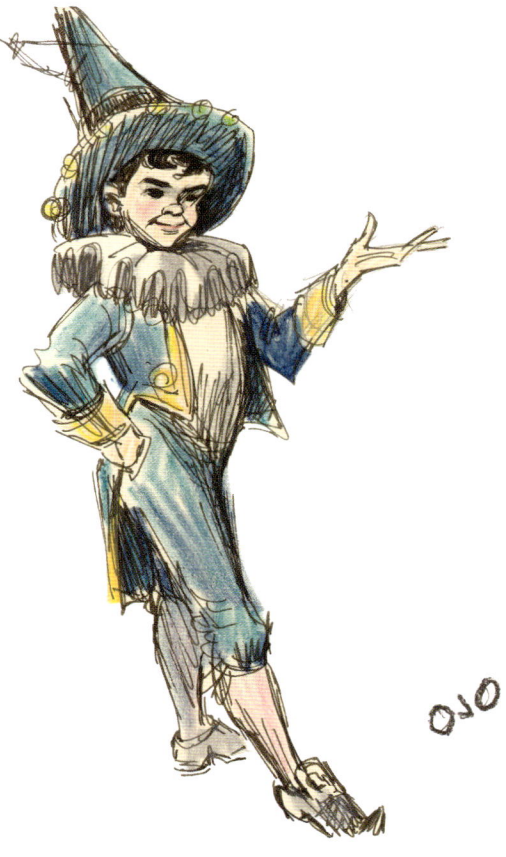

ABOVE: Concept sketches for one of the proposed Oz stories titled *The Rainbow Road to Oz*.

studio since the late 1930s.[57] On November 24, 1937, story artist Bianca Majolie had written a first synopsis, which was circulated among her colleagues. A few days later, the head of the Story Department, Ted Sears, and writer Al Perkins summarized their concerns with the story. Al Perkins wrote:

> I question the desirability of purchasing *Chantecler* [sic] for our reserve shelf, or even considering it as a feature. Except for a few situations, such as the love story, the plot against Chantecler, and his fight with the White Pile, I think we would have to construct an entirely new story. I believe that we could construct a story of our own that would be much better than anything in *Chantecler*, which impresses me as being highbrow. The experience with *Bambi* illustrates the difficulty of working entirely with animals, unrelieved by humans, and I think *Chantecler* would possess the same problems. If we are going to use an all-animal picture, I think we should go the whole hog in a cartoon way, put pants on them and lean heavily on the comedy side, as could be done, say, in *Reynard the Fox* or *Penguin Island*.

Ted Sears added:

> The main problem would be to create a likeable rooster in appearance and character that would draw sympathy of the audience and keep them interested in his troubles and triumphs.[58]

In 1953, the project resurfaced as a musical, thanks to a story treatment by Dick Huemer.

The originality of Marc Davis and Ken Anderson's 1960 approach was that it combined the story of Chanticleer with that of Reynard the Fox.[59] Marc Davis remembered:

> [Chanticleer is] a vain rooster who believes that crowing makes the sun rise. It takes place in France. He ruled the roost, was a favorite with all these hens. He becomes mayor and abuses his authority. Of course, it is eventually discovered that the sun comes up even if he doesn't crow and that takes some of the wind out of his sails. There was a con man fox named Reynard who preyed on the hens so he has to get Chanticleer out of the way. He's going to run for mayor and take over the place. He has his night people who are like carnival performers, jugglers, strolling bands, but unsavory types; and they seduce the townspeople into voting for him. I did many different versions of the fox.[60]

Walt at first was enthusiastic. He focused on Reynard, who offered the most exciting possibilities for character development. On the evening of May 11, executive Ken Peterson sent a note to Ken Anderson about a meeting with Walt that had taken place a few hours earlier:

> Walt opened by saying that the purpose of the meeting was to consider the potential of *Chantecler* for a good musical picture . . . He said, "Go for fun stuff . . . We should really have a ball with this type of picture." Walt saw Reynard as a fast-talking manipulator, who plays on people's bad traits and appeals to their gullibility . . . Through cutbacks to historical times, the story is told by Chantecler of how Reynard and all his descendants have been held in ill repute by the other animals. Chantecler tells of his wrong doings and the trial of animals, which was held and Reynard condemned. There has been a curse on the House of Reynard ever since.[61]

But in the end, the same issues that had been identified by Ted Sears and Al Perkins in 1938 killed the project. On August 24, Walt weighed in with his artists:

> These characters will not be warm and sympathetic . . . Chantecler is a pompous character. Reynard is a scoundrel. [It's] always tough to make a story around a scoundrel . . . [The] fox could be pathetic . . . [We] have to get characters with sympathy, warmth, heart. [We] have to capture the imagination of the public.[62]

The writing was on the wall. Ken Anderson explained how things finally came to a head:

ABOVE: Character designs for the abandoned project *Chantecleer*. Courtesy: Wendy Greer.

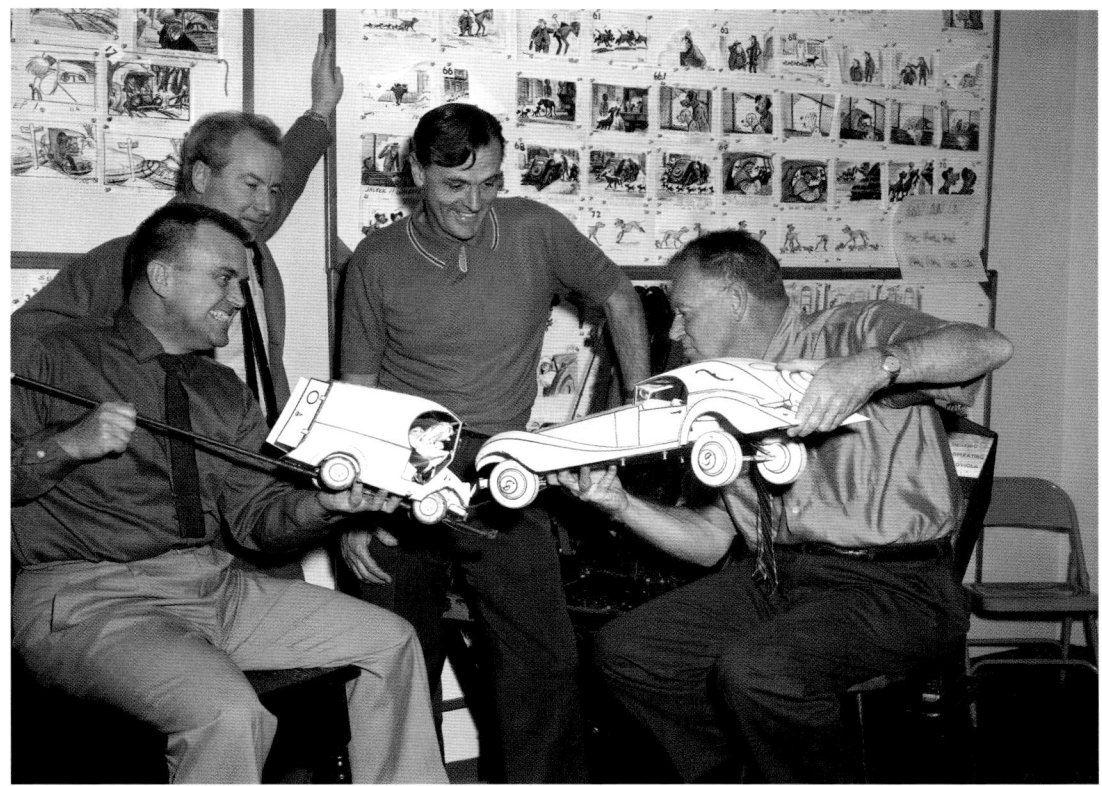

ABOVE: From left to right: Ken Anderson, Bill Peet, Woolie Reitherman, and Ham Luske goofing around during the making of *One Hundred and One Dalmatians*.

Bill Peet was on [*The Sword in the Stone*] and I was on *Chanticleer*. We liked it: it was good music and good characters. Marc Davis was working with me, doing beautiful drawings . . . But [animator] Milt Kahl couldn't see a hero being a chicken. Chickens were bad. That was strike number one. And a lot of animators agreed with him. They couldn't see a chicken being the kingpin. The other thing was that we had to hurry. We were having a late start with Walt having us beat this other picture by Bill Peet. I didn't quite know what his anxiety was . . . Walt came in and said, "Ken, why don't you come up by tomorrow with some other angle on this thing: something with kids." So I worked like hell at night developing kids, young chickens, young pigs . . . and I was running the whole story through them. I brought that into Walt, but his mind was already made up. He was looking at Bill Peet's stuff and Bill Peet's stuff on [*The Sword in the Stone*] won up.[63]

THE XEROX REVOLUTION

Ken's most innovative initiative in the late 1950s and early 1960s was well intentioned and very bold, but would end up affecting his life in a traumatic way. It all started with his noticing an intriguing technique being used by the department headed by Walt's niece, Phyllis Hurrell, which in the 1950s produced commercials featuring Disney characters.

There was a unit under Phyllis, a commercial unit, and they were using Xerox. They were using it in a much different way than I thought we should use for a feature. They were making nice, definite, finished, heavy lines, and it worked out well, eliminating the cost of ink[ing]. So, I reasoned that it would be a double benefit in a feature. It would cost an awful lot less and eliminate ink[ing] . . . Ub Iwerks had developed the equipment for transferring the lines to a cel and ours was the first method of doing that, with an electromagnetic process . . . All I had to do was sell the idea.[64]

Ken knew exactly when to do so:

[Walt] was very unhappy with the cost [of *Sleeping Beauty*] . . . He had said, "We're not going to make any more animated features. This'll be the last one. We've come to the end of everything. The animators, the top guys, I'll have special jobs for you, so don't worry about that, but everybody else . . . " I didn't believe that. I thought that we could make [the next feature] *One Hundred and One Dalmatians* for a reasonable amount.[65]

KEN ANDERSON 39

And Ken's idea would have an added benefit: the animators had always been frustrated by the fact that their original animation drawings lost their vitality after they were inked. With the Xerox process, not only would costs be reduced but the animators would see their drawings make it directly to the screen.

I conferred with the animators, Milt [Kahl] and Marc [Davis] and Ollie [Johnston] and Frank [Thomas]. They echoed my enthusiasm for this thing.

On May 21, 1958, executive Ken Peterson wrote Walt about *One Hundred and One Dalmatians*:

Ken Anderson is making some very interesting experiments on a new style of background and layout handling for this picture. Everyone is very enthusiastic about the possibilities. You may have seen some of this material in room 2F-8.⁶⁶

To convince Walt, Ken even went as far as animating three test scenes himself:

One of them was a long shot down a street and Roger up in his bedroom. You could see him through the window and he was working on something and he looked out the window and tossed the paper out. The other one was a close-up of Pongo looking out the window, and the third one was a close-up of Roger playing the piano.⁶⁷

Walt, who was focusing most of his efforts at the time on the development and expansion of Disneyland, approved Ken's plans rather distractedly, and Ken started focusing on the actual art direction of the movie, with the help of background artist Walt Peregoy. Ken Anderson explained:

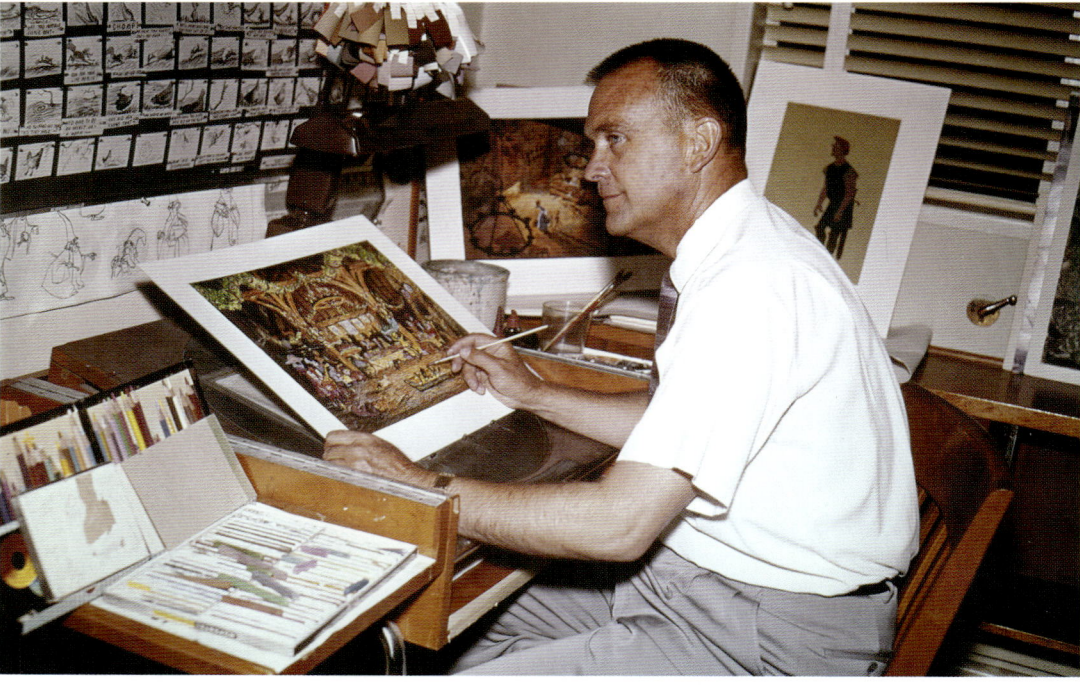

Ronald Searle was a very good friend of mine and I was always enamored of his work . . . [In *One Hundred and One Dalmatians*] I very definitely went for his English style. I loved that soft color, muted greys, and tonal values. To get the authentic feeling of London and England I had a little talk with Ronald Searle and his wife Kaye Webb and he helped me a lot in getting the Englishness in the film . . . They sent me photos of Regent's Park and we discussed color.⁶⁸

But when Walt discovered the final result on the screen he was appalled: the Xerox process accentuated the angularity of the animated drawings; the backgrounds were much too sharp, much too modern.

[Walt] wouldn't even speak to me for a year; he wouldn't speak to me at all. I was cut out of meetings and the job of head of design and head instigator of how the pictures would look was removed from me. The directors [of the next animated feature, *The Sword in the Stone*] were supposed to take over

ABOVE: Ken Anderson at work on *The Sword in the Stone*.

40 THEY DREW AS THEY PLEASED

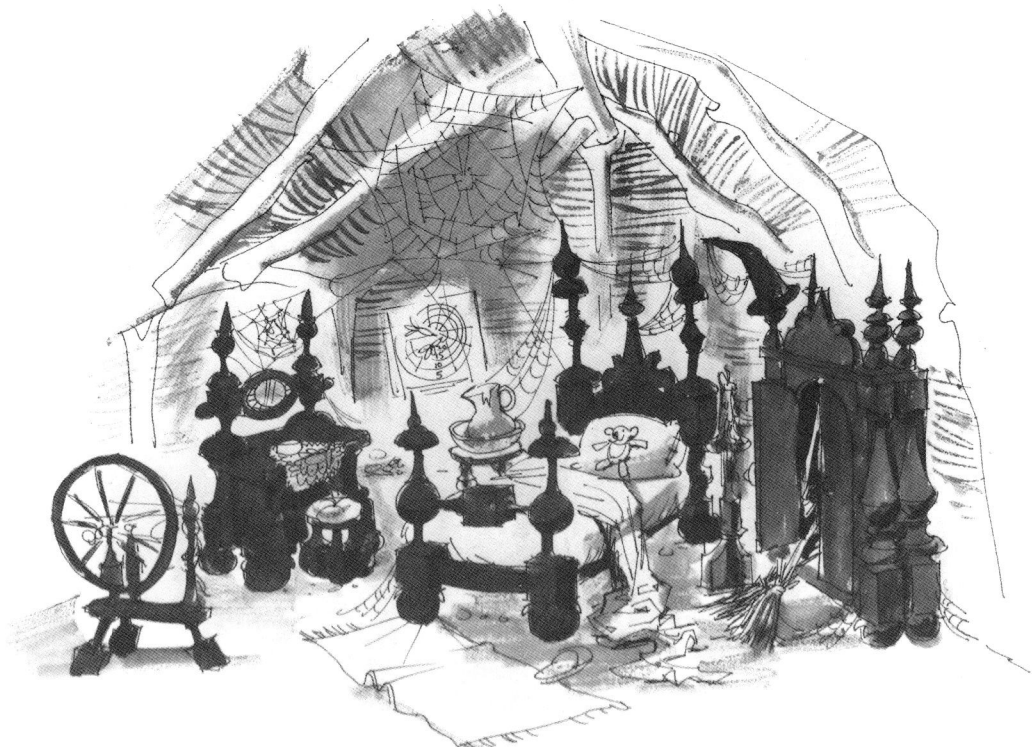

ABOVE: Concept sketch for *The Sword in the Stone*.

and do what I was doing for the whole thing. Instead they'd all call on me. Even though I was removed from the position they'd call on me for the same answers that I had given them before . . . I was crestfallen, because Walt wouldn't speak to me and might even fire me, but he didn't.[69]

In 1962, the emotional stress weighing on Ken was so heavy that he suffered two strokes in one week, which left the right side of his body partially paralyzed for close to three years.

[After the strokes] I was very, very concerned with the future of Disneyland. And, so while I was invalided, I tried to think of things that would be possibly interesting to the public and therefore to Walt and suggested [them] to him. I made very, very poor scribbles of those ideas. Those were probably the first things that I got involved with [after the strokes]. In a pond there were frogs. They were huge frogs, three times the size, but exact reproductions. All this croaking and singing and so on and so on. It got into a big water spectacle. Everything was music and water and the way the frogs spouted water to the music. They had an impresario and a leader. They had an orchestra and they could make really fantastic sounds that would be wonderful to hear. They played this music, and different fountains and different colored things went on. It [would have been located] near the hub.[70]

When Ken returned to the studio, the artists were still hard at work on *The Sword in the Stone*.

Walt had dropped out of this [project] and he didn't seem to be pushing . . . He left it up to us. Those of us who were willing and interested in taking hold did. And those of us who were interested in taking hold were Bill Peet and myself. We kind of filled the niche where once Walt had been, both pictorially and verbally. We had a strong animator in Milt Kahl and we had a pretty good story. Either Bill or I would be on a new sequence and we'd be critical of each other's work and it would lead to re-dos that were better than the original.

Ken, however, was dissatisfied with the movie. *One Hundred and One Dalmatians* had achieved a unity of design between backgrounds and characters, with modern backgrounds a perfect match for the hard lines generated by the Xerox process. Not so this time around: stylistically this new feature pulled into two opposite directions:

The Sword in the Stone was not completely planned for the *Dalmatians* treatment. It was . . . a toothsome thing; it was an original backdrop painting, soft and foggy and a spotlight effect with characters on top of it, but at the same time it couldn't help but be affected by the looks of *Dalmatians* in most cases . . . We were unable to make it be a picture in which it had the unified effect of one drawing that was appearing on the screen at the same time rather than two drawings.[71]

KEN ANDERSON

THE CHARACTER DESIGNER

With work complete on *The Sword in the Stone*, Ken could feel that Walt's attitude toward him was softening as he started working on his next big project, *The Jungle Book*. It was a movie full of truly memorable scenes and characters, a movie that played to Ken's key strengths: character designs and arresting drawings that suggested full sequences. While looking at a drawing of Baloo in *The Jungle Book*, animator Ollie Johnston explained:

> [Ken] has a rare ability to do drawings that have what you might call a "big concept." In other words, we relied on him, particularly in the last fifteen or twenty years [of his career] to come up with drawings that suggest a whole sequence of action, not just a little gag. [For example] what these [drawings] did was to suggest to us a whole sequence of having the bear scratch. He scratches on the tree, goes to rocks, and finally pulls the tree out of the ground and scratches with it. It was based on these imaginative few drawings that Ken did . . . It takes a special kind of guy to think of these things. It's more than just the drawings; it suggests something with an open end and a whole lot of ideas.[72]

While Ken helped design all the characters in the movie, his biggest challenge was Shere Khan, the tiger. According to animator Milt Kahl, for months the artists had envisioned him as a Jack Palance type of character.[73] Ken saw things differently:

> All of us involved, particularly the animators, were very interested in the development of this Shere Khan as a personality. And we felt that he should be worked throughout the whole picture, so that whenever we had a meeting on any story sequence, we kept bringing up Shere Khan, much to Walt's dislike. He became annoyed with this, finally, to the extent of excluding the animators from the story meetings. I was lulled into a false sense of security that made me feel we didn't need any Shere Khan after all. Because Walt said, "[T]his isn't a story about a tiger; this is a story about the boy. Let's get the boy . . . the boy and his compatriots." And so it went on and on like that until one day, in a meeting, Walt turned to me and said, "Ken, it's time for you to come up with Shere Khan," which, of course, stopped me in my tracks, and I agonized that night until I thought in terms of Basil Rathbone, who, to me, was a very menacing, underplayed villain. So I made these drawings of the tiger with that attitude, supercilious, so confident of his power and so confident of his ability that he didn't need to rant or roar. [I] made these drawings and showed them to Walt the next day. He said, "Hey, that's it. I know who that is. That's George Sanders. He's a friend of mine, and he'll do it," which it turned out he did.[74]

In parallel to his work on *The Jungle Book*, Ken was also handling visual development for another cartoon based on a literary property: *Winnie the Pooh and the Honey Tree*. The studio had considered adapting the stories of A. A. Milne since the late 1930s. In 1941, artist Jack Miller had even written some proposed treatments, and Mary Blair created a few concept sketches for a planned musical adaptation set to Schumann's Symphony No. 4 and Bach's Suite No. 3. *Winnie the Pooh and the Honey Tree* was a much less ambitious project: a simple featurette released on February 4, 1966, with the movie *The Ugly Dachshund*. It was so charming and so well received that on May 31, Walt Disney sent a note to his artists encouraging them to look into producing a sequel.[75]

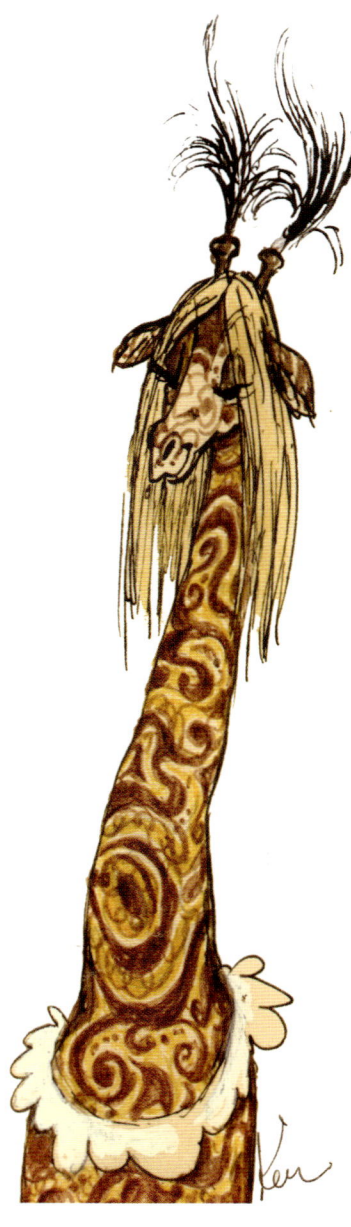

ABOVE: Character design created for an article released in 1970 in the *Wonderful World of Disney* magazine. Courtesy: Erika Thorpe.

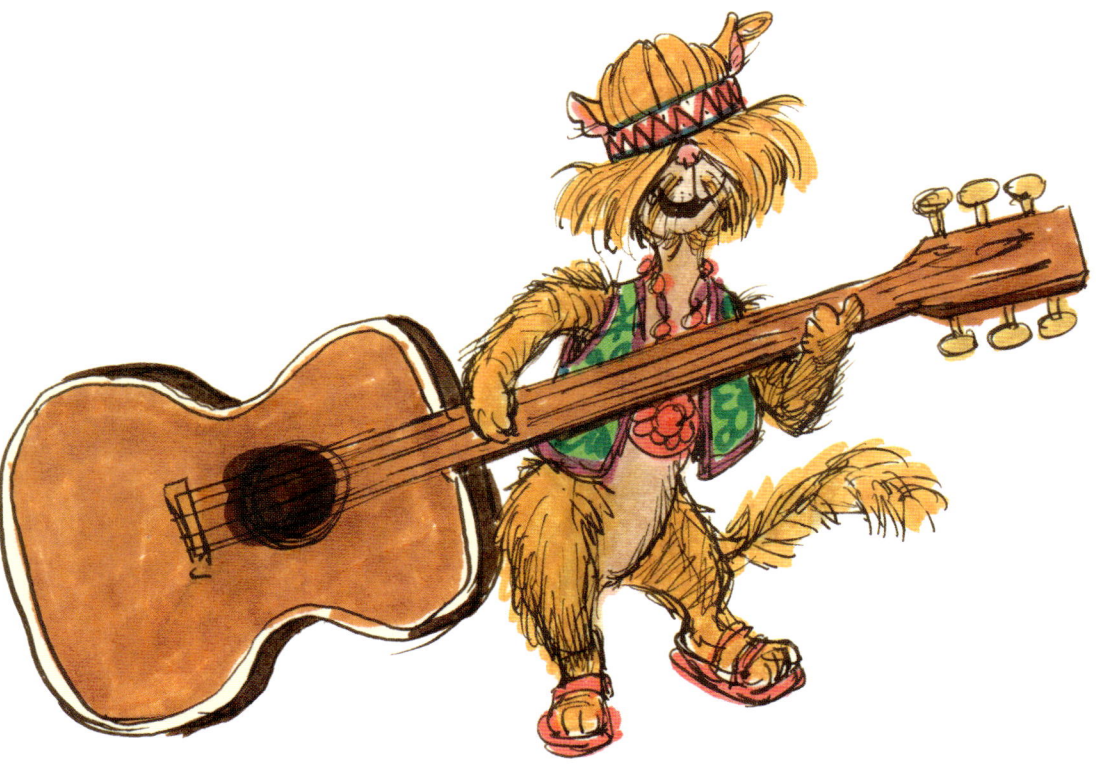

ABOVE: Character design for *The Aristocats*.

THE ARISTOCATS

While the animators were finalizing production on *The Jungle Book* and *Winnie the Pooh*, Ken was already focusing on the next movie, along with Walt, executive Harry Tytle, and veteran story artist Otto Englander.

Drafted by director Tom McGowan and writer Tom Rowe in 1962, under the incentive of Harry Tytle, *The Aristocats* was initially conceived as a live-action, two-part television show, and then as a live-action feature. The following year Tytle convinced Walt that the story should be adapted as an animated feature. Walt concurred, and in April 1964 Otto Englander was assigned to work on the project.[76] Ken Anderson most likely joined the *Aristocats* team at some point in 1965, by which time he started designing some of the characters and visualizing key scenes.

But the original story was too long and too complex. On the human side, the key characters included Madame Adelaide Bonfamille; her butler, Edgar; Edgar's wife, Elvire; as well as Madame Bonfamille's doctor, nurse, and lawyer: Doctor Pilule, Minou, and Monsieur Hautecourt. The cats Duchess and O'Malley were already there, but also five kittens: Marie Antoinette, Berlioz, Renoir, Escoffier (the gourmet cat), and the black cat Waterloo.[77]

Publicity shots would later show Ken Anderson surrounded by boards filled with photos of all types of cats. The shots might have been staged, but they gave a real sense of Ken's work ethic when tackling a new assignment:

> I research everything I can. For an actual creature, I get every photograph or book that I can find. I immerse myself in as much knowledge of the creature as I can, make it a part of me. Then I decide that some things [I] have to adapt but I can make the adaptations based on what I know. The material leaves me better prepared to come up with something new . . . In order to translate [*The Aristocats*] into film I had to study Parisian architecture and style. I did a lot of research and went to the library and had stuff brought in . . . I thought Paris was a rich feeling, and so I tried everything I could to make it appear to be that, including the characters [who] were very Frenchy (sic): Berlioz, these little cats, you could imagine, were the animal counterparts of their illustrious human namesakes.[78]

As he had done for *One Hundred and One Dalmatians*, Ken even animated a test sequence to give a feeling of what he was trying to achieve:

KEN ANDERSON 43

I did a scene of a couple of servants for the house. [Edgar] was caught in a wheelchair, and what I animated was him going down the Seine River, and falling in and being attacked by his wife. She banged him over the head and she was banging him over the head until the end of it.[79]

With *The Jungle Book* scheduled for release in 1967, there was no real pressure to nail down the story or the characters of *The Aristocats* very quickly. What the artists could not imagine, however, was that the clock was ticking. On December 15, 1966, Walt Disney passed away. As Ollie Johnston recalled, they were on their own:

[For] *The Aristocats*, none of us had been in any meetings with Walt; Ken Anderson had been in one, and had made several drawings. But the rest of us didn't know what Walt had seen in the picture or what he wanted, and yet that had been designated as the next picture.[80]

Less than two weeks after Walt's death, on December 28, 1966, director Woolie Reitherman, art director Ken Anderson, story artists Don DaGradi and Vance Gerry, writer Larry Clemmons, animator Dick Lucas, and executives Bill Anderson, Winston Hibler, and Bill Walsh met to discuss the future of the feature. They agreed that the story needed to be simplified and the number of characters pared down.[81] By April 10, 1967, the studio had a working script that was close to what would eventually make it to the screen: Doctor Pilule and Minou were gone, so were Escoffier, and Waterloo (who became Napoleon for a short while). Renoir had been renamed Toulouse in homage to Toulouse Lautrec, and the cast gained one new character: the mouse Roquefort.[82]

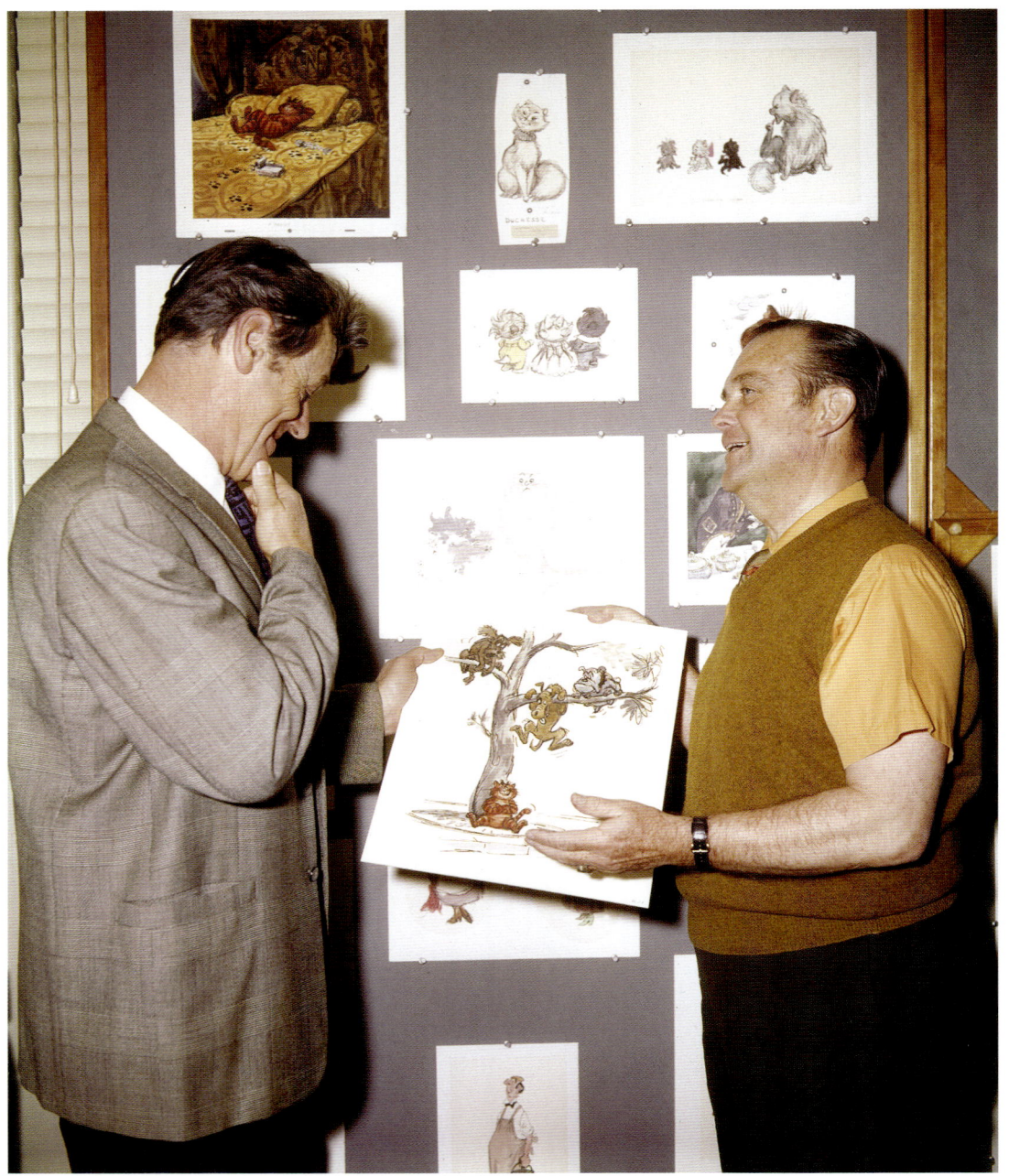

ABOVE: Ken Anderson and director Woolie Reitherman in 1970 in front of a storyboard from *The Aristocats*.

44   THEY DREW AS THEY PLEASED

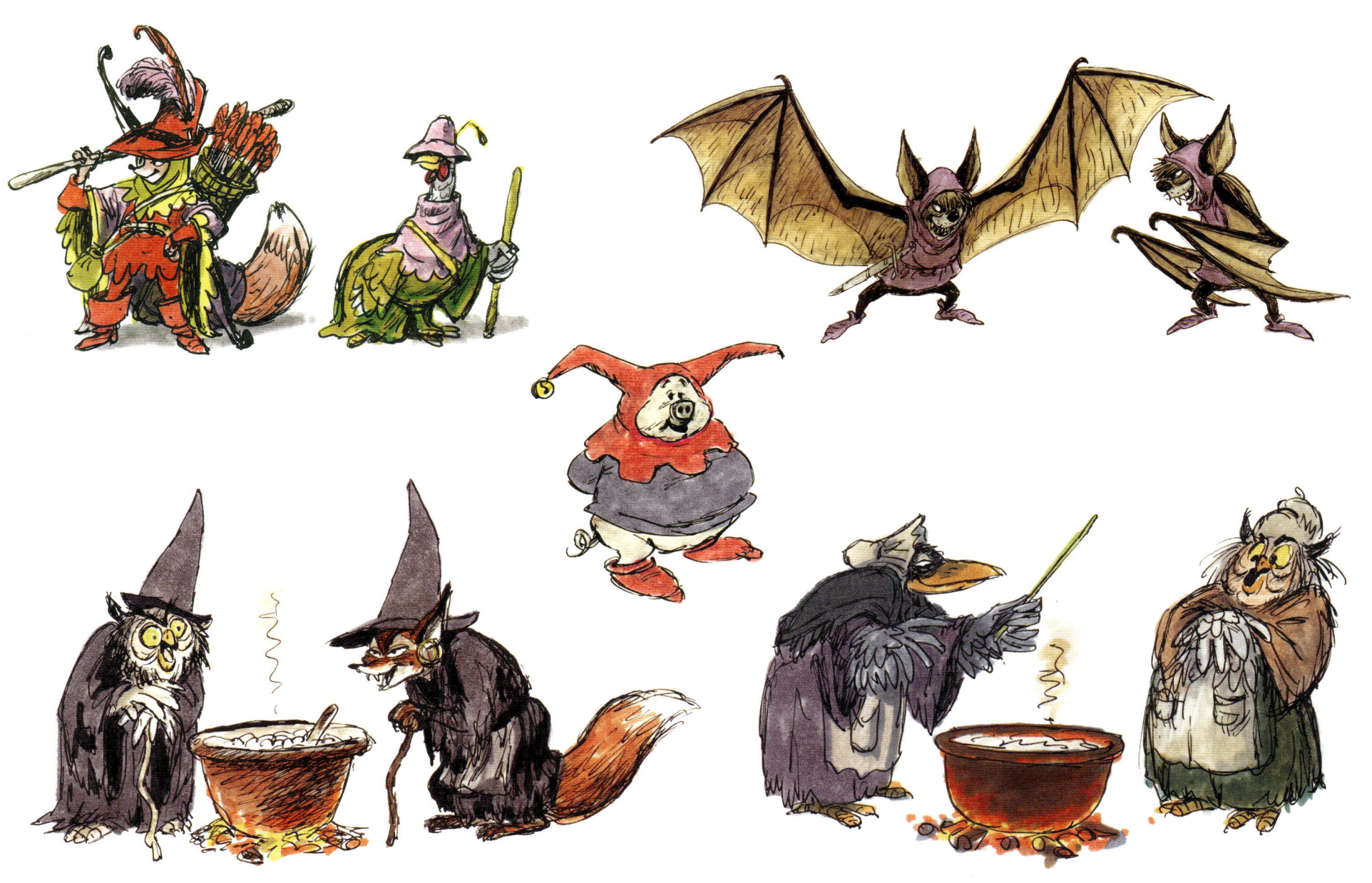

ABOVE: Character designs for *Robin Hood*.

ROBIN HOOD

With *The Aristocats* well into preproduction by 1968, the studio had to decide what to do for an encore. Thankfully, Ken Anderson soon provided the answer:

On a fishing trip to [Hot Creek in] the High Sierras, accompanied by [our chief operating officer] Card Walker, in October '68, he indicated that he was concerned about the lack of a property to follow *Aristocats*. He suggested that a classic story might be found that would lend itself to suitable adaptation for a cartoon with the substitution of animal characters in place of humans. What did the animators enjoy doing? They most enjoyed working in the manner in which we worked on *Song of the South*. Where could I get animal creatures that were somewhat like *Song of the South*, and what kind of a picture, sort of a charade, a burlesque of some well-known fantasy story? *Robin Hood*? Aha! The happy thought of *Robin Hood* occurred to me and Card was enthusiastic about it. He urged me to pursue the idea when we returned to the studio.

At the time I was deeply engrossed in *Aristocats* but I took time out to relay the idea to Otto Englander. Otto had been assigned the project of researching for a suitable property which might serve as a basis for a feature cartoon and the idea of *Robin Hood* with animal characters had so far eluded him. He immediately warmed to the idea. We discussed the similar elements in the one-time activated property *Reynard*, and felt that in *Robin Hood* we had a superior story line and a subject with all the necessary elements for quality development of personality business. Accordingly, Otto sent a digest of our discussion to Bill Anderson for his reaction or approval. This turned out to be ironical since it had apparently been Bill Anderson's idea in the first place to adapt a classic story and use animals for humans if such a story could be found. Naturally Bill was in favor of the idea, too. I then broached the idea during an *Aristocats* story meeting and once more everyone approved. No one was more enthusiastic or seemed to immediately see more in the project than Woolie.

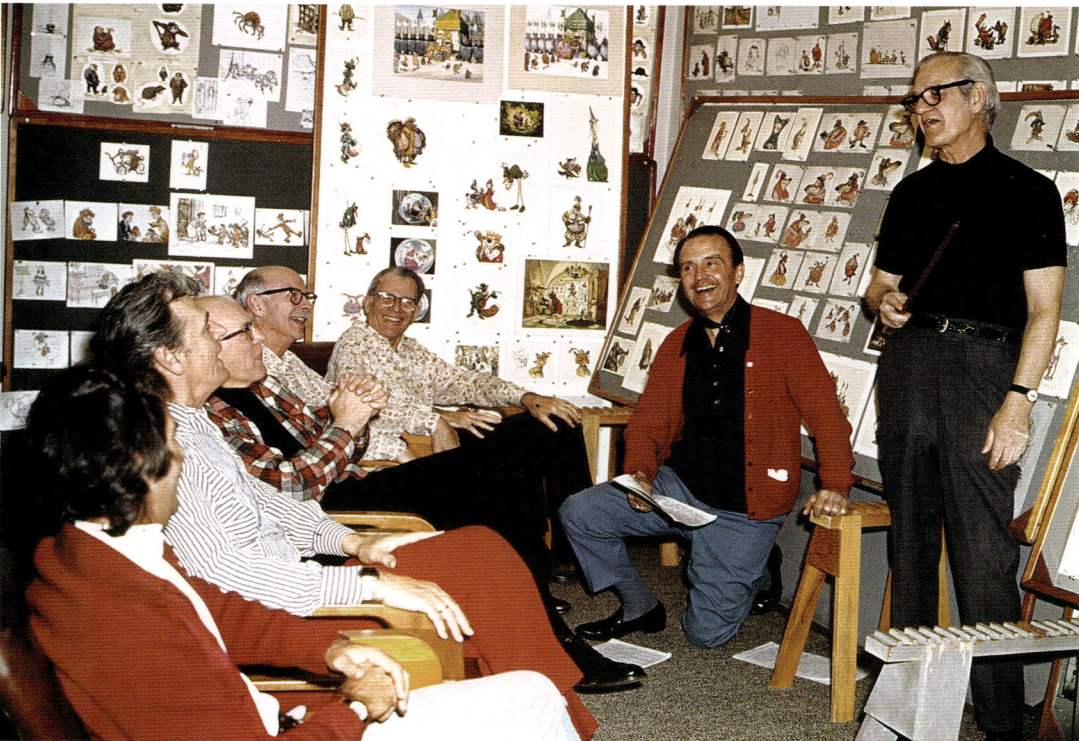

Next followed a meeting with Bill Anderson, Woolie, and Larry Clemmons to set direction. As a result I was assigned to start exploratory animal character drawings and so *Robin Hood* was finally launched into production.[83]

From a character design point of view, along with *The Jungle Book*, *Robin Hood* is one of Ken's masterpieces. Working almost nonstop, he created dozens and dozens of arresting characters, many of which did not make it to the screen.

I worked on the development by myself for about four or five months. The very first step, before I started digging into any of the drawings, was to read the stories. So I read what existed and then I even made little sequences to sell the idea. I had a little thumbnail sequence of Friar Tuck and Robin Hood crossing each other, going back and forth across the water, showing ways that it did work. And the tournament . . .

ABOVE: From left to right: Dave Michener, Woolie Reitherman, Milt Kahl, Ollie Johnston, Frank Thomas, Ken Anderson, and Larry Clemmons working on *Robin Hood*.

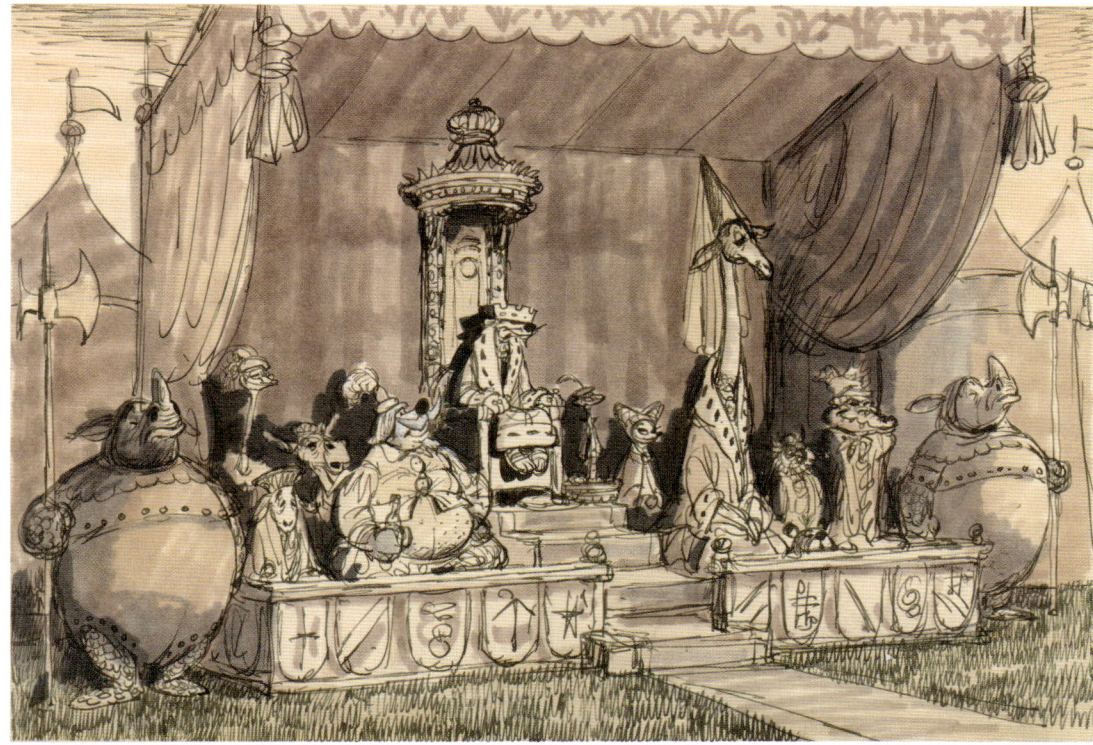

ABOVE: Concept sketch for *Robin Hood*.

I had all down in thumbnails . . . I did sequences at the same time I was doing the characters. Those sequences were of interest to the animators and to Woolie. There are no rules for developing characters. Or rather, for each character there is a different set of rules. Each character is a different personality, has different problems, and is conceived in a different way. What we are after is to visualize a personality that is strong enough so that an actor can get hold of it. You don't think of the actors first. You create a character that the actor can work with . . . [For] Maid Marian, the first person I had in mind was Goldie Hawn.[84]

And so, under Ken's pen, the characters started taking shape:

I knew right off that sly Robin Hood must be a fox. From there it was logical that Maid Marian should be a pretty vixen. Little John, legendarily known for his size, was easily a big overgrown bear. Friar Tuck is great as a badger, but he was also great as a pig, as I had originally planned. Then I thought the symbol of a pig might be offensive to the Church, so we changed him. Richard the Lionhearted of course had to be a regal, proud, strong lion and his pathetic cousin Prince John, the weak villain also had to be a lion but we made him scrawny and childish . . . The idea of the snake, I think, came from Larry Clemmons . . . I had a snake but the snake was a common, ordinary garden variety snake, one of Robin Hood's men, and he was an infiltrator, like the mole. I had the mole as a spy and the snake as a spy. And the mole would dig holes and the snake would go with him. The mole would always get there and eavesdrop. When Larry came on the picture and saw that, he thought in terms of the snake being a good foil for King John. So I started to go with that. I thought it was a good idea. Then Woolie encouraged me in directions I might not have gone by myself. He said, "Why restrict yourself to just the animals in England? Why not take any animals?" So with tongue in cheek, I tried elephants, crocodiles, and they turned out great. In *Robin Hood*, all the domestic animals, all the nice animals were the outcasts [Robin's men], and the foreigners are all around King John: they are all imported animals. Once I began to visualize some of these things, then people began to aid me with lots of other ideas. I would develop along many new lines that they suggested, which I also thought might be possible.[85]

In parallel to his work on *Robin Hood*, Ken, who never stopped creating, even at home, was toying with several other intriguing story ideas. In 1969, for example, he offered his take on the story of *Hiawatha*,[86] which several Disney artists had already tried to develop throughout the years, including Holling C. Holling in 1944,[87] and Dick Kelsey in 1948.[88]

And in 1971, he suggested that the studio produce a movie based on the "it's a small world" attraction.[89] The concept of producing movies based on park attractions was ahead of its time though. It would take another leadership team at Disney to reinvent that idea, after Ken's death, at the dawn of the twenty-first century.

FROM *CATFISH BEND* TO *THE RESCUERS*

In 1973, Ken took a strong interest in the *Catfish Bend* book series by author Ben Lucien Burman, whom he saw as the modern Mark Twain.[90] The project obsessed him until his retirement and influenced several other studio projects.

The *Catfish Bend* stories took place in an imaginary part of the Mississippi River, close to Vicksburg. It featured a cast of anthropomorphized animal characters who were bound to fascinate Ken: Doc Racoon, the country squire, well-liked by all, leader of the good guys; the snake Judge Black, the solemn, motto-quoting pundit of great and unimpeachable integrity; J. C. Hunter, the flashy show-off red fox whom Ken converted into a hillbilly entertainer; and Gray Fox, the con man, riverboat gambler villain.

By 1976, helped at first by story artist Dave Michener, then by writer Steve Hulett, Ken was cranking outline after outline and even invited Ben Lucien Burman to visit the studio on June 14, 1977, to review his progress.[91] But finding a strong story arc to connect Burman's short tales was no easy task. After five years of intense efforts, when Ken retired in 1978, the project was still yet to be green-lit.

In July 1978, a few months after Ken's retirement party, Woolie Reitherman, Steve Hulett, and Mel Shaw met to summarize the rough plot ideas that were on the table: in one version, the young daughter of a poor family discovers the musical animal members of Catfish Bend jamming in the forest; in another, the daughter of a rich plantation owner is swept away in floodwaters and saved by the animals.[92] The following month, Ron Miller, Steve Hulett, and artists Mel Shaw, Brad Bird, and Randy Cartwright analyzed one more approach, developed by Mel Shaw,

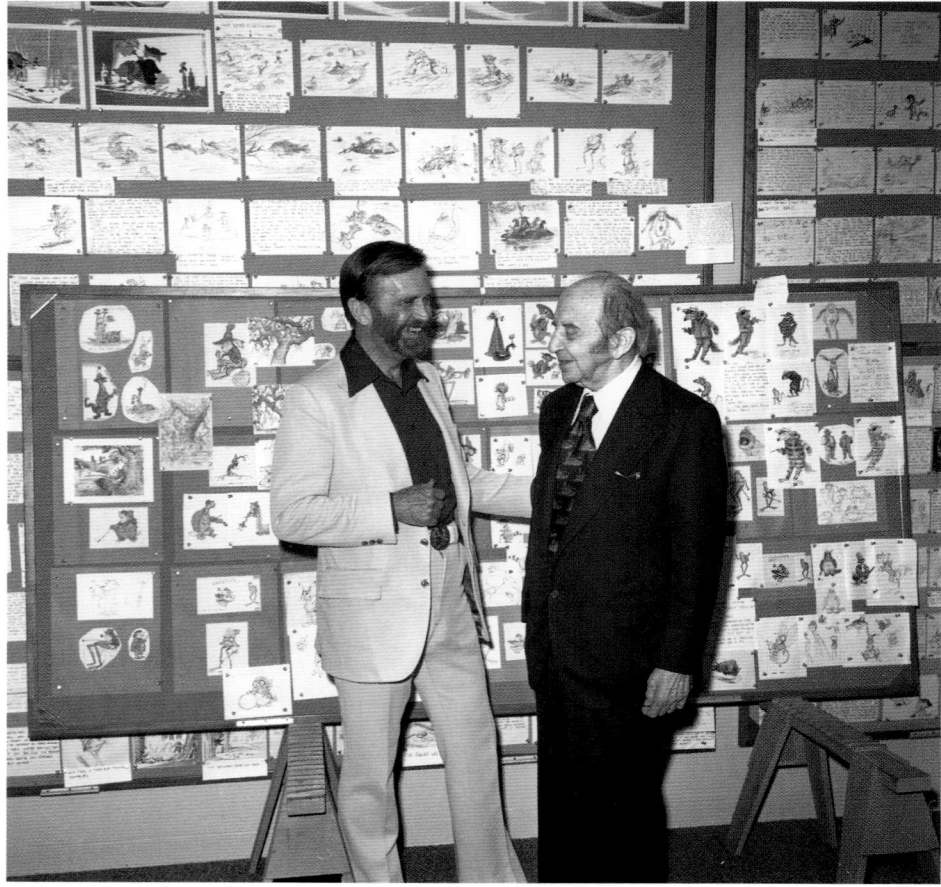

which centered on the daughter of an evil circus owner fleeing to Catfish Bend. No one in the room was totally convinced by what they saw, but Ron was unconcerned: the movie, in his mind, was to be released six to eight years later, after *The Fox and the Hound* and *The Black Cauldron*.[93] There was ample time.

With the success of Mickey's fiftieth birthday celebration in 1978, Woolie Reitherman decided to explore the possibility of developing a Mickey feature, an idea that had been considered often by the studio throughout the years since the late 1930s.[94] By November 26, 1979, a proposed outline described the movie as "a live-action picture containing several cartoon sequences, each one featuring Mickey and the gang interacting with the Catfish Bend characters."[95] The bizarre idea was eventually shelved.

ABOVE: Ken Anderson and Ben Lucien Burman (author of *Catfish Bend*) on June 14, 1977.

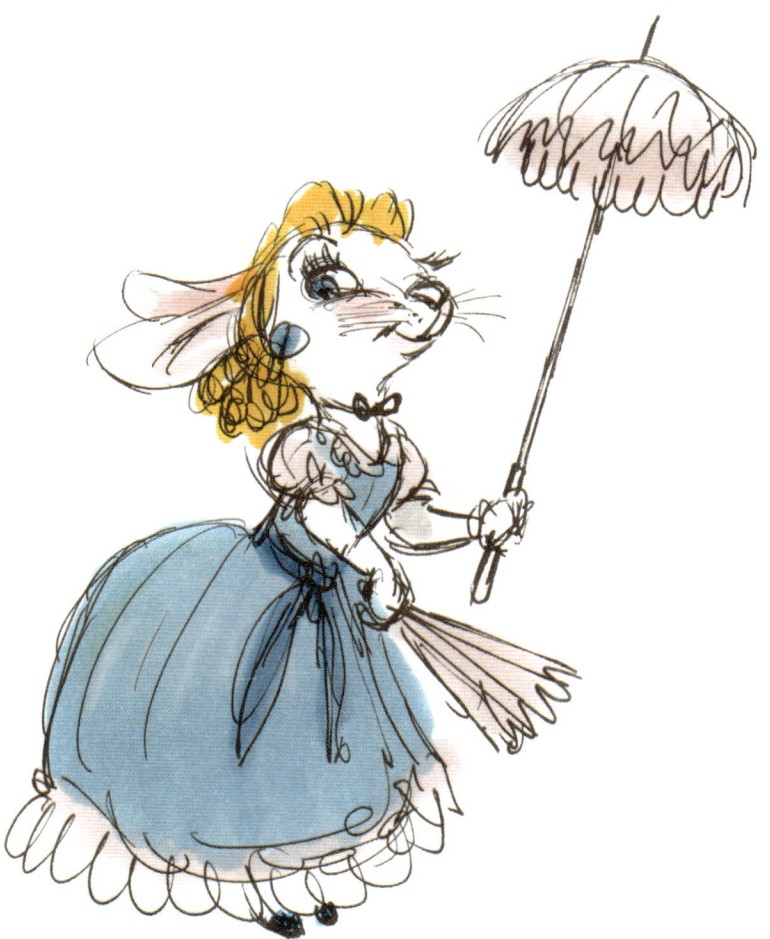

ABOVE: Character design for *Catfish Bend*. Courtesy: Wendy Greer.

Most of the critters that Ken Anderson had designed for the Catfish Bend project actually made it to the screen . . . as part of *The Rescuers*, the studio's next feature after *Robin Hood*. Animator Frank Thomas explained:

> Ken Anderson did probably the best preliminary work [on the swamp critters]. He had drawn them way back for another picture [*Catfish Bend*] . . . We found the old drawings and adapted them to this.[96]

Walt was still alive when some artists at the studio started working on *The Rescuers*. On January 2, 1963, story artist Otto Englander had written an outline based on the novel by Margery Sharp, and by April 1964 four large storyboards had been created by artist Joe Rinaldi.[97] The story at the time revolved around the rescue by Bernard and Bianca of a Norwegian poet. In August 1968, a little less than two years after Walt's death, Otto Englander penned another treatment, this one featuring Bernard and Bianca in the Middle Ages trying to rescue Richard the Lionheart.[98] This, less than two months before Ken Anderson suggested *Robin Hood* to Card Walker as the studio's next feature project! It was in early 1972, however, that *The Rescuers* started to take center stage in the story artists' minds. The plot was still uncertain: Bernard and Bianca were going to rescue a bear deceived by a con man penguin, or maybe it would be a little girl, as in Margery Sharp's second *Rescuers* novel, *Miss Bianca*.[99] Woolie Reitherman recalled:

> The [plot] never got anywhere, because it never had a villain . . . I remember that I went to Europe, I think it was for [the release of] *Robin Hood* . . . I took Margery Sharp's books along and there was in there a mean woman in a crystal palace. When I got back I called some of the guys together and I said, "We've got to get a villain in this thing." I mean, a real honest to goodness villain . . . We got Ken Anderson and Larry Clemmons and three or four of the animators on it. We started to develop this villainess with a kidnapping premise . . . And Ollie [Johnston] met with Ron Miller in the elevator one time and he said, "We've got a new villainess. And she's kidnapping a little girl, dah, dah, dah." And in a classic understatement [Ron] turned around and said, "My, it has changed, hasn't it?"[100]

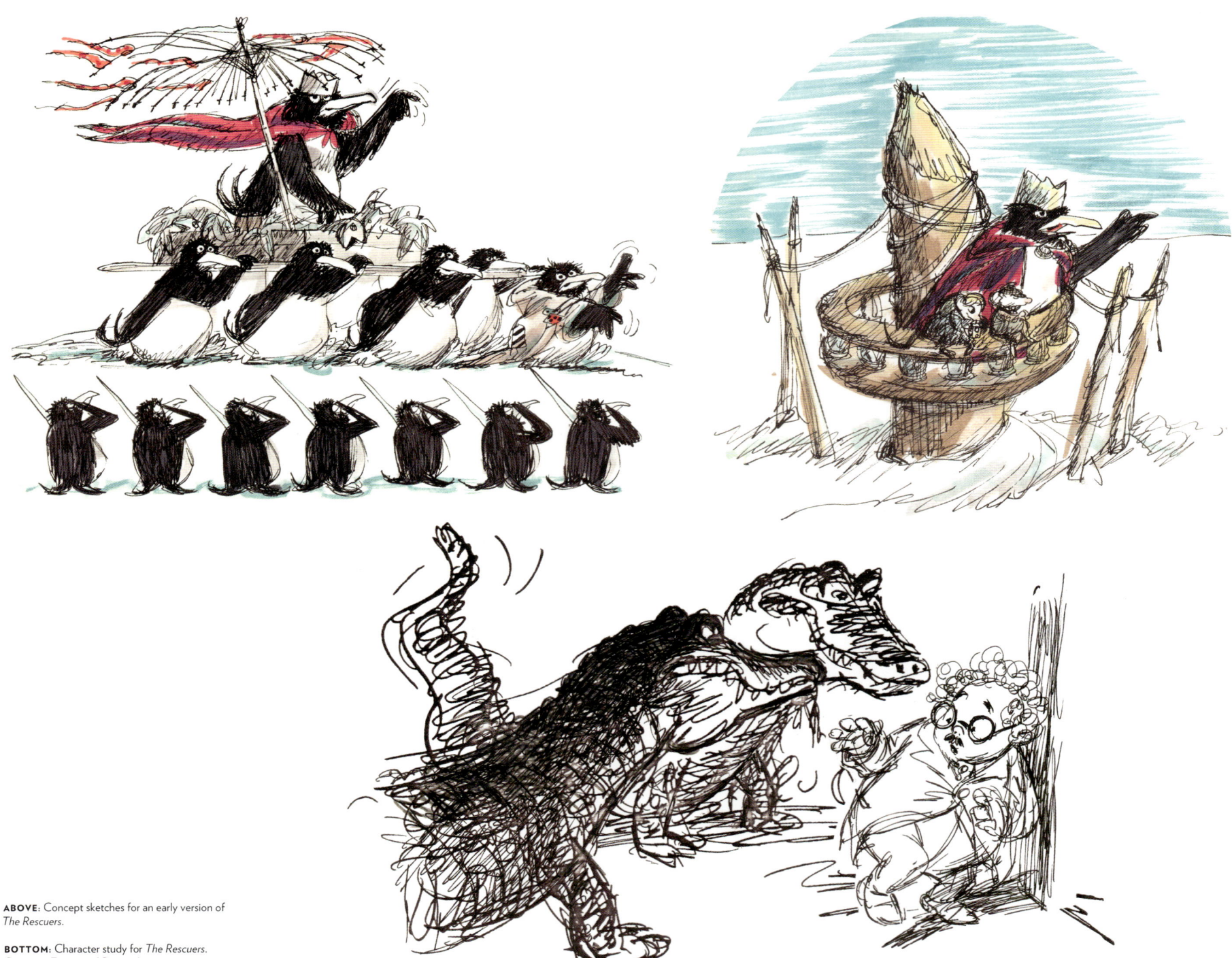

ABOVE: Concept sketches for an early version of *The Rescuers*.

BOTTOM: Character study for *The Rescuers*.
Courtesy: Emmanuel Bourmalo.

When the story finally became that of the rescue of Penny, Ken was able to start designing the missing characters. He based Mr. Snoops on the bubbly journalist John Culhane who spent days on end at the studio interviewing the Disney artists for *Reader's Digest* and the *New York Times Magazine*. As for the villainess, Ken decided at first to propose an unconventional idea: repurposing Cruella De Vil from *One Hundred and One Dalmatians*. The idea was short-lived, as story artist Burny Mattinson explained:

> It was talked about because Medusa and Cruella had a lot in common. But [animator] Milt [Kahl], of course, was very strong against that, "Oh, no no. We're gonna have a new character. I'm not gonna do Cruella," Because he felt that Marc [Davis had animated] Cruella beautifully. He was not gonna go and take his character.[101]

There was also the question of Evinrude, one of the only swamp animals from *The Rescuers* that Ken had not originally designed for *Catfish Bend*. He recalled the character's evolution:

> He was a complete invention. He had nothing to do with the original story. In the story the way we developed it, the way we planned it and pruned it and worked it out together, Evinrude became not only a delightful character, as far as his personality, and the business that he performed in the picture, but that the little part that he played fit into the rest of the picture. I used to have a place in Lake Sherwood. We'd go up there at night after work and then we would get up early in the morning and go out in a little rowboat and go fishing for bass. And many were the Evinrudes that would accompany us around the lake. I started calling [the character] Evinrude in jest, and it stuck. [Writer] Larry Clemmons glommed on it. He just loved that.[102]

Along with *Catfish Bend* and *The Rescuers*, there was one last project that Ken was passionate about in the early 1970s, the story of *Scruffy* by author Paul Gallico. Starring a Barbary ape living on the Rock of Gibraltar during World War II, the idea, which Ken worked on from 1971 to 1975, was a tough sell.[103]

In 1976, Ken admitted to John Culhane that *Scruffy* had been tabled.[104]

And yet, at sixty-seven, after forty-two years at the Disney studio, Ken was busier than ever. He was involved with the early efforts to adapt *The Black Cauldron* to the screen, designed characters for a TV animated project inspired by the upcoming Energy Pavilion at EPCOT, and was still developing his pet project, *Catfish Bend*.[105] It was a request from Walt's son-in-law and president of the studio, Ron Miller, however, which would provide him with his last great hurrah.

PETE'S DRAGON

Pete's Dragon had first been envisioned by the Disney studio back in 1957 as a property that could be adapted as a two-part TV episode for the "Disneyland" show. Disney historian Max Lark explained:

> In December 1957, Walt Disney Productions hired author Seton I. Miller as a film writer to write *Pete's Dragon and the U.S.A. (Forever After)*, based on an unpublished short story of the same name that Miller had co-written with S.S. Field . . . In March 1958, productions #5815 and #5816 were opened for *Pete's Dragon and the U.S.A., Part I & II*—this time envisioned as a Fantasyland-branded two-episode entry for the "Disneyland" television show. Records pertaining to that production date to spring 1958, when writer Noel Langley was hired to craft a screenplay, a work which he completed that April. Although he was drawn to the story and its potential, Walt was still deciding the best way to approach the property, and *Pete's Dragon* was soon put away to mellow.[106]

Fast forward to 1976: by then a new screenplay for a movie that would combine live action and animation had been written by Malcolm Marmorstein and the studio was serious about bringing that version to the screen. In a newspaper article released in December 1977, journalist Bob Thomas told what happened next:

> [Ken Anderson] was ready to retire from Walt Disney Productions a year or so ago when executive producer Ron Miller tossed a challenge at him: help pull a full-sized dragon on the screen and make him perform with human actors. "Why not?" Ken Anderson agreed . . . "I had finished doing the characters for another feature, *Catfish Bend*, and was about ready to retire," said Anderson. "Then Ron gave me an original story that he said Walt had been interested in. It was about a boy and his dragon, but the dragon never appeared to anyone. The village had to keep making up excuses for all the damage that happened—a freak storm or something. The dragon came into the story only in the boy's dream, and then he was just a storybook dragon with no intimation of personality. I was really on the spot. I thought I shouldn't be critical of something both Walt and Ron had believed in. I could have drawn a dragon out of any book, but I decided to operate on the ploy that Elliott appears to those who are in need of help." From 9 a.m. until noon one morning, Anderson made a series of sketches for his concept of the star of *Pete's Dragon*. Ron Miller and co-producer Jerome Courtland saw the result and were charmed. Miller convinced Anderson to stay on and direct the young animators who would bring Elliott to full, fire-breathing life.[107]

Ken was designing his last great character, Elliott, and he loved it:

> I thought dragons normally to the Occidental mind are vicious, mean, terrible creatures . . . In [some cultures], dragons are beneficent. They are the ones that bring the rain to the farmers. They are the ones that make the crops succeed. They save people when things are wrong. So I felt, why not a big, bumbling Wallace Beery type of dragon? He doesn't shave, he can't shave. He's got a stubble on his chin, and yet he's warmhearted, but crude. And also it would be kind of nice if he

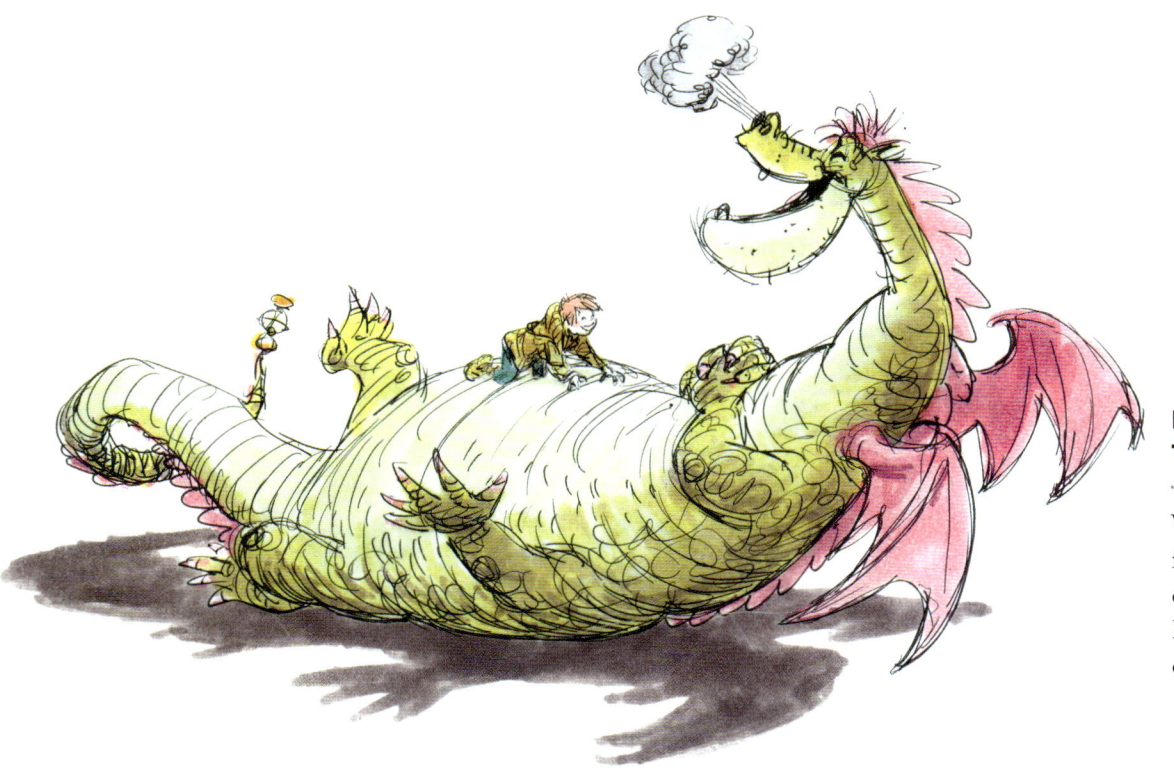

ABOVE: Concept sketch for *Pete's Dragon*. Courtesy: David P. Smith and Wonderful World of Animation.

wasn't really able to be facile. He wasn't able to fly too well, and he'd allowed himself to get a little paunchy. And so no longer were his wings capable of lifting him off the ground without a great deal of effort, which would make people feel a little bit for the dragon if he was a nice fellow. And at the same time he should be fancifully colored. All these things together led to the concept of this dragon, which isn't too different from many other dragons. He actually isn't too different, in body shape, from the Reluctant Dragon, except he's fatter, and I think he would have a harder time getting off the ground. But he's an entirely different personality. And he served his purpose as a training ground for these young animators.[108]

NEW FANTASYLAND, EPCOT, AND THE DISNEY CHANNEL

With this last character design for the studio under his belt, Ken finally retired, on March 31, 1978. And yet, this was not the end of his Disney career. From 1979 to 1983, he was hired by WED Enterprises, later known as Walt Disney Imagineering, as a show design consultant. Imagineer Tony Baxter remembered:

> Ken and I worked on the New Fantasyland for Disneyland after he had already retired. But I knew he had been so involved in the first Fantasyland that I called and said, "It would be wonderful if you could come and give us some help on the new Fantasyland." Ken was great because he was someone who had been there the first time, with Walt. So, all of us, "the new kids," had a father. When someone wanted it this way and others that way, Ken would be able to come and say, "No, look, look, look, this is what we need to do in here." So Ken would kind of soothe everybody's egos and do a quick little sketch of what it should look like and that would be it. So much of the architecture on [the] Snow White and Mr. Toad [attractions] is from Ken. Ken was very strong on those two designs; he had a very strong influence on the rest of us during that whole process.[109]

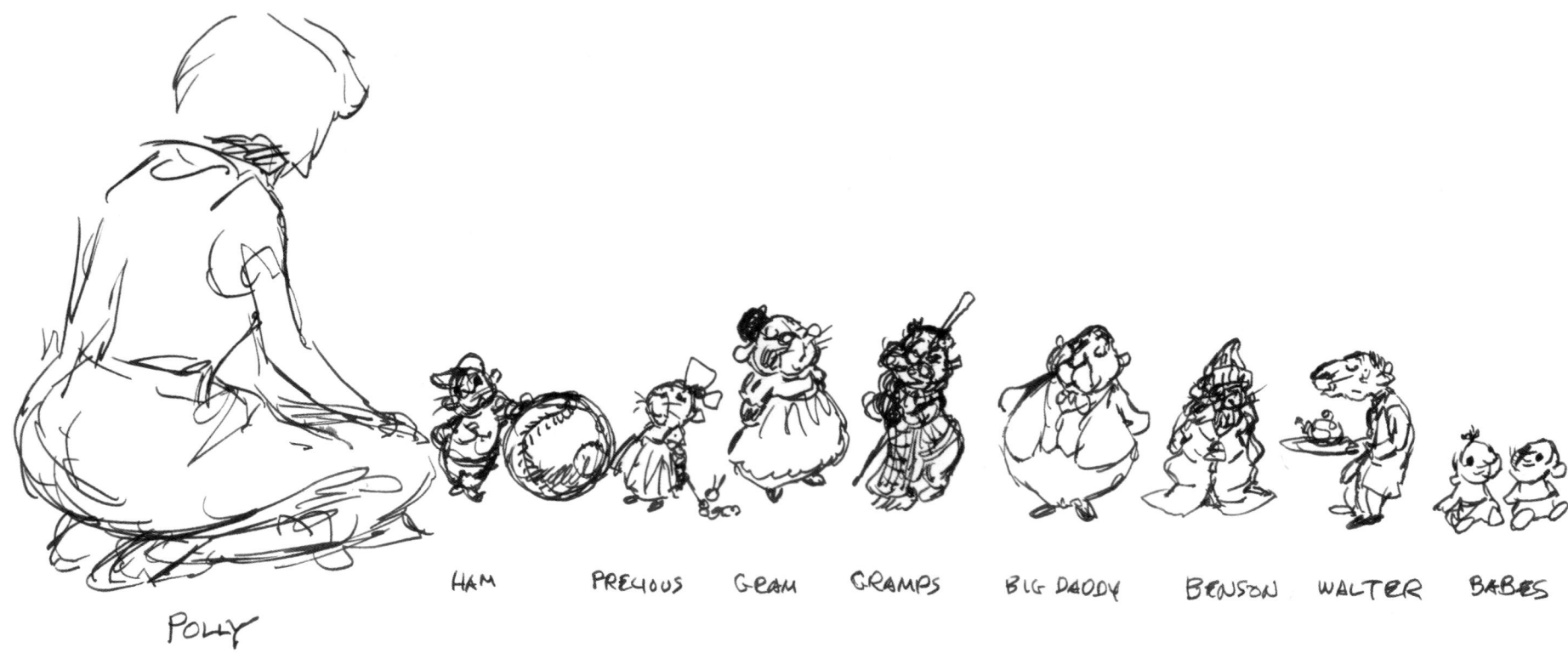

On May 25, 1983, the new Fantasyland opened to the public. And yet, Ken carried on working for Disney on a freelance basis. This time, for The Disney Channel. In 1982, he had developed concepts for a planned daily half-hour science program titled *Wizards*, which was supposed to originate from EPCOT Center.[110] He was now designing the characters for the series *Dumbo's Circus* and *Disney's Adventures of the Gummi Bears*. Then in 1984 he helped develop *The Wuzzles*, and in 1986, he submitted several outlines for a proposed animated series titled *Hamster Hamlet*, which unfortunately did not make it to the screen.[111]

On January 22, 1985, more than fifty years after originally joining Disney, Ken signed a new agreement with WED Enterprises to work as a consultant on the proposed African Pavilion for EPCOT Center.[112] Also involved with the project were Alex Haley, world-famous author of *Roots*, director Jack Couffer, and Ken's colleague and friend Herb Ryman. Collaborating once again with Ryman must have signaled to Ken that his career had come full circle. After all, he had first met Herb in the early 1930s, before joining Disney, when the two men were still young artists at MGM.

Ken passed away on December 13, 1993. A few years later, his former colleague Don Bluth wrote about him:

> He liked to think of himself as just a guy in the art game slugging it out, but I think he knew deep inside that he was a bird of rare plume. There was an impish grin always challenging those in the room to a friendly duel, as if to say, "Come on, let's see what you've got." The sparring for excellence was never about besting another artist, but always about mining to the million-dollar idea.[113]

In other words, Ken was the consummate concept artist: always at his best when he succeeded in inspiring all around him, changing the Disney legacy and the world, one drawing at a time.

ABOVE: Character designs for the abandoned TV project *Hamster Hamlet*. Courtesy: Wendy Greer.

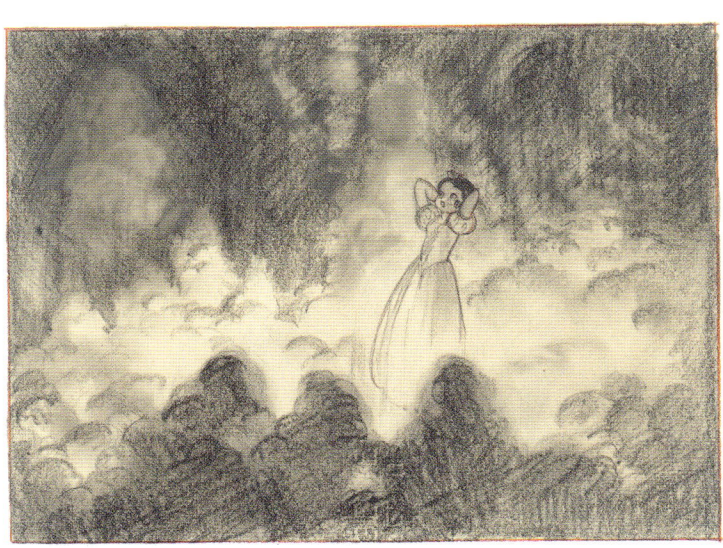
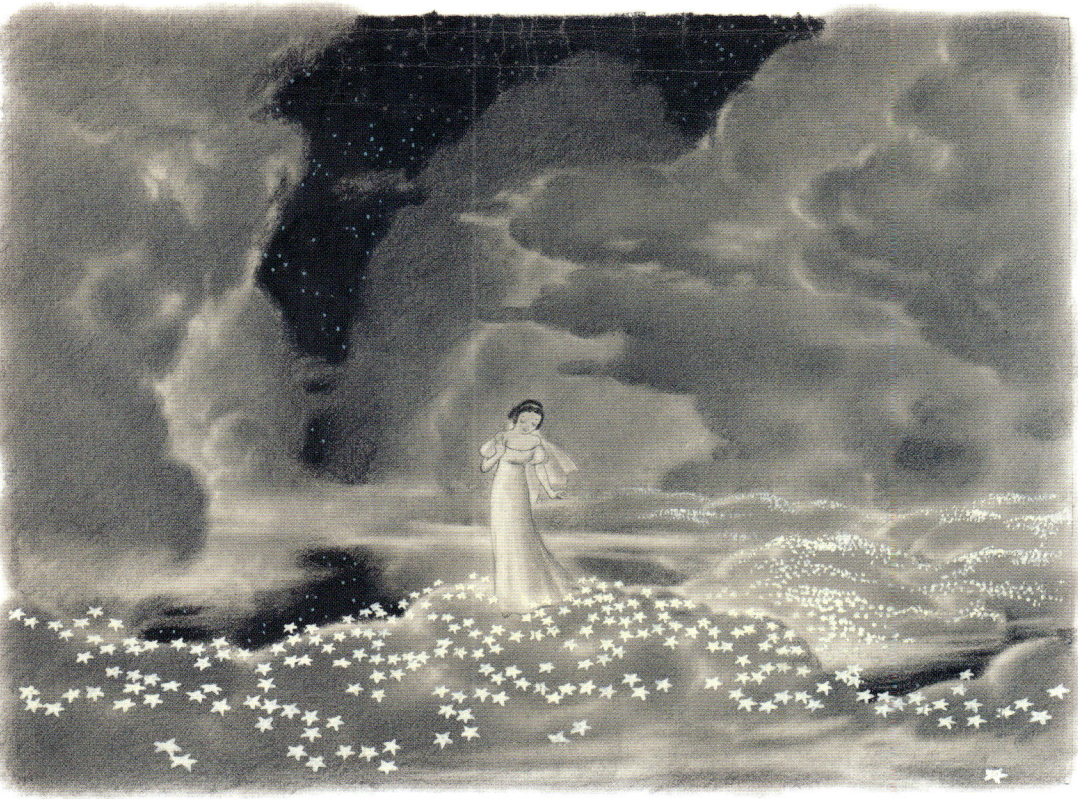
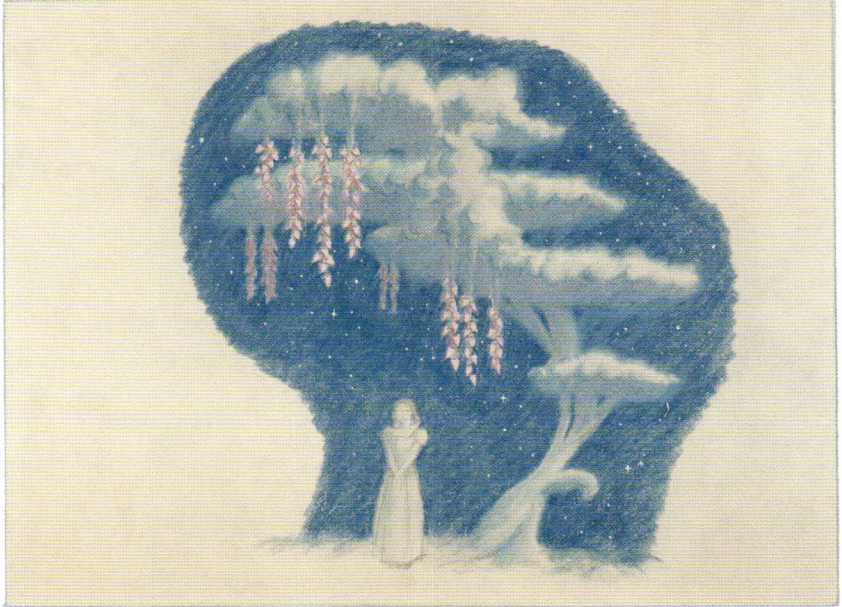

ABOVE: Story sketches for the abandoned dream sequence in *Snow White and the Seven Dwarfs*.

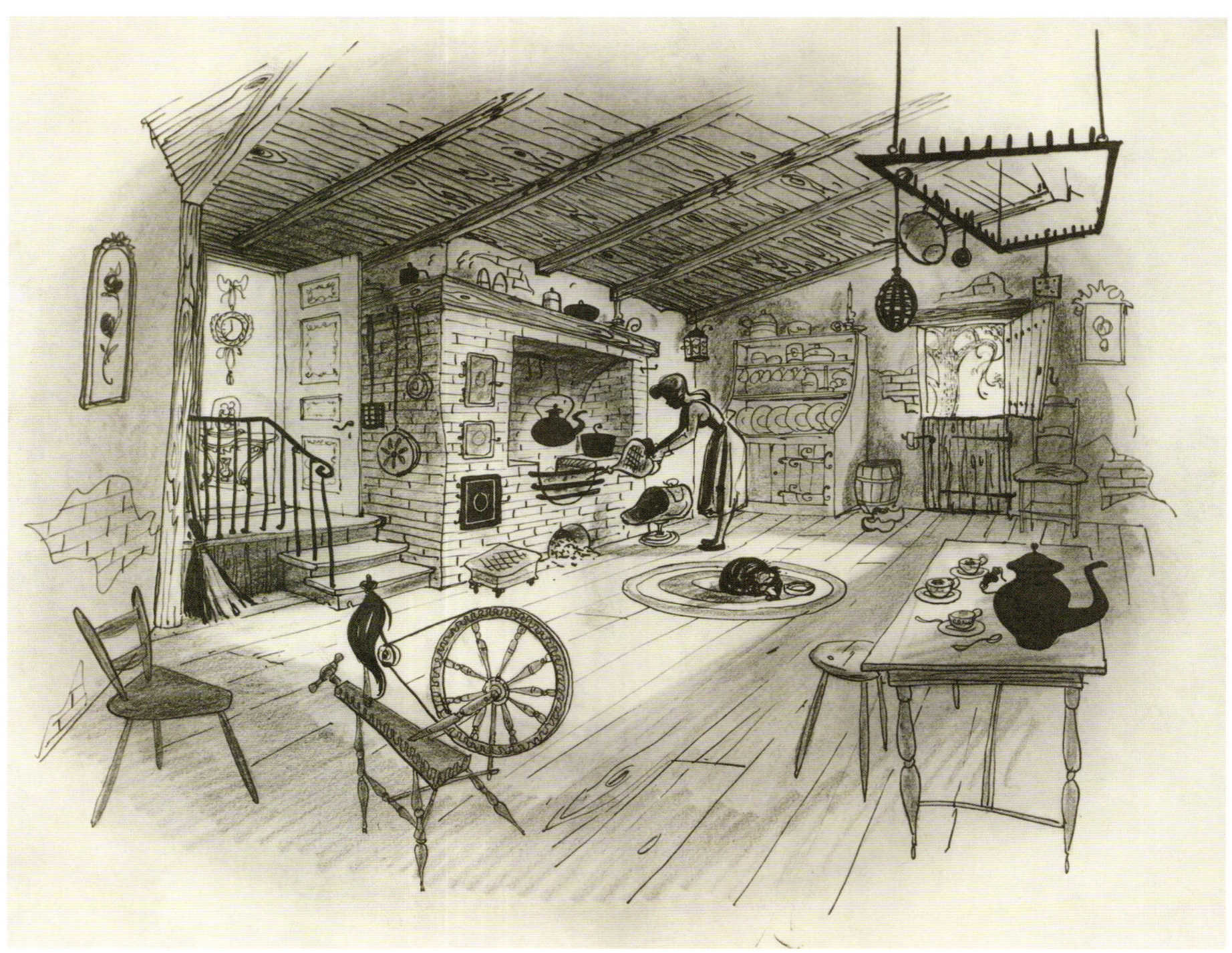

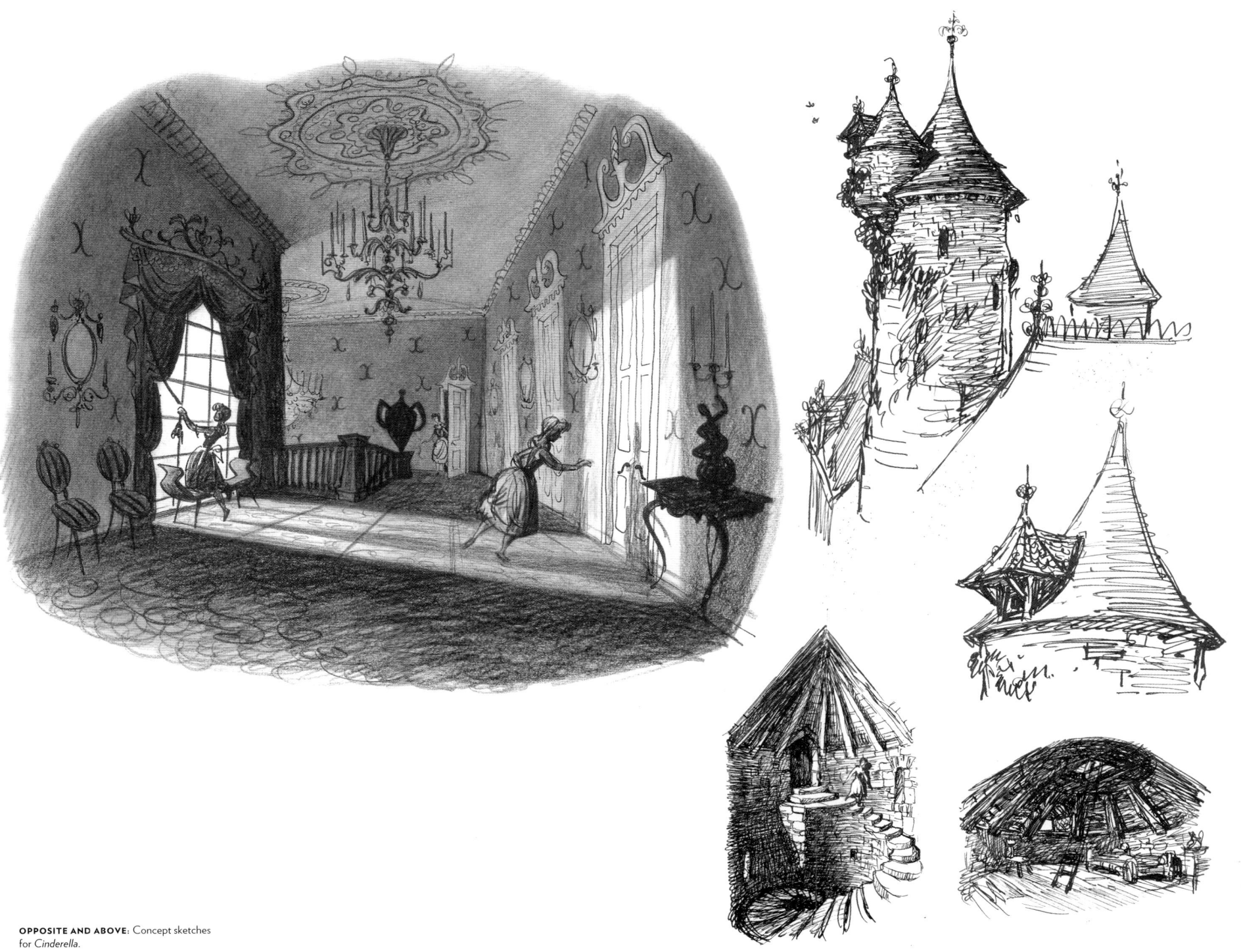

OPPOSITE AND ABOVE: Concept sketches for *Cinderella*.

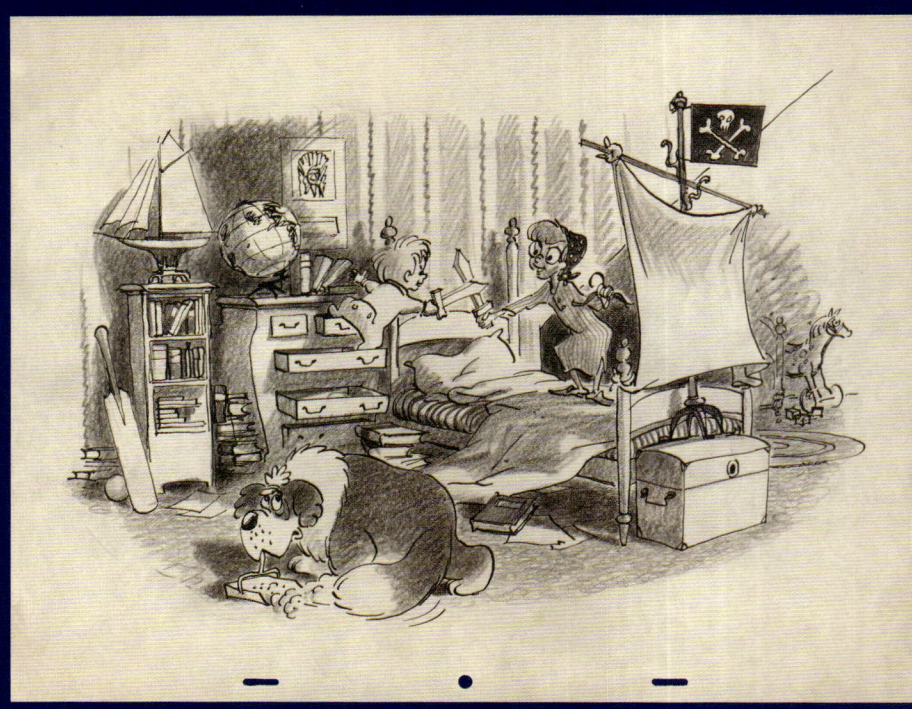
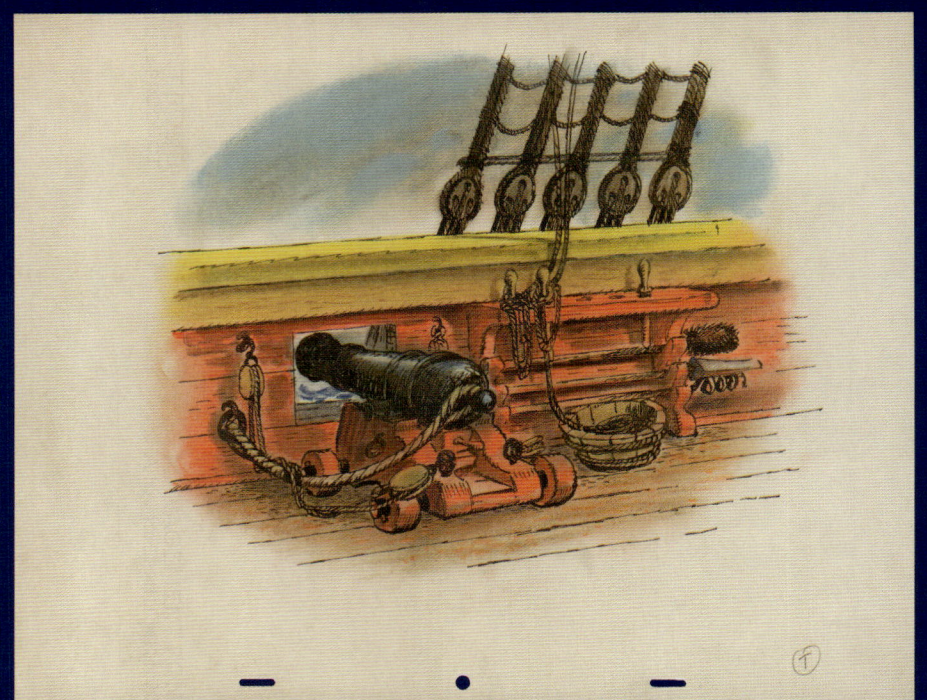
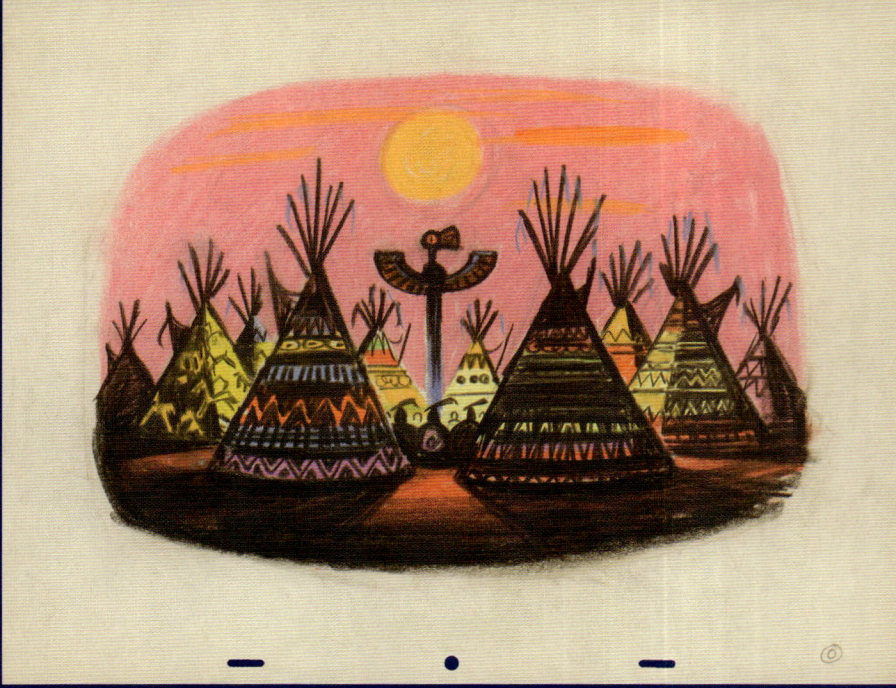
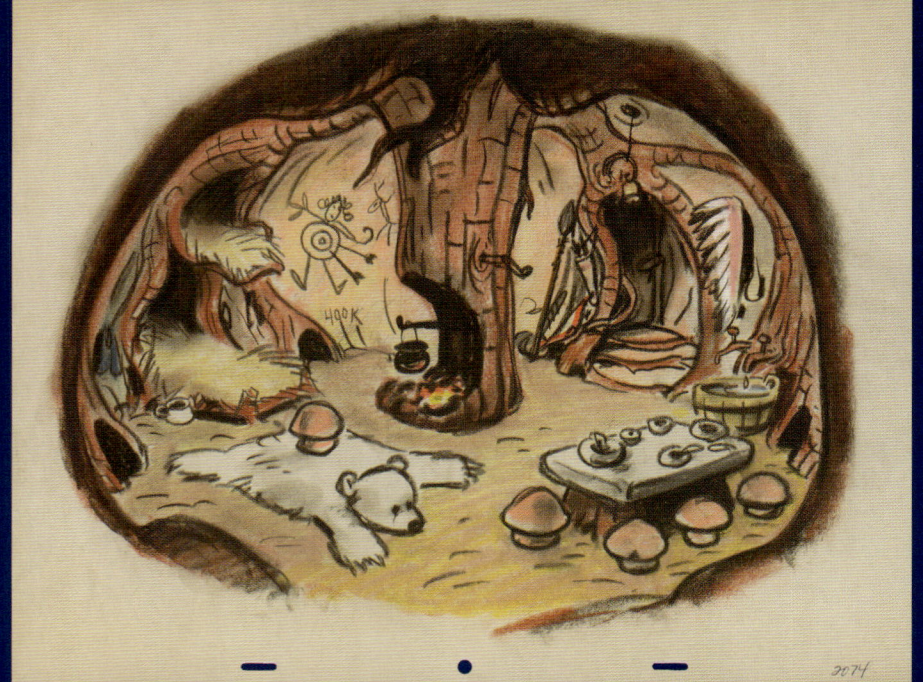

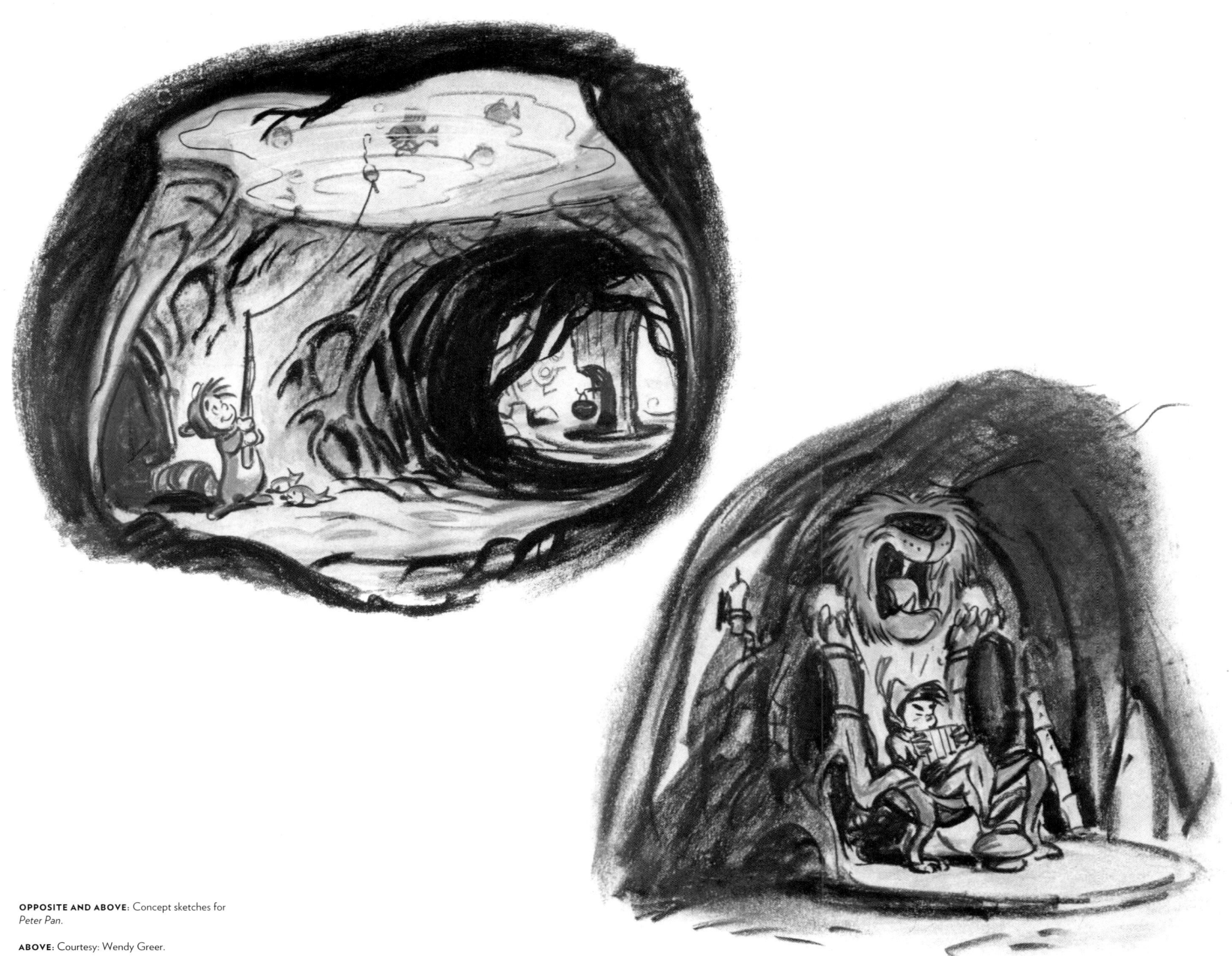

OPPOSITE AND ABOVE: Concept sketches for *Peter Pan*.

ABOVE: Courtesy: Wendy Greer.

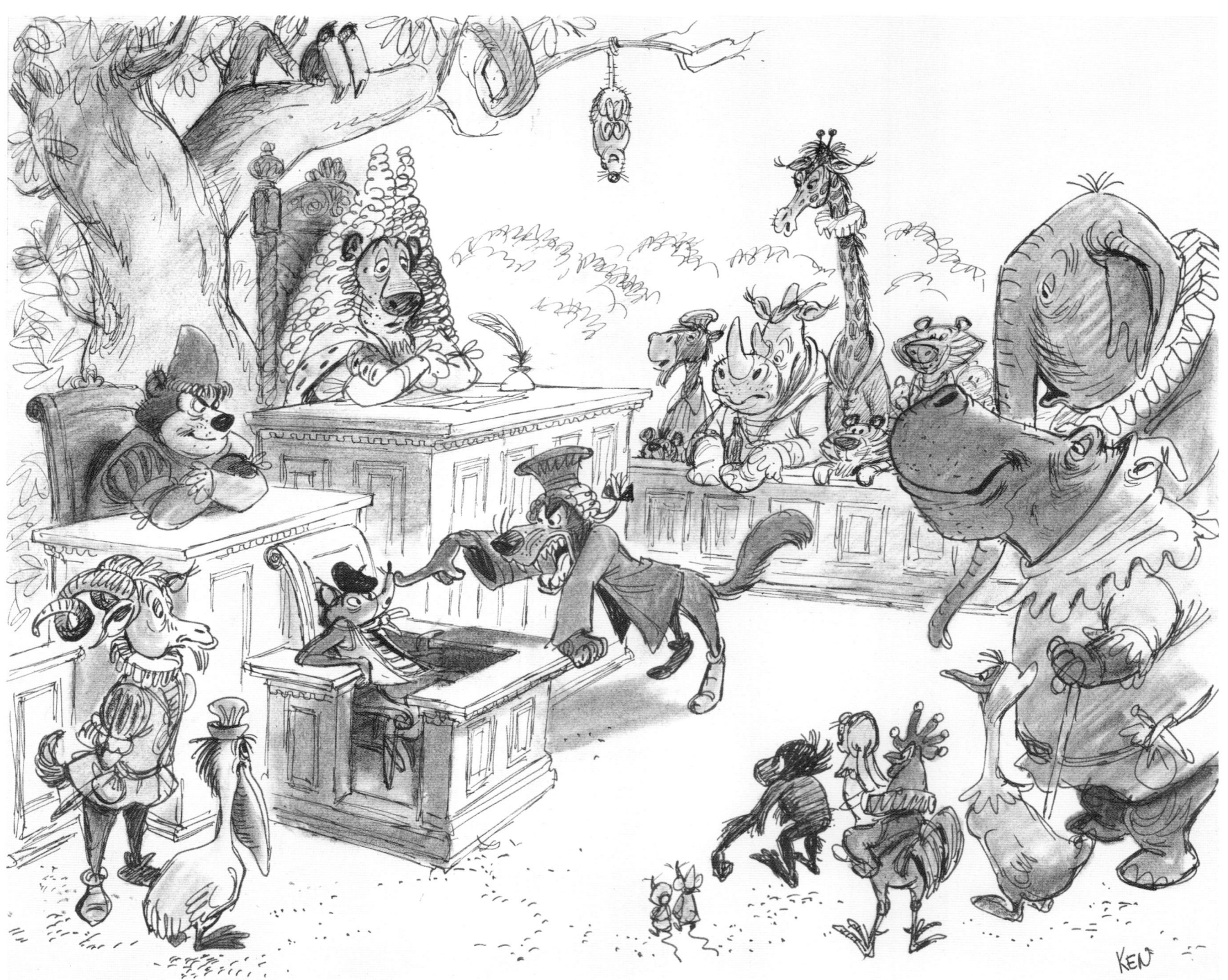

OPPOSITE AND BELOW: Early concept sketches for the abandoned project *Chanticleer and Reynard the Fox*.

KEN ANDERSON

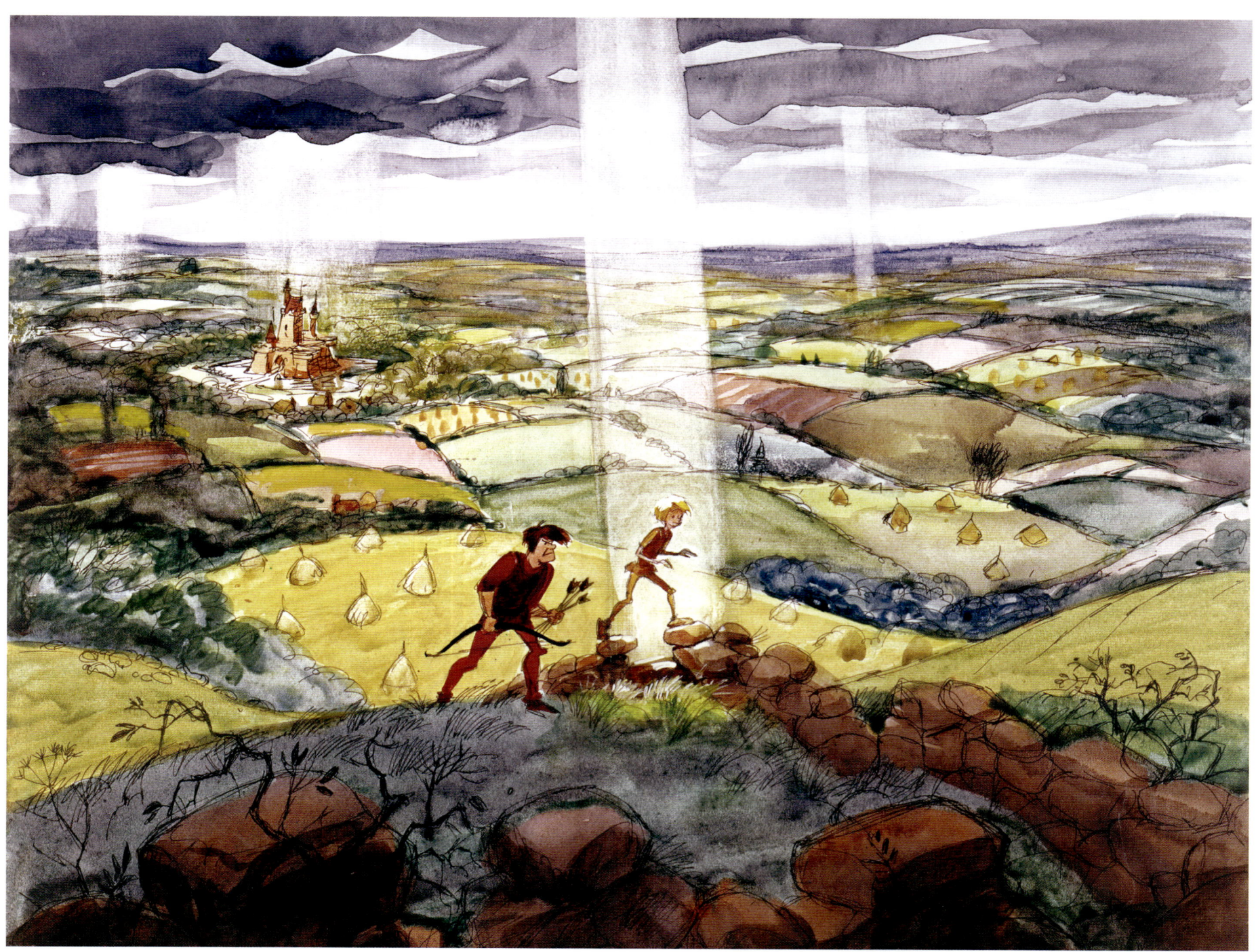

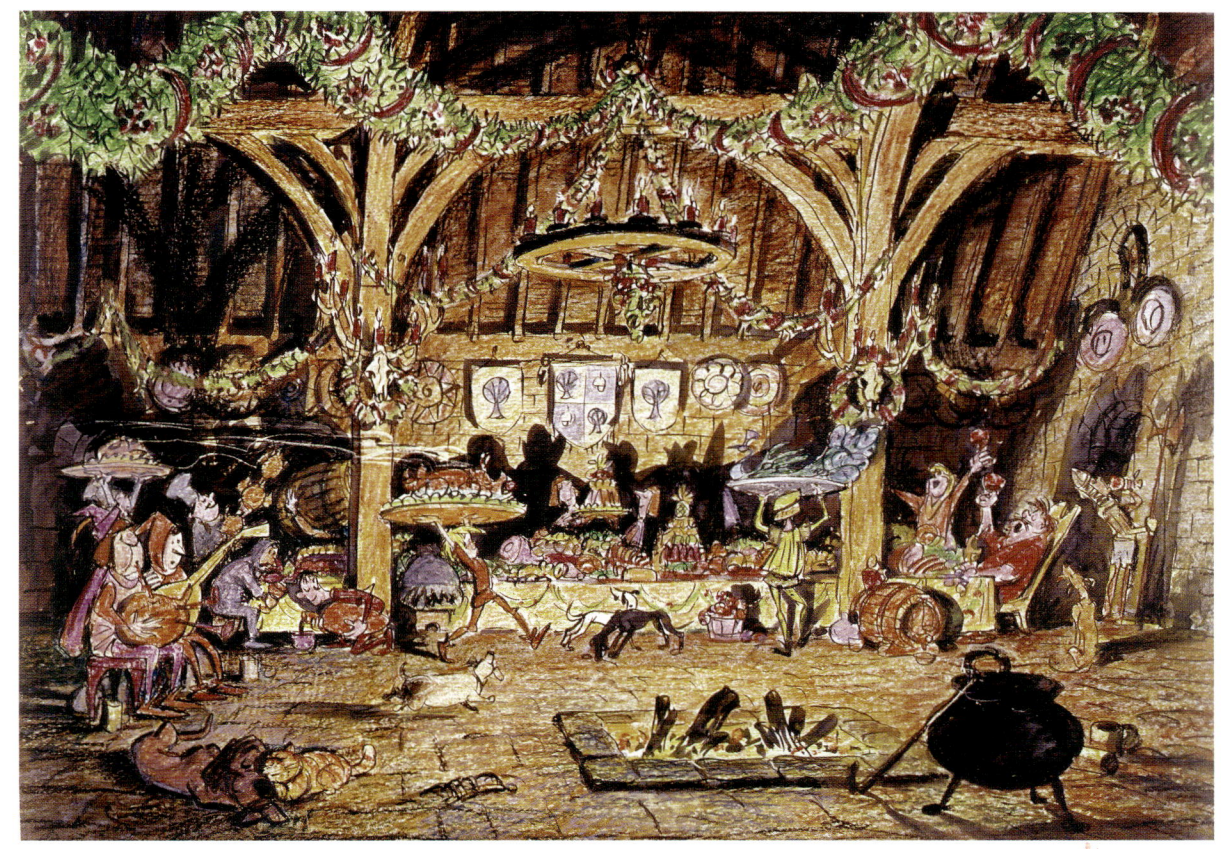
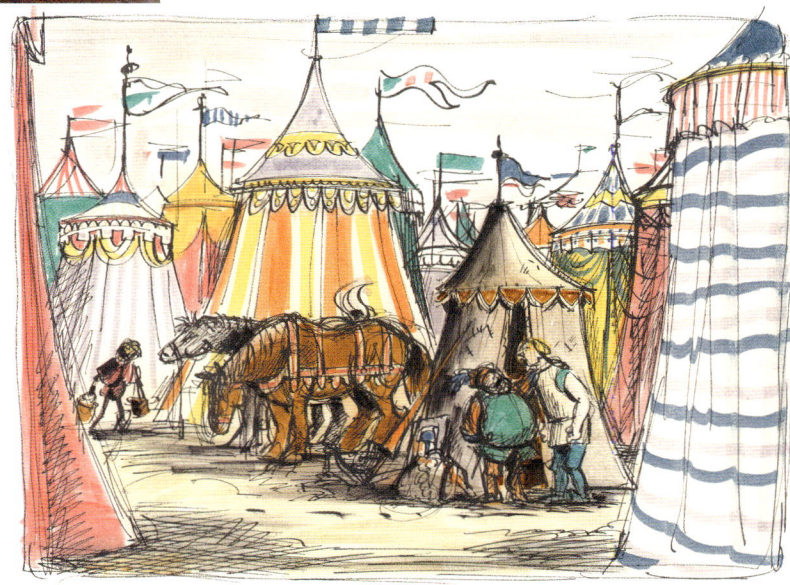

PAGES 62–67: Concept sketches for *The Sword in the Stone*.

KEN ANDERSON

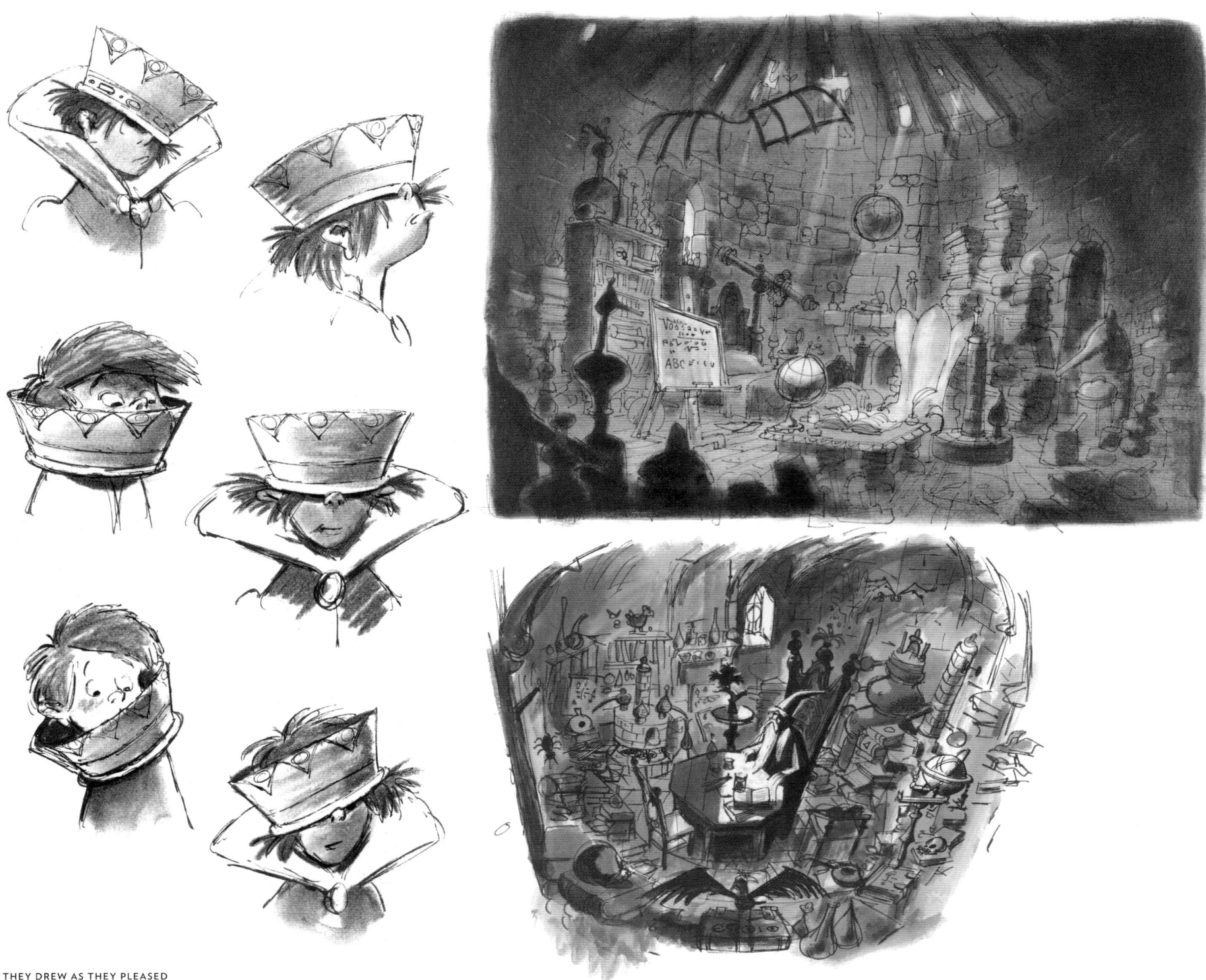

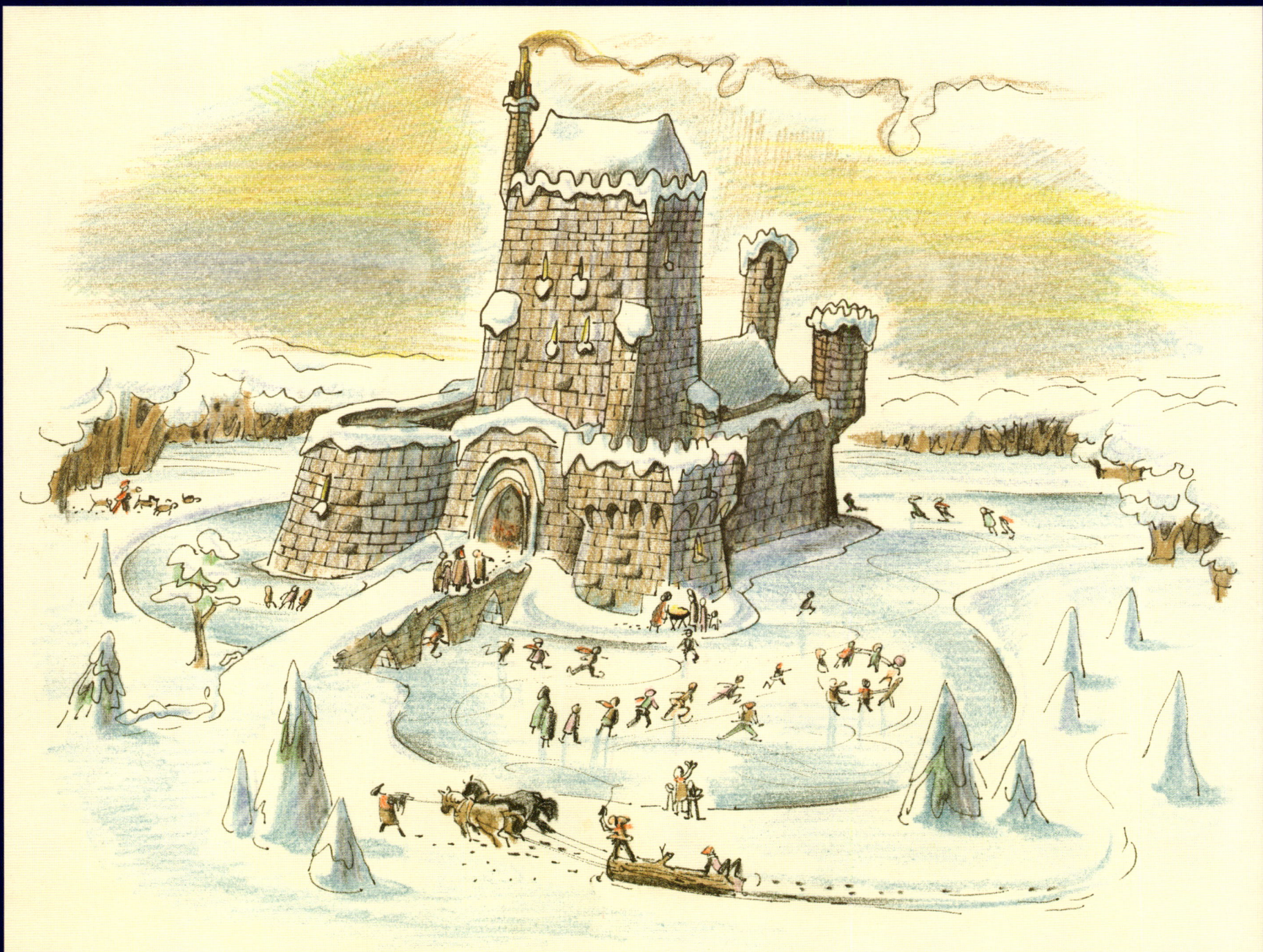

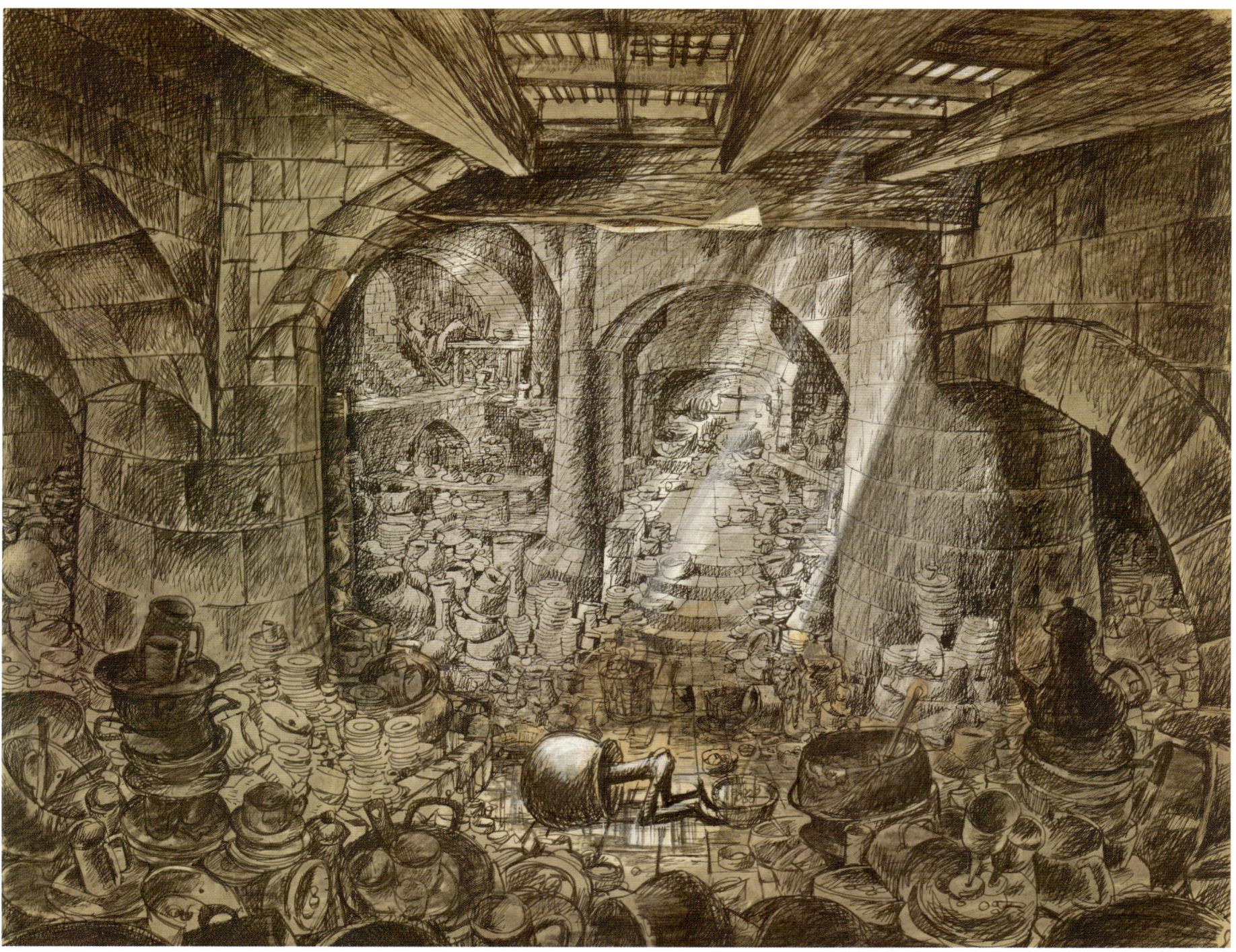

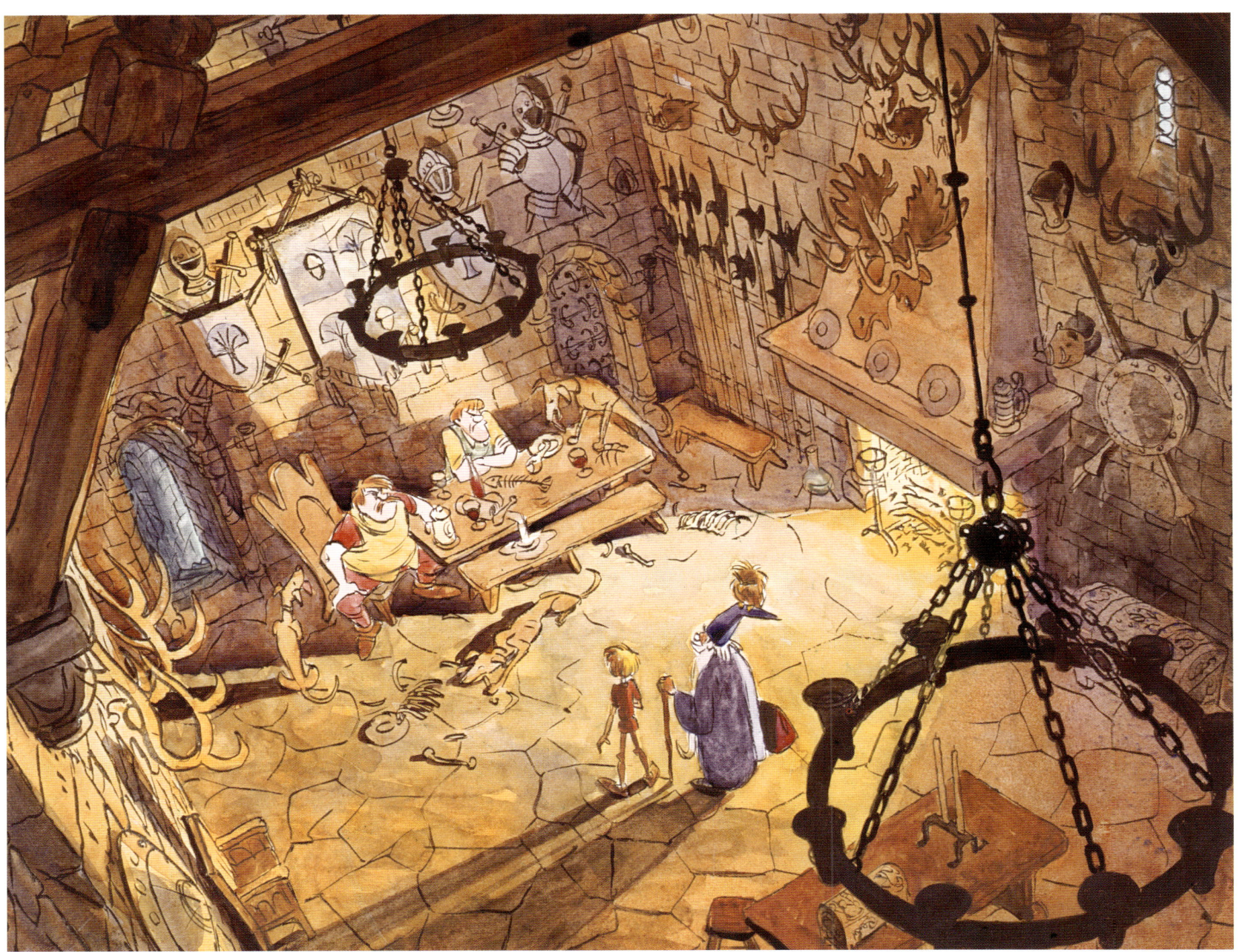

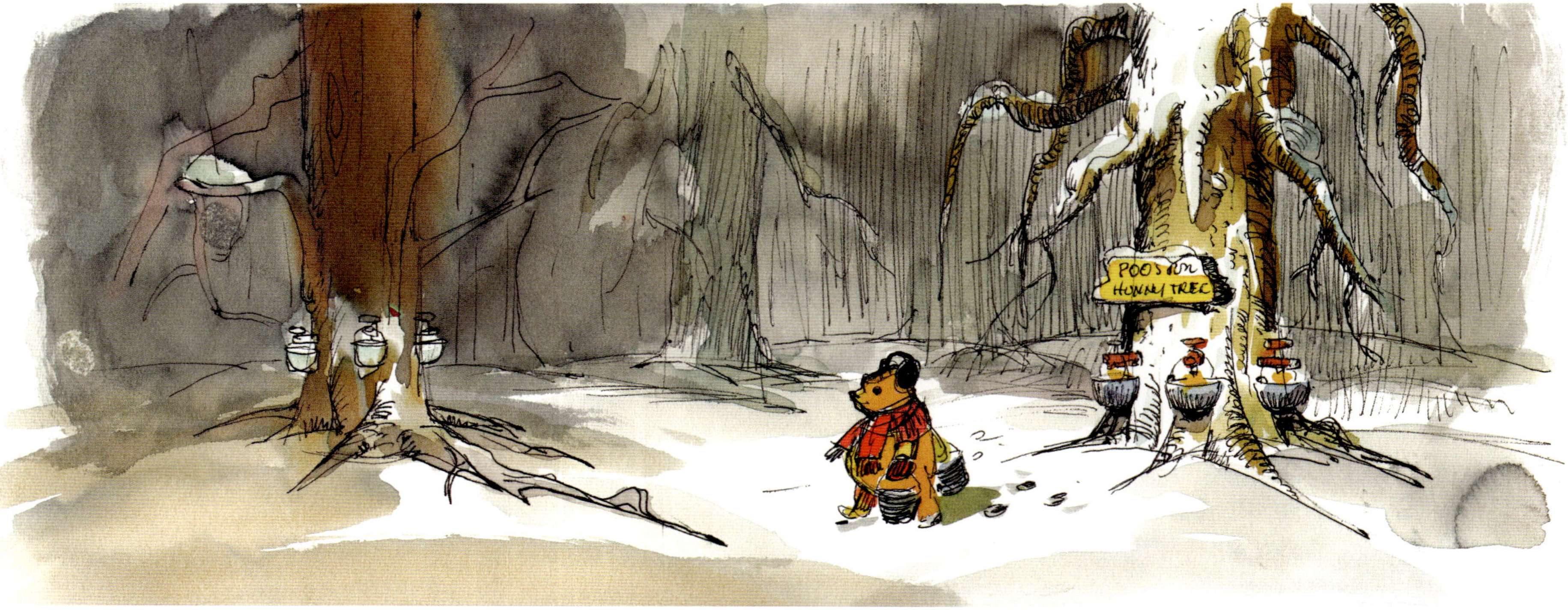

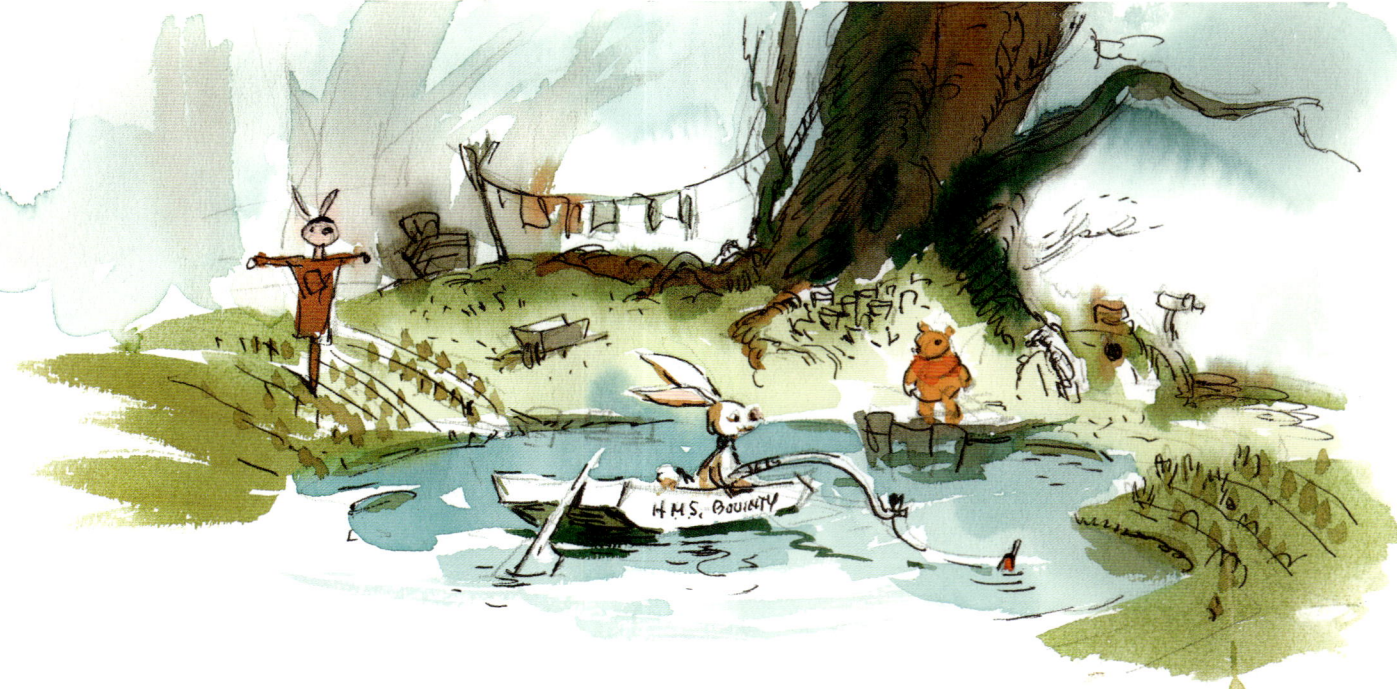

PAGES 68–72: Concept sketches for *Winnie the Pooh and the Honey Tree*.

68 THEY DREW AS THEY PLEASED

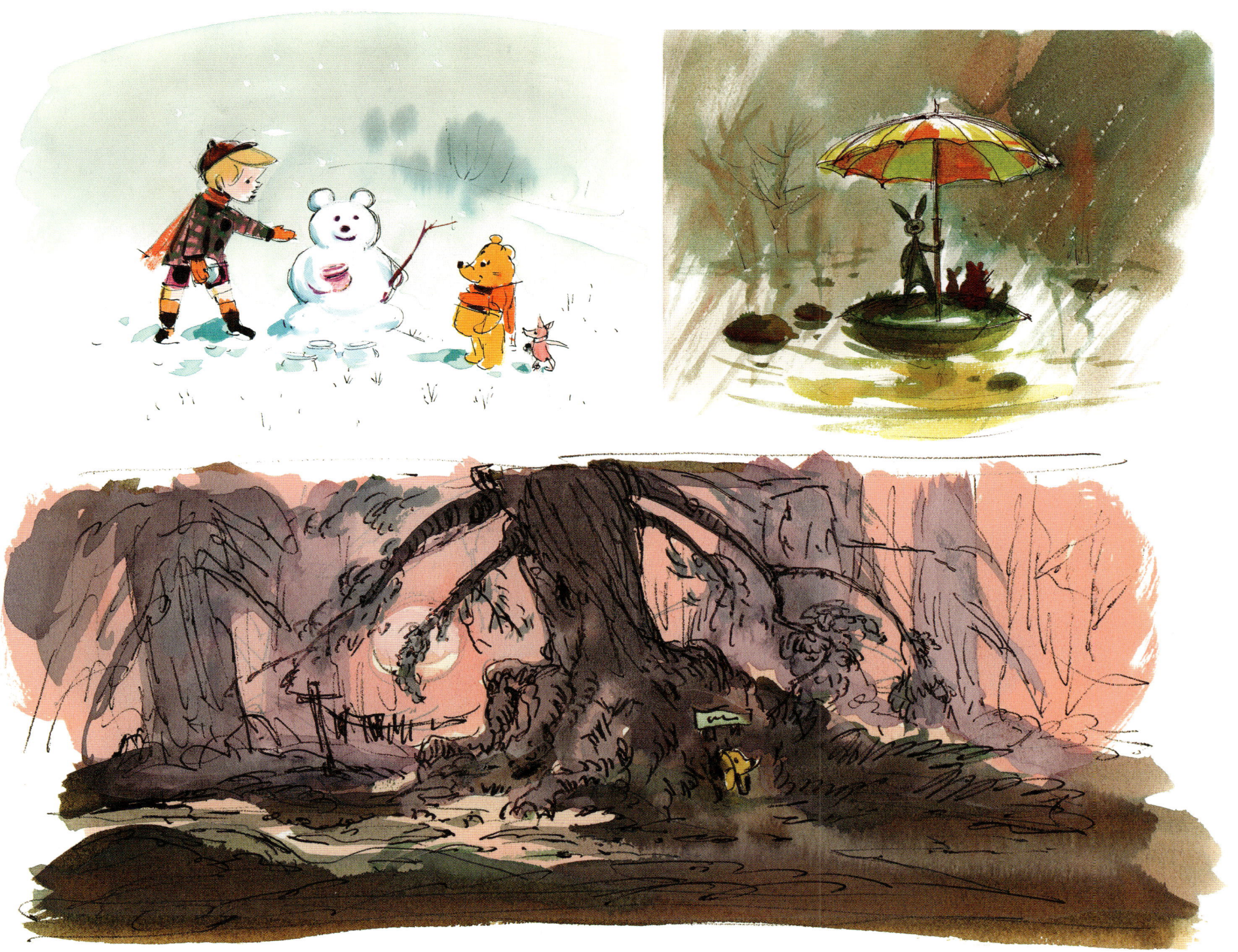

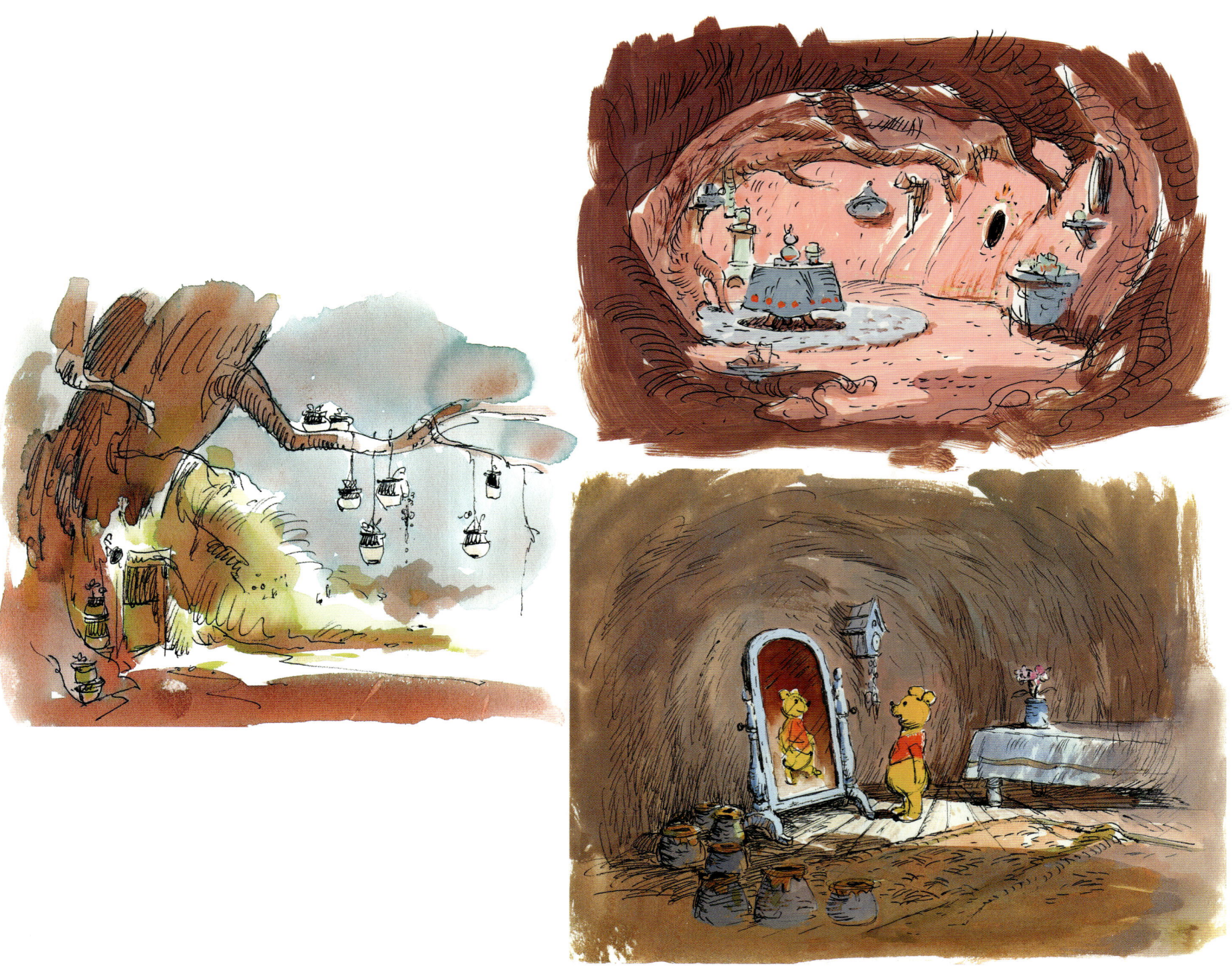

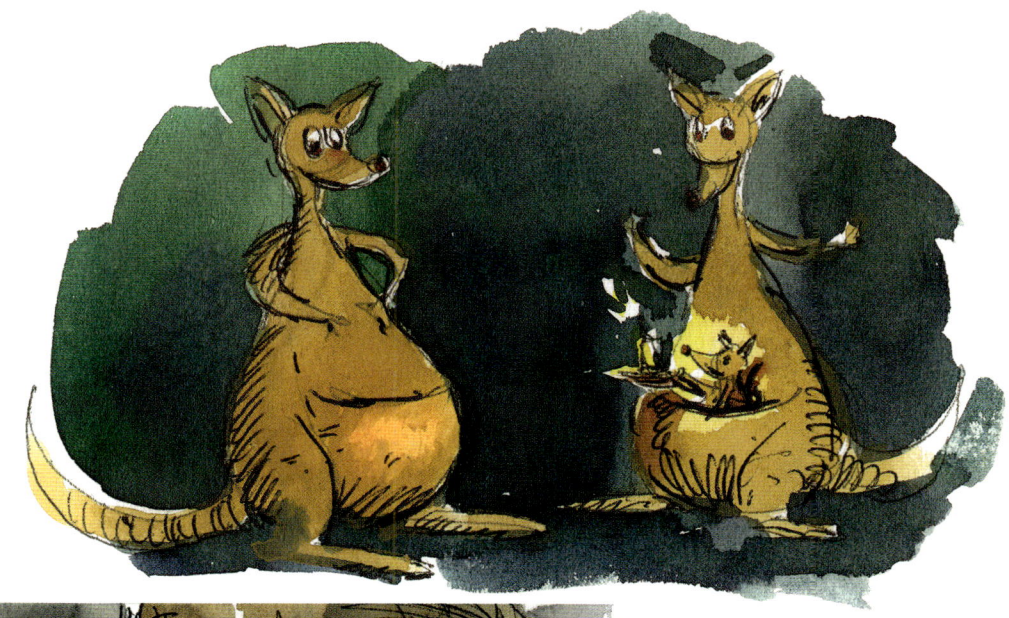
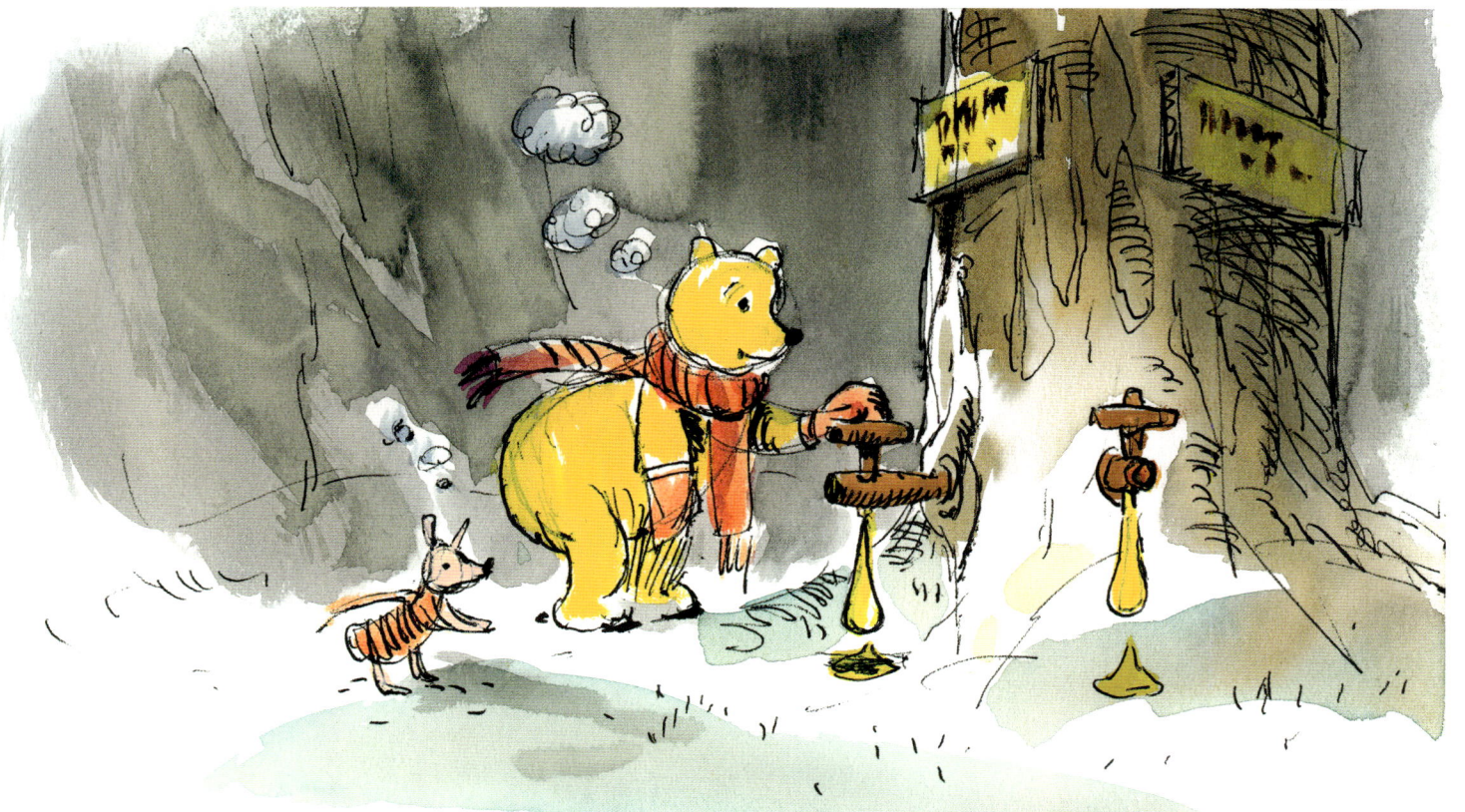

KEN ANDERSON

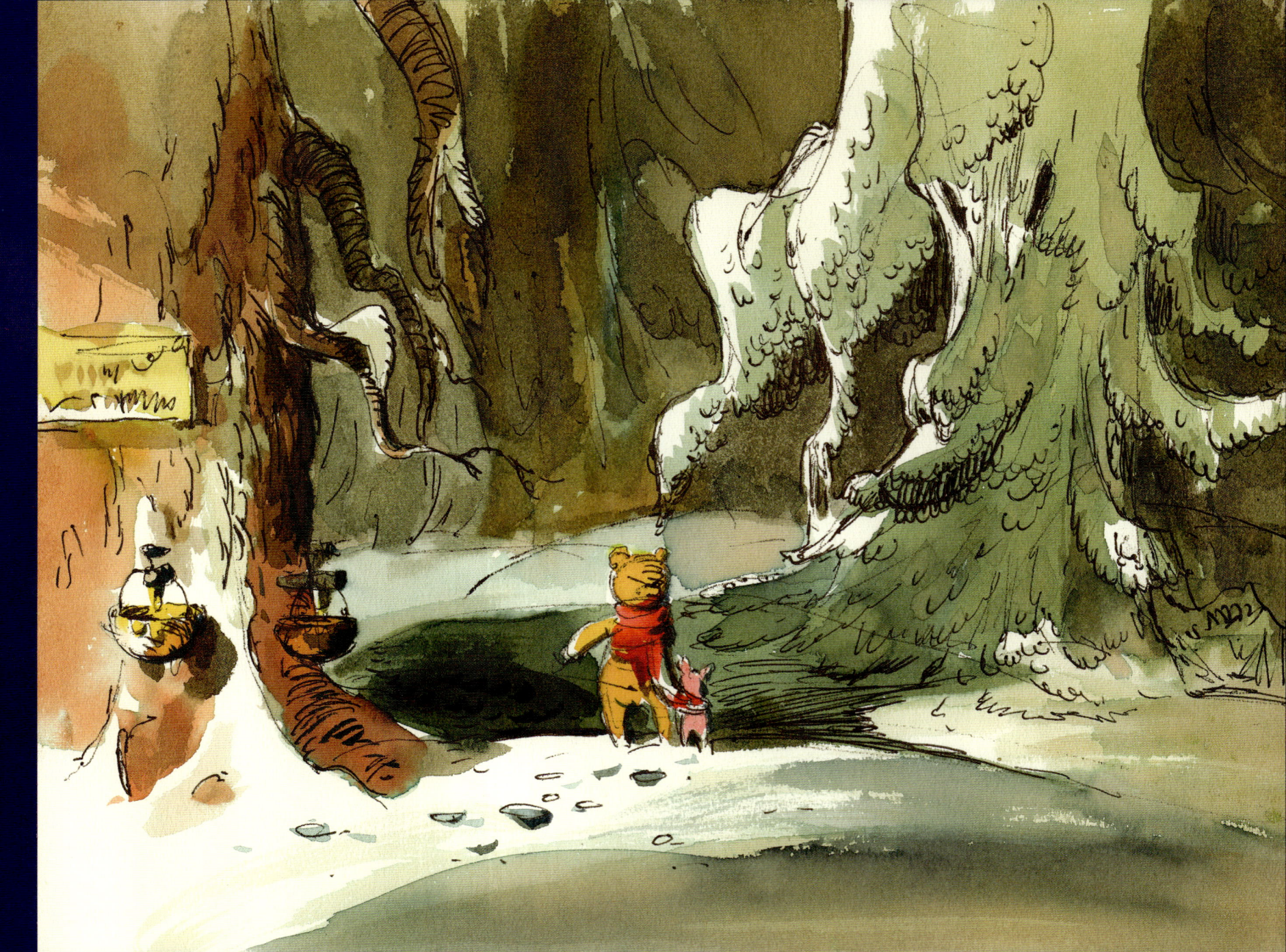

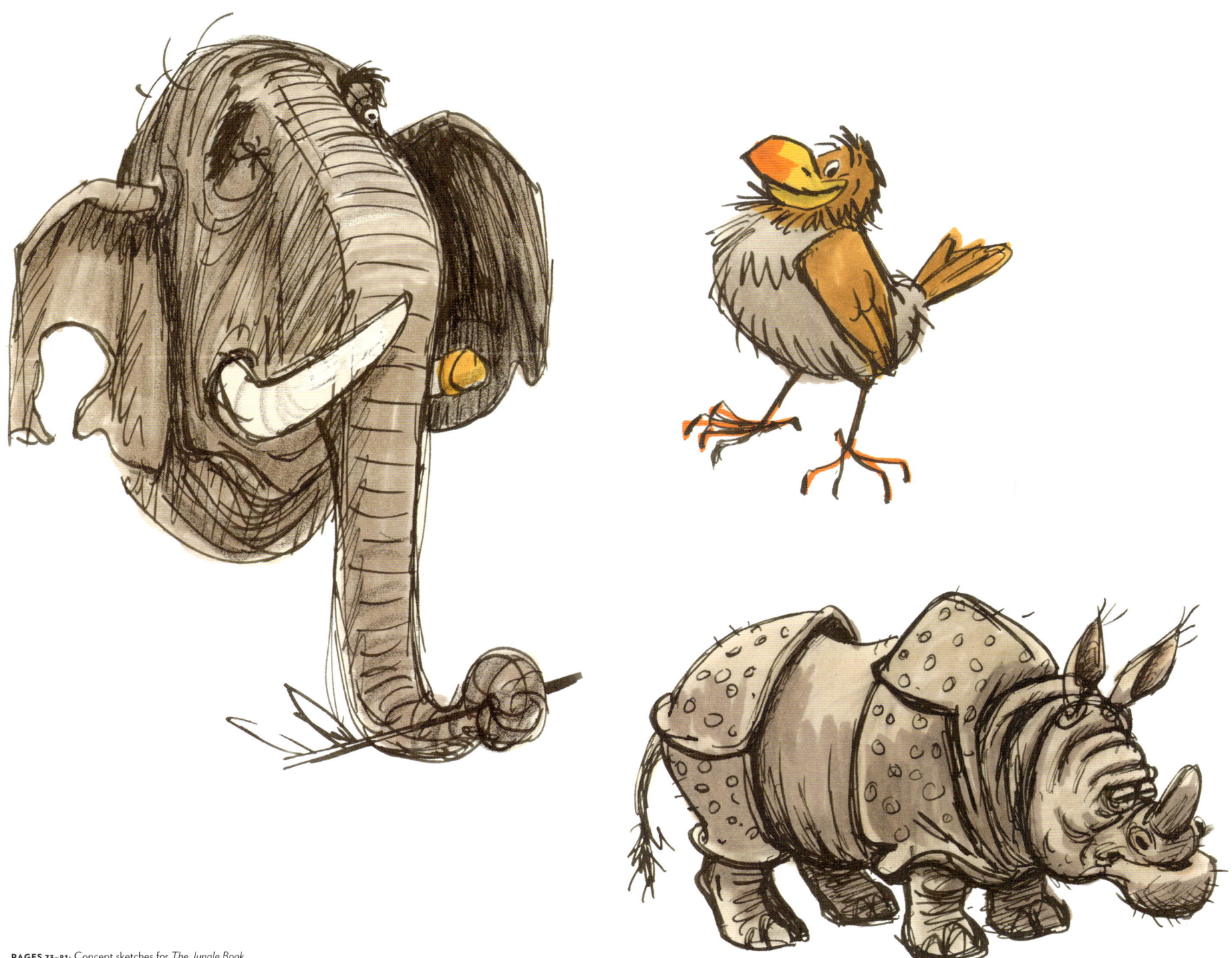

PAGES 73–81: Concept sketches for *The Jungle Book*.

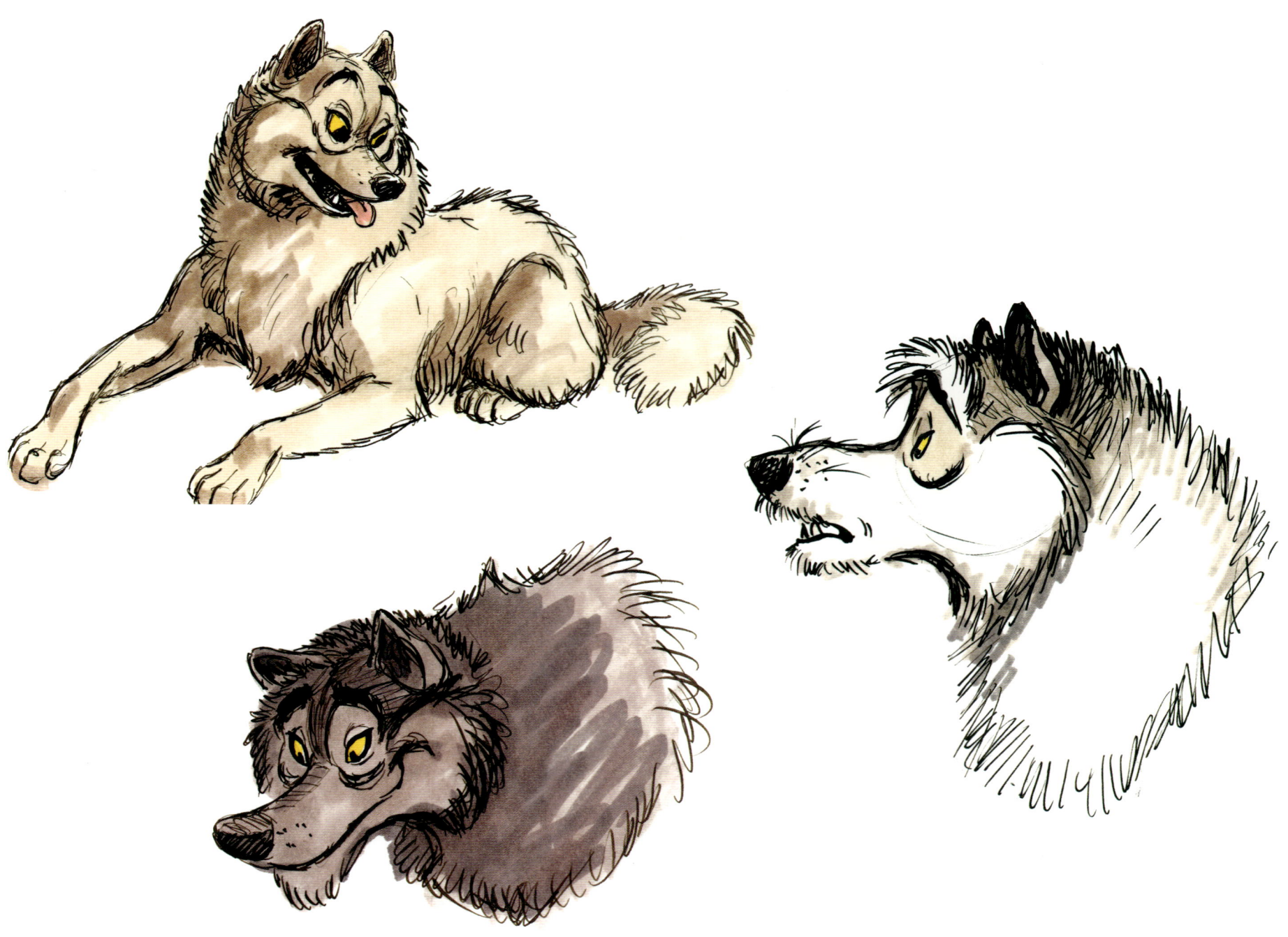

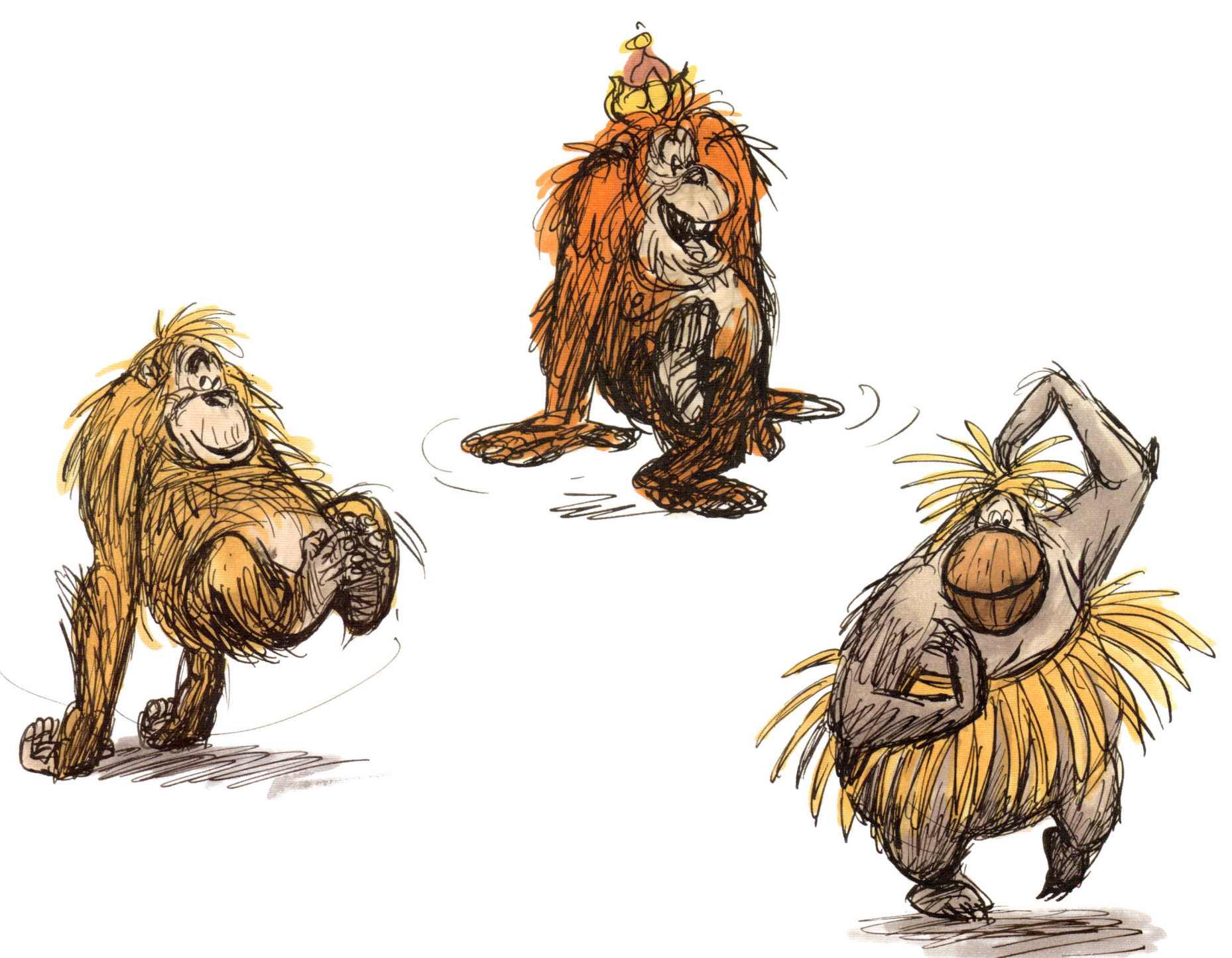

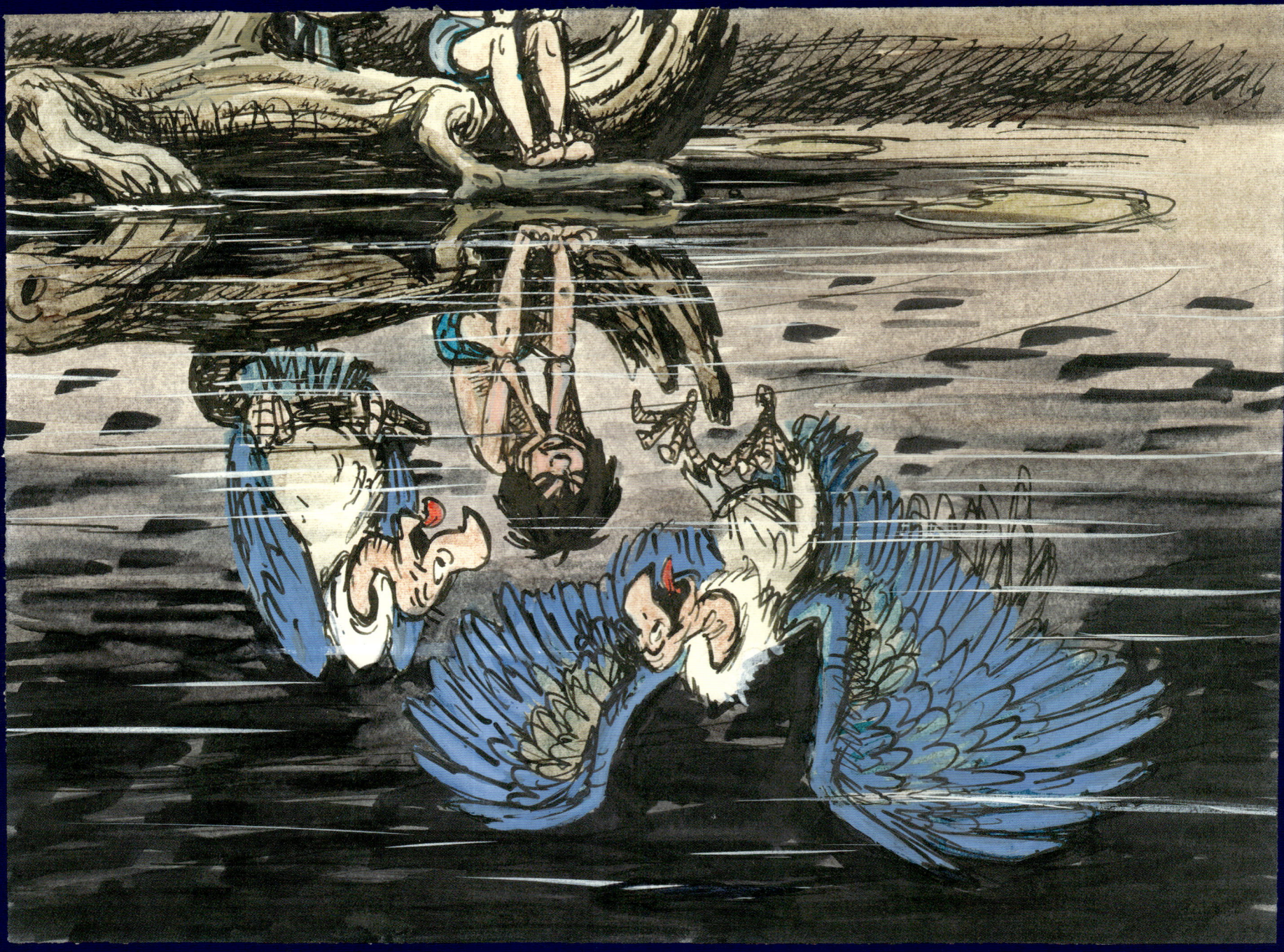

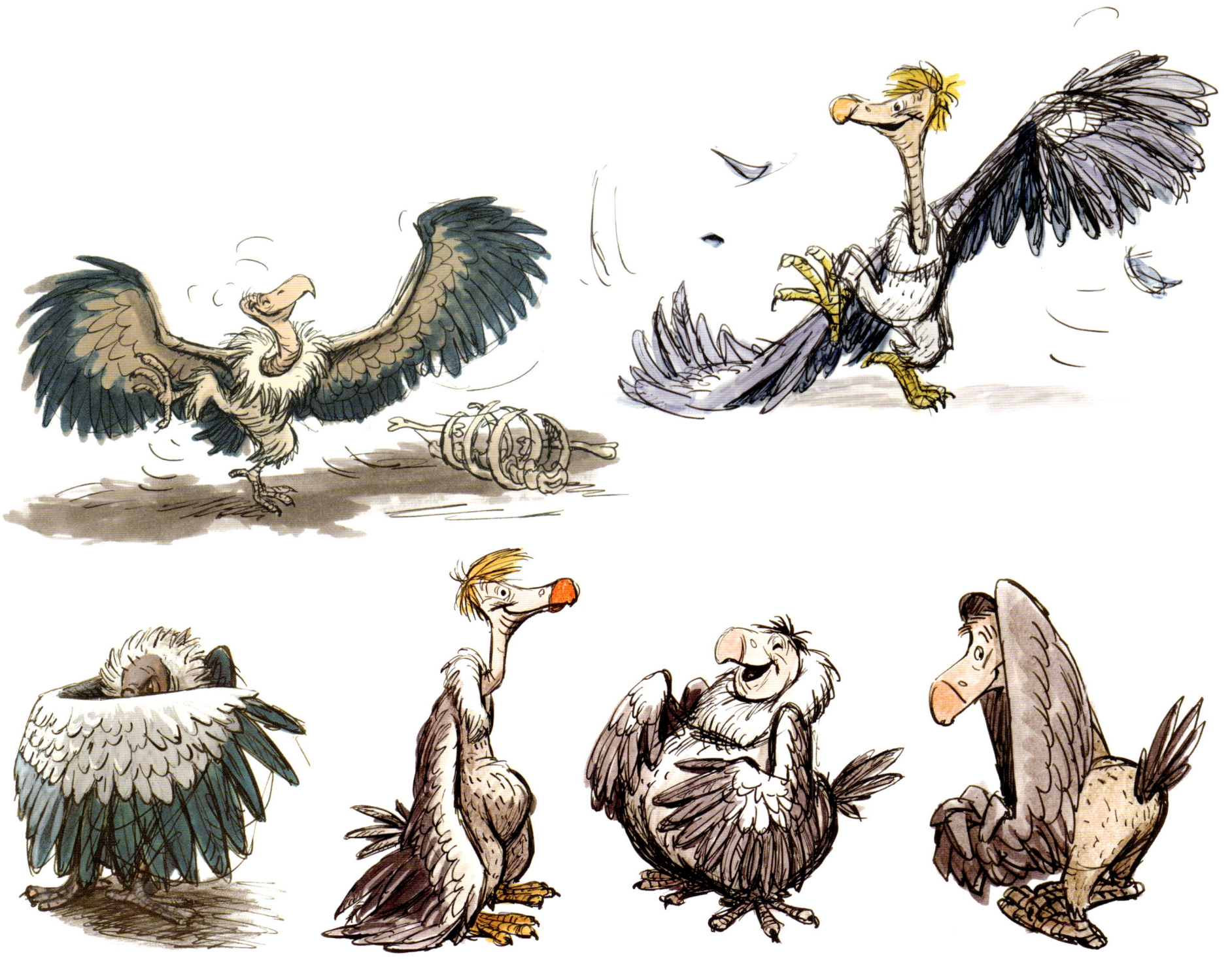

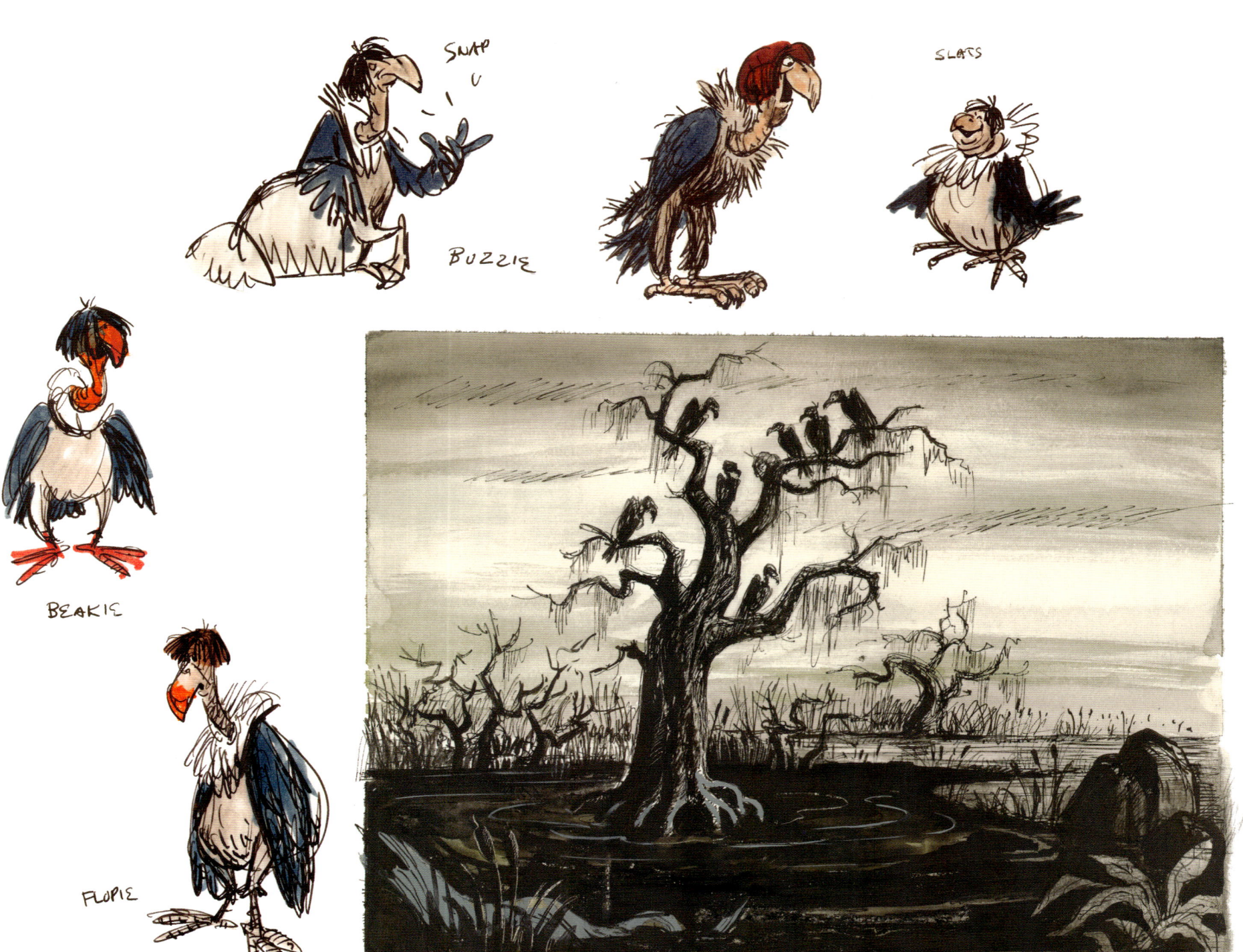

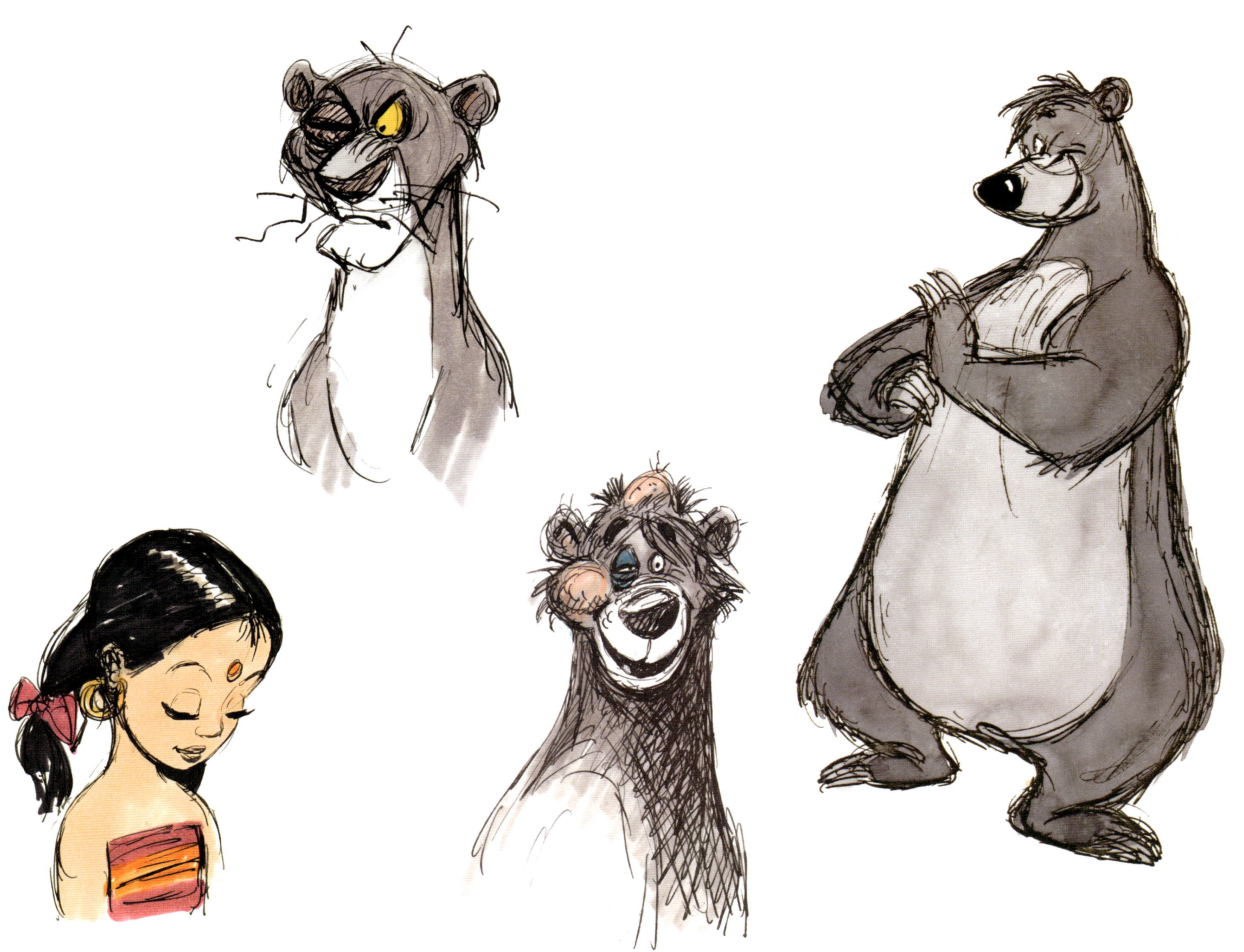

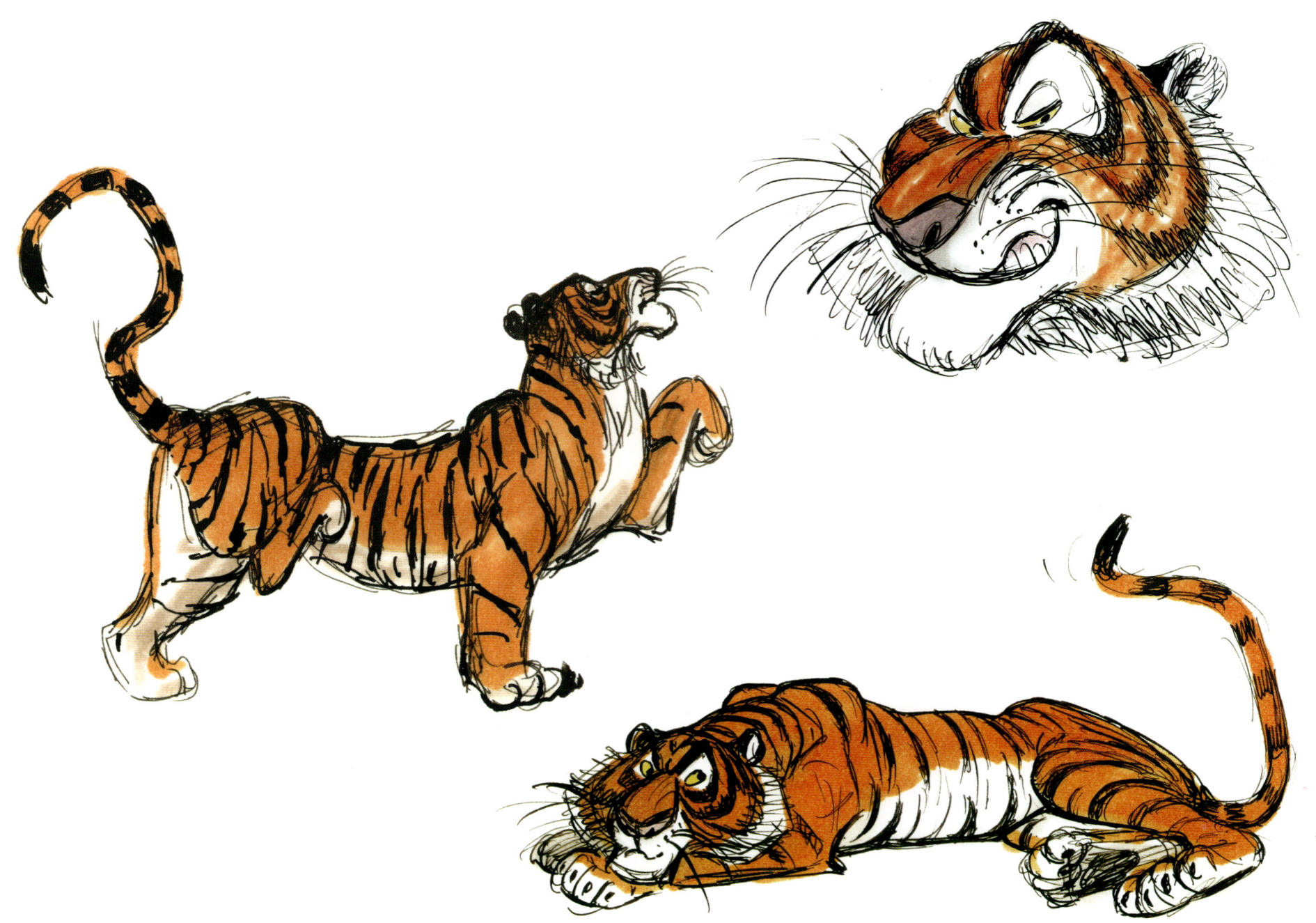

ABOVE: Courtesy: Bruce Reitherman.

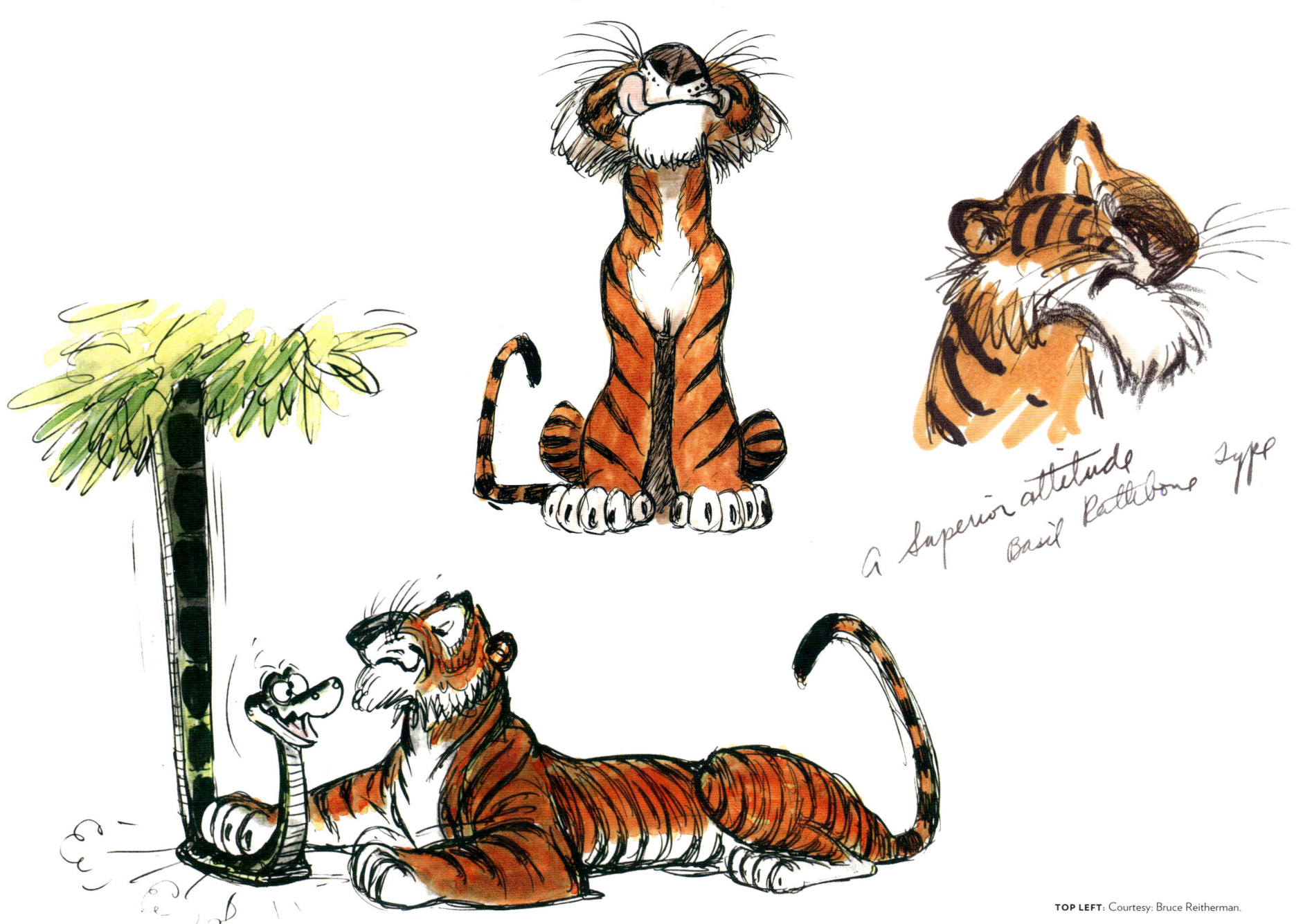

TOP LEFT: Courtesy: Bruce Reitherman.
BOTTOM: Courtesy: Gretchen Vander Weide.

PAGES 82–89: Concept sketches for *The Aristocats*.

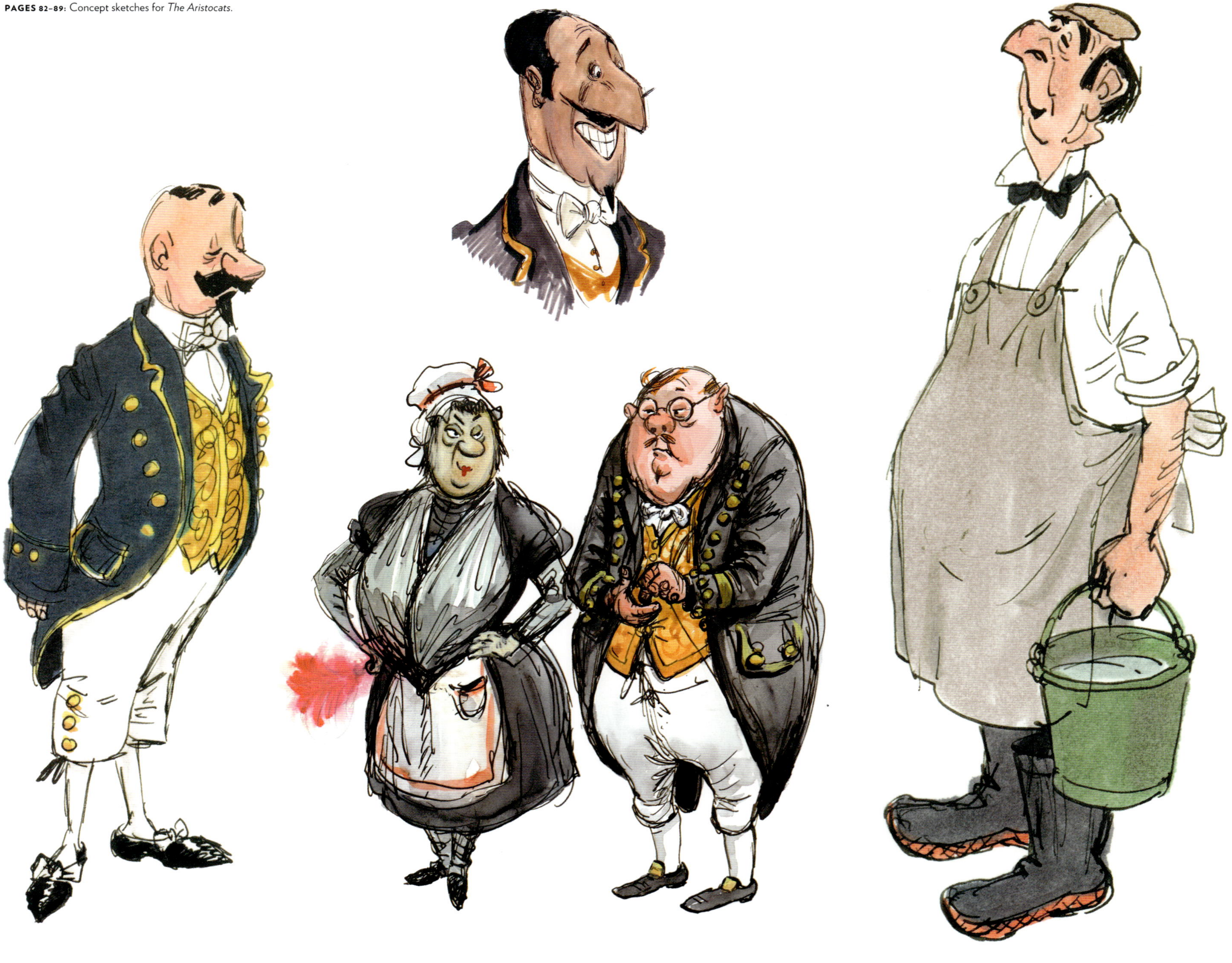

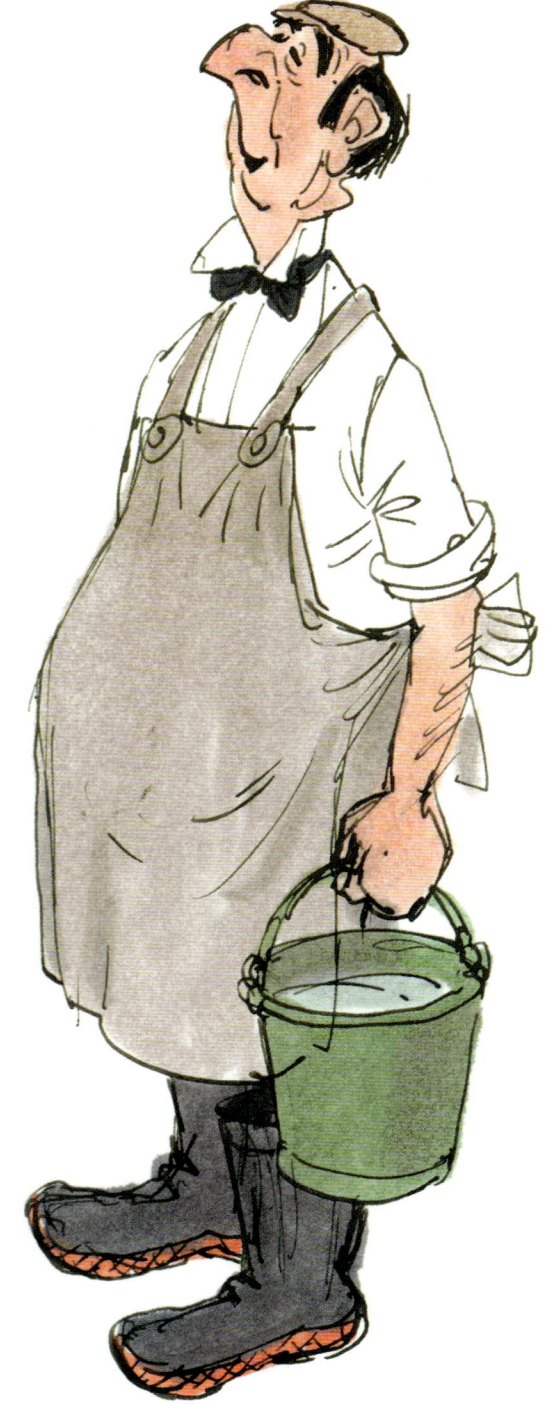

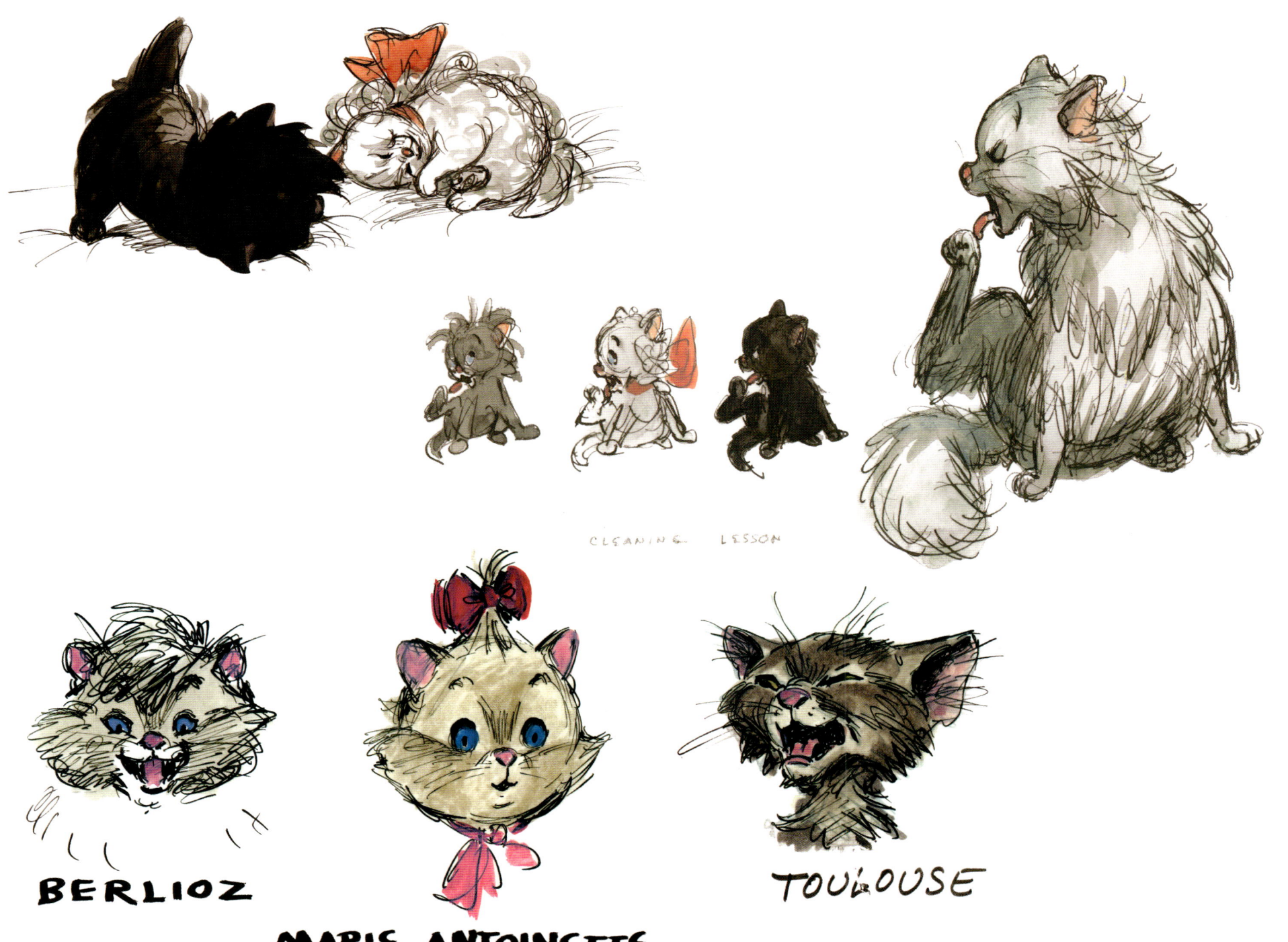

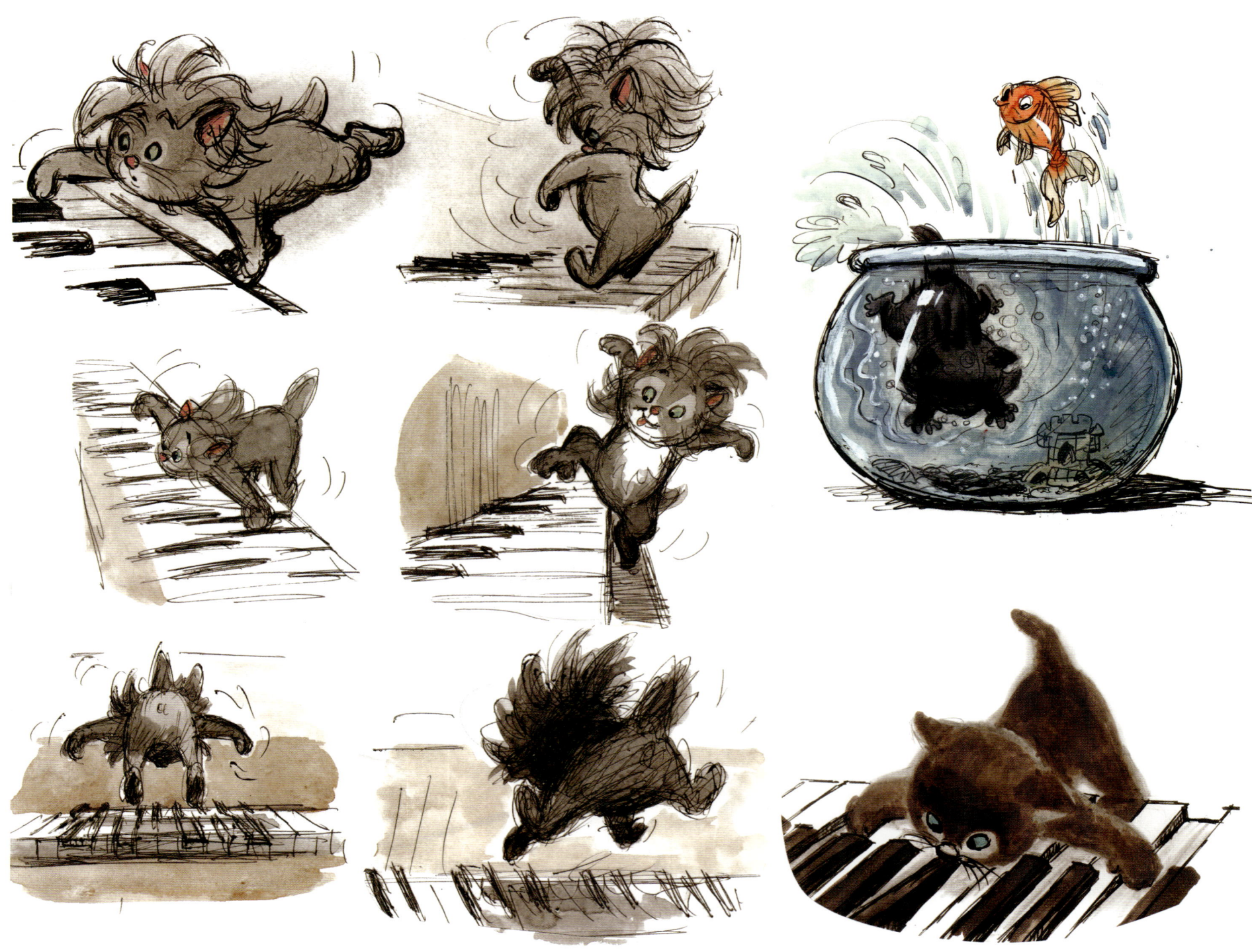

BELOW: Courtesy: Van Eaton Galleries.

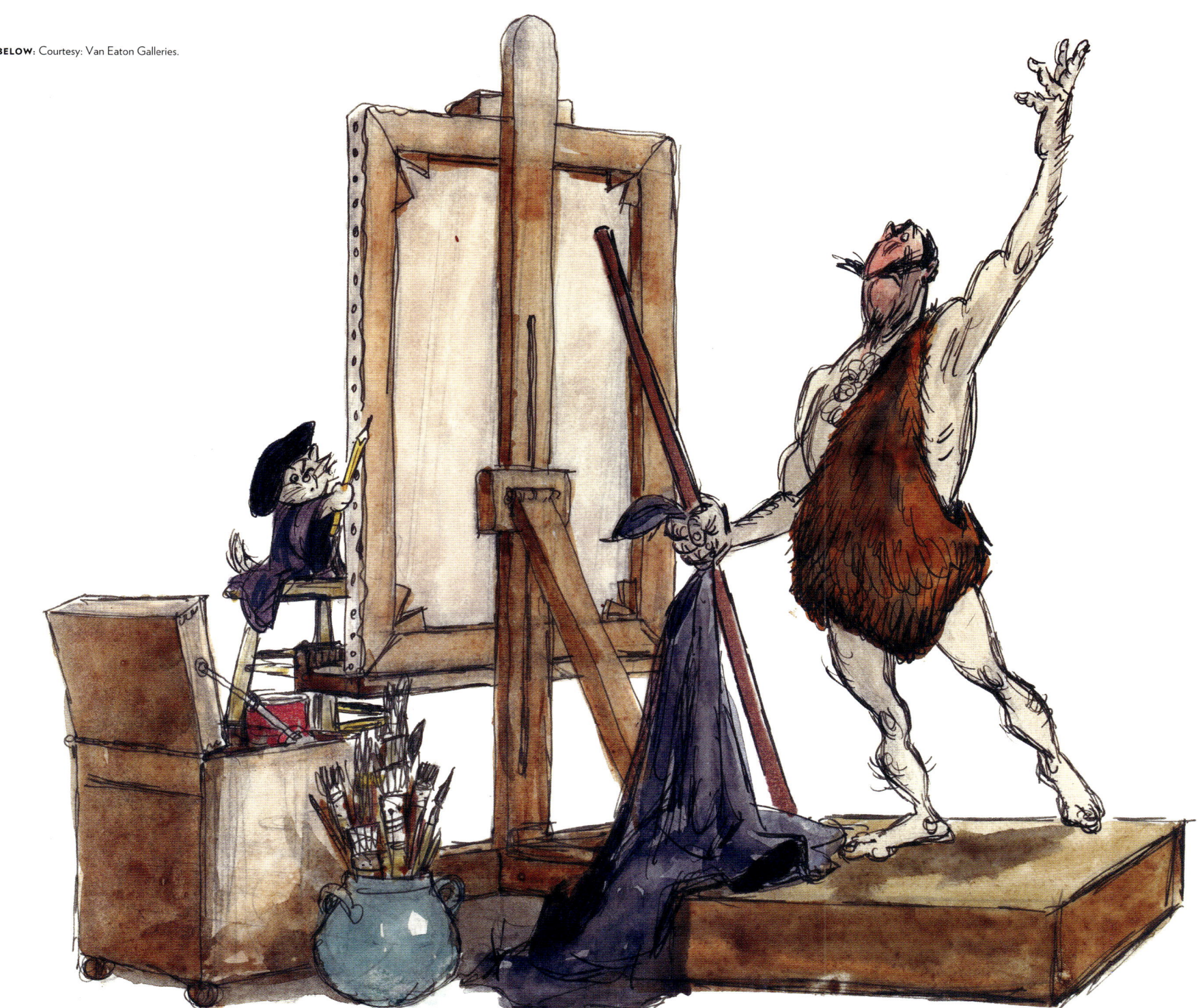

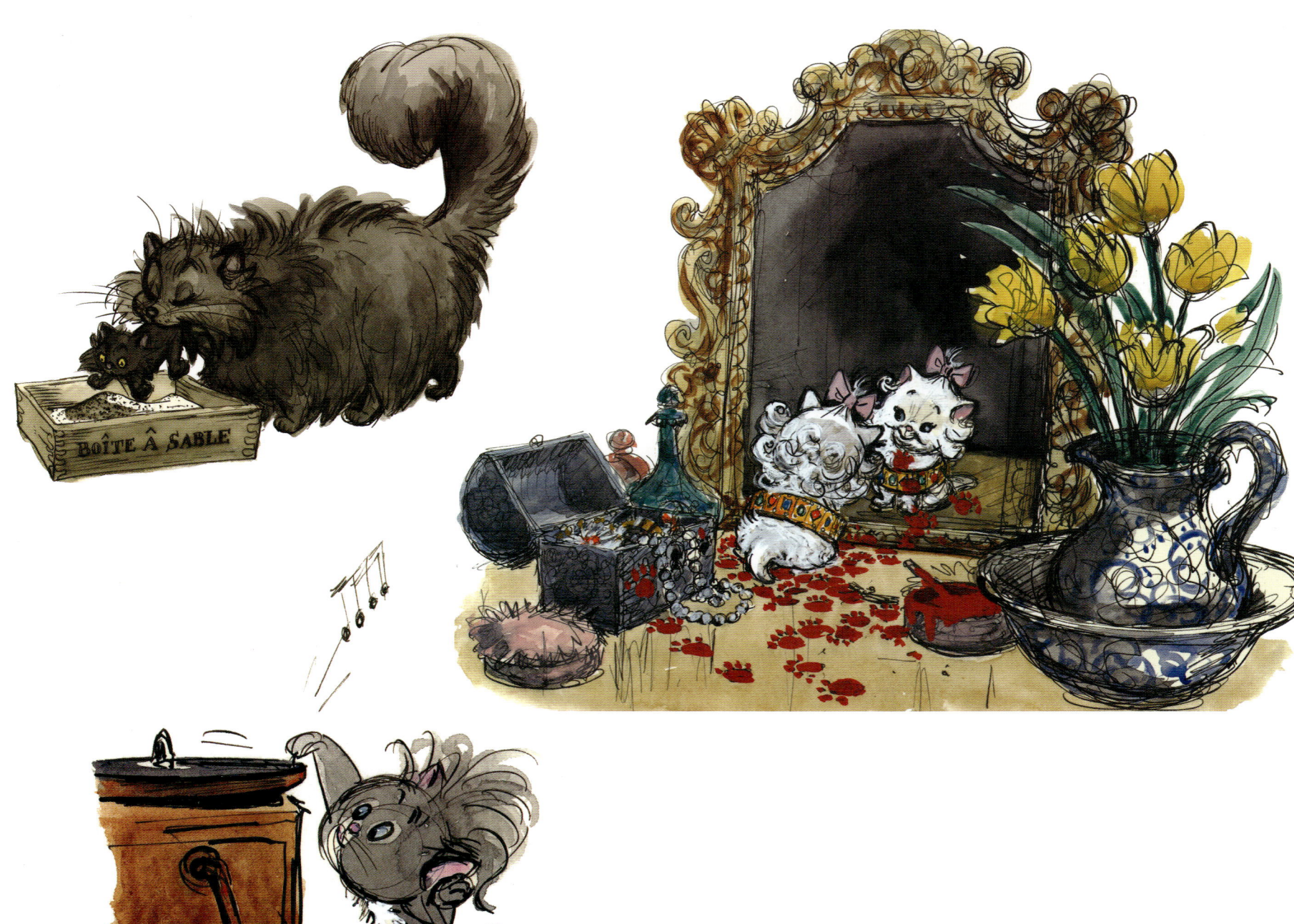

BOTTOM: Courtesy: Van Eaton Galleries.

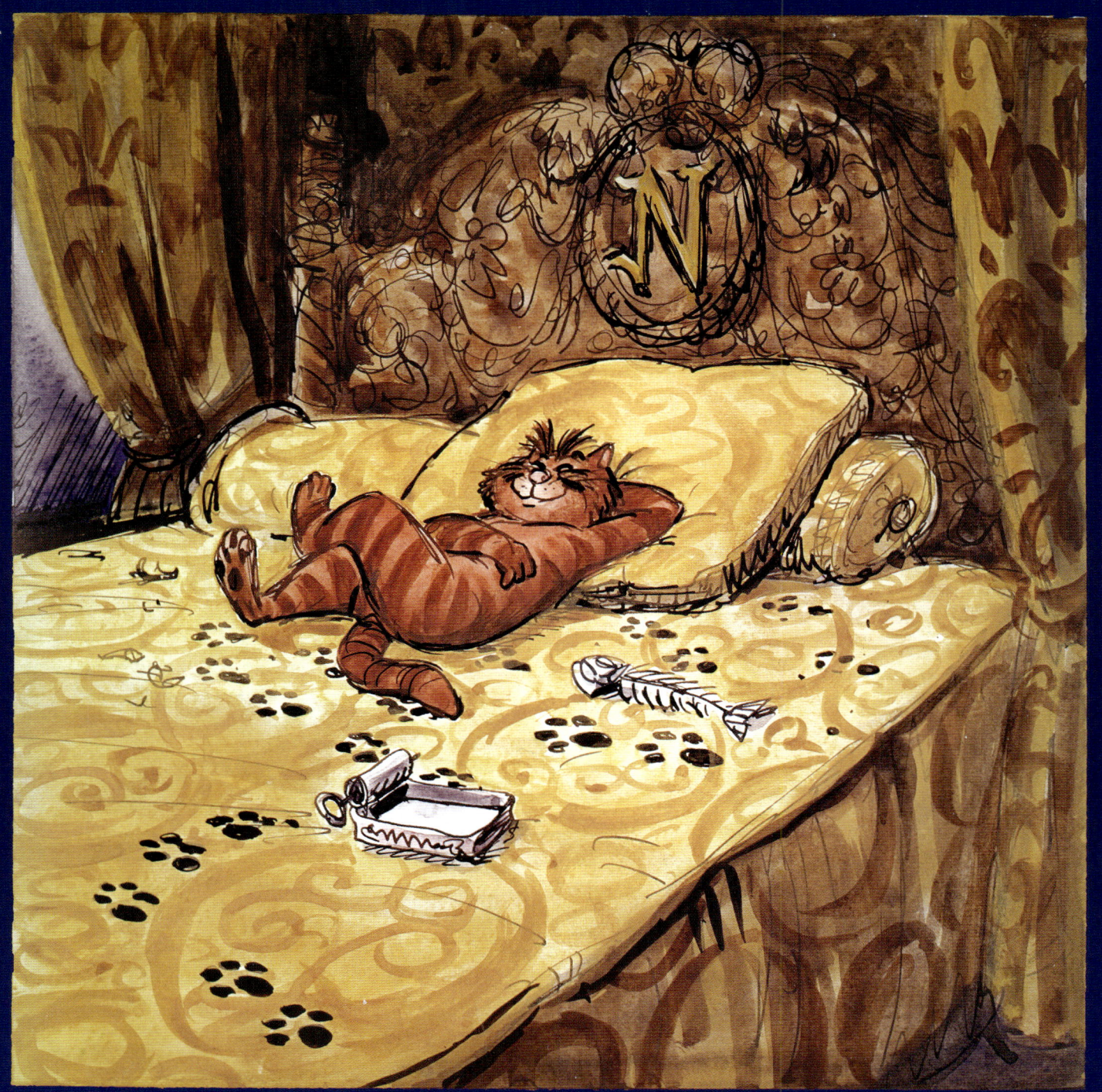

KEN ANDERSON

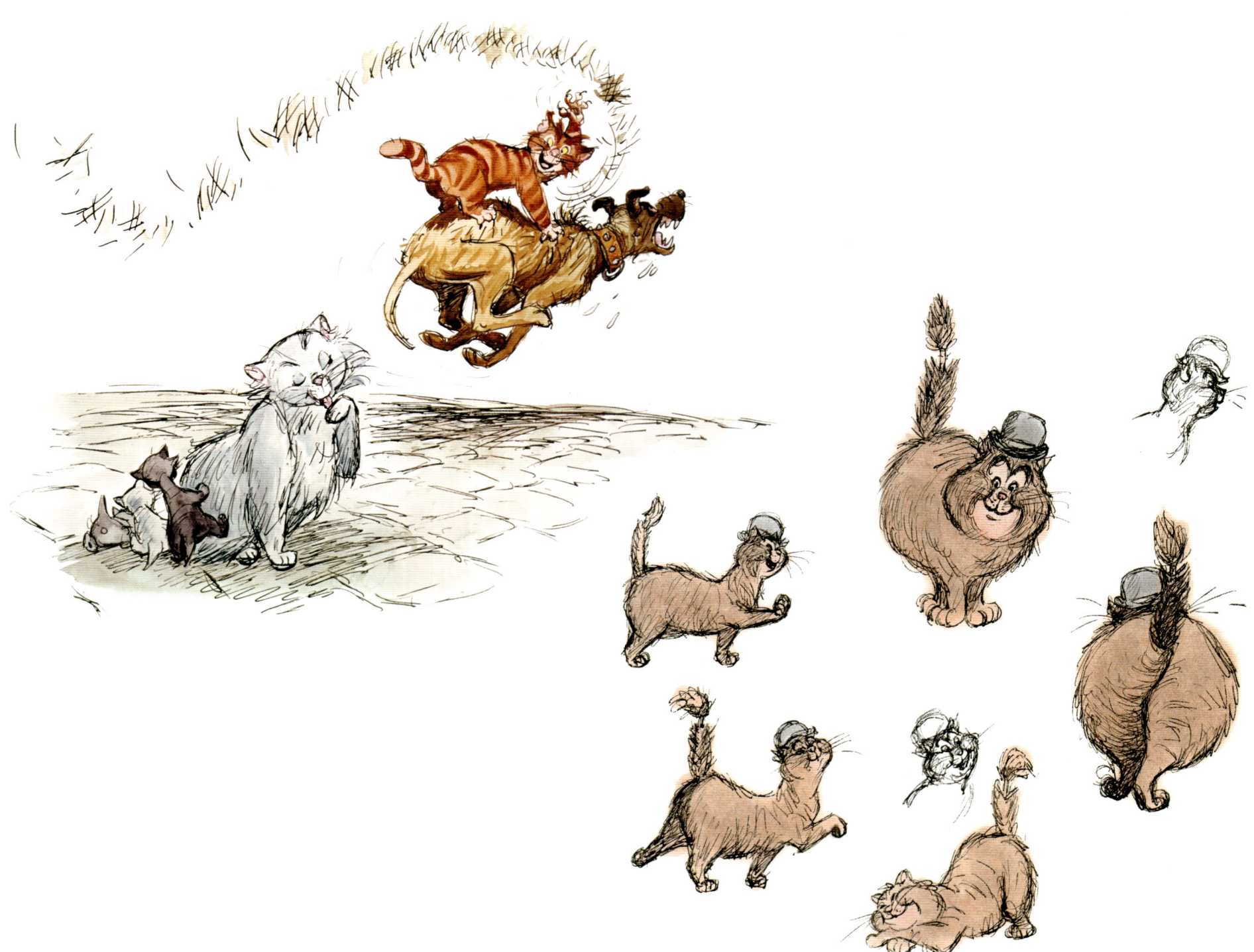

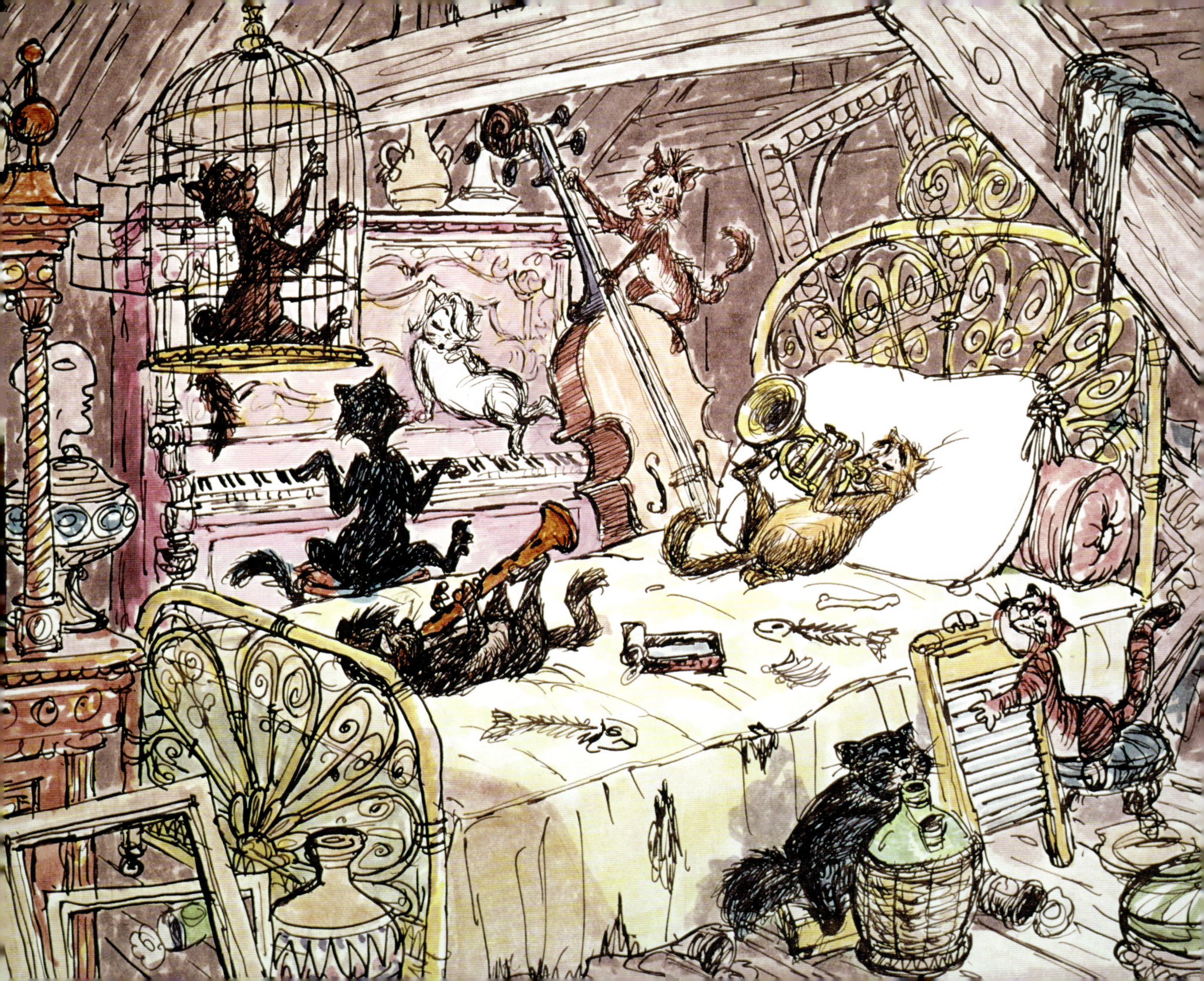

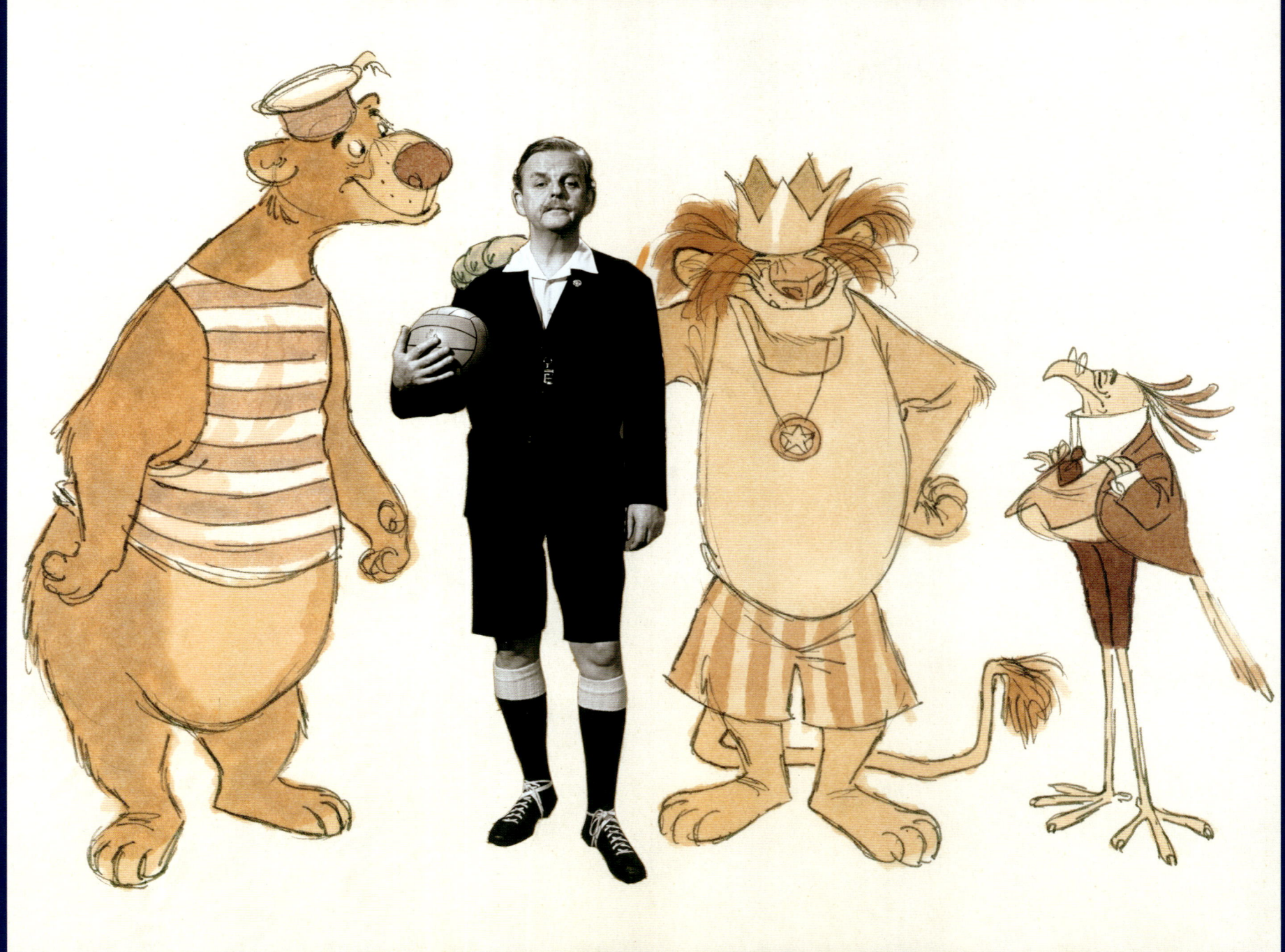

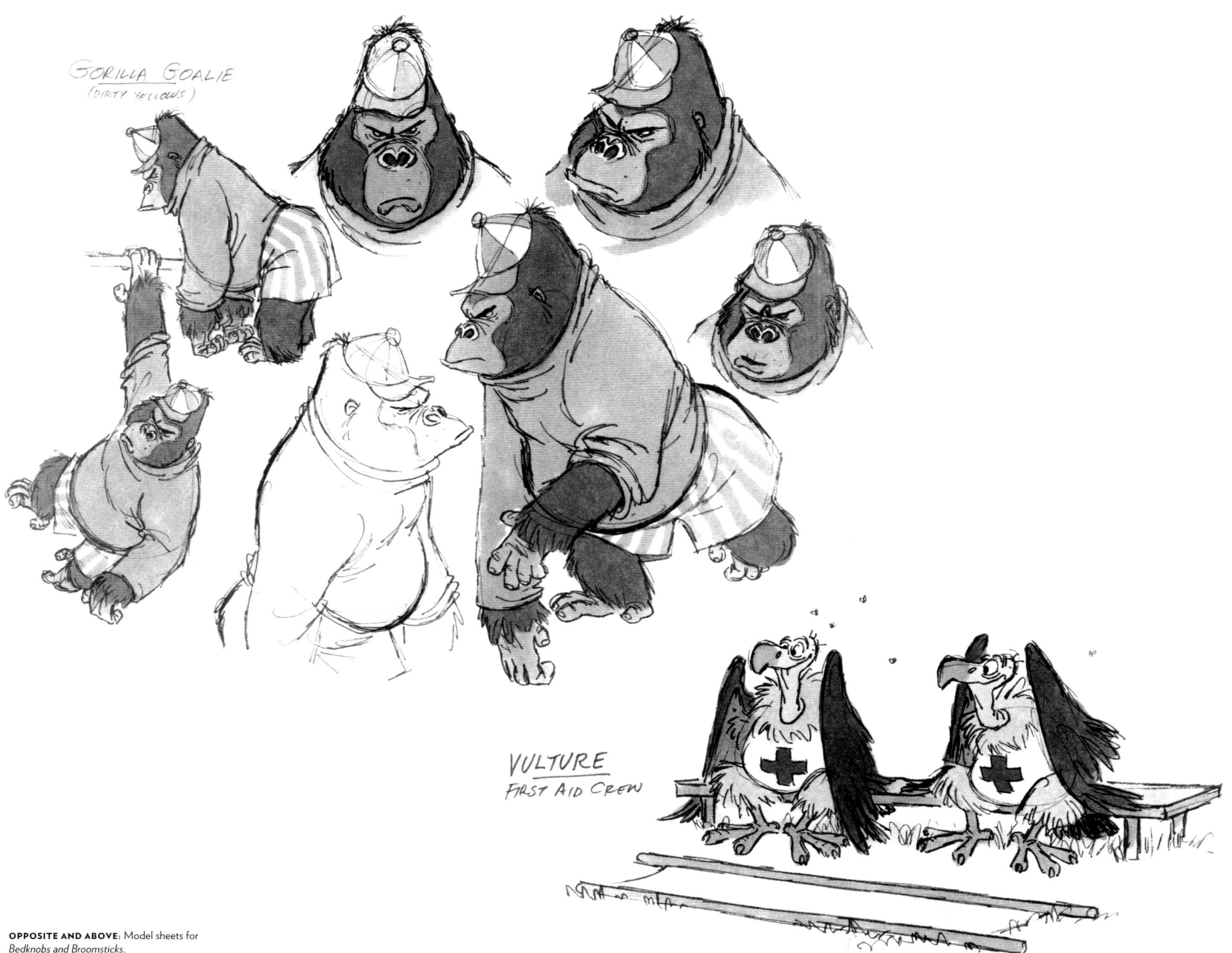

OPPOSITE AND ABOVE: Model sheets for *Bedknobs and Broomsticks*.

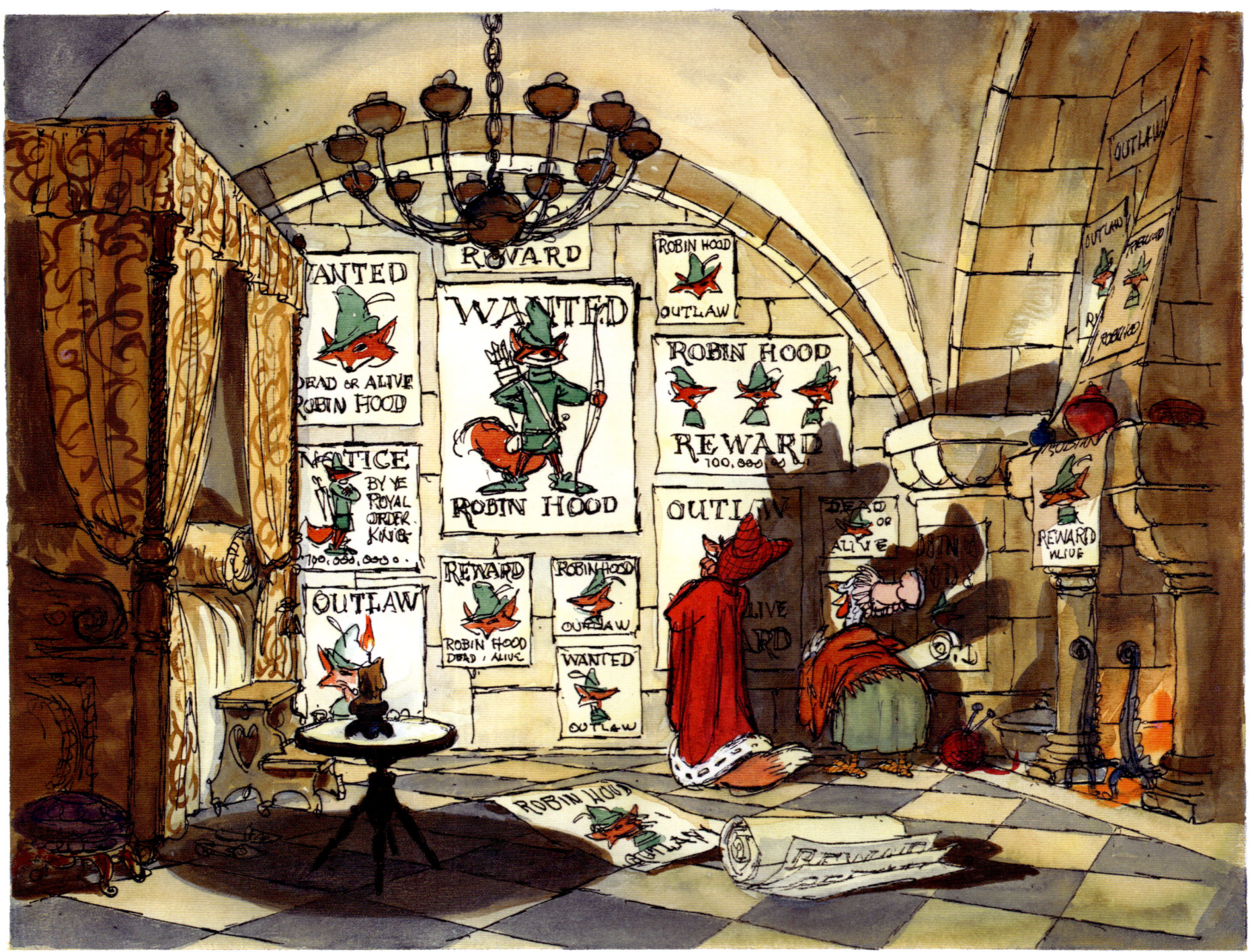

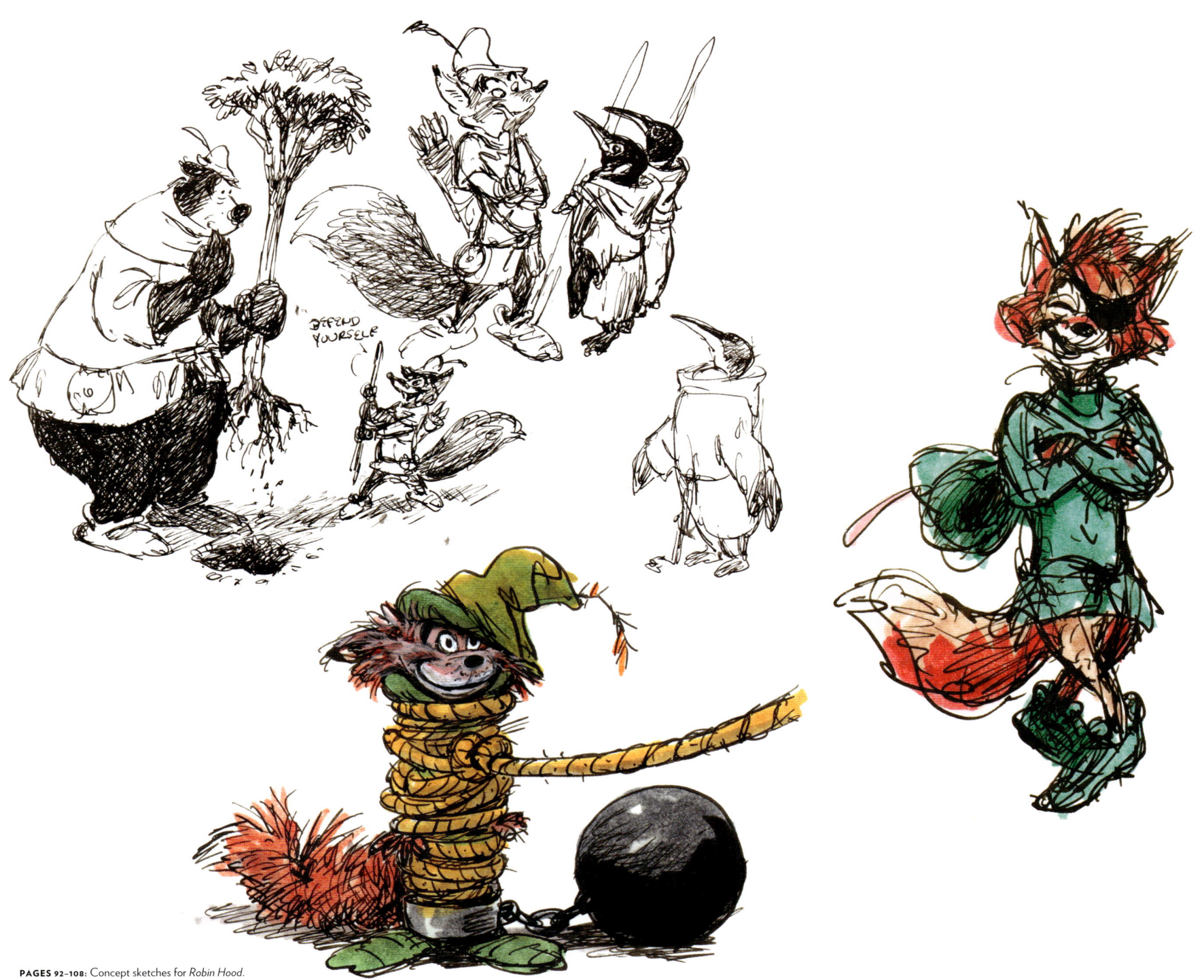

PAGES 92–108: Concept sketches for *Robin Hood*.

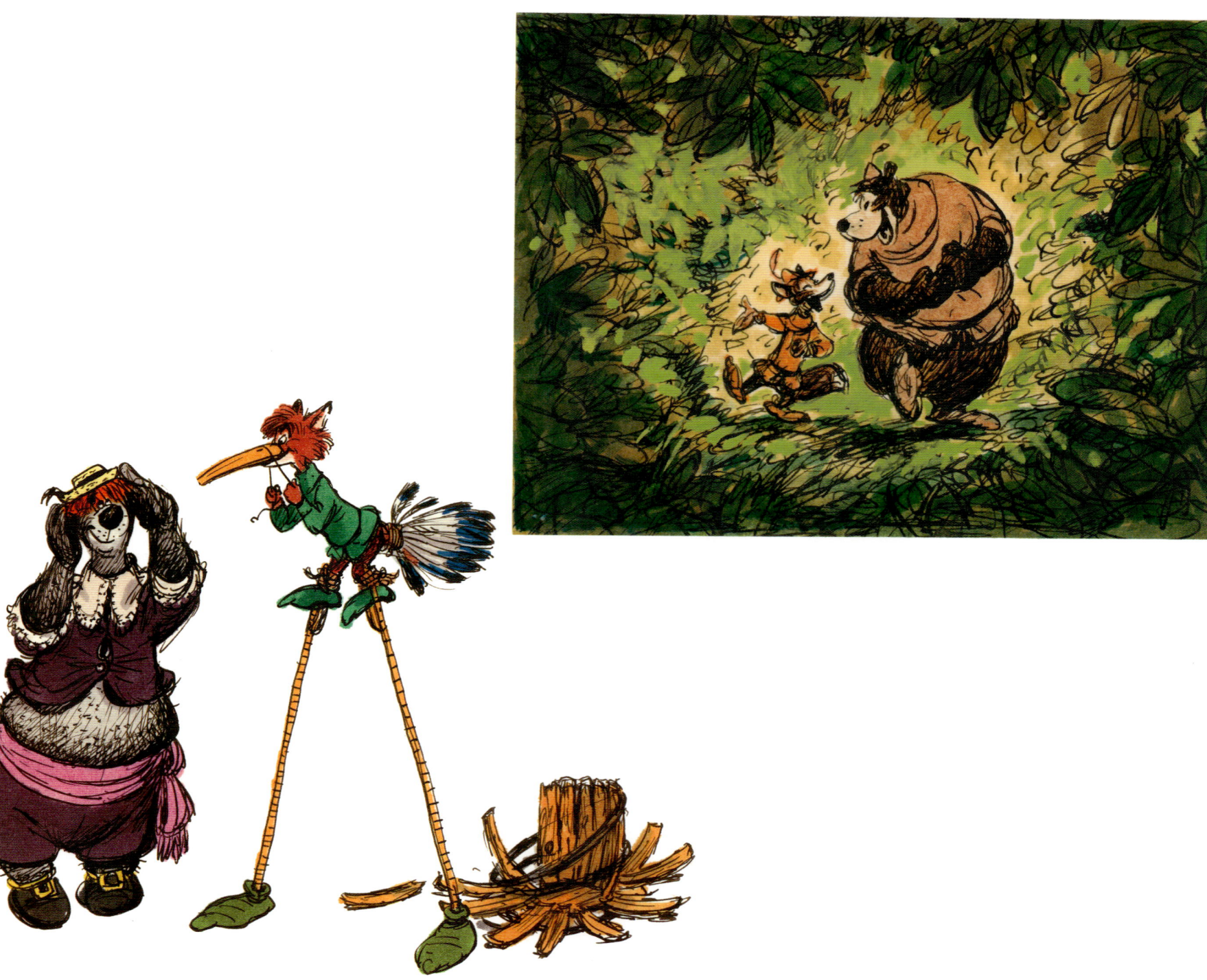

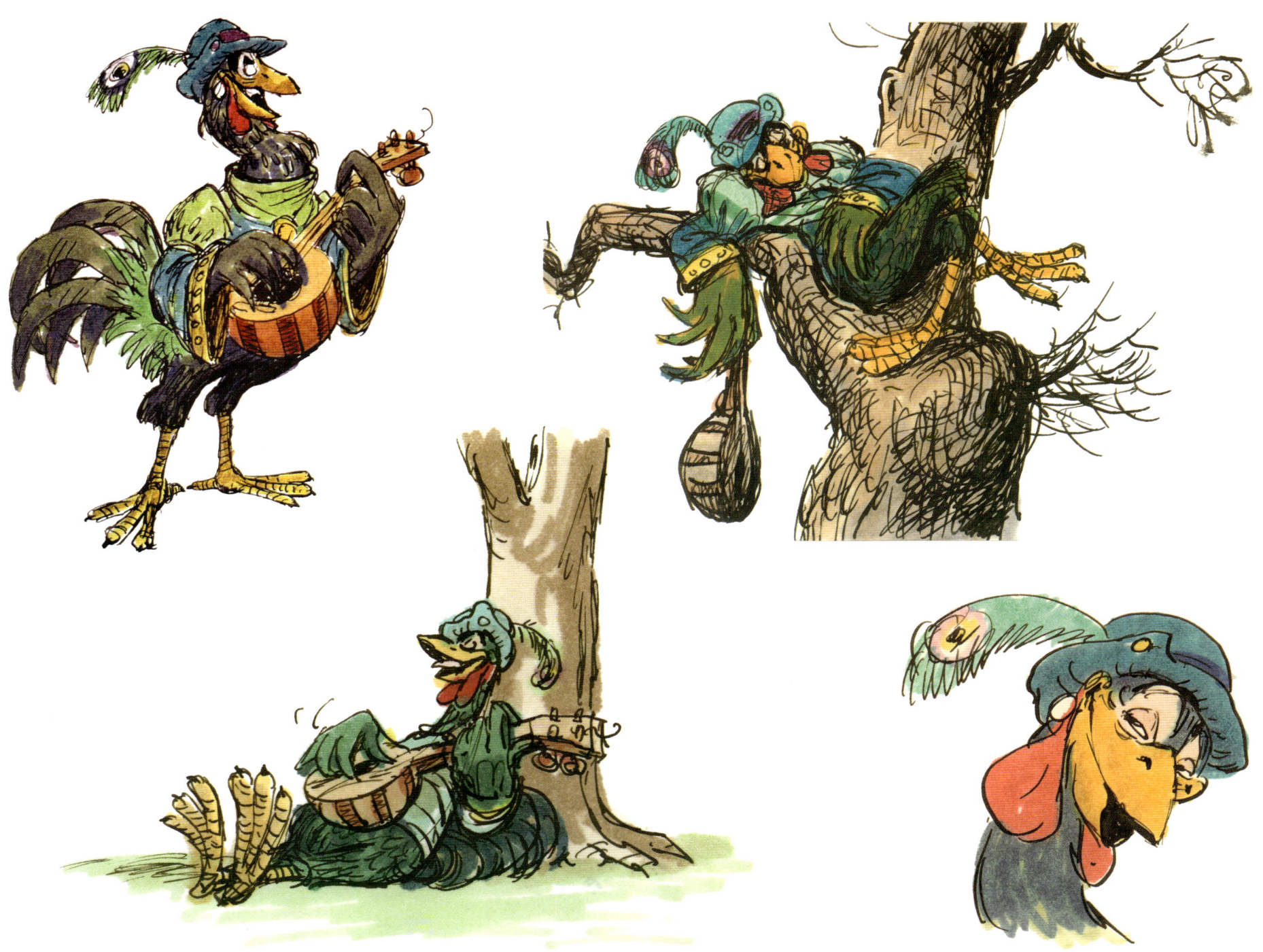

BOTTOM LEFT: Courtesy: Gretchen Vander Weide.

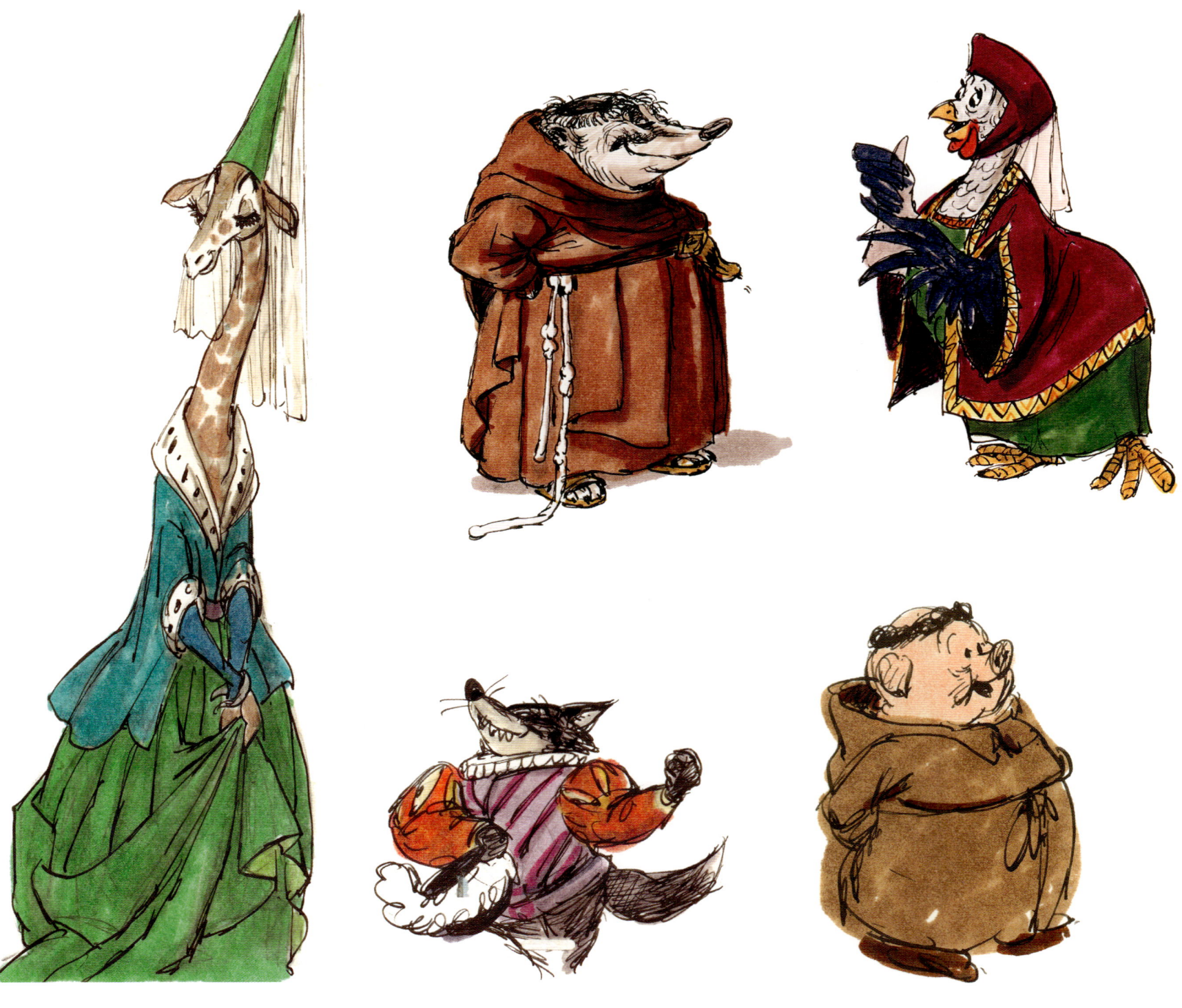

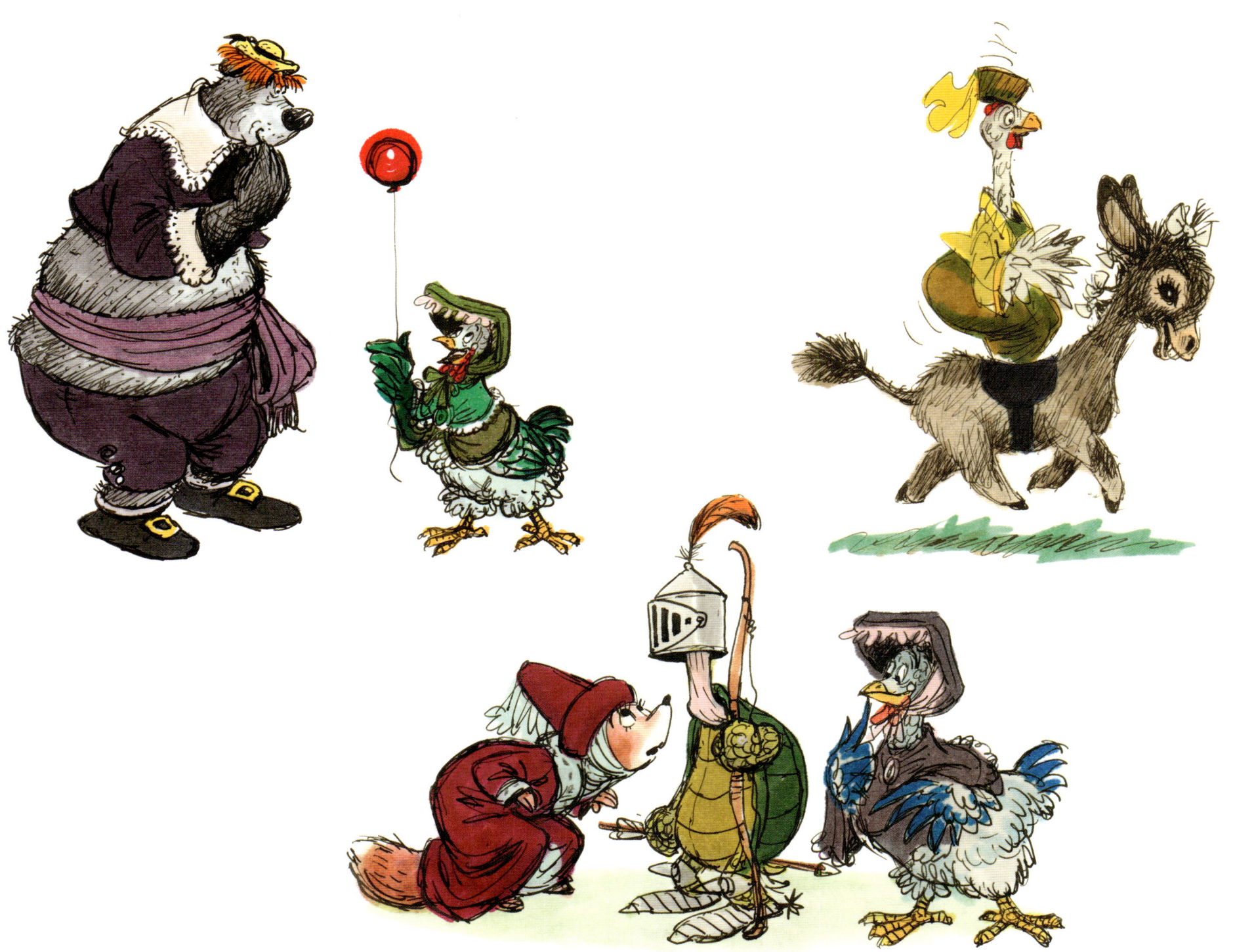

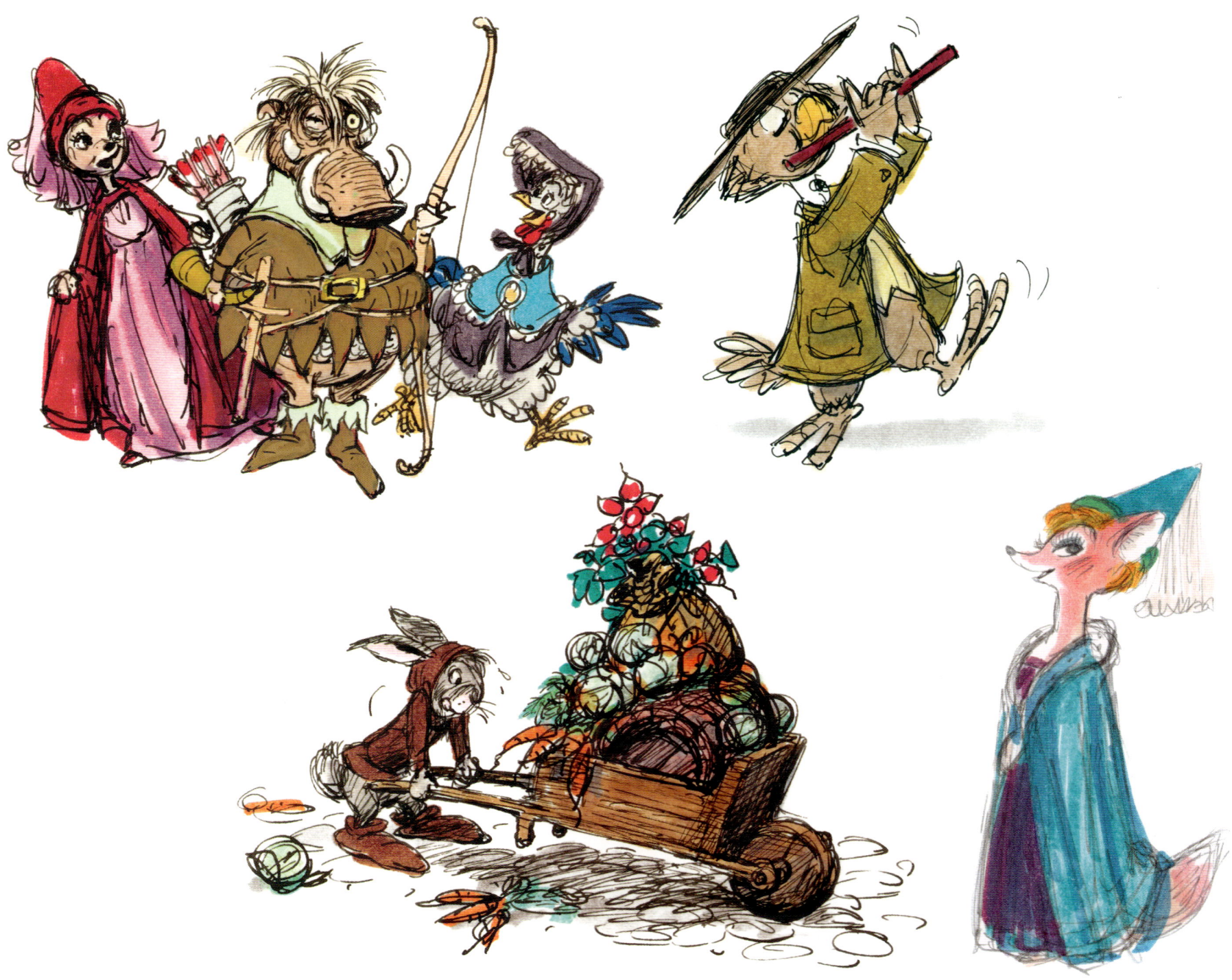

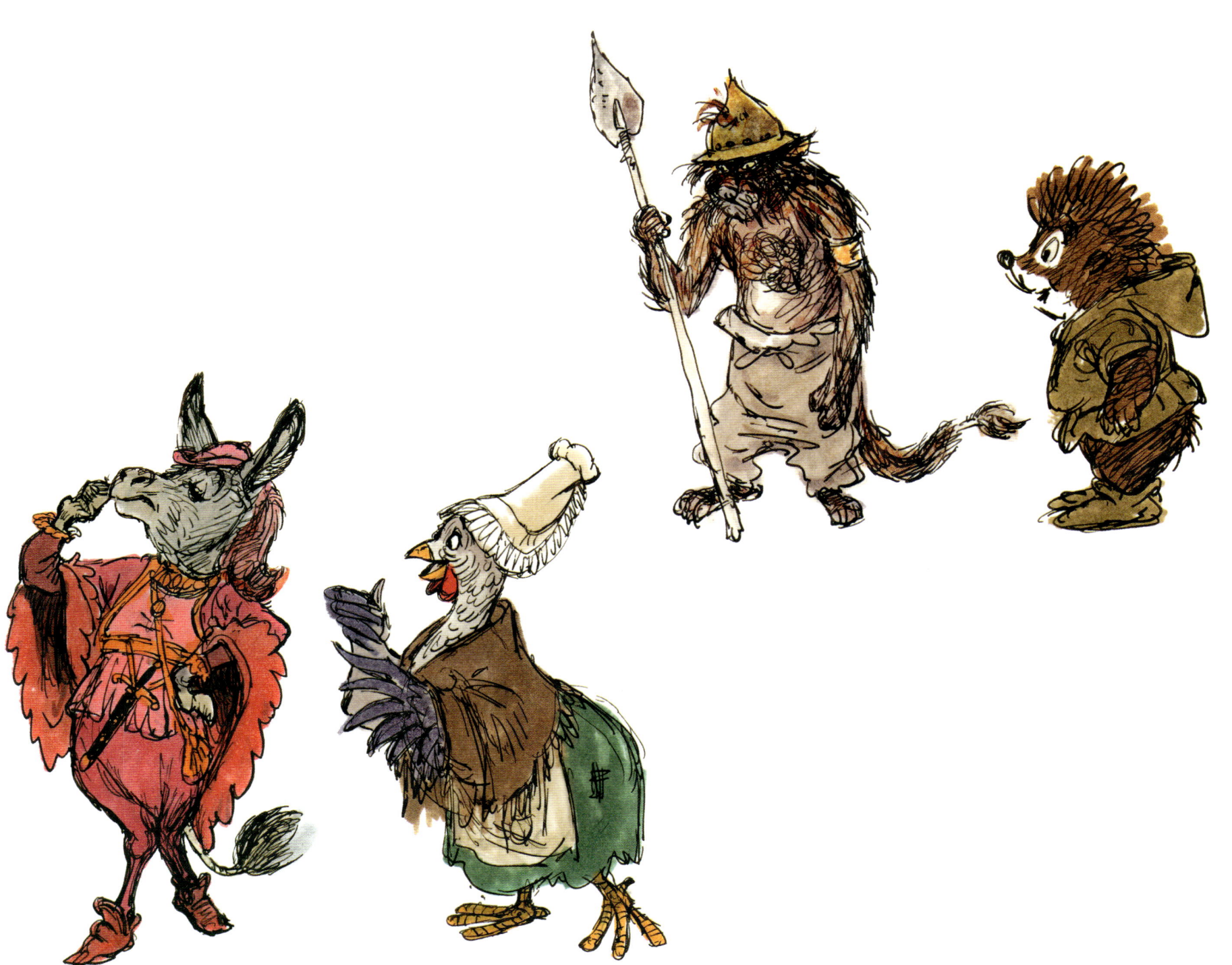

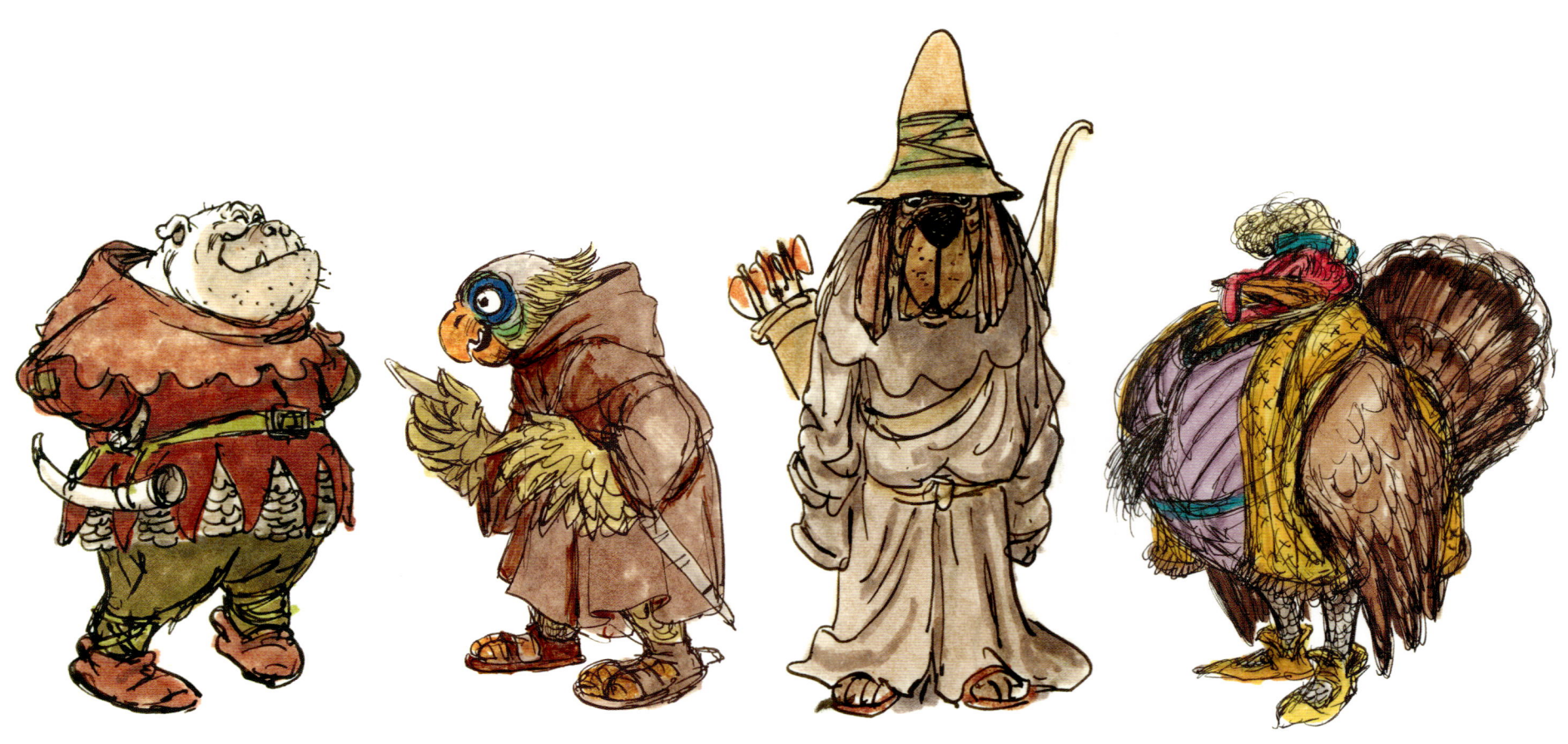

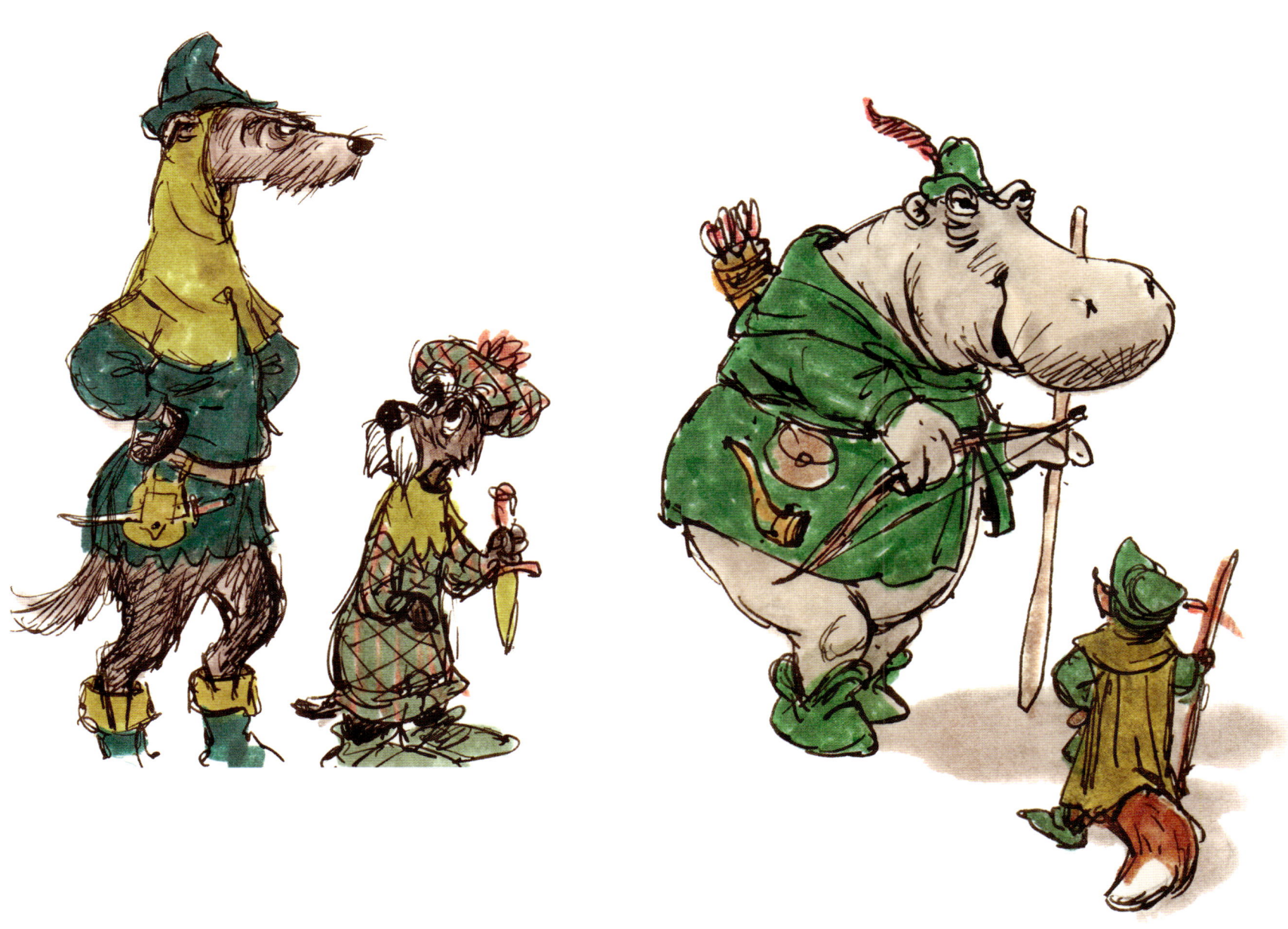

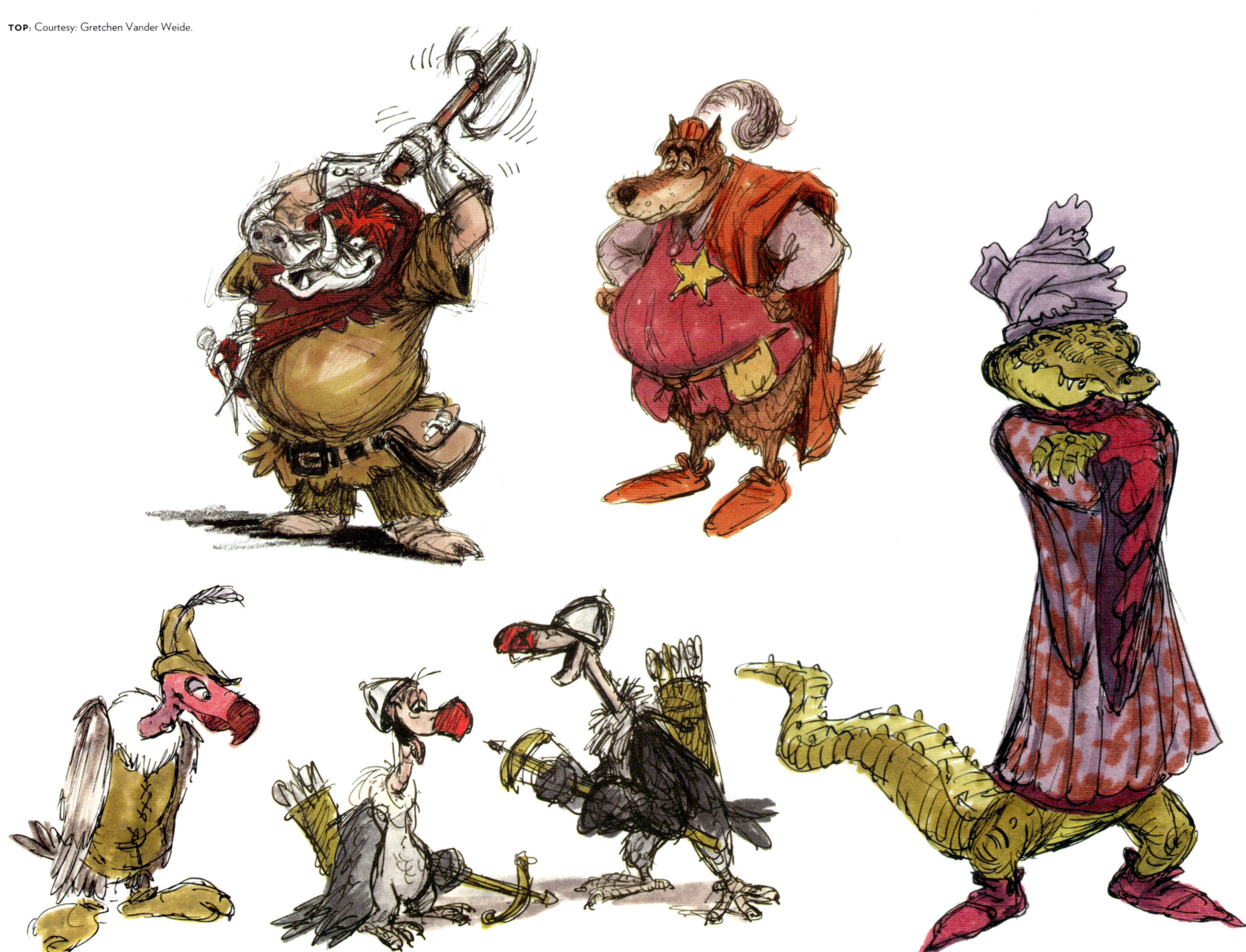

TOP: Courtesy: Gretchen Vander Weide.

TOP LEFT: Courtesy: Gretchen Vander Weide.

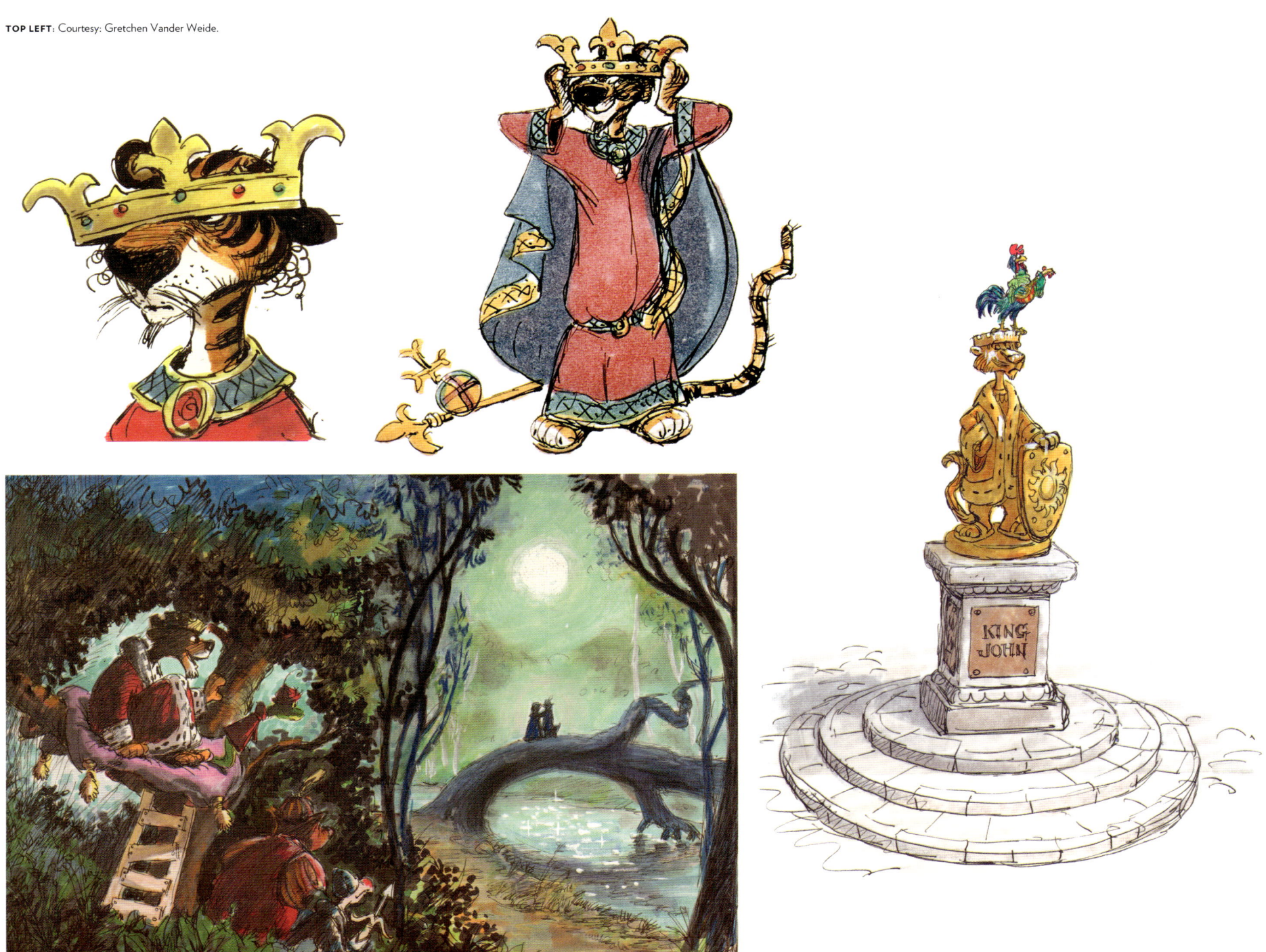

KEN ANDERSON

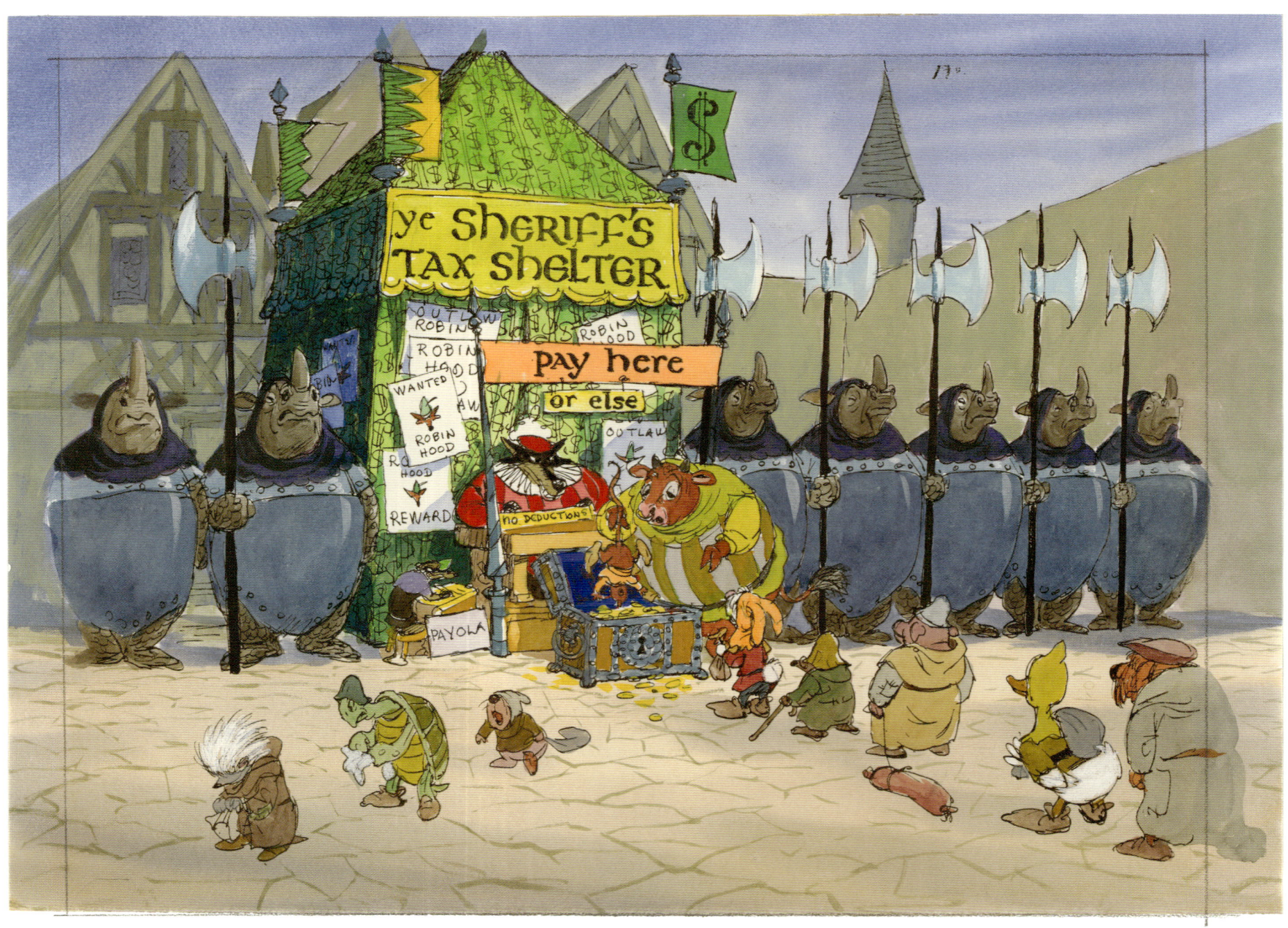

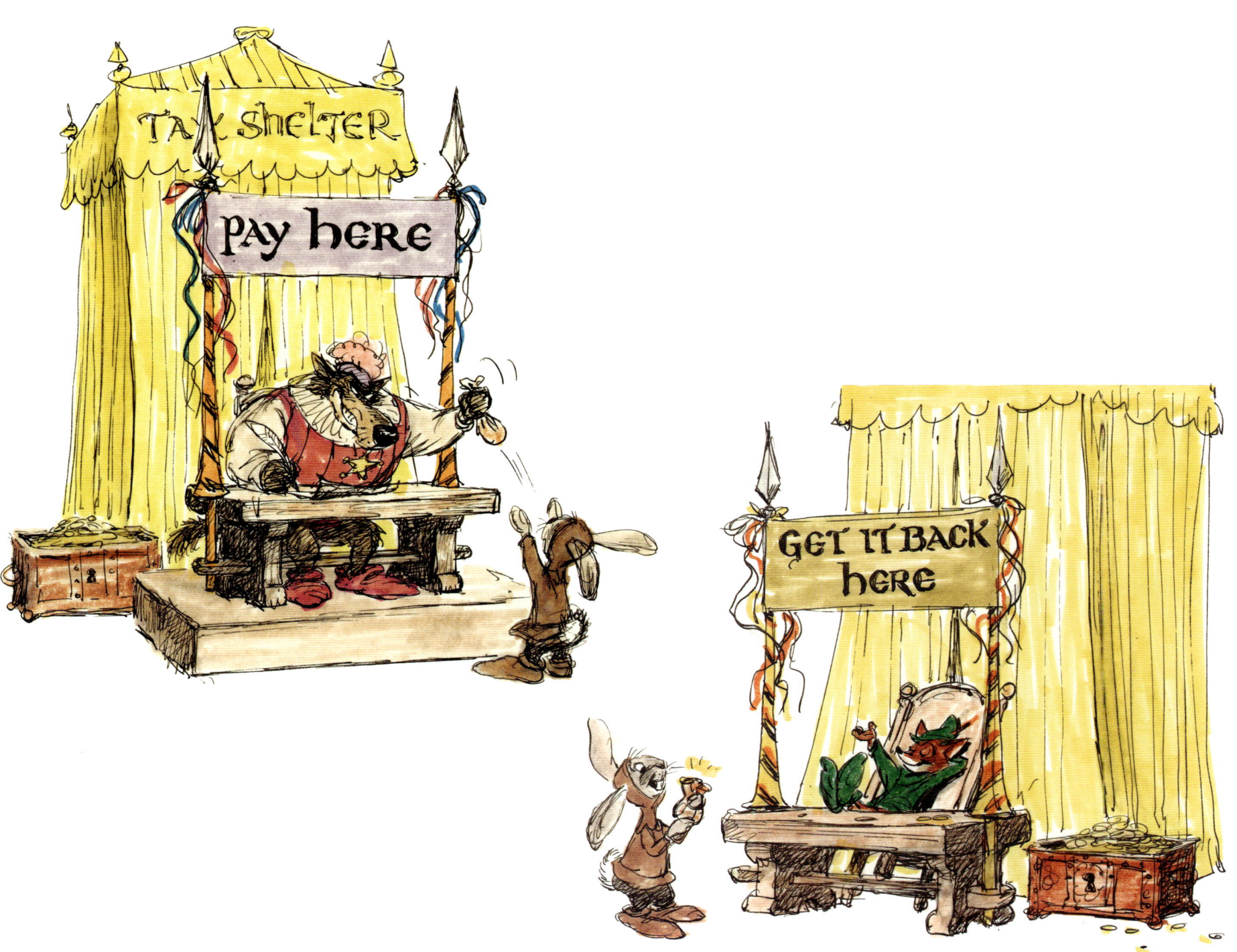

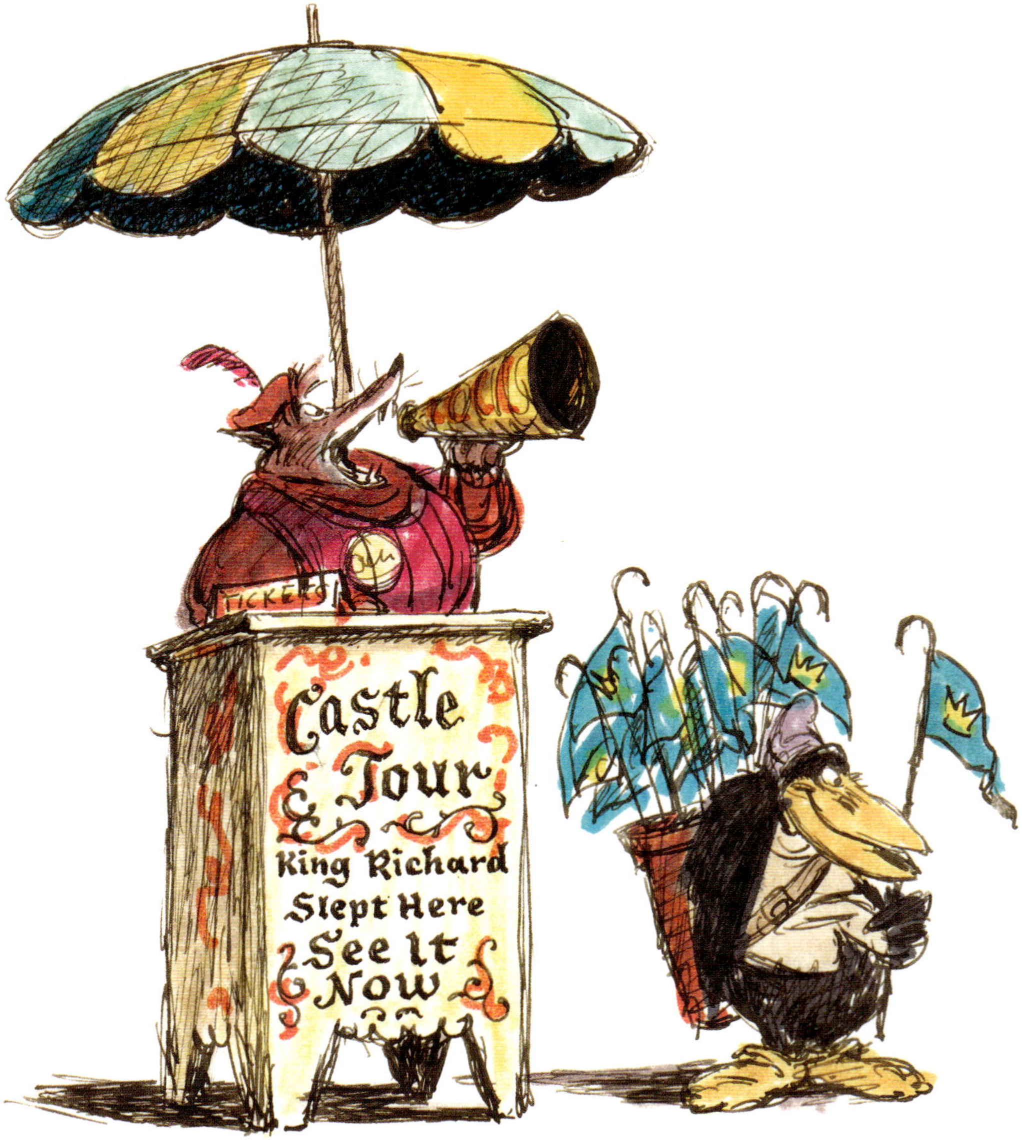

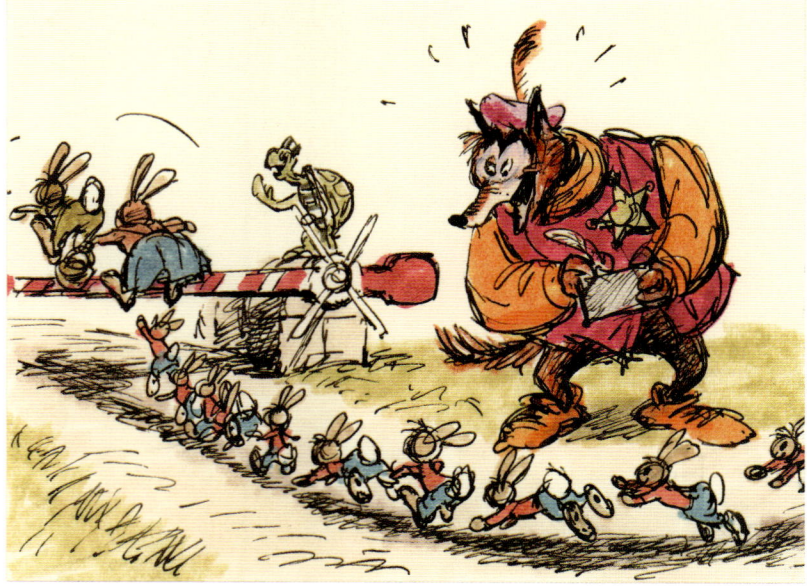
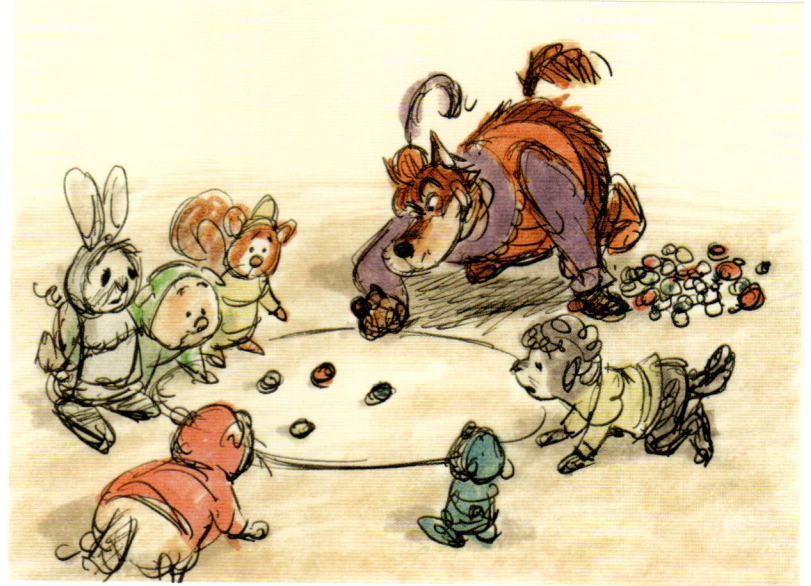

106 THEY DREW AS THEY PLEASED

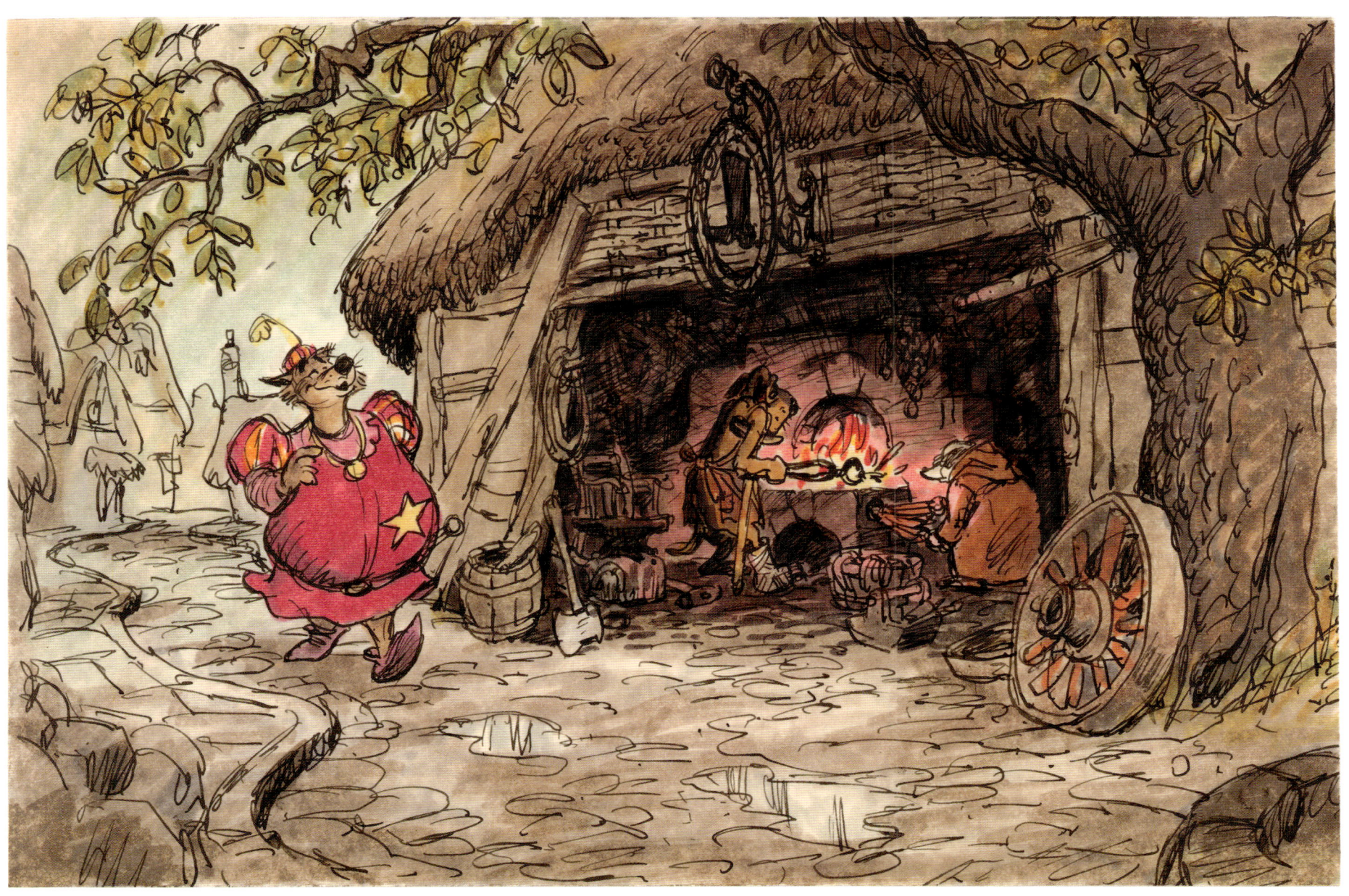

KEN ANDERSON

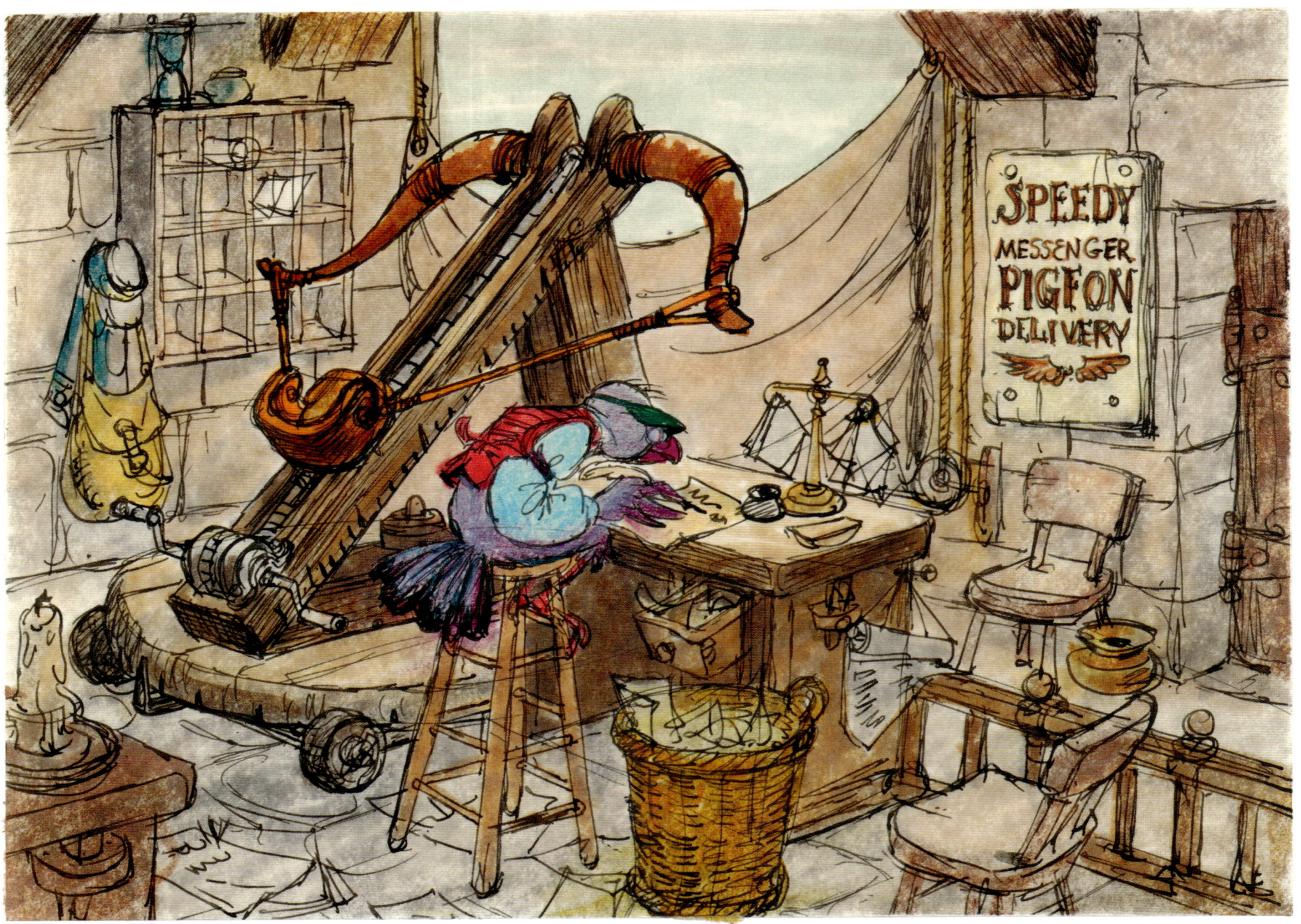

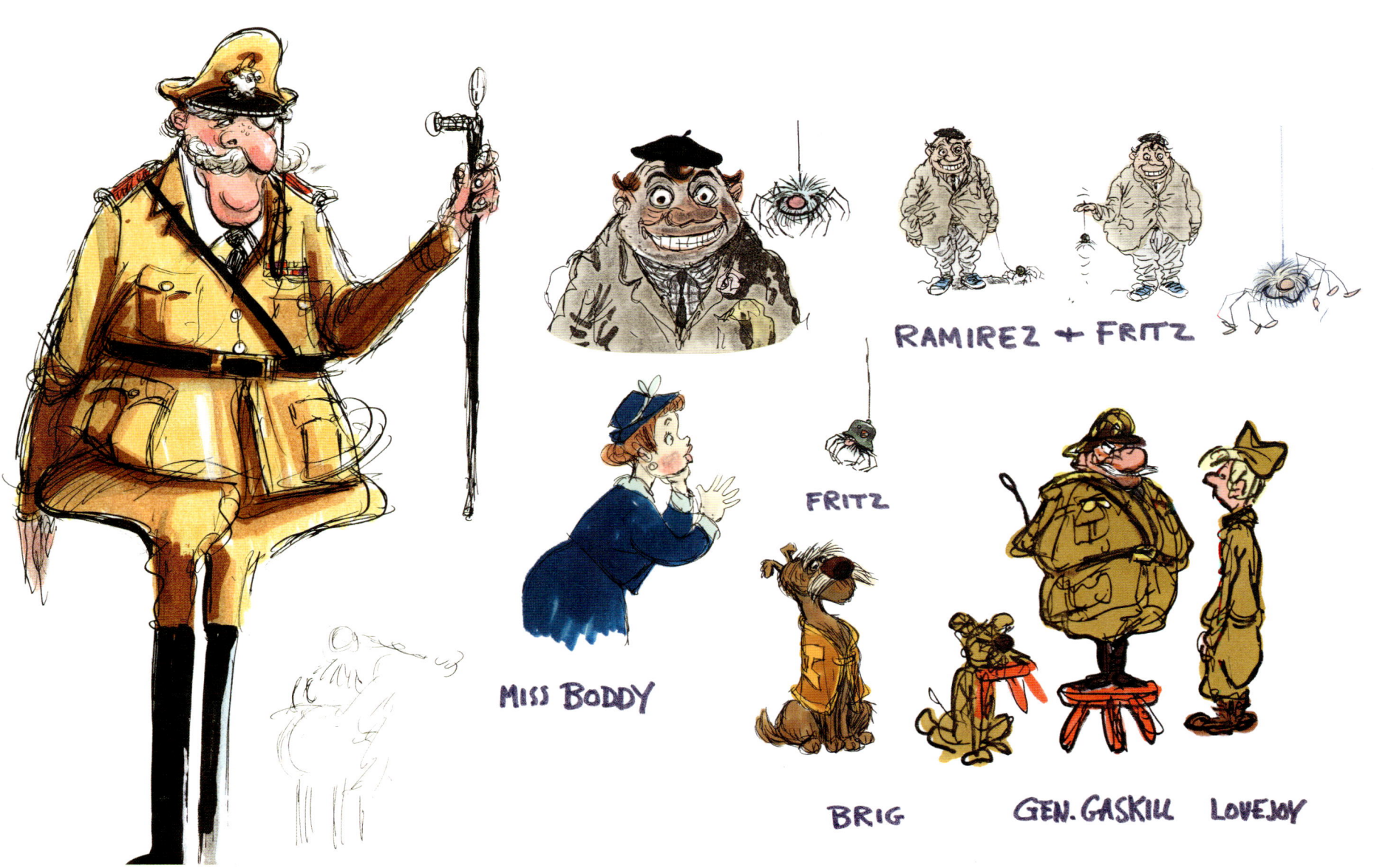

PAGES 109–111: Character designs and story sketches for the abandoned project *Scruffy*.

KEN ANDERSON 109

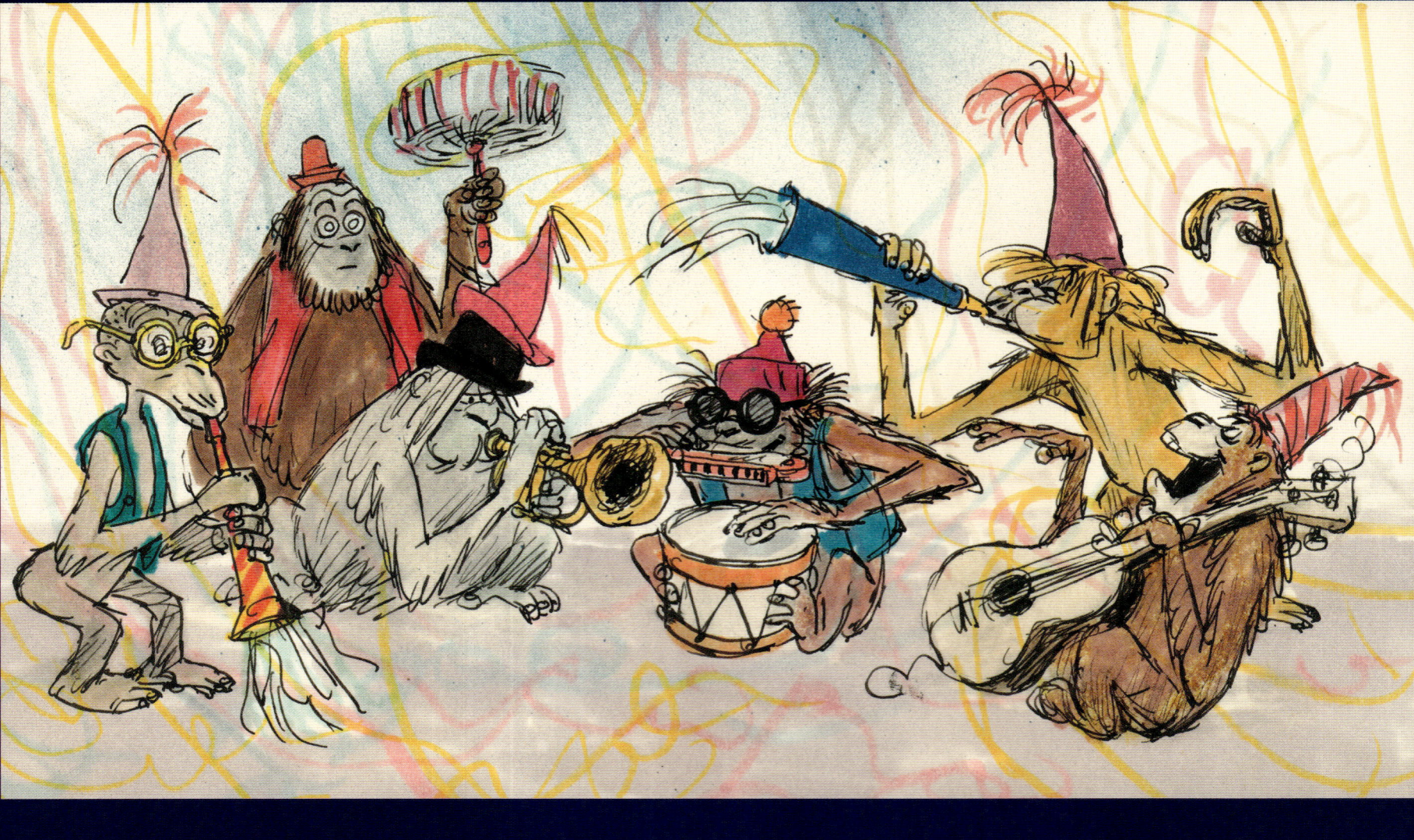

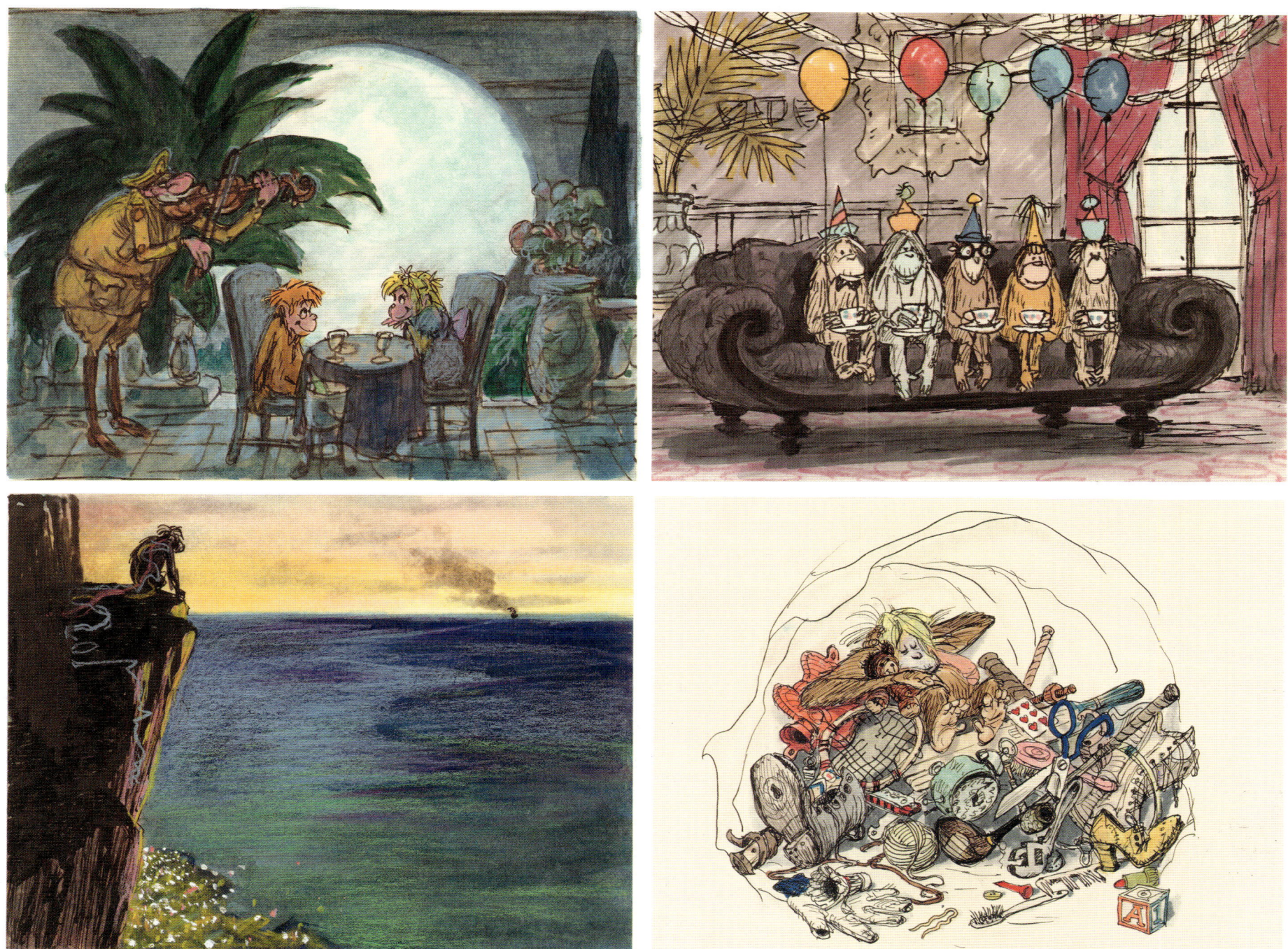

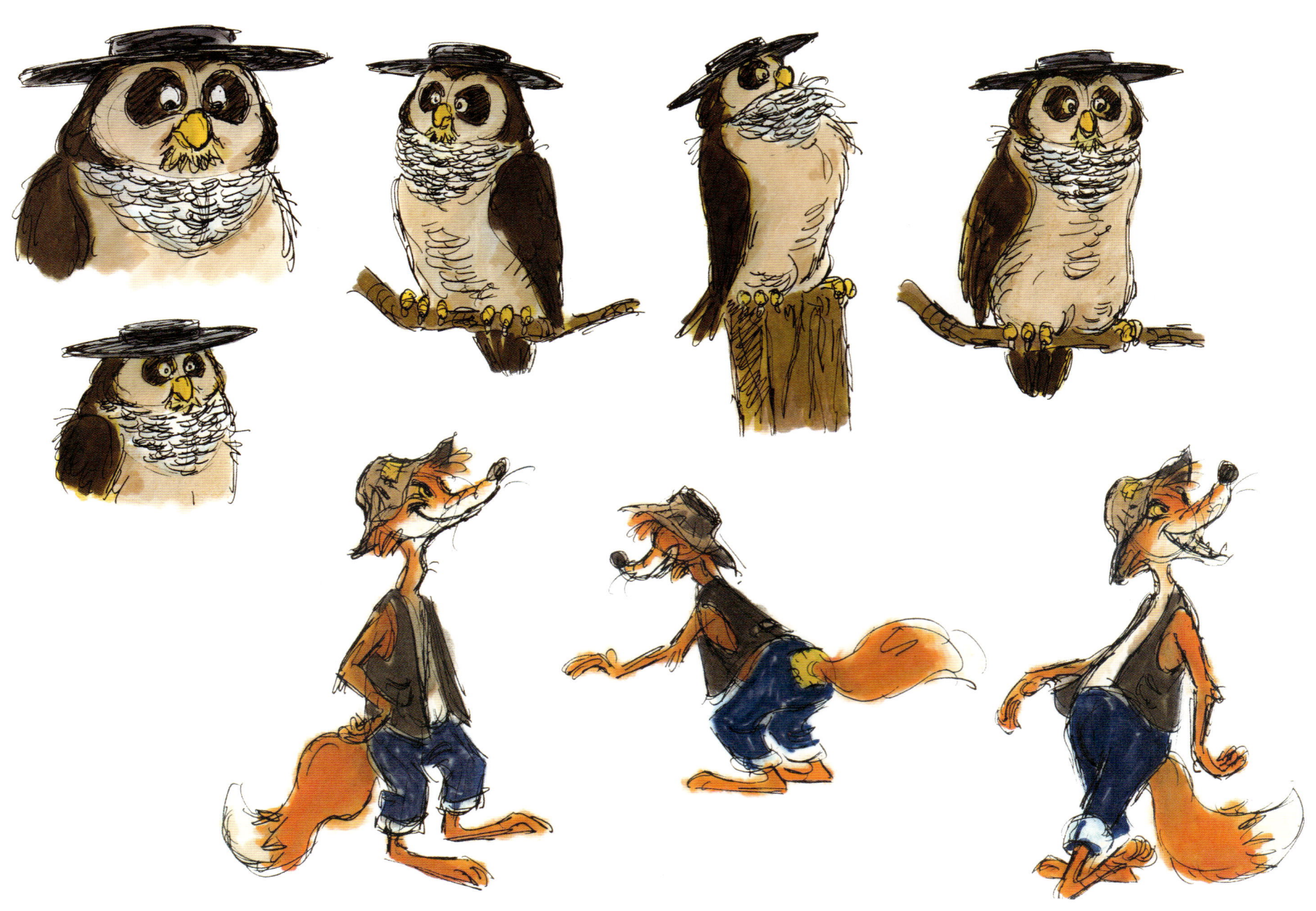

PAGES 112–115: Character designs for the abandoned project *Catfish Bend*.

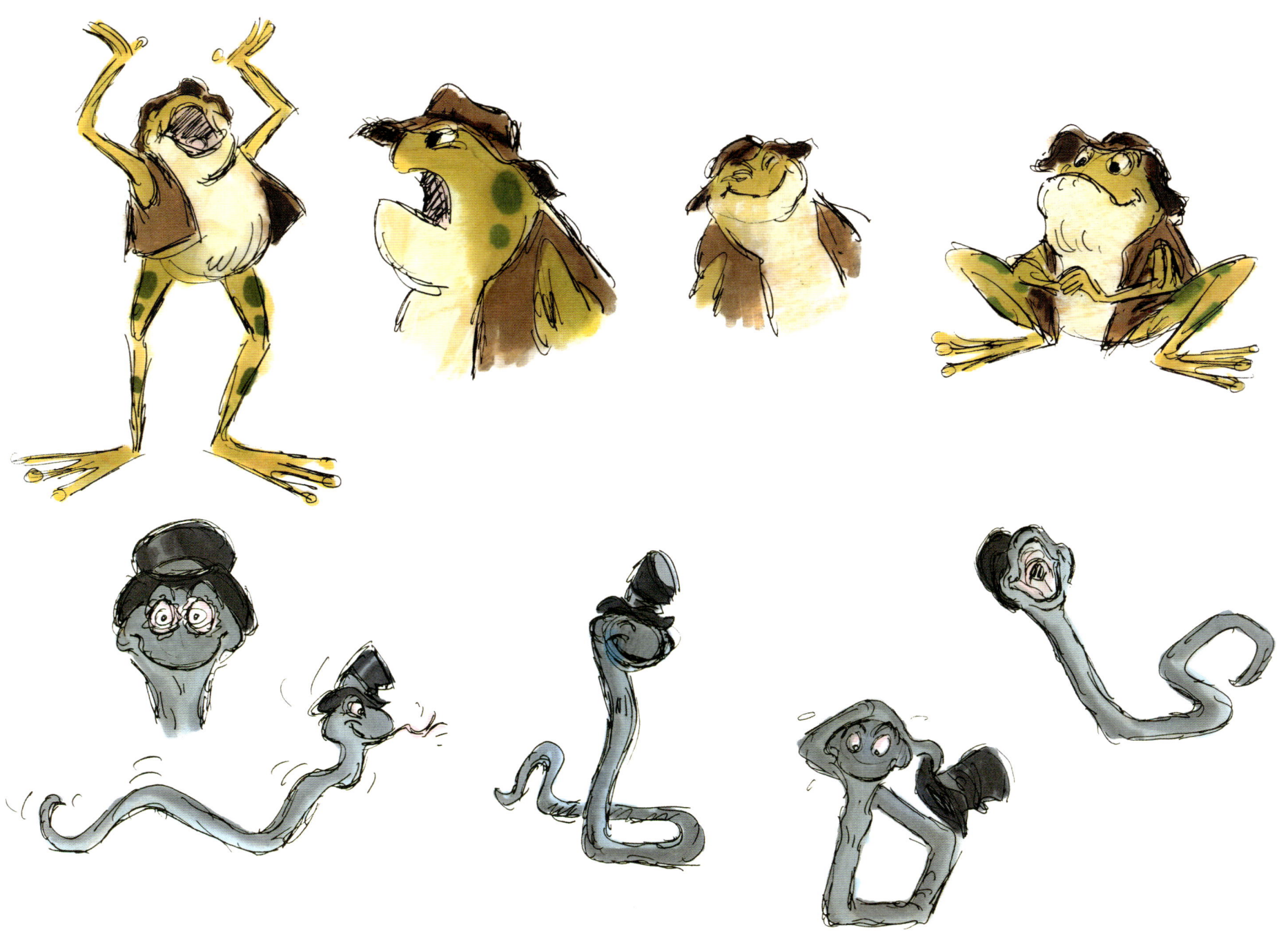

KEN ANDERSON

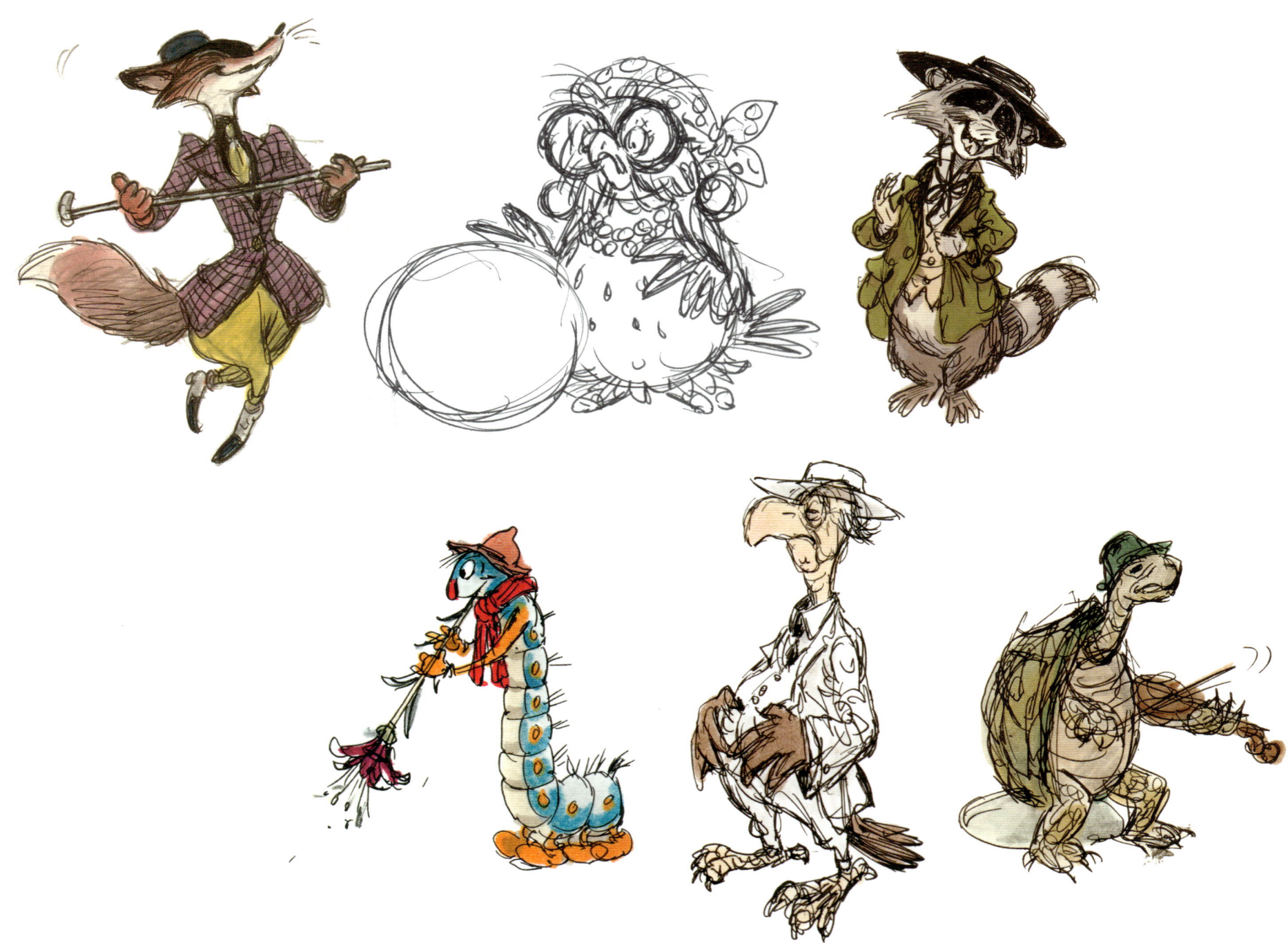

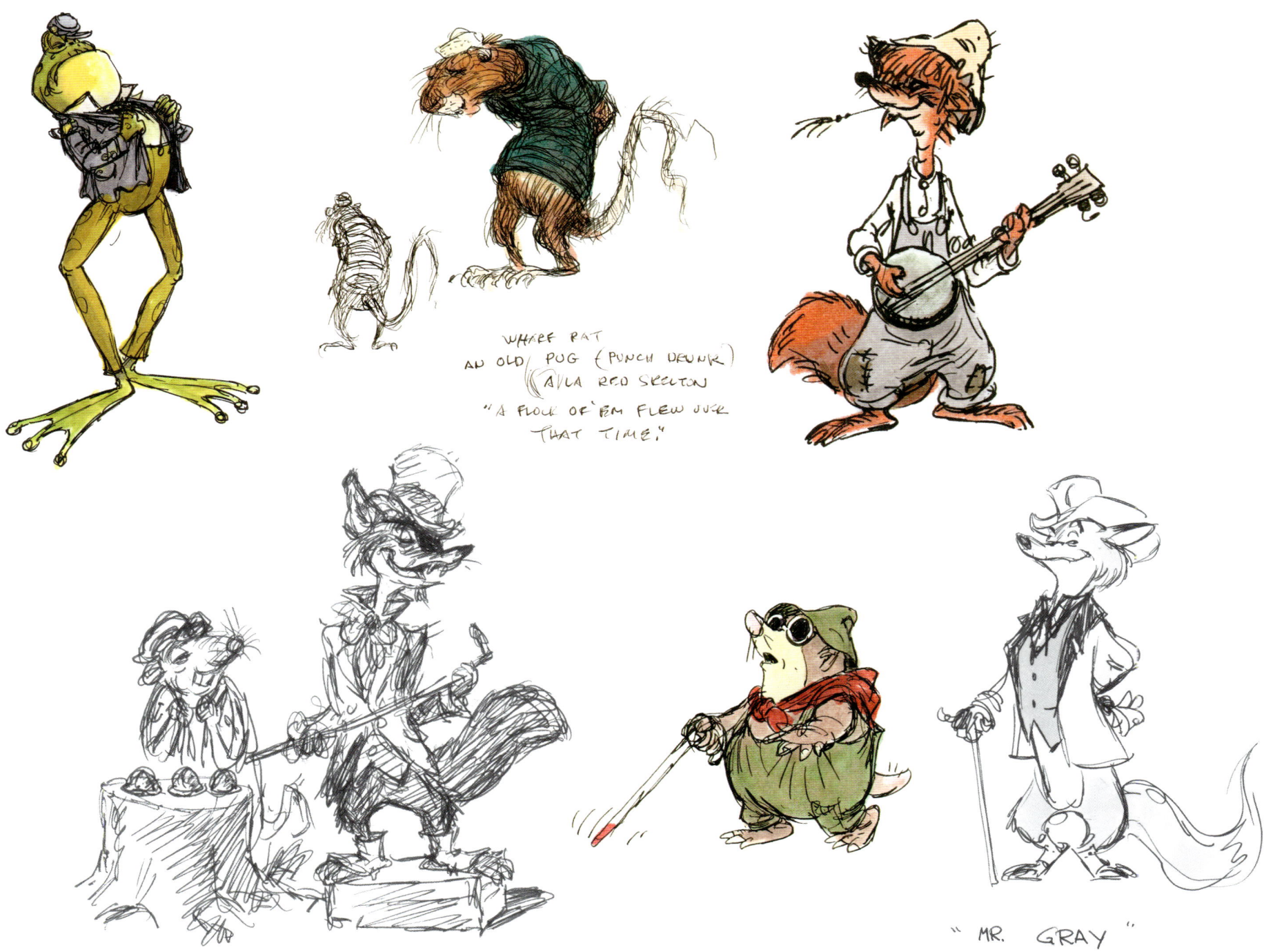

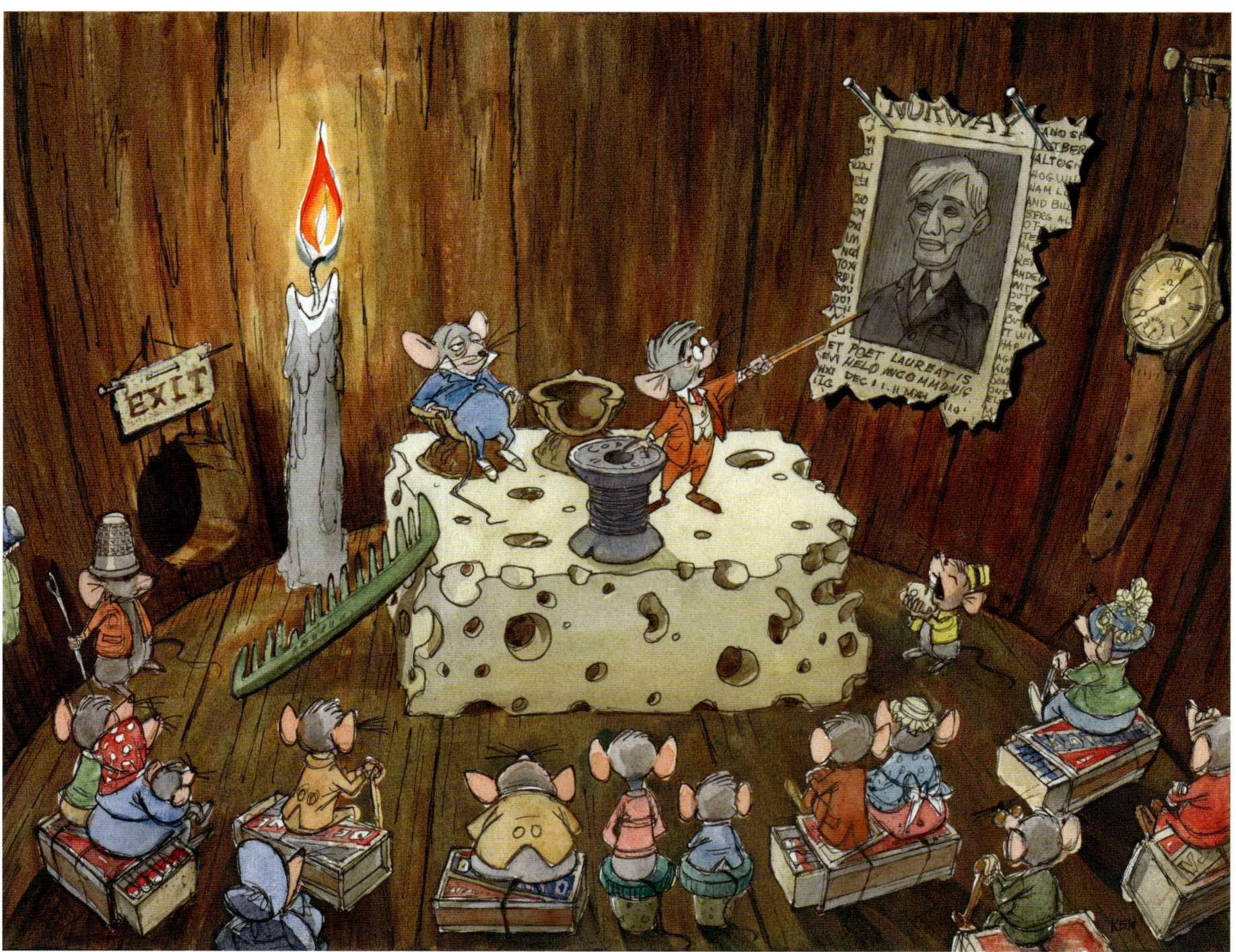

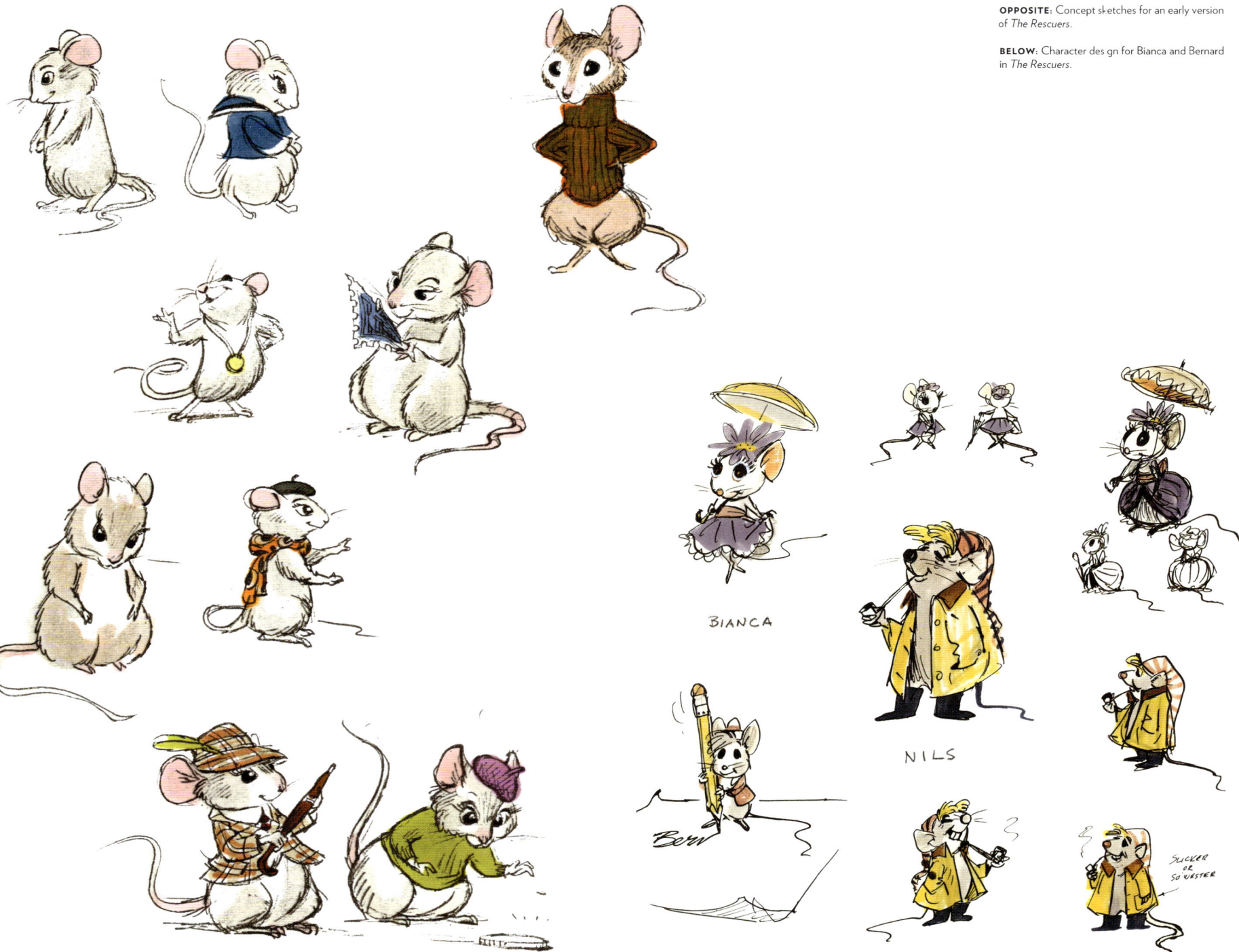

OPPOSITE: Concept sketches for an early version of *The Rescuers*.

BELOW: Character design for Bianca and Bernard in *The Rescuers*.

KEN ANDERSON

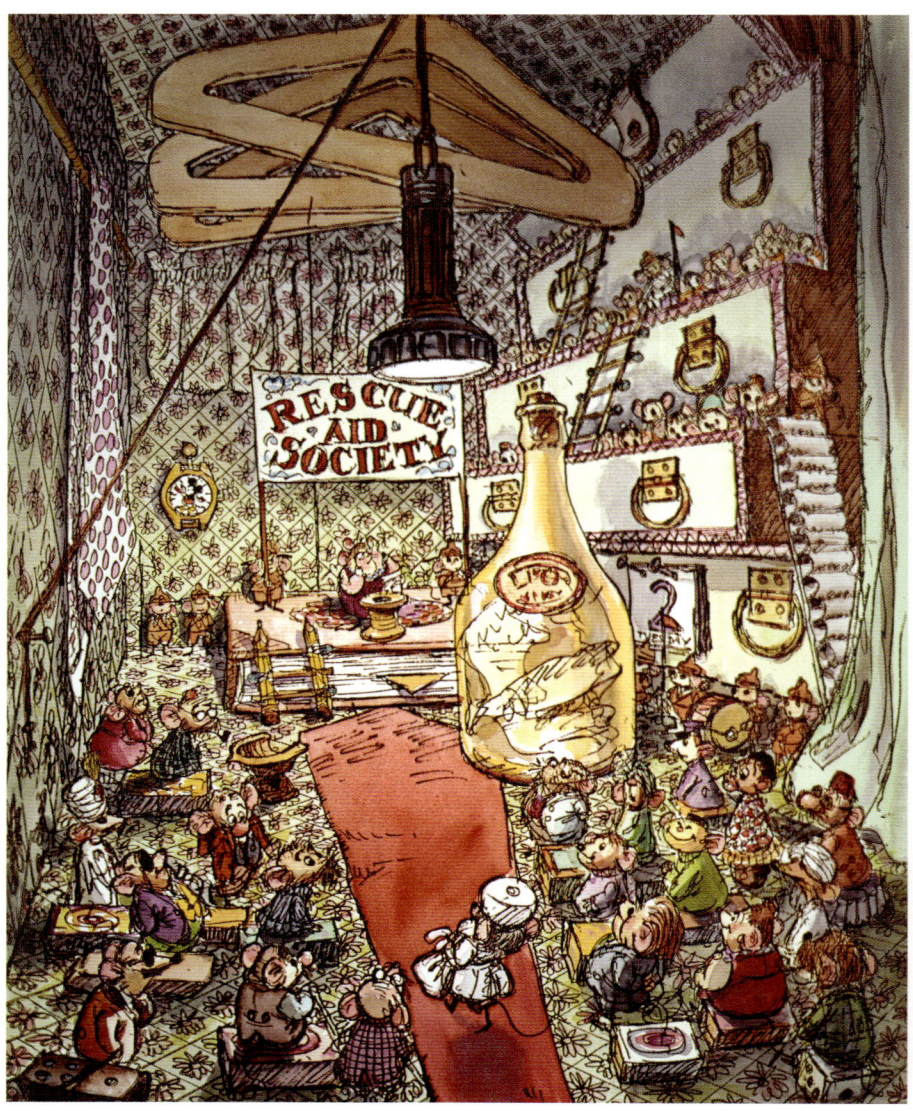 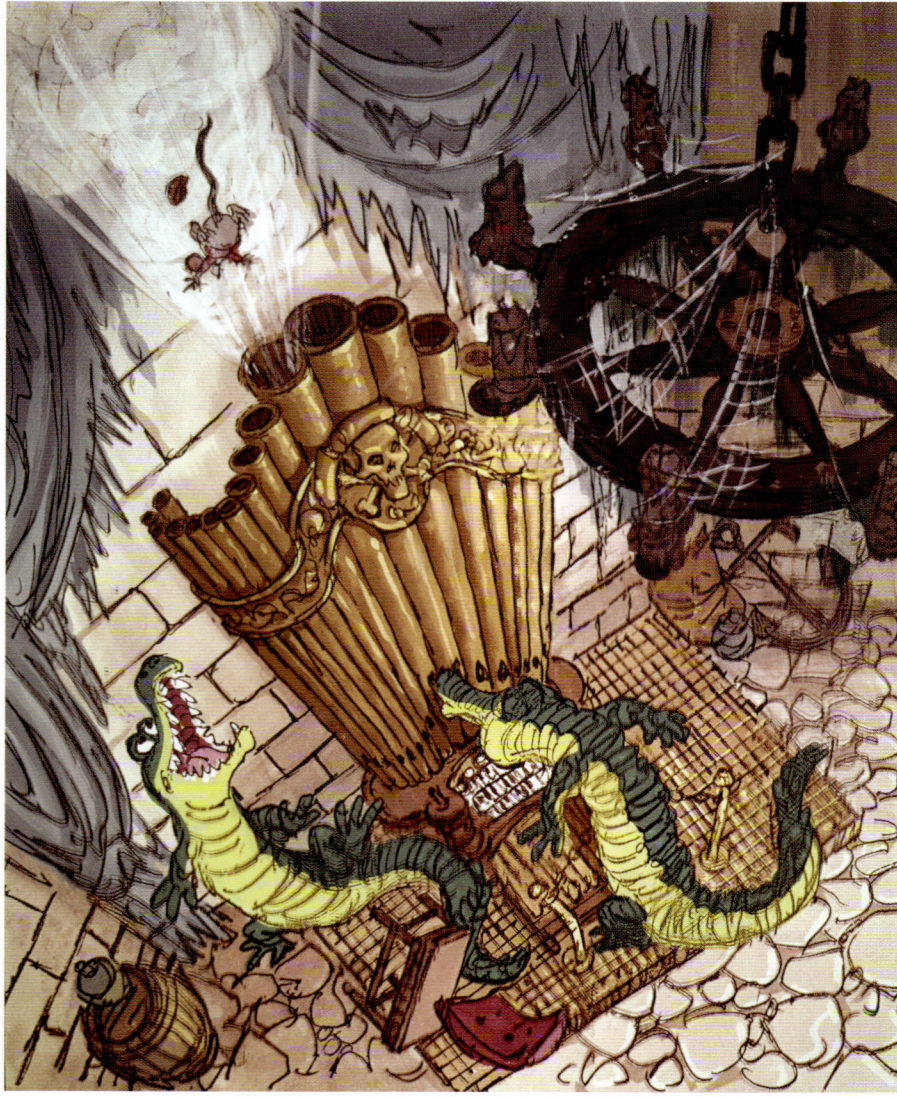

ABOVE: Concept sketches for *The Rescuers*.

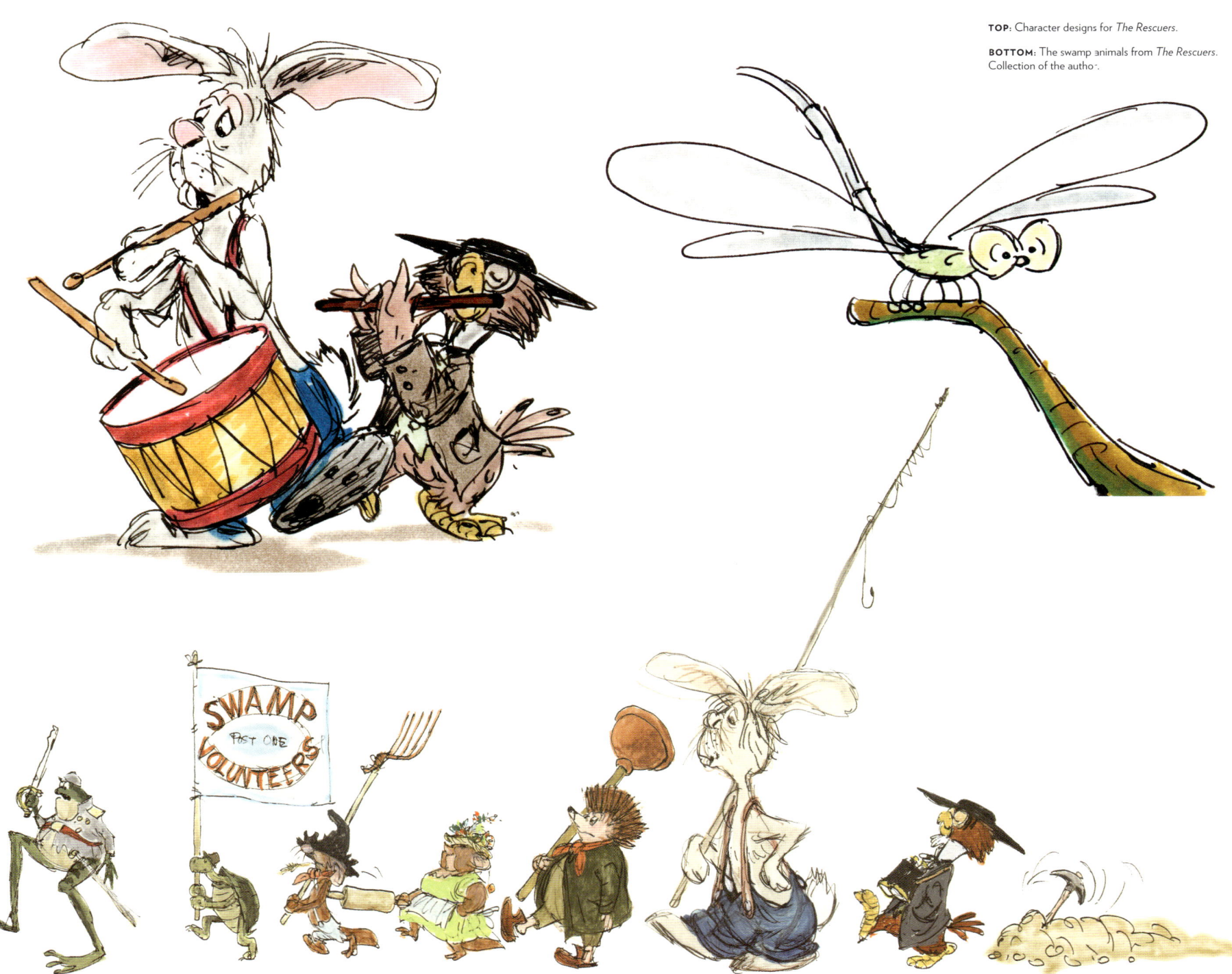

TOP: Character designs for *The Rescuers*.

BOTTOM: The swamp animals from *The Rescuers*. Collection of the author.

KEN ANDERSON

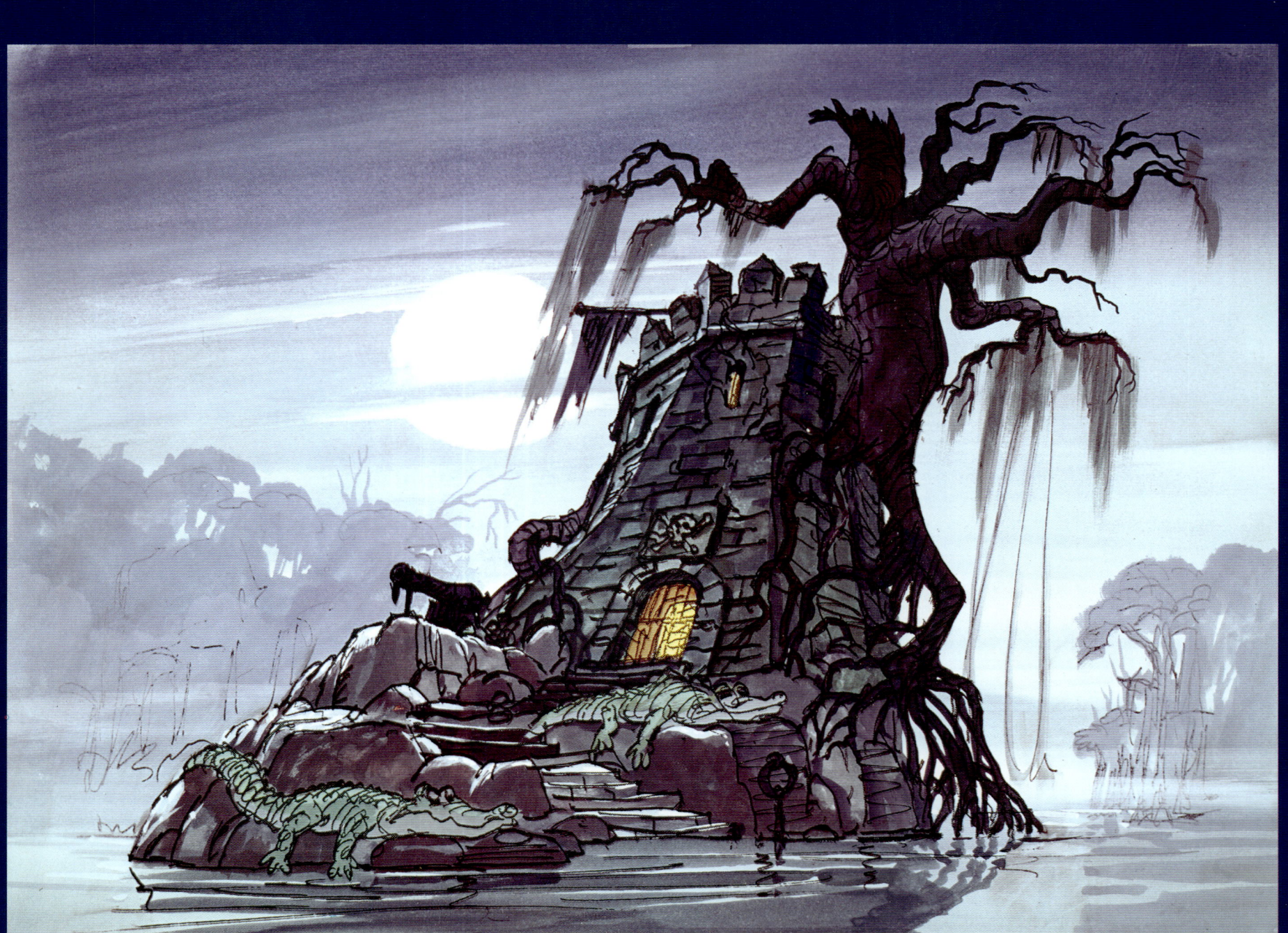

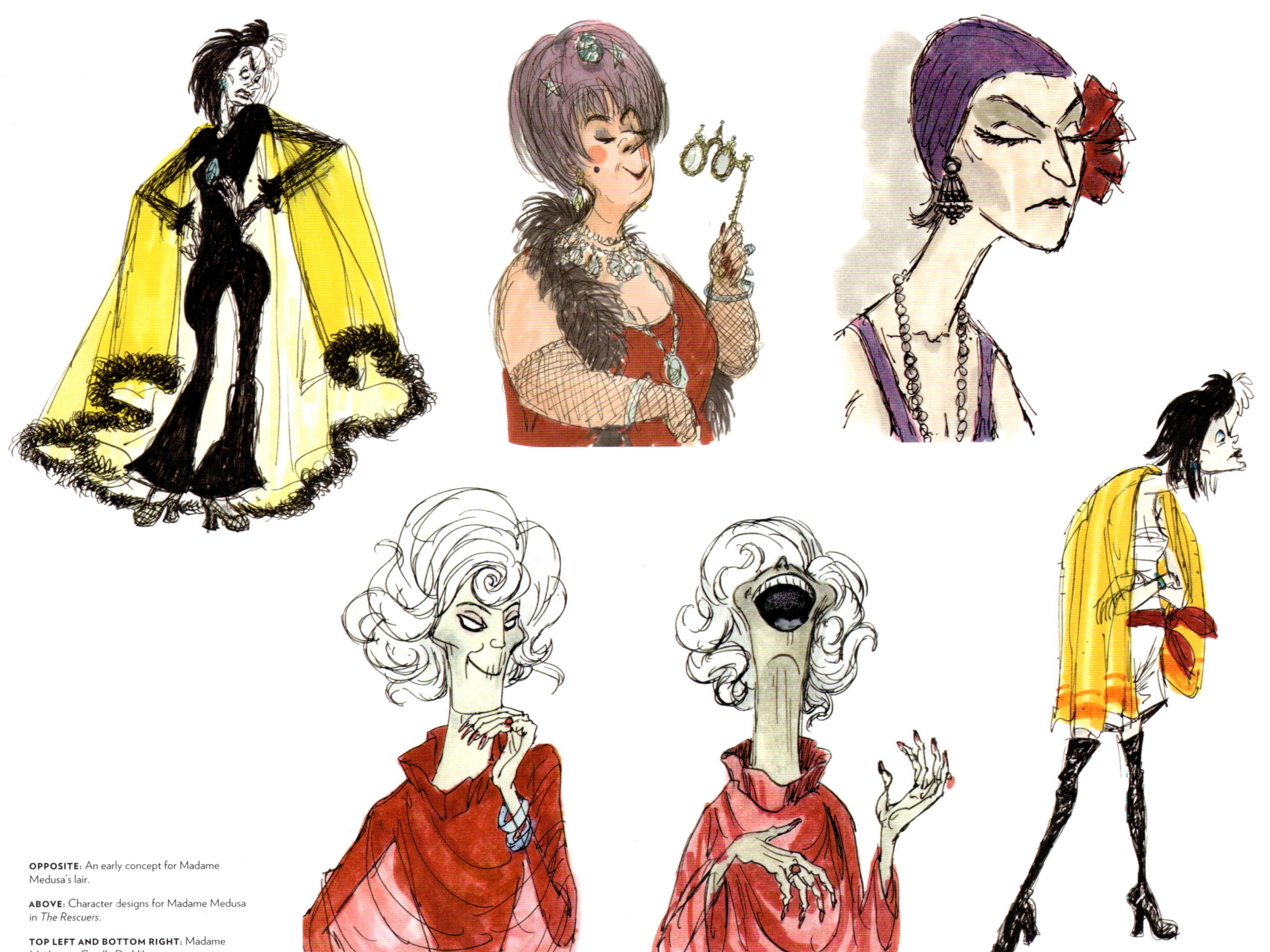

OPPOSITE: An early concept for Madame Medusa's lair.

ABOVE: Character designs for Madame Medusa in *The Rescuers*.

TOP LEFT AND BOTTOM RIGHT: Madame Medusa as Cruella De Vil.

KEN ANDERSON

LEFT: Character design for *Pete's Dragon*. Collection of the author.

RIGHT: Character designs for the abandoned TV project *Wizards*. Courtesy: Andreas Deja.

OPPOSITE: Character designs for Disney's *Adventures of the Gummi Bears*. Courtesy: Wendy Greer.

122   THEY DREW AS THEY PLEASED

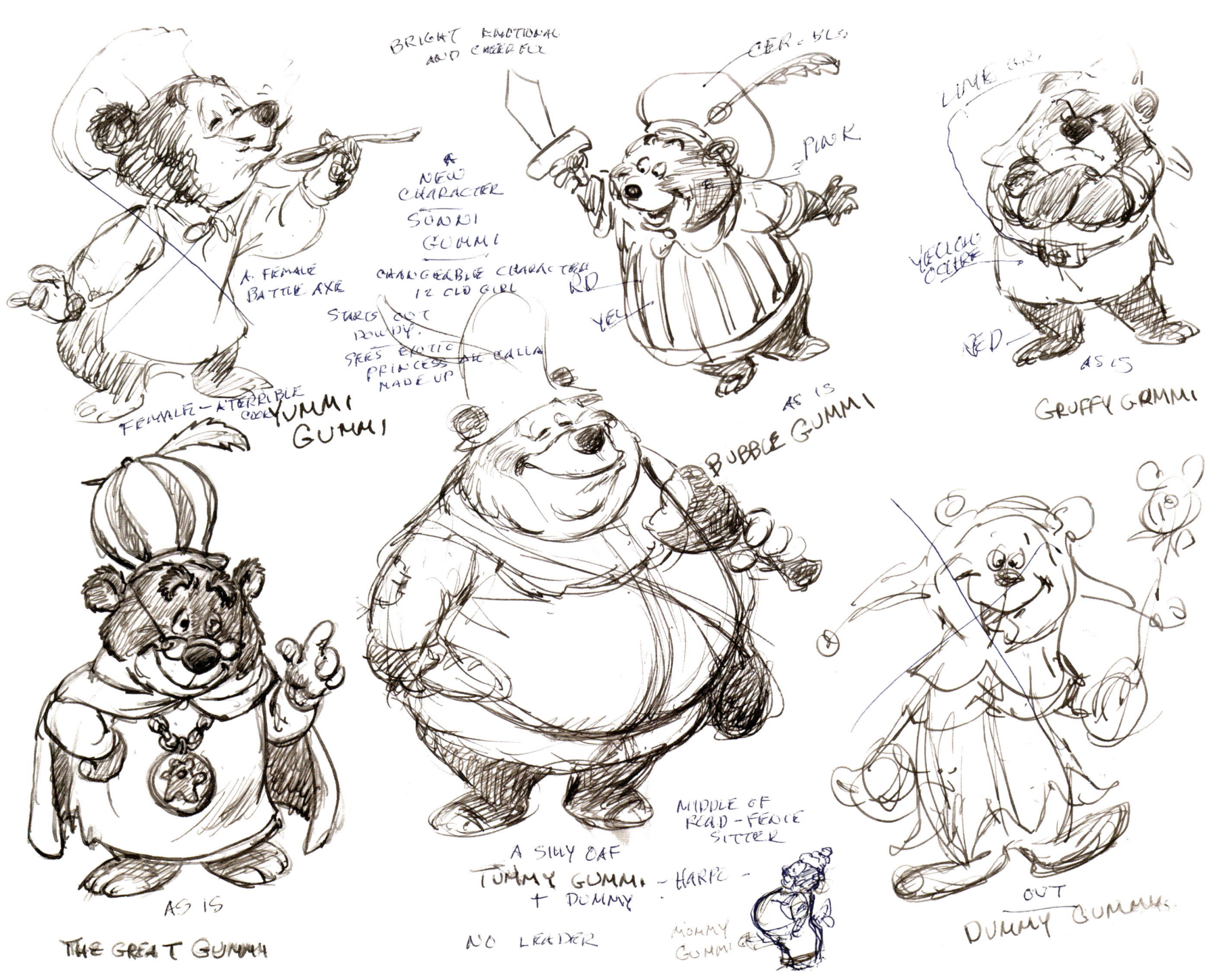

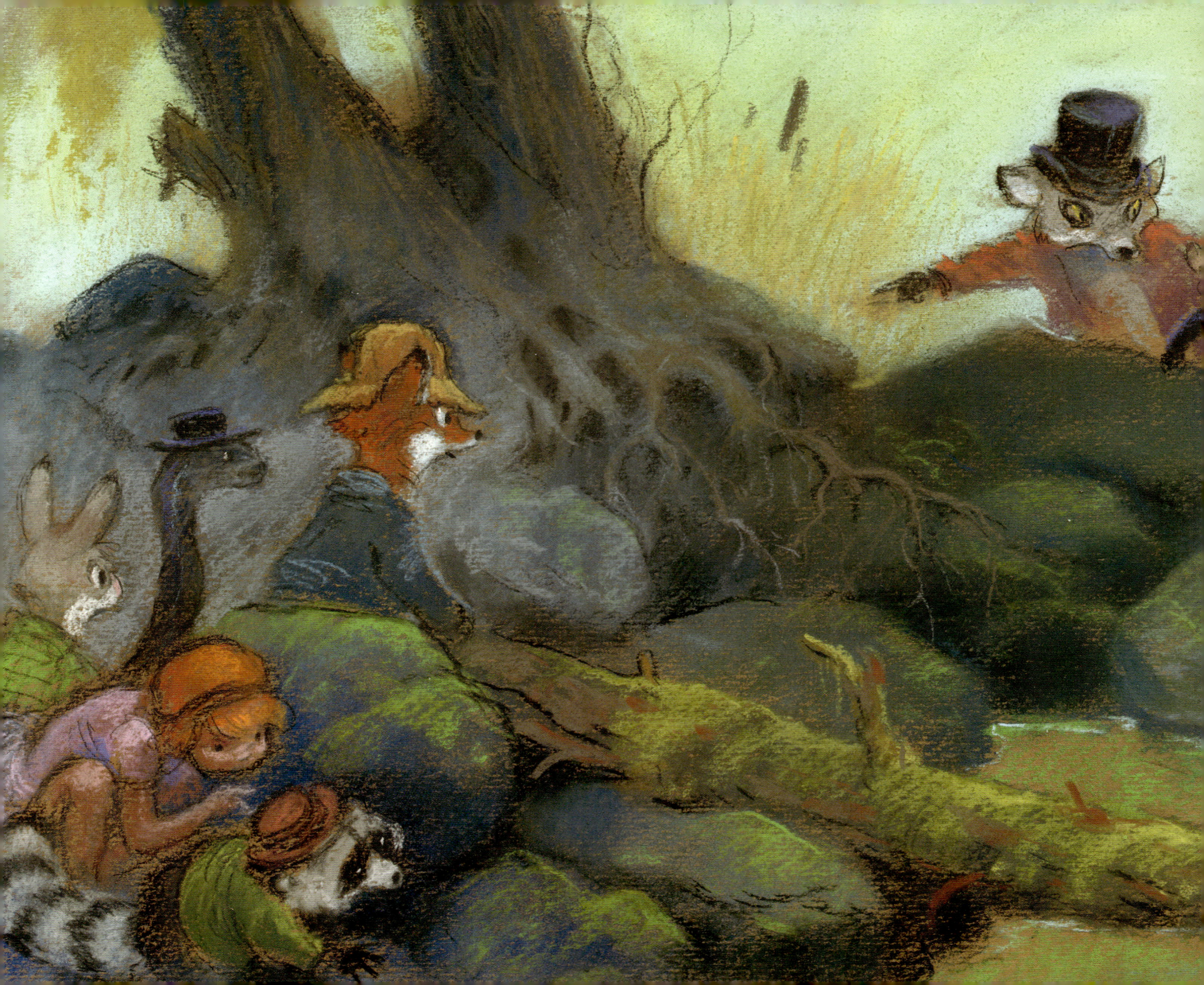

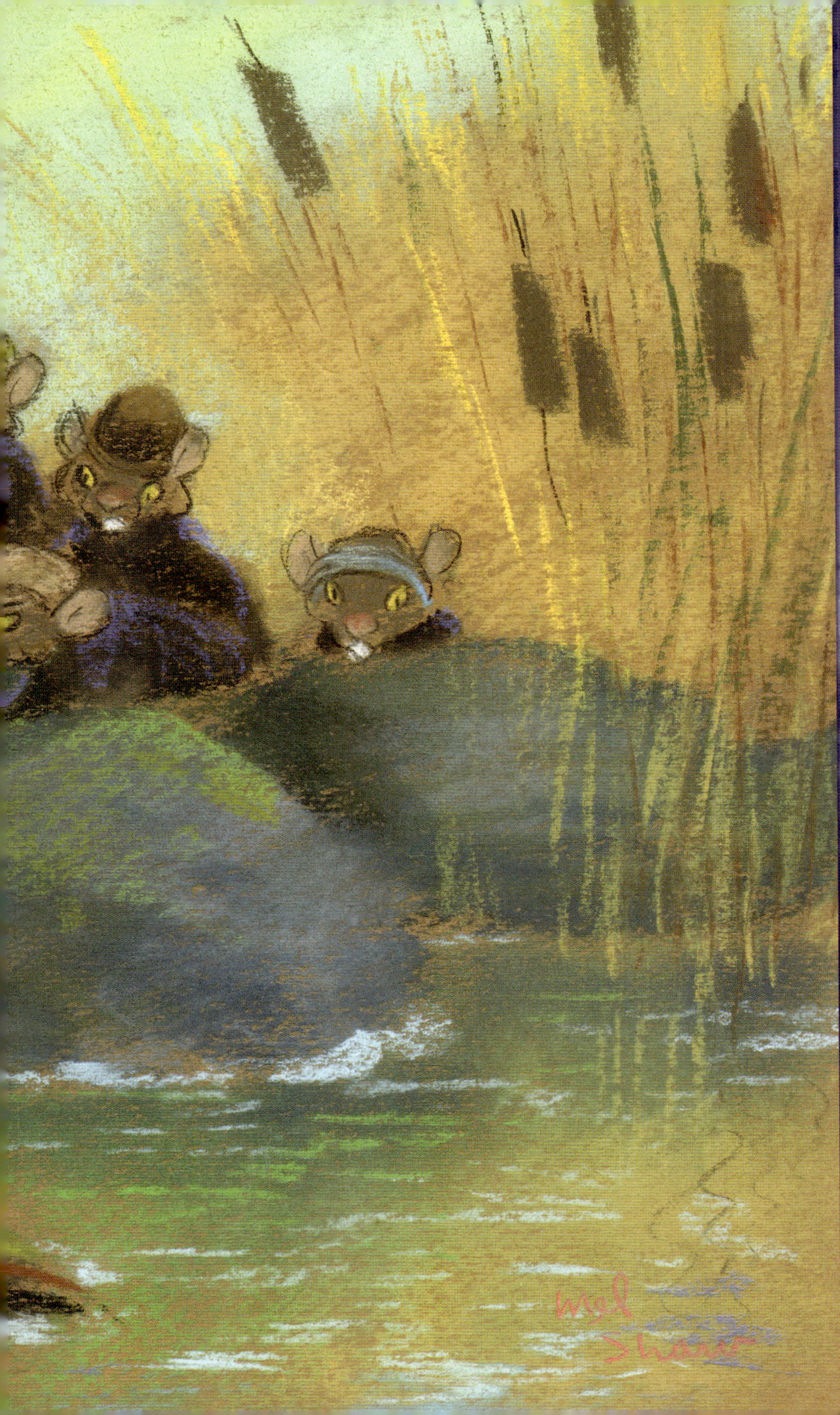

2
MEL SHAW

"[Mel Shaw] could do a pastel [drawing] in nothing flat ... He'd do two or three a day, and everybody admired his work."
—STORY ARTIST BURNY MATTINSON

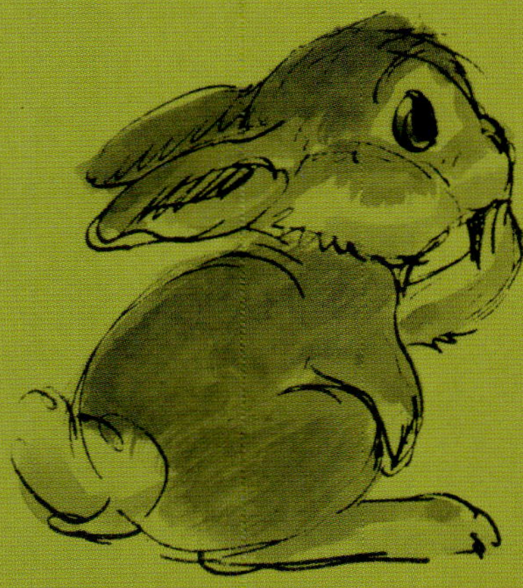

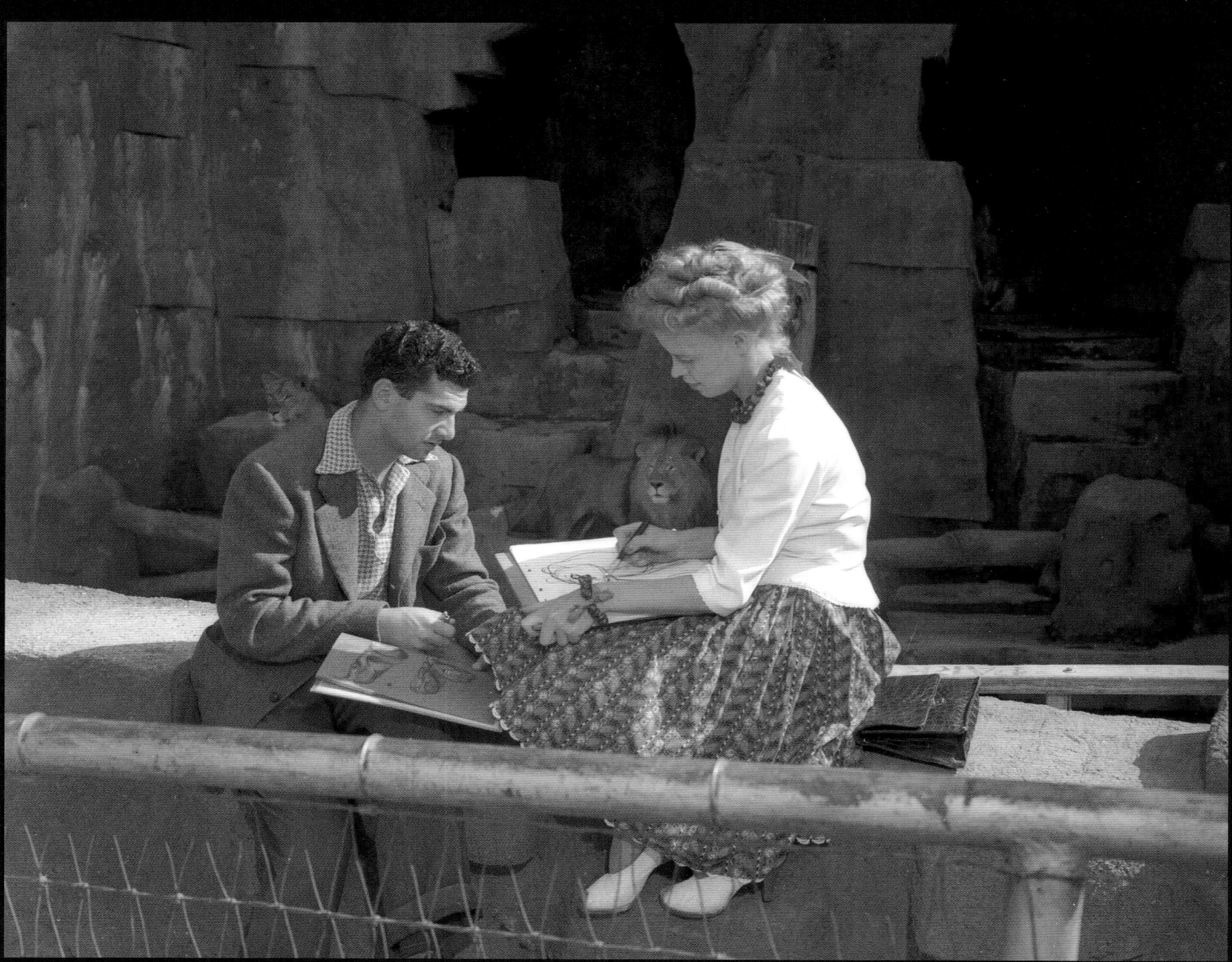

ONE DAY IN THE MID-1970S, effects animator Ted Kierscey was roaming the halls of the Animation building at the Disney studio when he stopped in his tracks. His attention was drawn to a set of drawings done by Mel Shaw. Without a doubt, they were stunning, totally captivating works that would later frame the visual style for the studio's current film, *The Rescuers*.

> I remember seeing a whole bunch of beautiful story sketches that had been drawn in pastel by Mel Shaw, and they were for *The Rescuers*. His storyboards inspired you to work harder on the film, because they weren't just flat sketches, they were colorful beautiful pastel sketches of ocean and characters. Really inspirational. And I remember [director] Woolie [Reitherman] putting the word out, "We want to make our movie look like Mel Shaw's sketches."[114]

Like Ken Anderson, Mel Shaw was an immensely versatile artist: he had once been an animator and was an accomplished sculptor. He drew in pastels, but also in watercolors; he knew how to build a story and how to sell it, and he had even been a successful businessman. Like Ken Anderson, Mel Shaw's Disney career had started in the 1930s. Unlike Ken Anderson, however, he hadn't spent his whole life at the studio. And yet, in the 1970s, along with Anderson, he became one of Disney's two most influential visual development artists.

Melvin Schwartzman was born in Brooklyn, New York, on December 19, 1914, the son of Lillian and Theodore Schwartzman, a successful lawyer and businessman. His childhood was one of ease and luxury, as Mel remembered in his autobiography, *Animator on Horseback*:

> Life in Brooklyn was wonderful for young families and children. At times my father would collect up many of our playmates from the neighborhood and have our chauffeur drive us to Coney Island for a day at Luna Park.[115]

It was not, however, a childhood totally free of trouble. Mel's brother Clarence passed away at a young age from liver cancer. Beyond this, his family faced problems from people holding fast to anti-Semitic views, which were rampant in the first half of the twentieth century. These troubles were so deep and at times so personal that Mel decided to shorten and Westernize his name to Shaw in the 1940s.

Mel was just ten years old when his undeniable artistic gifts were noticed by his school teachers.

> One of my teachers had submitted some work that I had done to the [Art Students League], which was an organization that sponsored young artists from the age of ten on up . . . They accepted my work and I became one of their scholarship students. What I had done at that time was mostly sculpting and modeling, and some of the little [animal] characters that I had modeled . . . were submitted . . . They thought that I had talent, so I was accepted to the Art Students League. Shortly after that I had done some work under the tutorship of their school and I'd won a national prize in modeling which was sponsored by Procter & Gamble, the soap company. I modeled out of a large cake of soap a Mexican and a pack donkey, and it won first prize. So they felt vindicated in choosing me as a future sculptor. After the scholarship I got from that, I did models, and one was exhibited in the Metropolitan Museum of Art, in the children's department there.[116]

His family's situation, however, was about to take a turn for the worse:

> October 24, 1929, was called "Black Thursday," and our lives were turned upside down as the stock market crash stopped the world in orbit. It took a stout heart and a brave soul to look ahead. My dad had lost everything . . . He decided to move to California to start life over.[117]

OPPOSITE: Mel Shaw and Retta Scott at the Griffith Park Zoo.

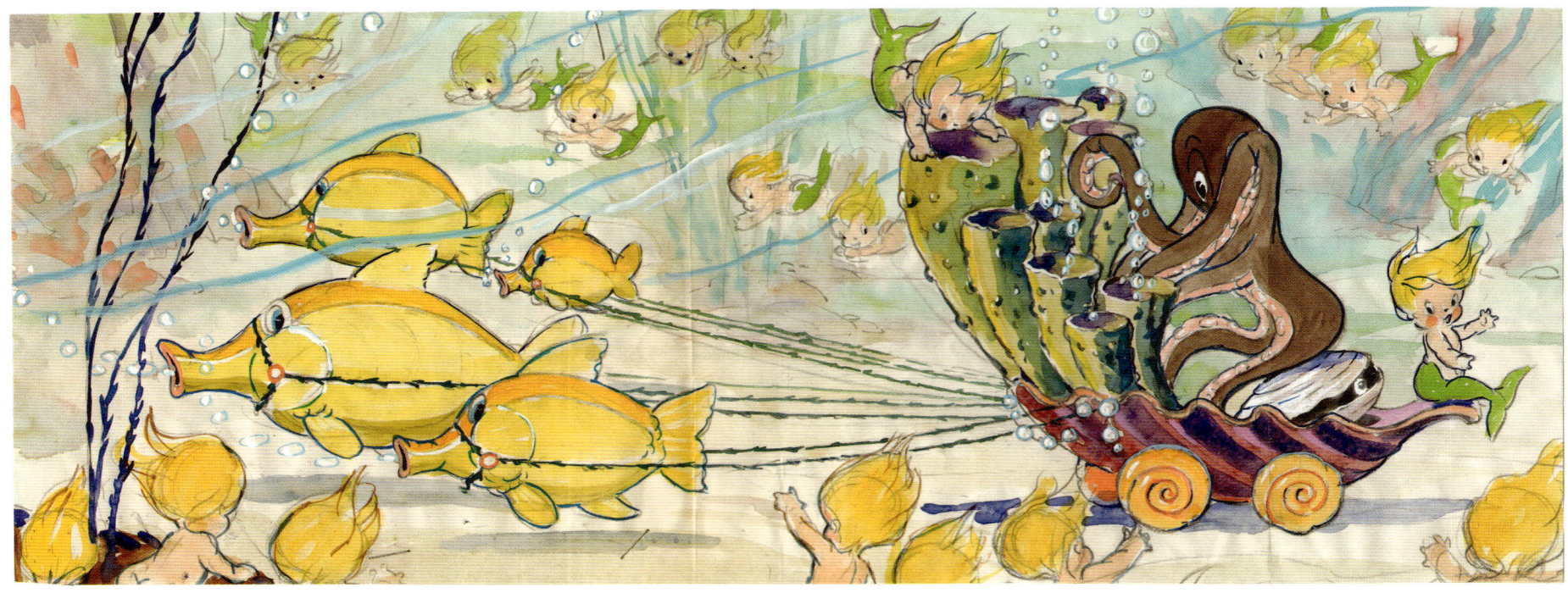

FROM COWBOY COUNTRY TO HARMAN-ISING

A few months after the move to the West Coast, Mel decided to go on an adventure which would mark him forever.

> When my family moved out to California, I thought it would be great to be a cowboy. I was just fifteen and a half. I was going to L.A. High [and] I met a boy there whose father owned a ranch in Utah. I didn't get along with my father at the time, so I just ran away from home and got a job on the ranch. The first winter that set in just scared me to death. They were sending me out to [repair] fence[s] in the snow and things like that.[118]

A short while after Mel's return to Los Angeles, a letter arrived, which helped launch his long and successful artistic career:

I can only imagine what my parents must have felt as they opened the letter with intrepid fingers. What had Melvin done now? To their surprise, the letter was good news from the Art Students League in New York City. They wrote to my parents of their concern about what was being done to continue the development of my art abilities while living on the West Coast. We were excited to hear that the Art Students League had contacted the Otis Art Institute in Los Angeles and they had recommended me to be accepted there as a student on scholarship! It would be a very small class with only three of us attending on Saturdays. I was happy to find that there were other students who had the same interests and talents and quickly became friends with Tyrus Wong, who worked with me, years later, on *Bambi*, and Dorothy Jenkins, who would become a renowned costume designer.[119]

Mel's parents were now convinced of their son's gifts and

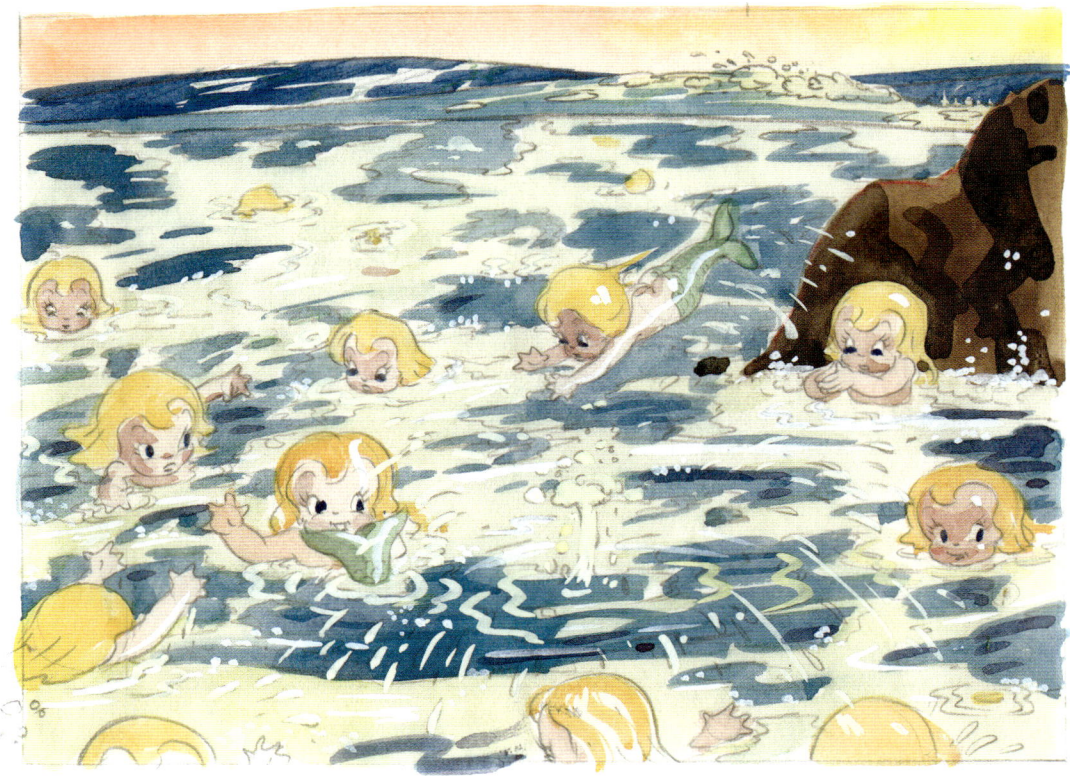

OPPOSITE AND ABOVE: Story sketches for *Merbabies* in the style of Mel Shaw.

decided to try and help him as best they could through their personal connections and with limited family resources:

> [My father] had a friend by the name of Leon Schlesinger that owned Pacific Title. He spoke to Leon and Leon said, "Send him over." My father told him that I was basically an artist, and [Schlesinger] said, "I think we can put him to work." So they put me to work sweeping the floor at Pacific Title. I learned about title-making and trick photography. In those days there were still titles [for silent films]; sound pictures were just coming in. [This was] about 1930, just after the crash. I saw the first rushes that came into the lab of Bosko . . . animated cartoons which Hugh [Harman] and Rudy [Ising] were just starting. They had their own lab at Pacific Title. I thought, "That looks like something I could do without any trouble."
>
> I met Sid Ising, who brought the rushes in. He was the cameraman at Harman-Ising. I asked him if he could talk to them and see if I could get a job. He said, "Just bring your drawings in." The only drawings I had were straight art work, and a few statues I'd made . . . Rudy said, "You saw the things on the screen; they are completely different from straight art drawing." So I went back and copied some Sunday newspaper comics and brought them in, and he hired me as an inbetweener, for ten dollars a week.[120]

At Harman-Ising Mel met many of the artists who would later become his colleagues at Disney. Two among them had a particularly important influence on him: Bob Stokes and Lee Blair. Mel recalled many years later:

> [At Harman-Ising, I animated] mostly for Hugh [Harman]. Rudy [Ising] had his prized animators that he liked working on his pictures, and Hugh liked me to work on his. I worked under Bob Stokes for a while, which helped me a lot, because Bob was a teacher of the human figure in art school, and while I worked for him I learned a lot—not animation so much as draftsmanship, drawing the human figure . . . [And] I got into watercolors because Lee Blair, who was the President of the California Watercolor Society, came to work at Harman-Ising. I liked some of his watercolors and I asked him if he would help me in learning to do watercolors. So we went out watercolor painting together quite a few times . . . I think I picked up some of his styling, although not near as bold and as beautiful as his stuff. I just do what comes naturally.[121]

Mel's horizons were expanding in several other fields: beyond animation, his responsibilities at Harman-Ising slowly expanded to include layout and story; and outside of the studio he took on a sport that helped change his career forever.

After I'd been at Harman-Ising about two or three years, Disney had organized a polo team. Les Clark and some of the key [Disney] animators started to play polo. That seemed to be the thing. So Harman-Ising organized a little polo team, and we went out and we started to play, and we played against them every once in a while, or just the local polo groups in the San Fernando Valley . . . I seemed to be a better horseman and player than they were, so I was the captain of the Harman-Ising team. Through that I was offered a couple of opportunities to play semi-professional for some of the big clubs around Los Angeles. And this leads on to how I met Walt Disney himself.[122]

In 1937 the Harman-Ising studio lost its distribution contract with MGM. This dealt a huge blow to the viability of the company, and on September 10, 1937, the studio had to shut its doors for three weeks.

During the time that I was out of work at the studio, I was playing polo semi-professionally for the Riviera Country Club. Walt had a membership there, and he was playing there, and he knew that I was one of the animators of Harman-Ising . . . He asked me what I was doing and I told him, "Nothing now." He asked me if I'd be interested in coming over and showing my work to the head of the studio there at the time. Which I did, and then Walt asked me if I was interested in animating or going into story and character development, and I said, "I think I would rather do [development] than

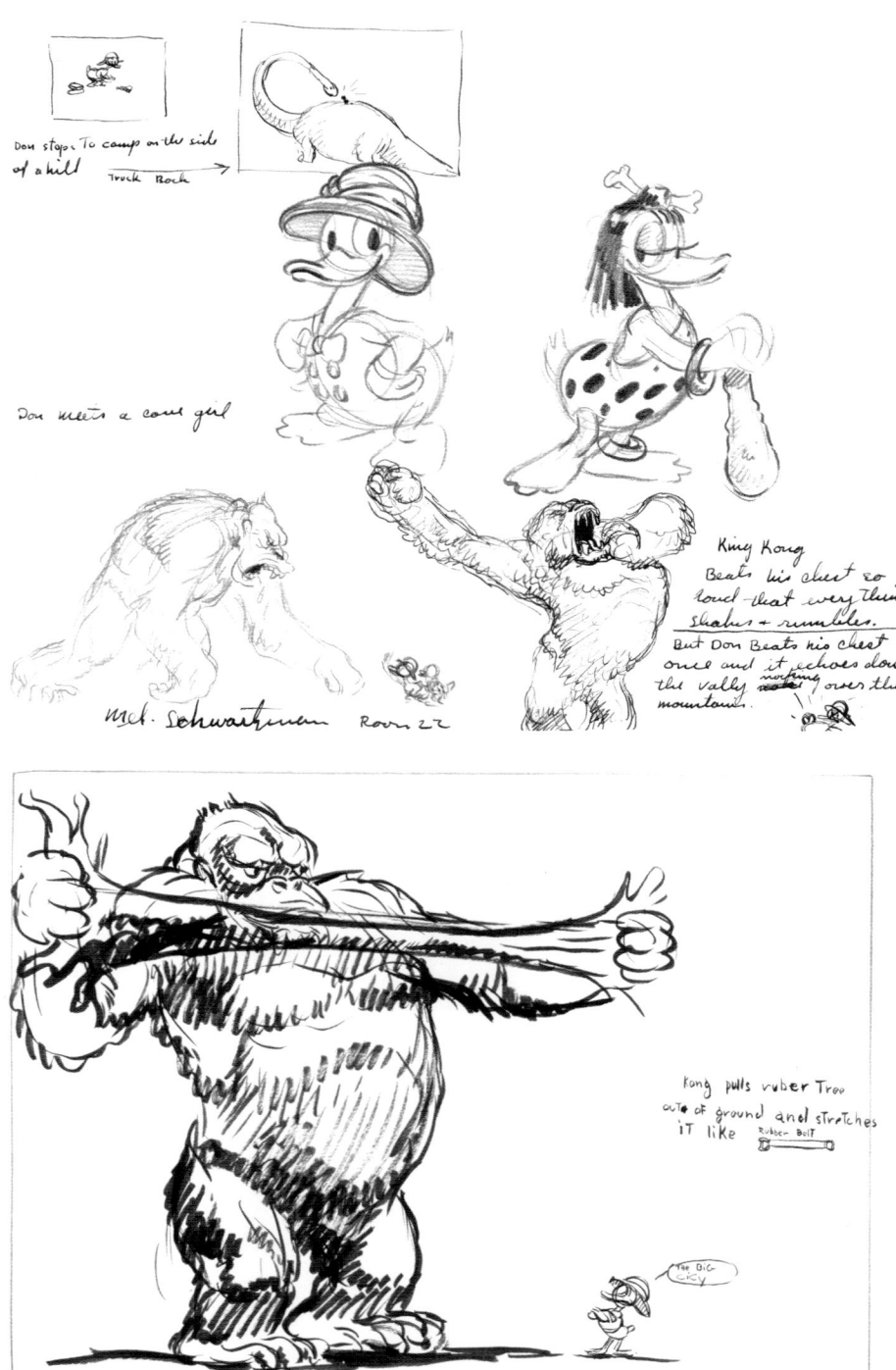

130 THEY DREW AS THEY PLEASED

do the other." The reason for that was that when Harman-Ising started to lose a lot of their animators, I got involved in helping them with layout and working on the stories. And I enjoyed that end of it a little more than I did the animation end itself.[123]

The Harman-Ising studio managed to reopen in October ... with the help of Disney! Walt was busy completing work on *Snow White and the Seven Dwarfs* and decided to subcontract the making of the Silly Symphony *Merbabies* to his former colleagues Hugh Harman and Rudy Ising. In a reciprocal arrangement, Harman-Ising loaned its painters and inkers to the Disney studio to help on *Snow White*. *Merbabies* moved to animation in October 1937. Mel Shaw tackled some of the layouts and animated at least one scene, which involved a crab and a lobster in a cage.[124] When animation on *Merbabies* was nearing completion, Mel was presented with an offer to come work for Disney. He joined Walt's studio on March 21, 1938.[125]

A few weeks later, Disney story artists Carl Barks and Chuck Couch started developing a short featuring Donald Duck, based on the adventures of the Baron Munchausen. The first paragraph of their outline read:

[Donald's nephews] are reading a book on prehistoric adventuring. Don[ald] tells them such stories are "kid stuff." He begins to tell them: "One time I was in Africa . . ." We cross-dissolve to Don[ald] in Africa discovering a strange, goofy valley in the crater of an extinct volcano.[126]

Inspired by the theme and eager to impress, Mel submitted two gag drawings to the Story Department, which featured Donald's encounter with King Kong.

OPPOSITE: Gag drawings for the abandoned short *Donald Munchausen*.

FROM FAUNS TO FAWN

Mel's first official assignment, however, was a musical one. In February 1938, Walt Disney started toying with the idea of producing a "concert feature" with Paul Dukas's *The Sorcerer's Apprentice* at its core.[127] Walt and his artists were analyzing many possible pieces of music that could be included in the feature. Among them: "Babes in Toyland," "Don Quixote," "Midsummer Night's Dream," "Pinafore," "Moto Perpetuo," "Brementown Musicians" (for which Stravinsky was offering to write the score!), "Bolero," "March of the Little Lead Soldiers," "Grand Canyon Suite," "Nibelungen Ring," "Idilio," and "Dance Macabre." And then there was story number 1034, "Cydalise Suite," which was detailed as including "Dance of the Little Fauns," "Afternoon of the Fauns," and "Flight of the Bumblebee." On April 12, 1938, the studio secured a license for the use of "Flight of the Bumblebee" by Rimsky-Korsakov, and around the same time it tried to acquire the authorization to use Debussy's "Afternoon of a Faun." As to "Dance of the Little Fauns," it was probably a slightly mistaken title for "March of the Little Fauns," a jaunty little piece from *Cydalise et le Chèvre-Pied* by Gabriel Pierné.[128] By the time Mel joined the team, most of the ideas for *The Concert Feature* were little more than figments of the artists' imagination. "Cydalise Suite," however, was put under active development.

On his first day at the studio, Mel Shaw was asked to handle the project, along with director Perce Pearce, and composer Leigh Harline.[129]

As I walked through the main entrance, [director] Dave Hand's secretary ushered me into his modest office and Dave proceeded to put me at ease by informing me that he had heard of the work I had done. After a short discussion, he assigned me to a musical short using the score from

"The Flight of the Bumblebee" and informed me that my workroom would be an apartment-sized kitchen, inside the apartment house behind the main Hyperion studio.

Enthusiastically, I went right to work. The droning cadence of "The Flight of the Bumblebee" was usually performed as a violin instrumental and suggested the rapid fluttering of a bee moving from flower to flower. I developed a sleepy mythical faun whose nap was repeatedly interrupted by an intrusive bee collecting pollen from the faun's bed of wildflowers. Most storyboards at this time were done in black and white but I decided to do my "Flight of the Bumblebee" presentation storyboard with pencil and watercolor. I felt that this would bring out the brilliant colors of the flowers and trees and help everyone visualize my idea for the setting of the story. A few weeks later Dave Hand and Walt came to see my work and when Walt paused in front of my colorful storyboards for a moment, he suddenly let out a big "WOW!" From his reaction I thought that this must have been the first color storyboard ever presented to Walt.[130]

By early July, Mel was ready to show Walt even more of his work. To do so, he was about to use an exciting new tool for the very first time: the Leica reel.

In a memo dated June 20, 1938, titled "New Method of Presenting Story Sketches," [Disney's chief engineer Bill] Garity had explained to all the artists:

As you are probably aware, there has been under consideration for some time a new method of displaying story sketches in story conferences by which the individual sketches are photographed on standard 35 mm film, a single frame for each sketch, and this film is made into a loop and during the story meeting, the film is projected by means of a stereopticon Leica projector on the screen.[131]

Two weeks later, on July 5, Garity noted in his daily report:

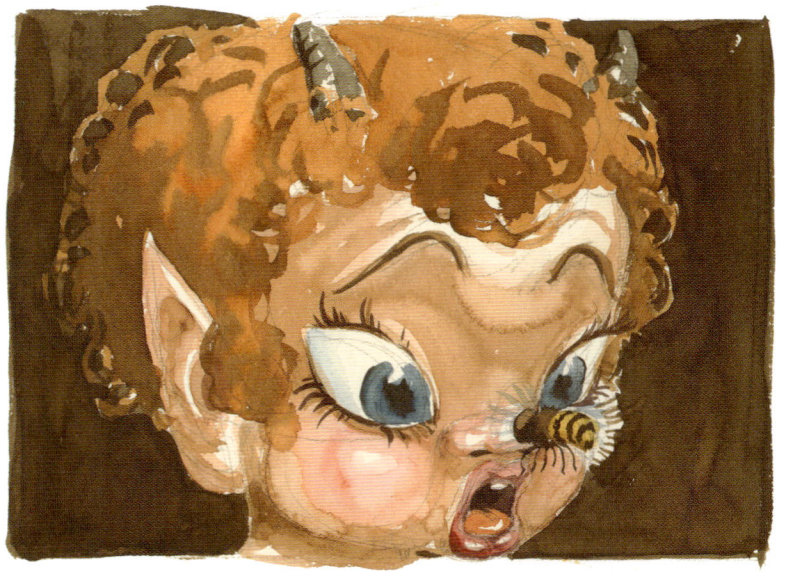

Checked with Mel Schwartzman the Leica sync loop on "The Afternoon of the Faun." It seemed to work very nicely.

And on July 7, he added:

Went up to sweatbox 4 and demonstrated Schwartzman's reel to Walt and the story conference he had in session at the time.[132]

"Cydalise Suite," however, was one of the toughest sequences from *Fantasia* to nail down and on January 5, 1939, Walt Disney opted to keep its mythological theme but to drop the Cydalise music. He decided to replace it with Beethoven's Pastoral Symphony.[133] By that date, Mel had already moved on to another memorable endeavor. Toward mid-September 1938, Walt had startled him with an unexpected proposal.[134]

"You like to draw animals, Mel?" Walt asked. "How about starting on an adaptation for this?" he inquired as he handed me the *Bambi* book with a script by Sidney Franklin. Franklin had intended to make the story in live action, similar to the picture *Sequoia* which he had directed. This did not suit the approach that animation offered. Walt wisely saw that he

ABOVE: Story sketch for the abandoned "Flight of the Bumblebee."

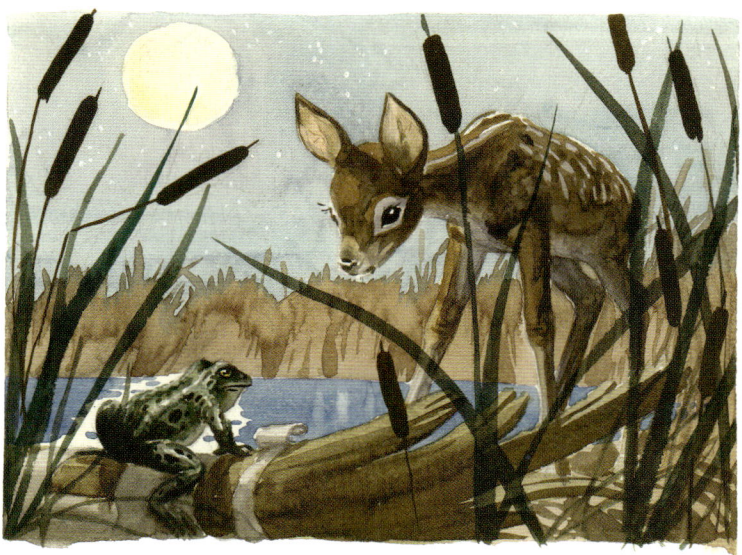
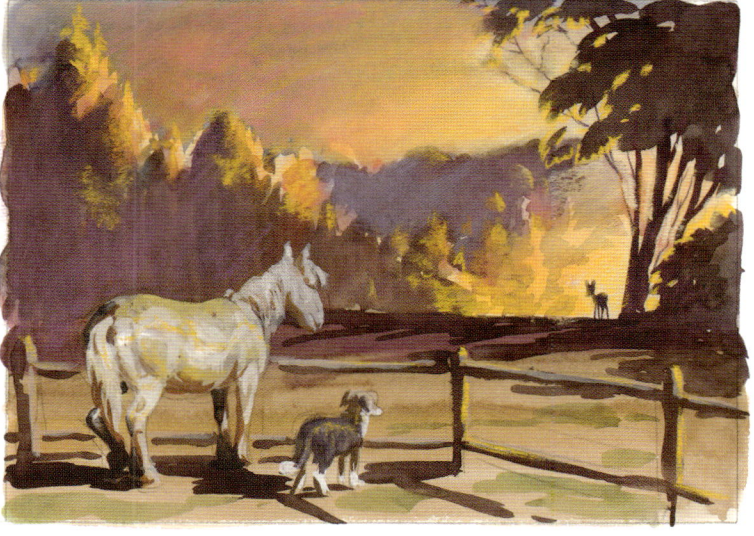

could have us rework the approach to *Bambi* by leaving the live-action ideas and script behind.

As the first [artist] on the story, I had assumed I would be the producer or supervising director. What a break for a twenty year old! But that was my dream and not Walt's intention as I discovered that Walt had assigned Dave Hand and Perce Pearce to be the producer and the director . . . Regardless of the disappointment I might have felt when I found that I was still a story director and not a producer, this would prove to be a great break for me as the twists and turns of the studio kept us on our toes. I still looked forward to the creative challenges facing me. *Bambi* was a wonderful project![135]

Mel was delighted by the challenge, but soon found that his work environment was changing yet again.

I was immediately assigned a new gag man, Roy Williams, and another storyboard sketch artist, Carl Fallberg, to assist in my story development unit. My expanding *Bambi* unit began storyboarding in the old Hyperion studio but as we and all other departments were growing, many units had to continue their work spread out over several sites. The irony was sending my unit to Seward Street and renting the old Harman-Ising Studio where I had been just a few months before. When Hugh and Rudy lost their contract with MGM, their lease ran out on this building so Disney rented it [in October 1938] for our use until the new Disney studio in Burbank was available. Now, I was working back in my old haunts.[136]

As he started storyboarding the movie and designing characters, Mel realized that inspiration could come from the most unexpected sources.

While I was exploring the many animals to be presented in *Bambi*, I attended a lecture [on March 28, 1939] by a very fine short story writer, Alexander Woollcott. In his lecture he described how he had carefully and scientifically studied parrots in preparation for writing about them. As I sat there intently listening to his discourse, I found that he was becoming the inspiration behind my model for "Friend Owl." Woollcott looked very owlish as he stood on the sound stage before us. He gripped the podium with his hands as though they were talons on a limb and spoke to us while turning his head first to the left, and then to the right. As he carefully lectured, I noticed how his large glasses would catch the light. For all the world, he looked like my idea of "Friend Owl."[137]

ABOVE LEFT: Concept sketch for *Bambi*.

ABOVE RIGHT: Concept sketch for the abandoned project based on *Bambi's Children*.

One of the frustrations of the *Bambi* unit on Seward Street was their lack of access to Walt, which often led to misunderstandings, some of which could be quite farcical.

We had more or less a free hand for a long time, and our first meeting with Walt . . . was quite a few months after we started, six months or so, and we had gotten a lot of the storyboards up. I always remember a meeting with Walt where he said, "We want to get into all the creatures. How when Bambi is learning to walk, he might step on a place and frighten a frog, or maybe he'd step on an anthill, and maybe it would cause confusion in the anthill. Look down below under the ground and here are the ants scurrying, and the queen of the ants, and it causes a flood," and all that type of thing. So we started to develop this thing and we worked on it for a bit, two, three months. We were so far off the storyline of Bambi growing up, and Walt came back, and this was typical of Walt: he gets these hot ideas, and they sound good, and you start to develop them . . . After all he's the boss . . . We spent all this time developing the characters of the ants, and the queen of the ants, and all of this, going through all of these tunnels and trying to close up the dam that's breaking, and Walt looks at this and he says, "Gee, do you think we're getting off the storyline?"[138]

Toward the second half of 1940, with his work complete on *Bambi*, Mel was assigned to tackle a variety of projects: He drew a few sketches for a planned adaptation of *Don Quixote*, created some storyboards for *Dumbo*, and even illustrated a *Bambi* storybook using watercolors and pastels.

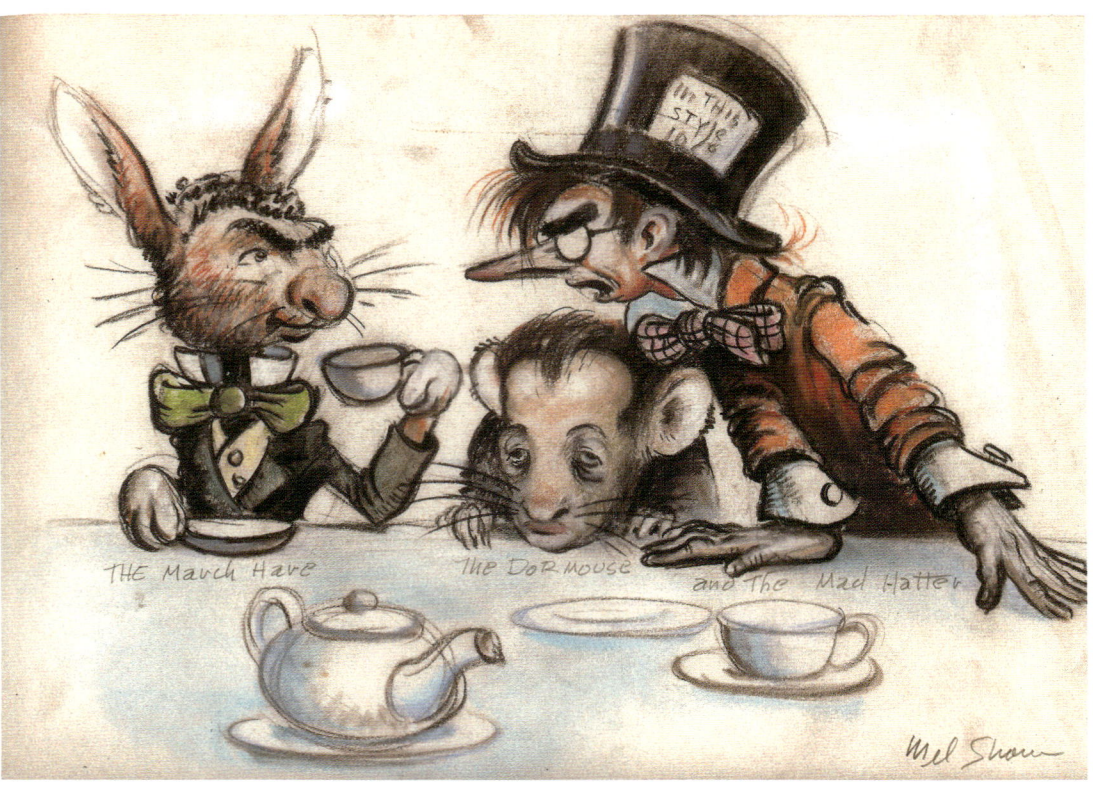

FROM *WIND IN THE WILLOWS* TO *THE LITTLE PRINCE*

Convinced that his next big project would be *Alice in Wonderland*, Mel drew himself and his colleagues Marc Davis and Carl Fallberg as characters out of the Lewis Carroll novel. But Walt had other plans for him. Mel was going to handle Kenneth Grahame's *The Wind in the Willows*.[139]

Wind in the Willows was a wonderfully whimsical subject, and I especially enjoyed the eccentric "Mr. Toad" portion of the book. I worked very closely with Larry Morey, who was a fine story artist as well as a lyricist for many Disney soundtracks. As we began to develop these creatures from the English countryside, we found that caricaturing our subjects with a British demeanor was interesting animation. The flamboyant

ABOVE: Mel Shaw's caricatures of himself (left) and of Disney artists Marc Davis (center) and Carl Fallberg as characters of *Alice in Wonderland*. Courtesy: Rick Shaw and Melissa Couch-Deranleau.

OPPOSITE: Concept sketch for *Wind in the Willows* (which became one of the sequences of *The Adventures of Ichabod and Mr. Toad*). Courtesy: Rick Shaw and Melissa Couch-Deranleau.

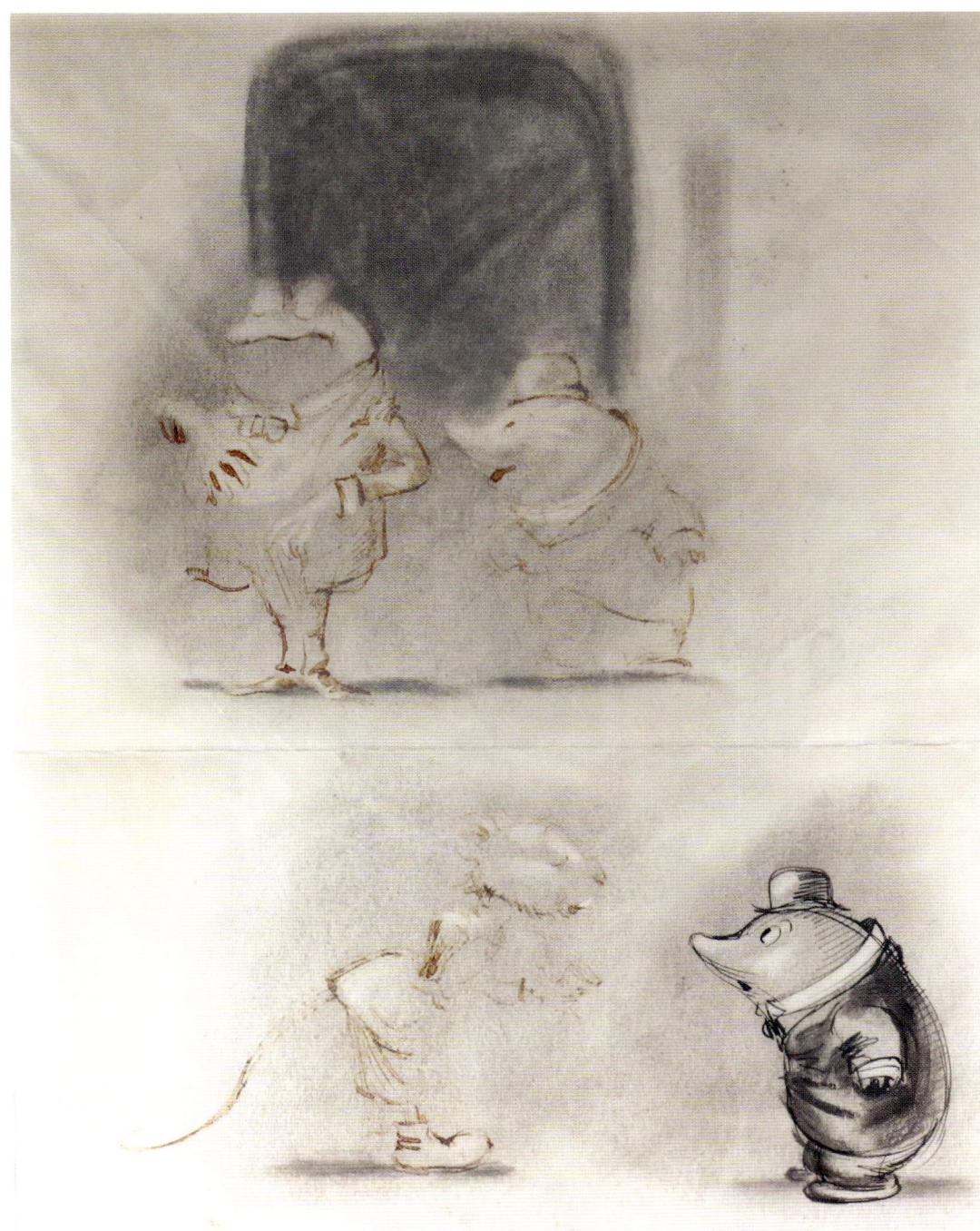

"Mr. Toad" had his close comrades, "Ratty," "Moley," and the conservative "McBadger," (sic) all in a dither during most of the story. I worked on the storyline for about eight months before it was ready to be turned over to the animators.[140]

When the Disney studio strike started in May 1941, Mel was still working on *Wind in the Willows*, but Walt also asked him and story artist Moe Gollub to start sketching a few ideas for a sequel to *Bambi*, titled "Forest Friends," featuring Faline having twins and based on Felix Salten's book, *Bambi's Children*.[141] The project was eventually shelved.[142]

In November 1940, while on his way to the premiere of *Fantasia* in New York, Walt decided to stop in Atlanta to visit the house of Joel Chandler Harris, author of the *Uncle Remus* stories that the studio was thinking of adapting to the screen.[143] A little less than a year later, toward the end of the strike, Mel and story artist George Stallings were assigned to explore the project visually.

While I was working on *Uncle Remus* I started doing my sketches in a style similar to [illustrator A. B.] Frost, if you remember his illustrations of [the] *Uncle Remus* [books]. And George Stallings was working on the story with me. We got the idea that you could do a comic strip in that style, with the *Uncle Remus* tales. Each one could be a separate tale. So, being that the studio was closed down [from August 15 to September 15, as a result of the strike], I went to [Walt's brother] Roy and I said, "Could I have the rights to this thing? You're not going to do anything with it right now." And Roy said, "Yeah, go ahead and do a comic strip on *Uncle Remus* if you want."[144]

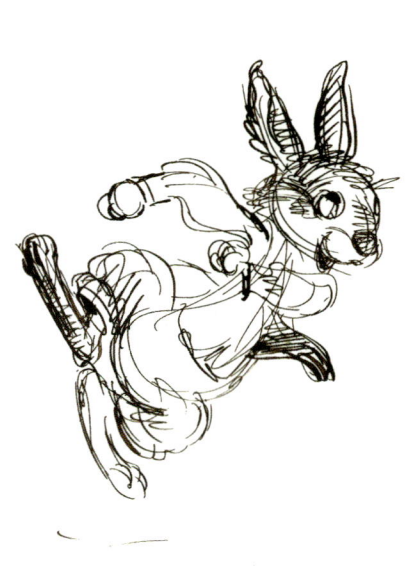
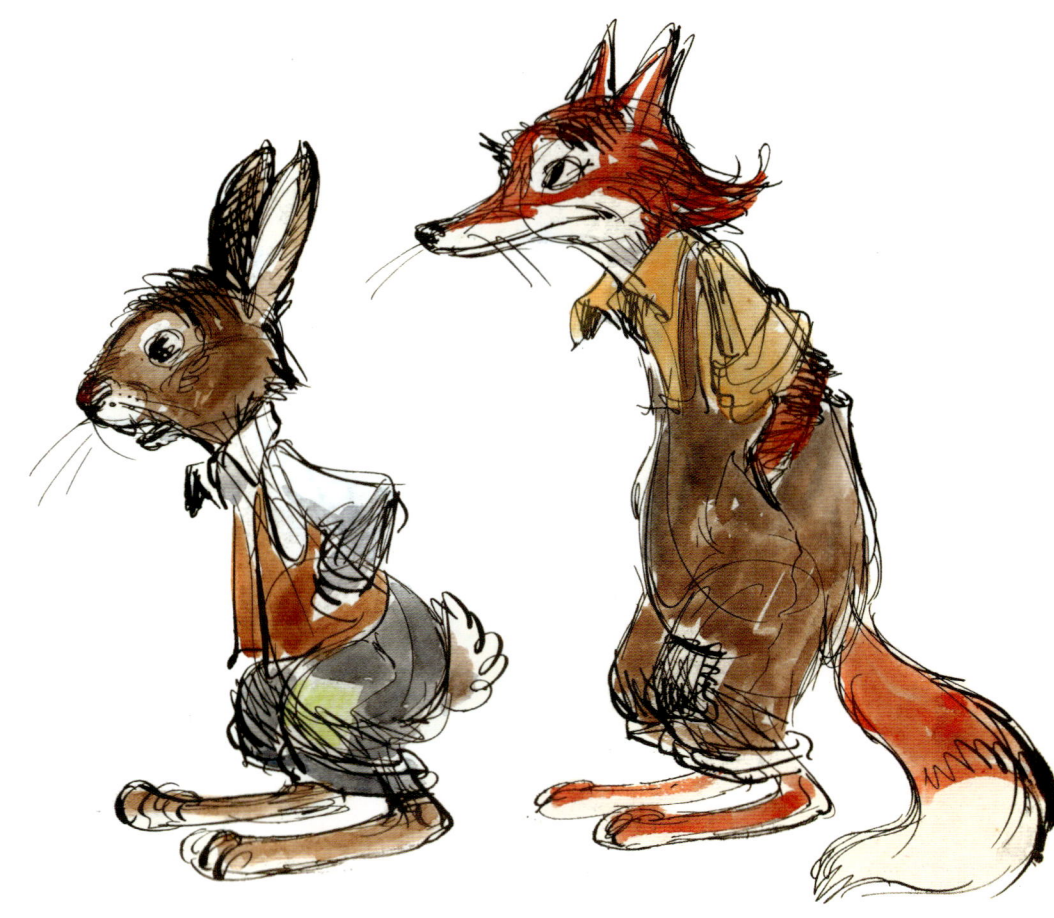

Unfortunately, after the studio reopened, Mel realized that Roy and he were not on the same page when it came to the financial conditions linked to the *Uncle Remus* comic strip project, and toward the end of 1941 he decided to leave the Disney studio.

Mel's first move after Disney involved his former colleague Hugh Harman. Mel and Hugh became partners in a new venture, Hugh Harman Productions.

Hugh didn't have any experience in doing features, so he asked me if I would be interested in being his partner, and he was going to do *King Arthur*. So I agreed to that, and we started on the *King Arthur* thing, and I did some models. We decided to develop that, and we were doing also war work. We were doing training films for the Army on booby traps and mines and artillery and everything else, which helped us . . . I found the book *The Little Prince*, which I was interested in, and we bought the rights for five hundred bucks to do [it] as an animation/live-action picture. Orson Welles was interested in the same thing. Orson approached us, and asked if he could work on it with us. He would do the live action, and he would be in the picture, playing the lead role as the aviator who's shot down in the desert. I started to work with Orson on that, and doing the training films and working on *King Arthur*.[145]

With Hugh Harman focused on the war productions, Orson Welles's attention moving to other creative ventures, and Mel Shaw being drafted in 1943, the *Little Prince* project was eventually shelved.

ABOVE: Character designs for *Song of the South*. Courtesy: Rick Shaw and Melissa Couch-Deranleau.

THE ALLEN-SHAW ADVENTURE

When he came back from India and China where he was sent as a war photographer, Mel soon launched a new creative venture, this time with artist Bob Allen.

> It's called Allen-Shaw [Associates]. We designed products. And [Disney's merchandizing representative] Kay Kamen made us the only outside designer of Disney products other than the people designing [them] in the studio: toys, ceramics. Evan K. Shaw was the company that hired Bob and myself... We did the whole early line of the little miniatures. We did dinnerware... We did all their products... Evan was a polo player, and that's how I met him.[146]

The Allen-Shaw partnership would last for twenty-five years. And from 1945 to 1970, Bob and Mel had the occasion of working on a few other projects for Disney, in addition to merchandising designs.

> When television started to come in [Walt Disney] contacted me through [executive] Harry Tytle... Harry Tytle was my old polo buddy... I never saw Walt personally on that. Walt told Harry to see if I'd be interested in doing some stuff on the outside. Because at that time he realized that he was going to have to use outside talent to do all of the television stuff. [For *Antarctica:*] *Operation Deepfreeze* [a program released on TV on June 5, 1957, as part of the *Disneyland* TV show, we] did the twelve-foot diorama. I had a big staff of guys at that time in my studio. We were doing architecture and everything else. And we built this out of fiberglass. We built the whole polar cap with all the little ships that explore all over the places. That thing is [on exhibit at] the Maritime Naval Museum in Quantico, Virginia, now. It's twelve-feet across...

> [In July, 1958, Bob Allen and] I wrote a script [for another Disney TV program] and developed it. [It] was called *The Look of Things*, and it was about how design has changed through the years... how people would change their clothing, how people changed their ideas of what housing should look like, and so forth. And it was all done tongue-in-cheek.[147]

The Look of Things was eventually shelved.

In 1970, Bob Allen decided to retire and the company became Shaw Associates. What Mel didn't know at the time, however, was that 1970 would also become a year of even greater professional changes, a year that would bring him back to the Disney studio for the second time.

> During the 1970 holiday season a friend who was also in the design field invited [my wife] Louise and myself to his Beverly Hills home for a party. Years earlier his wife had attended USC and had been a close acquaintance of [Walt Disney's daughter] Diane Disney, so she had also invited Diane and her husband, Ron Miller, for the evening festivities. Ron learned that I would be coming to the party, so when I arrived he sought me out because some of my friends at the studio had recommended me to him. As we talked, it became clear to me that he was anxious to revitalize the animation department. As he put it, "Animation is what made the studio in the first place and it should be rebuilt!" He then asked me if I would be interested in coming back to help out. I reminded Ron that I had my own studio to run but that I would be glad to return to the studio on a part-time basis. This was an intriguing opportunity to return to a medium I thoroughly enjoyed... Although I was trying to keep up my design studio, I found that I was gradually spending more and more time at the Disney studio. I realized that my interest in the design business was overshadowed by the sense of exhilaration I felt as I worked on the films again.[148]

BACK AT DISNEY

When Mel visited Disney's animation studio in the early-to-mid 1970s, quite a few interesting projects were under consideration.

[The studio] had bought the rights for *The Chronicles of Prydain*, and they had the Mannix book on *The Fox and the Hound* . . . Ron said, "Would you be interested in working on any of these things? Why don't you talk to Woolie?" So I went over and talked to Woolie. And he said, "You know what I need? I need an opening for *The Rescuers*. We're running out of money. We spent a lot of money on it." So I went over and I looked at the thing. He played the music for the thing. And I said, "Why don't you give me the tape?" (The music) "I'll take it back to my studio and see what I can do." So I took the tape and I did a whole bunch of pastels to illustrate that song, going in. I invited Woolie up to the studio with [his wife] . . . and I showed them the thing with the music. He was so impressed with the thing that he said, "You know, if I could just get that feeling on the screen . . ." I said, "Why, you can do anything you want." And he said, "Maybe I'll use it just like it is." So I went back to the studio and I worked with Burny Mattinson . . . on the thing. We put it together so that you could just dissolve and move in on the pastels . . .

The next one I did was *The Prydain Chronicles* . . . I read the books. There were [five] books, and I met the author [Lloyd Alexander]. He was out here at the time, and that impressed me, and he impressed me, so I started on that one [*The Black Cauldron*] . . . And on that one I spent a lot more time. They gave me a great big room up there, so I could bring in the drawings and put up the storyboards.[149]

In the 1930s, Mel had been the first Disney artist to use a Leica reel to pitch his ideas. In the 1970s, he decided to give a modern twist to this old technique. After a visit to the studio in 1978, journalist John Culhane reported with wonder on this powerful new way of presenting story sketches:

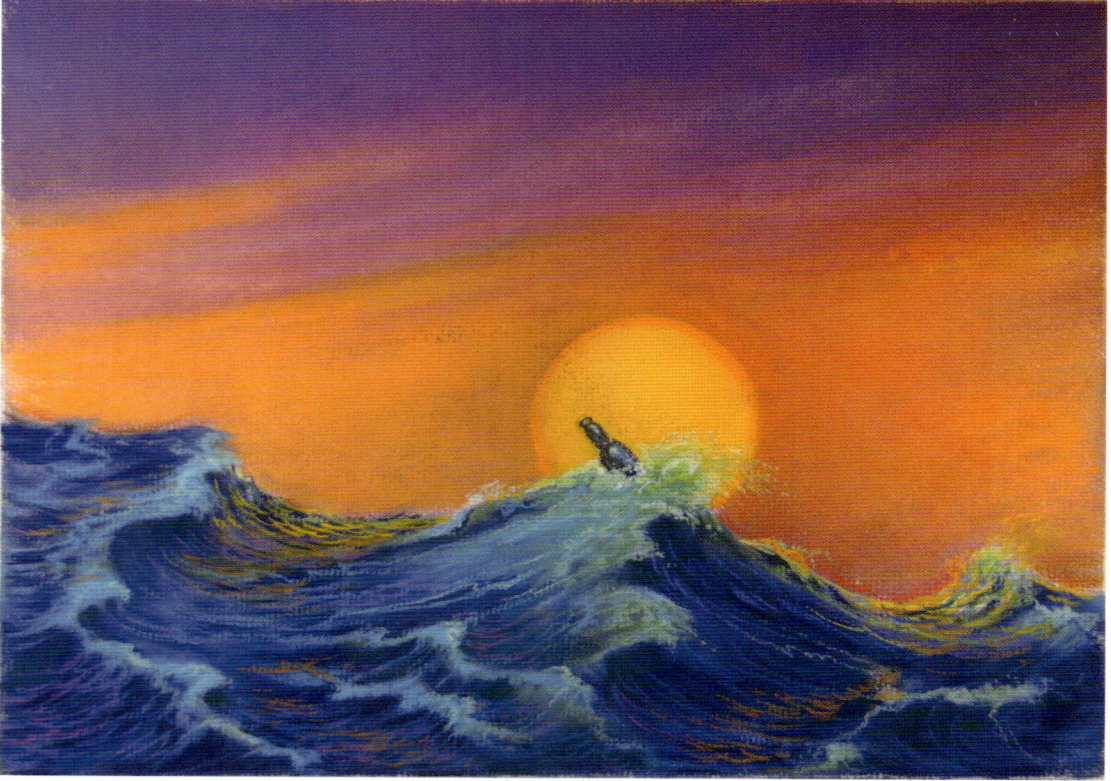

[Ron] Miller sent me to a big room in the animation building whose walls an artist named Mel Shaw had covered with dramatically colored story sketches for *The Black Cauldron* . . . I sat in a comfortable chair and Shaw switched on ominous music from Carl Orff's "Carmina Burana." The soundtrack triggered a slide projector, throwing slides of Shaw's color sketches onto a screen sequence at precisely the right moments in the music. Over the music, Shaw told me the story as he saw it.[150]

Mel's presentation of *The Black Cauldron* boards impressed Ron Miller. But the Disney veterans, director Woolie Reitherman and animators Frank Thomas, Ollie Johnston, and Milt Kahl among them, wondered if the new artists that the studio was in the process of training to replace them would be up to the task. Mel recalled:

ABOVE: Concept sketch for the opening titles of *The Rescuers*. Courtesy: Burny Mattinson.

OPPOSITE TOP: Concept sketch for *The Fox and the Hound*. Courtesy: Bruce Reitherman.

OPPOSITE BOTTOM: Mel Shaw in his office at the Disney studio, surrounded by drawings and models from *The Fox and the Hound*.

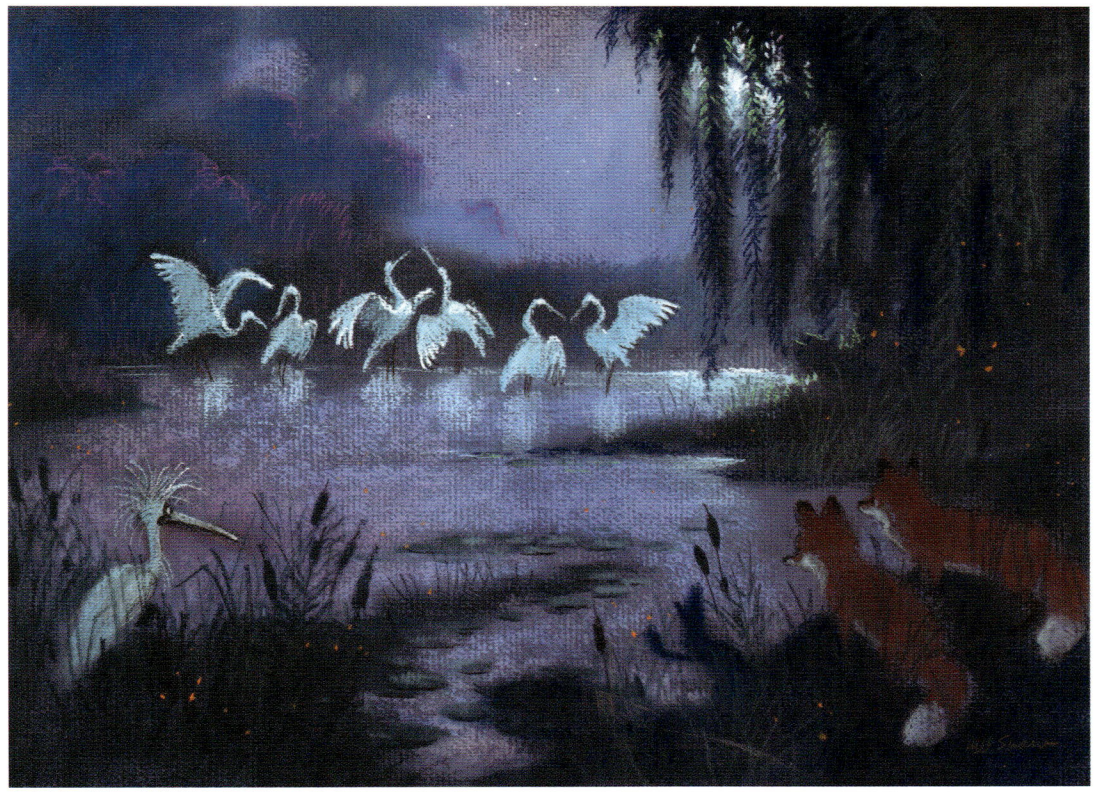

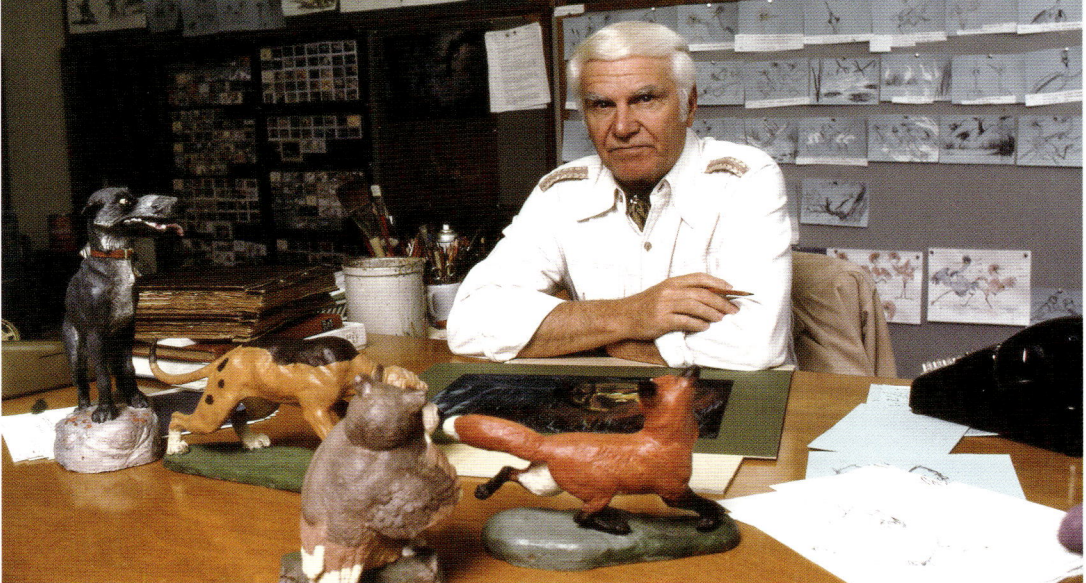

In the meantime [in 1974], they asked if I would look at this other thing, *The Fox and the Hound*. That was a story like *Bambi* . . . I did my interpretation of the thing and then Woolie said, "I think this one is something the guys can handle," and so did Milt Kahl.[151]

The Fox and the Hound was seen as an easier project than *The Black Cauldron*, and it was selected in 1975 as the next feature to move to production. And in addition to *The Fox and the Hound*, there was at least one additional training ground opportunity for the new artists, according to Mel:

It was also agreed that the inexperienced animators could gain additional training by working on a short film for which I had already provided an adaptation. It was titled *The Small One*, and it was a Christmas story told of the old, retired donkey who carried Mary to the town of Bethlehem.[152]

When he had worked at the studio in the 1930s, in addition to the Leica reel, there was another tool that Mel had loved at Disney: the three-dimensional models of the characters produced by the Character Model Department. And since Mel was an accomplished sculptor, he decided to start producing models again, starting with the characters of *The Fox and the Hound*. Mel both sculpted and painted them. The animators loved it.[153]

Never one to rest for a minute, in 1975 Mel Shaw was also creating dozens of pastel concept designs for a planned feature that would combine live action and animation, *The Hero from Otherwhere*, based on the book of the same name by Jay Williams. The story revolved around two boys, enemies at school, who get sent to a parallel, magical universe and have to work together to save their world from the wolf Fenris. But the ambitious project, whose animated sequences would have been directed by Frank Thomas, never moved beyond preproduction.[154]

MEL SHAW 139

THE LITTLE BROOMSTICK AND *MUSICANA*

While production started on *The Fox and the Hound*, story development was progressing on *The Black Cauldron*, as well as on another story involving magic, *The Little Broomstick*, based on the novel by British writer Mary Stewart. The tale, published in 1971, centered on a little girl, Mary, who is led by a black cat, Tib, to discover a magic broomstick that takes her to Endor College, a dark and scary training ground for witches. Once again, the concept drawings that Mel created for the project were enthralling.

Woolie Reitherman and Mel Shaw wanted to make the movie a kind of tone poem, with minimal dialogue and a great deal of storytelling through visuals and classical music.[155]

Artist Mike Peraza, who worked with Mel on *The Little Broomstick* at the time, recalled:

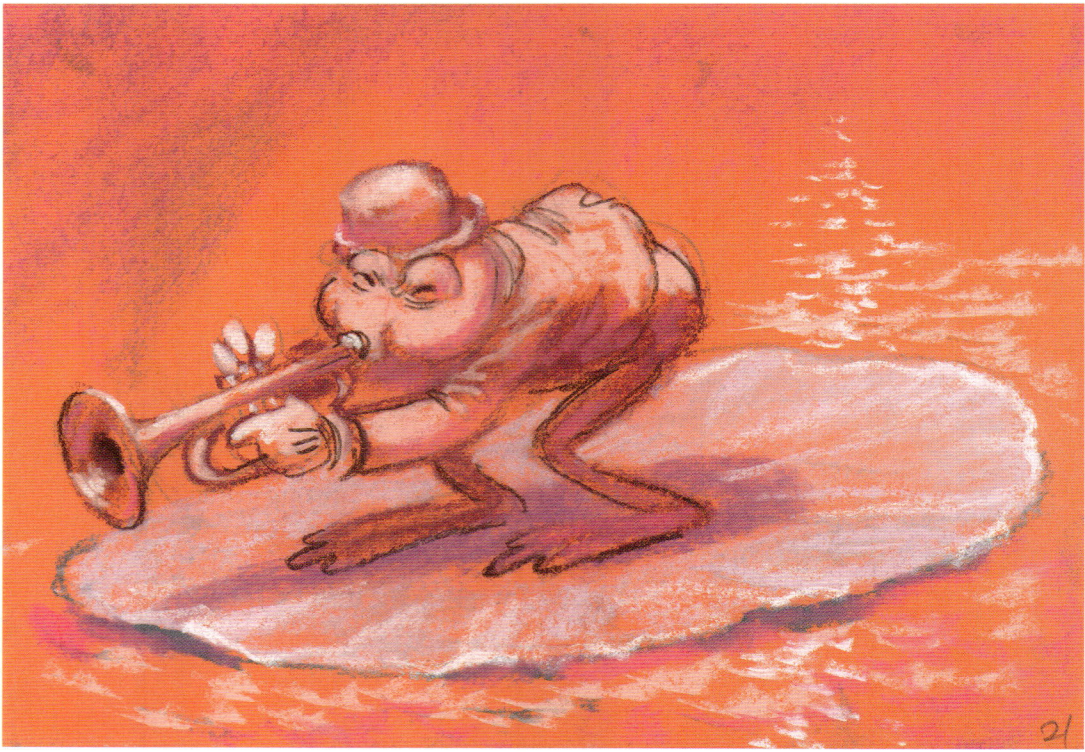

> I think when Ron [Miller] was seeing some of this stuff we were planning, he was like, "Wow, this is an epic." So it's, "Either we do this or we do *The Black Cauldron*" . . . They had to make a decision, because [*The*] *Fox and the Hound* was about halfway through production already, so they had to commit to something for the next one. And [*The*] *Black Cauldron* won . . . Mel was kind of undecided, because Mel liked *Cauldron* too, and he had a pretty large stake in it himself. He'd put a lot of work into it, even though *The Black Cauldron* film ultimately didn't reflect Mel's story. His version of *Cauldron* was amazing. The older generation, Frank and Ollie and all the other Disney veterans, liked *The Little Broomstick*. But the younger generation, almost to a person, was all excited about *The Black Cauldron*. You have to remember, though, we had been listening for a couple of years about how *The Black Cauldron* was our chance to do our own *Snow White*, something we could call our own . . . Woolie was very disappointed and he ended up leaving the studio not too long after that.[156]

The decision to shelve *The Little Broomstick* took place around July 1980.[157] Mel, never at a loss for new ideas, had already suggested another concept to Woolie: "Let's do something with *Musicana*."[158]

The Disney studio had been considering producing a sequel to *Fantasia* starting even before the release of the "concert feature" in theaters. The latest attempt dated from 1969, when the rerelease of the original movie had been promoted with a psychedelic-styled advertising campaign. At the time, the head of the Walt Disney Music Company, Jimmy Johnson, had written an internal memo titled "Neo Fantasia," which read:

> About a year ago, the idea of a live-action *Fantasia* came to my mind. It certainly was not original as I remember that years and years ago [effects animator] Josh Meador made some Fantasia type live-action footage . . . Several months ago, in a casual conversation with Ken Anderson, I told him of what I was thinking. It turned out that coincidentally he had been think-

ABOVE: Story sketch for the Dixieland jazz sequence of the proposed feature *Musicana*.

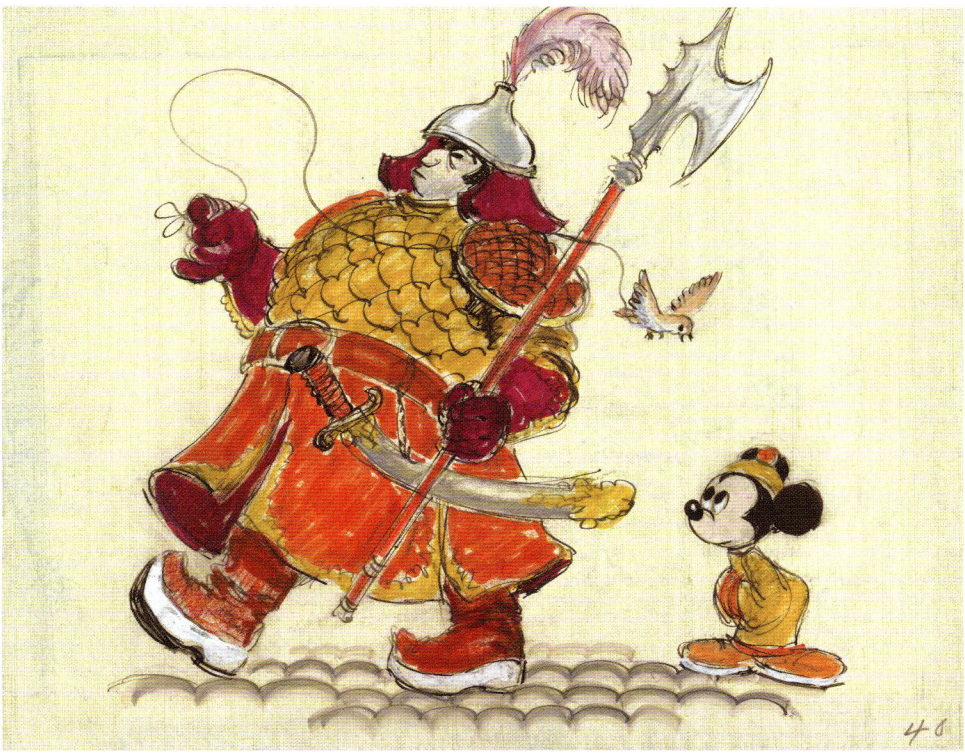

ABOVE: Story sketch for "The Emperor's Nightingale" sequence in *Musicana*.

ing along the same lines and had shot an eleven minute film to [composer Bedřich] Smetana's "The Moldau." This is a highly professional job and we include it in our show as the real highlight of what might be done along the lines of a neo Fantasia.[159]

According to an early treatment, the *Musicana* animated feature that Woolie and Mel worked on throughout the year 1980 aimed to present to modern audiences:

> Great music from around the world, combined with the Disney art of animation, told in a series of myths, tone poems, and occasional humorous folk tales: a "visual symphonic concert." The basic theme is that music is the "heart beat of the world"[160]

The movie would include six musical sequences: Chinese music to present the story of *The Emperor's Nightingale* from Hans Christian Andersen with Mickey as its main protagonist; "Scheherazade" by Rimsky-Korsakov featuring the story of Ali Baba with birds instead of humans; "Finlandia" by Jean Sibelius; traditional African music introducing viewers to the African myth of Maco the monkey, stealing the diamond from Ogaro, the rain god; a song by Yma Sumac for a South American sequence; and a frog choir singing Dixieland jazz in New Orleans on a song by Louis Armstrong and Ella Fitzgerald.

On June 24, 1980, Mel Shaw explained to Woolie what he had in mind when designing some of those sequences:

> I think maybe in the introduction, we should try to find a way of getting the basic ideas over, telling the reason for making a picture like this. And it's not really a *Fantasia II*, because this has more tales and more ethnic background using a Chinese orchestra, using an African orchestra, African drum music, using a phonic type of music that would be with "Finlandia," and also, the human voice, such as to be used with Yma Sumac as a South American Indian cultural [segment]. I think any kind of music that we would use, whether it be jazz or symphonic or just the most primitive type of music, I think they all have a common form and I think that's where we should start and try to explain what we have.

In each sequence the stylistic approach would be visually unique:

For *The Emperor's Nightingale*] the styling of the picture itself is part of the charm… and we're using the old Chinese technique, flat type of drawing with a line. I think it's a good idea to try to do it so that all the backgrounds look like they've been done on silk. Like the screen, that would be the introductory and then all of the colors would be [subtle] colors and the story itself would have that kind of a charm to it, with the music and with the introduction of Mickey . . . I think that Finlandia almost is dictated by the music there. It's heavy in the beginning and dark and gloomy and cold and it should be done very impressionistically and then when the sun starts to come through and it's fighting the storms that the Ice God is putting up, your colors would start to change and then when the sun comes out, of course then you go to your brilliant colors with the music that goes with it. I think there the styling of the thing is going to be more impressionistic. Kay Nielsen had a way of stylizing things like that.

And Kay Nielsen was not the only artist who had worked for the studio who Mel was using as a source of inspiration. He looked to other artists who had either contributed to Disney films in the studio's early years or whose work had inspired Walt decades ago.

[For the African sequence] you could say that would be like [Arthur] Rackham or [Gustaf] Tenggren or [Edmund] Dulac, that kind of a styling. Yet it should have a quality that would be indicative to Africa to it, because of the flat types of trees that they have out on the African veldt . . . [and] the background has to have a quality to it that is [like a] story book, because the animals are the characters that are going to be doing the dancing, etc. I feel about the animals [that] we're going to be using animal tones, and most of the animal tones are earth colors, because that's the camouflage of the animal. Consequently, I think that when we dress them, and we use a certain amount of dress, that they have to be harmonious with earth tones, rather than just picking colors abstractly. Consequently, the overall feeling would have a feeling of Africa; the veldt; the dry arid country alongside of the lush greens.

As to the Latin American sequence, its style was something else altogether:

I think you're led into it because the whole dream or hallucination is through the eyes of a naive person, supposedly. He is a peasant and he's carrying a heavy load of wood· and he comes into this area of this jungle that has flowers growing in it and the jungle has grown over the remains of the old Mayan civilization, in a naive way [like] that [Douanier] Rousseau stuff which is decorative, etc.[161]

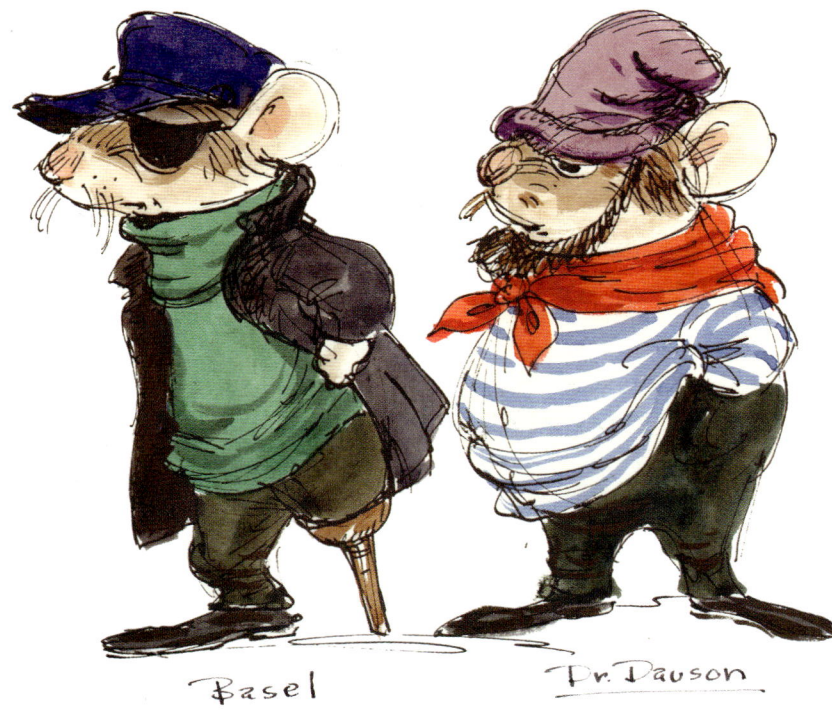

ABOVE: Character designs for *The Great Mouse Detective*. Courtesy: Philippe Cauvin.

A FRENCH PLAY AND A BRITISH TALE

When the *Musicana* project was shelved, Mel's attention moved to another idea that had obsessed Disney artists through the years: *Chanticleer*, based on the play by the French author Edmond Rostand. He wrote a story outline on February 11, 1981, and designed some beautiful story sketches. He even tried an approach that merged the story of *Chanticleer* with that of *The White Blackbird* by French author Alfred de Musset. His attempts at adapting the story, however, were no more successful than that of his predecessors.[162]

With the *Chanticleer* idea dead and Woolie Reitherman about to retire, the writing was on the wall, and Mel started thinking about retirement. There was one last story he tackled, however, in the spring of 1981: *The Great Mouse Detective* (then known as *Basil of Baker Street*).[163] He would end up having a decisive impact on it, as Burny Mattinson explained:

Ron [Clements] was in Story at that time, and then they moved John [Musker] in as the director on it. So when I came down there, I was sort of the outside director. [What Ron and John] had done was a very farcical approach to the story. It was really all done for laughs, and I didn't care for that style that they were working with. It looked nothing like what we used in the picture . . . Then I had these setups that Mel was doing, and everybody liked Mel's stuff. It was beautiful stuff, but [John and Ron] were persistent. They wanted to go in a whole different direction. Anyway, I went to Ron Miller and I said, "Ron, we've got to make a decision on this. Which way are we gonna go? Are we gonna go with the farcical they want to go with, that approach, or do you want to go with Mel's?" And, thank God he said "Mel's."

Not only was the overall tone of the movie set by Mel, but the most memorable sequence in the picture was also the fruit of his imagination, as his colleague Vance Gerry remembered a few years later:

Mel [Shaw] had drawn this picture of Big Ben in England and it was like a down shot—you were way up in the sky and looking down on it. But you were close enough to see that the two mice, Basil and his archenemy Rattigan, were having a fight to the end. Much like Sherlock Holmes had a fight with Moriarty at the falls. Here were these two mice at the very tip end of one of the hands of Big Ben. Now, that picture was so powerful and suggested such an image that you couldn't do anything but keep that in the movie. It was such a powerful image. And it stayed in the movie. That was done very early. That is when he was just exploring possibilities for what could happen. I don't think it was in the book; it was just something that occurred to him . . . That's one example I can remember of where one drawing suggested a whole sequence.[164]

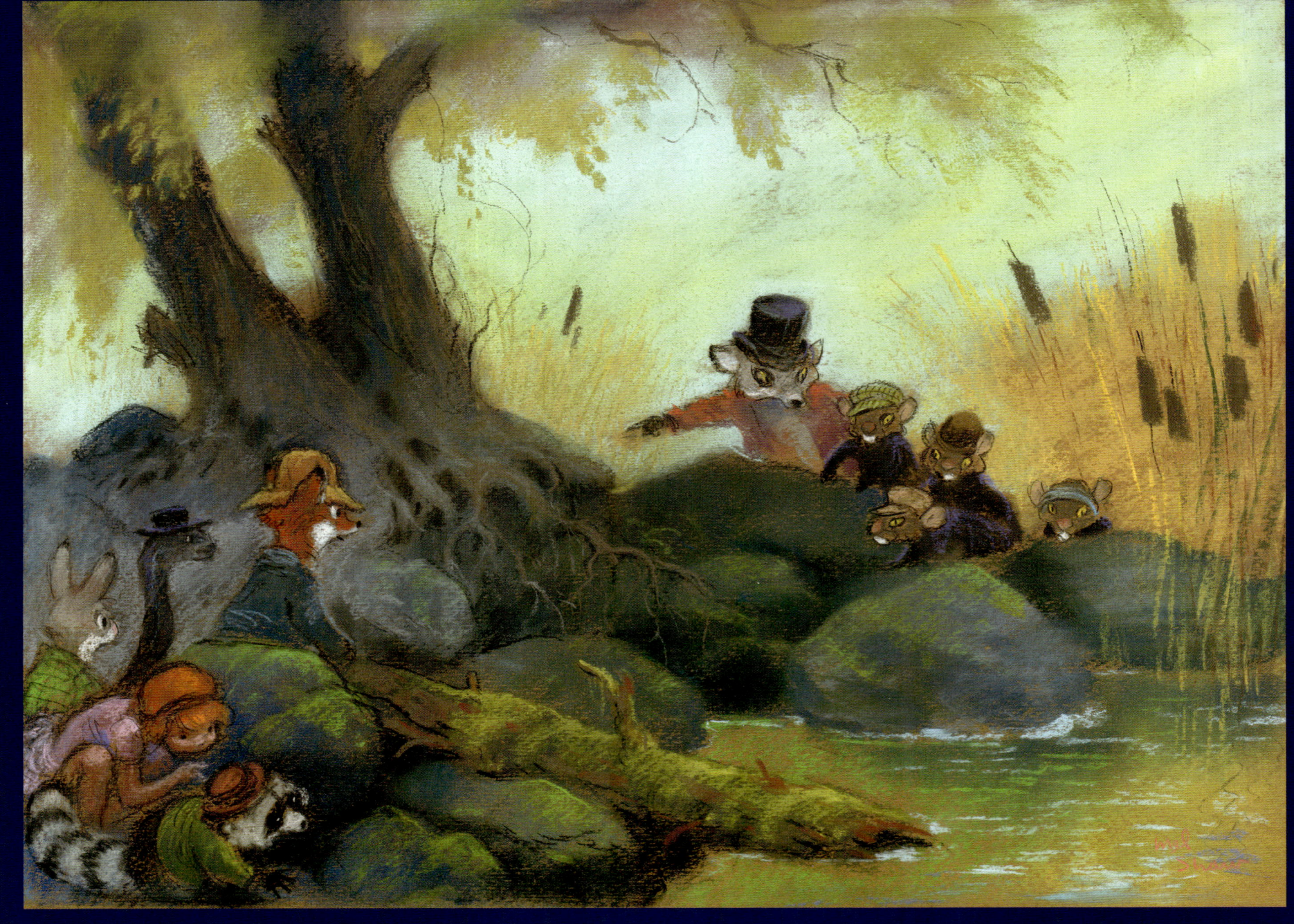

ABOVE: One of Mel Shaw's concept sketches for *Catfish Bend*. Courtesy: Philippe Cauvin.

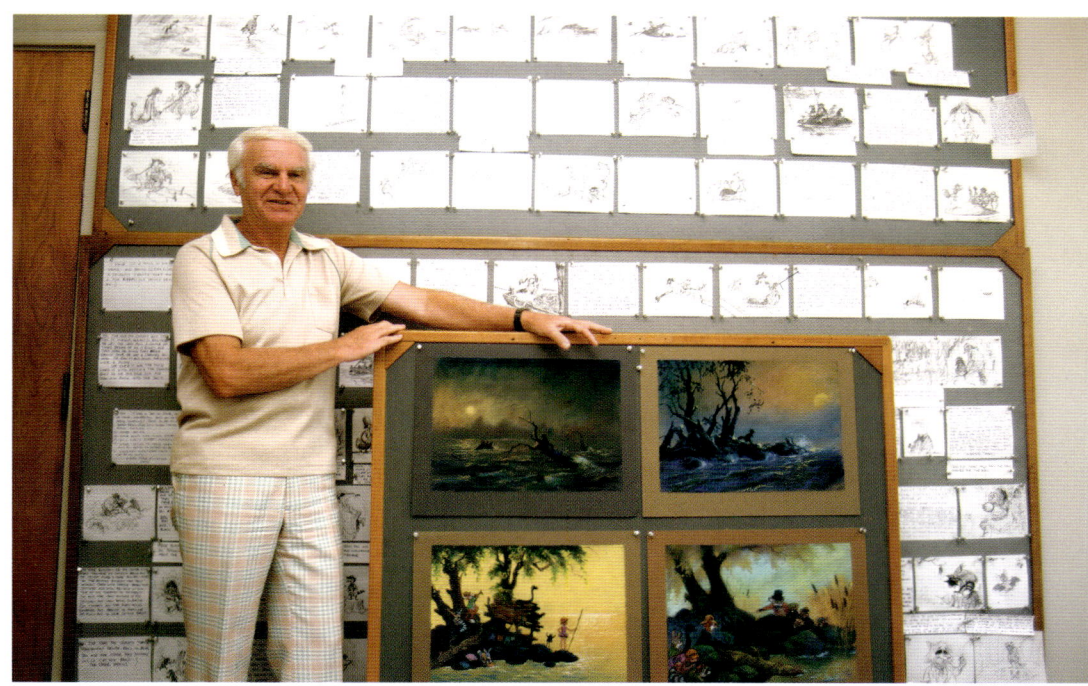
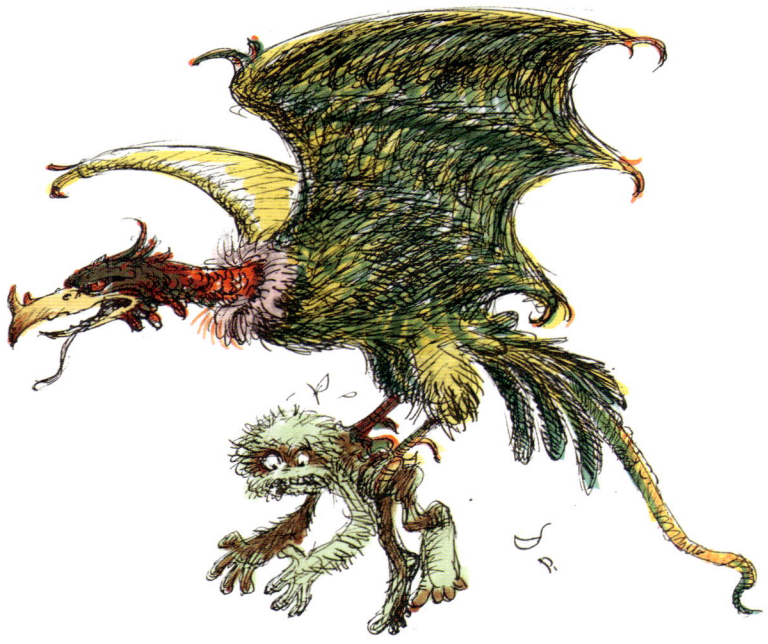
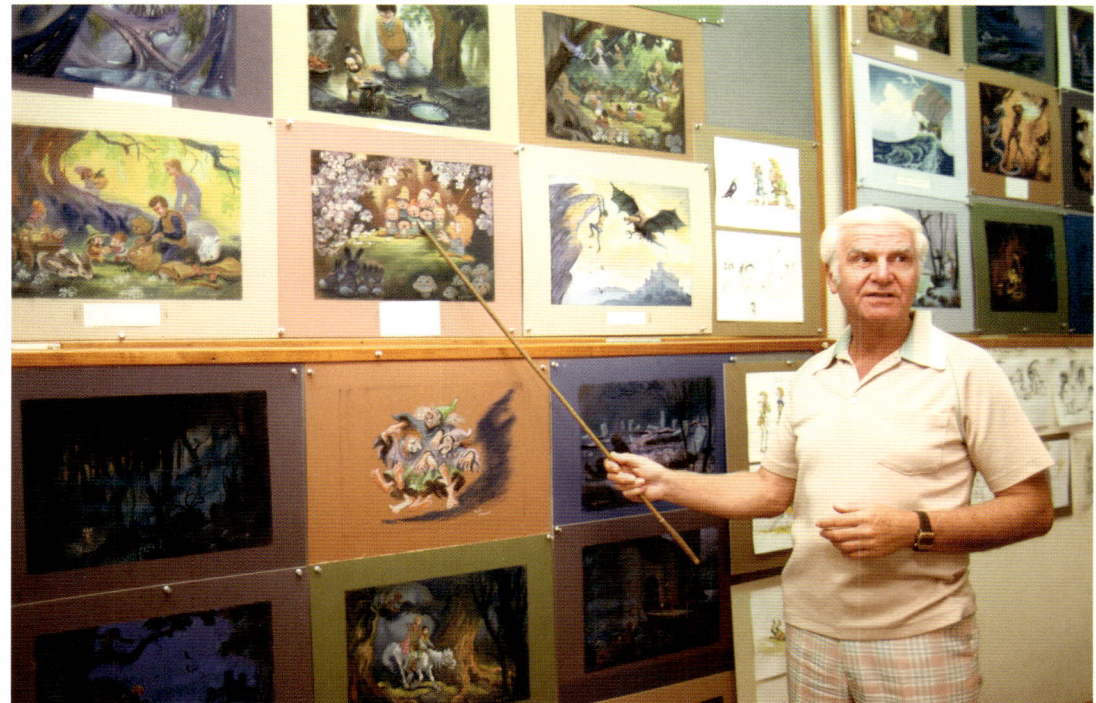

ABOVE LEFT: Mel Shaw pitching his version of the abandoned project *Catfish Bend* in 1978.

ABOVE RIGHT: Concept sketch for *The Black Cauldron*.

BELOW: Mel Shaw pitching *The Black Cauldron* in 1978.

FROM *BEAUTY AND THE BEAST* TO *THE LION KING*

After his short stint on *The Great Mouse Detective*, Mel decided to officially retire on September 5, 1981. A few years later, however, he received an unexpected phone call. A new management team led by Michael Eisner, Frank Wells, and Jeffrey Katzenberg was now running the studio, and a new Golden Age of Disney animation was about to begin. Mel was asked to be part of it:

> Don Hahn (an assistant director for *The Fox and The Hound*) remembered my work and contacted me for help developing a film he was producing for Disney, *Beauty and the Beast*. Since I [had] never considered myself "retired," I accepted the assignment and drove to the Burbank Disney studio to discuss their needs. I met with Don and he showed me the script that was prepared for the picture and asked if I would read it and make pastel sketches for an inspirational storyboard of the script. I took the script home to Santa Barbara for about two weeks and began making pastels of scenery and character sketches. Then I was informed that they had asked an English animation studio, Richard Purdum Productions, to produce the film and that I would be traveling to England to work with them on the picture. [My wife] Florence and I packed up, left Montecito for our rented flat near the London studio, and there I thoroughly enjoyed working with the fine young English and American talent of today.[165]

One of Mel's colleagues in London was the tremendously talented artist Hans Bacher, who, many years later, still remembered Mel's technique with a sense of wonder:

> Mel was there and he had brought all his equipment. He had brought all his special colored charcoals—a huge box of the most expensive Grumbacher charcoal—beautiful colors! He even had brought a very small vacuum cleaner, because whenever he was finished with his first layout of charcoal on his special colored cardboard, he had to vacuum-clean the dust from the drawings. That's how he worked. I'll never forget that sound. He went with this small vacuum cleaner over his illustration and he sucked up the dust of the colors. Then he continued and he smeared the colors and he went in all different layers on top until the painting was finally finished and was what he had in mind. In a way, he started very much like an improvised sketch. I never saw him do thumbnails of what he wanted to paint.

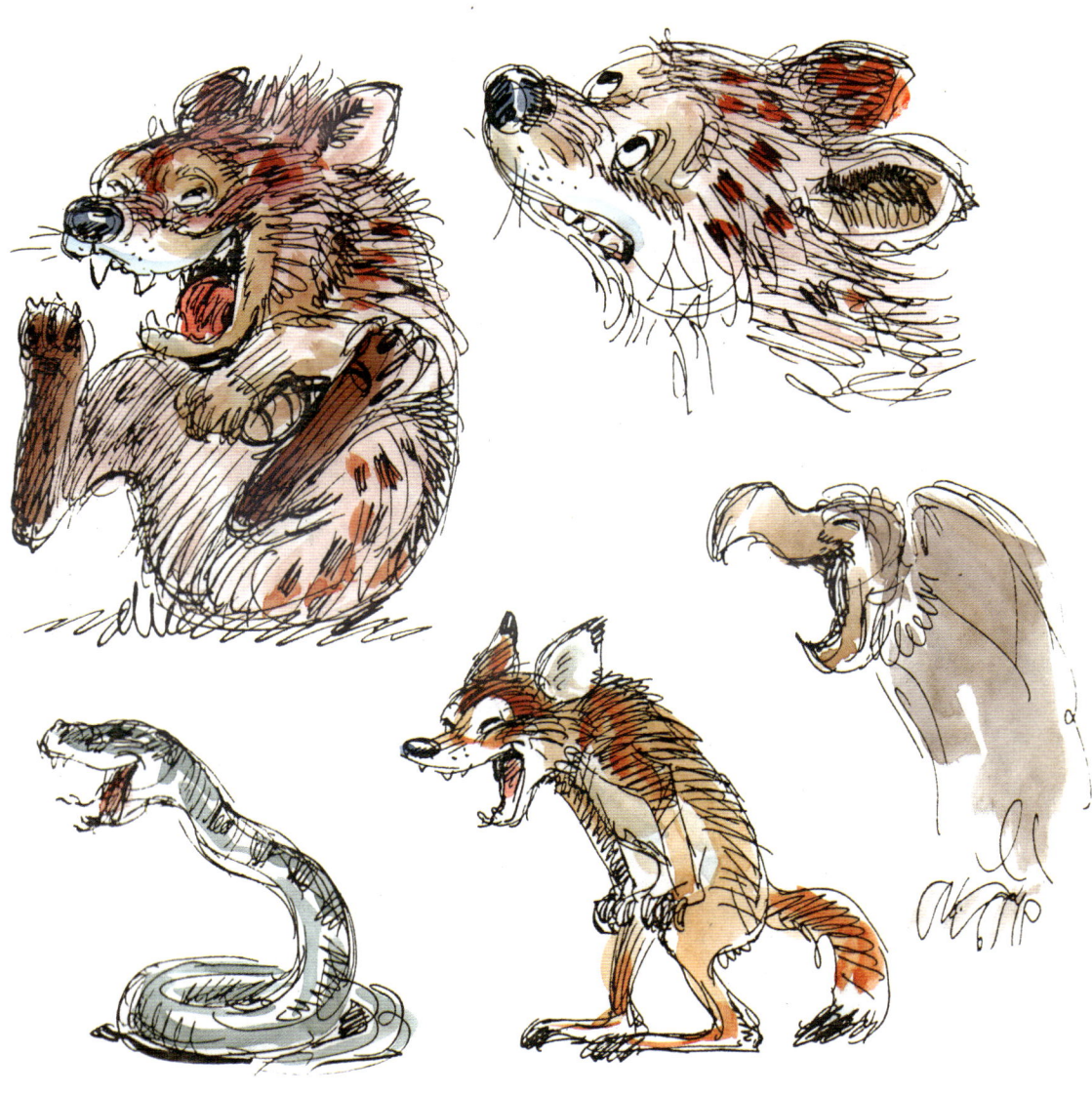

ABOVE: Character designs for *The Lion King*.
Courtesy: Rick Shaw and Melissa Couch-Deranleau.

He started with very rough sketches on his color cardboard. And he usually started just with a dark green or a dark brown or just some basic dark color and then he worked everything out of the darkness with lighter chalks and charcoal. And, following the first crude sketch that he did with a very hard, light grey charcoal pencil, he went straight in with color and he worked out first some of the background parts, like the sky and the basic atmosphere, so he got a feel for the color atmosphere and the color that he wanted to have. And then he went on top with another layer and another layer on top, and on and on until he finally came to the characters that were involved. He usually did the characters with finer charcoal pencils where he could do finer line work. So it was more like doing a sculpture than a painting. It was amazing... And he did one painting a day usually. He'd start in the morning and in the evening it was finished. So he was fast, he was light speed and he knew exactly what he wanted.[166]

Work in London on *Beauty and the Beast*, sadly, did not last long as disagreements on the story's approach within the studio led to a production shift from London back to California.

There was still one Disney project in the cards for Mel, *The Lion King*, the movie that would mark the apotheosis of Disney's new Golden Age.

Don Hahn gave me the script to read at home and asked me to submit my illustrated ideas on the picture. Apparently when Don had recommended me . . . he had informed [Jeffrey Katzenberg and the producer] that I would be turning out a minimum of five or six color renderings on the subject every few days. Not knowing that I was "under the gun," I returned to Northern California with the script and set about researching the subject. Having been to Africa and on safari recently . . . I enjoyed the challenge of drawing from my own experiences with the African landscape and animal life. I also gathered information from my own extensive morgue and worked on my visualization of the script until I had four renderings of my impressions of the characters and the dramatic Serengeti. With these four key scenes completed, I called the studio for an appointment to present my work to the new producer. I was informed that the animation department was no longer located at the Burbank studio but relocated about a mile away . . . This was the place that anyone in animation would report to because the Buena Vista studio was now reserved for the work of executives and live action . . . only. I found the [new location] and was ushered into the office of the producer . . . I took the wrapping off my four pastel renderings and lined them against the couch placed opposite his desk. He glanced at my work and then looked at me questioningly, "Four drawings? Is that all you did?" He then commented, "Don Hahn told me that you would complete five or six drawings in that time!" This producer never mentioned anything to me about the quality of my work or whether or not it illustrated the script.[167]

Fortunately, Mel's experience on the project ended on a happy note:

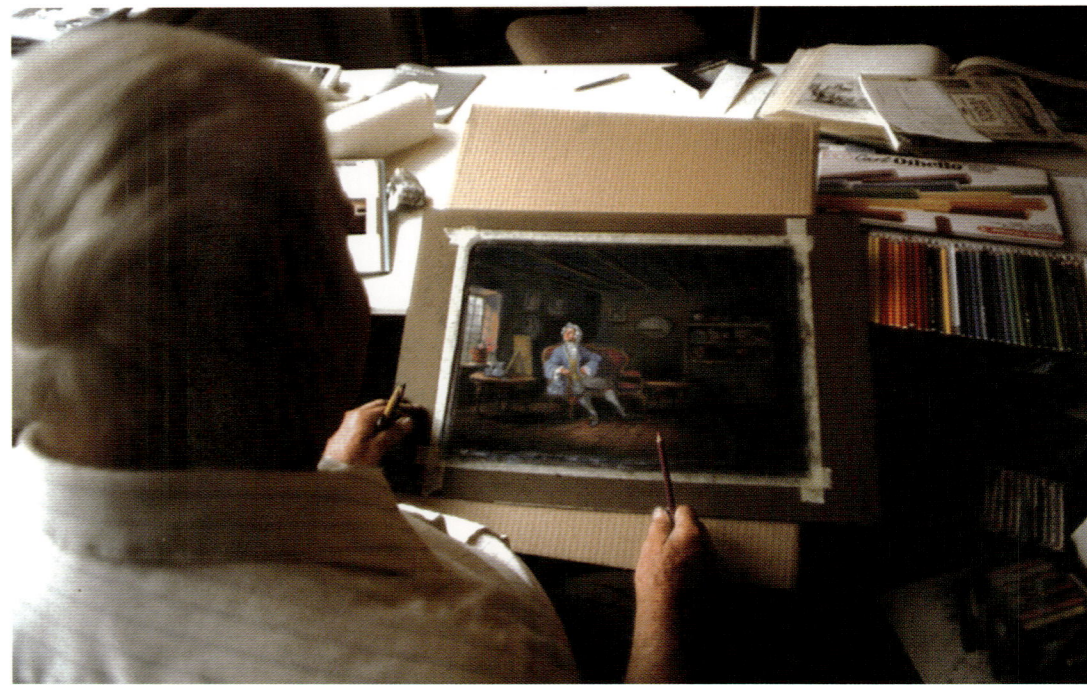

In a few weeks I returned to the studio with my latest pastels of the African terrain and my impressions of *The Lion King*. [The film] was now officially in the works and [a] new script was greatly improved. They asked me to do additional inspirational sketches to help illustrate the new storyline so I tucked a copy under my arm and commuted back to Northern California to continue my work. This time I felt as though my pastels were of some help to them as I had seen that they were being used in a storyboard form and had been received with enthusiasm. After presenting three or four more series of my pastel renderings, *The Lion King* went into animation and my work with the film was complete.[168]

The Lion King also marked the end of Mel's Disney career.

In the years that followed, Mel kept painting and sculpting for his own enjoyment. He was a month shy of his ninety-eighth birthday when he passed away on November 22, 2012. The "animator on horseback" was no more, but his work would ride on for generations to enjoy.

ABOVE: Mel Shaw working on *Beauty and the Beast* in London. Courtesy: Hans Bacher.

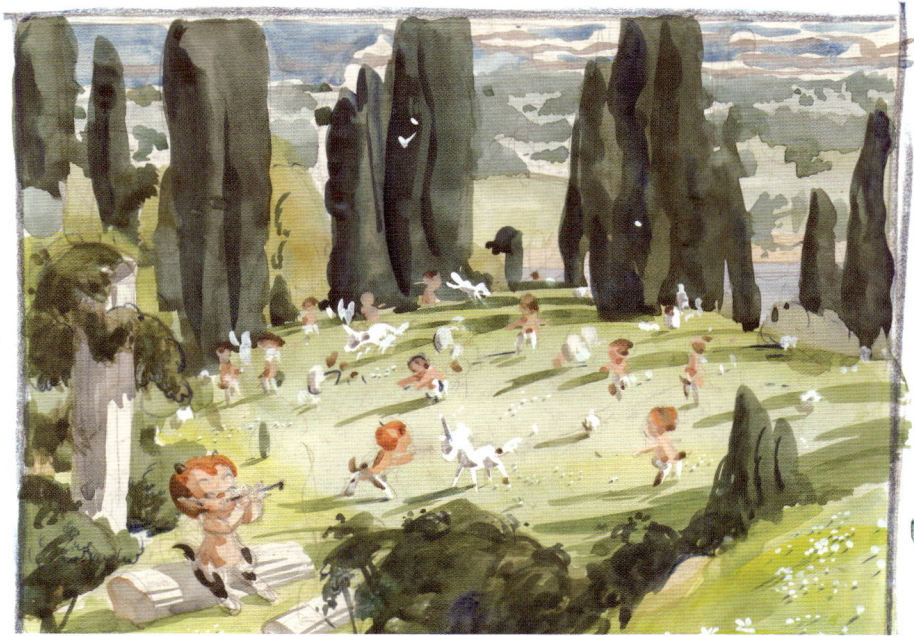
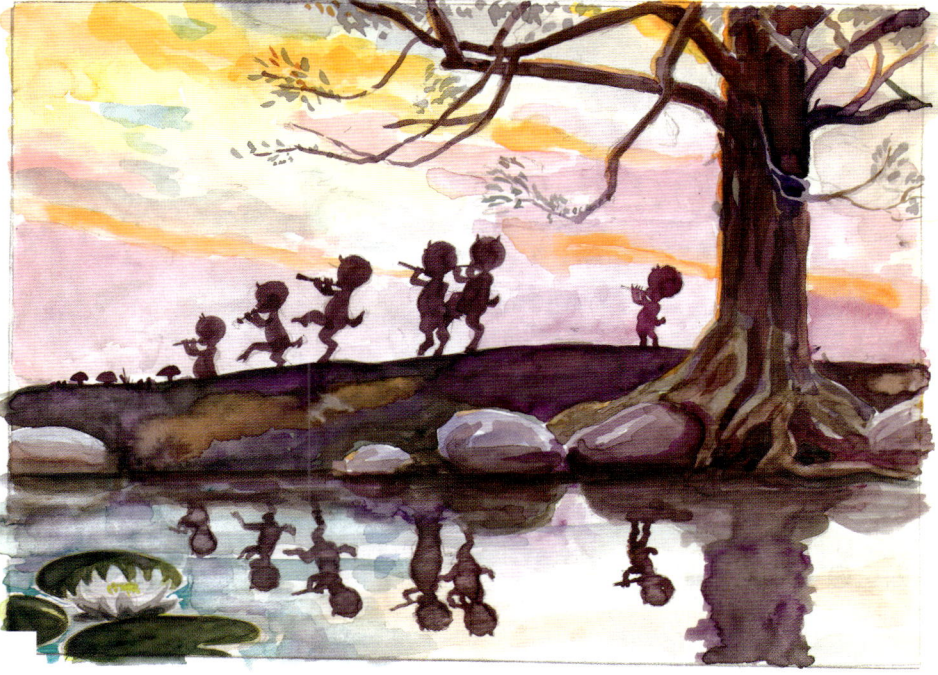
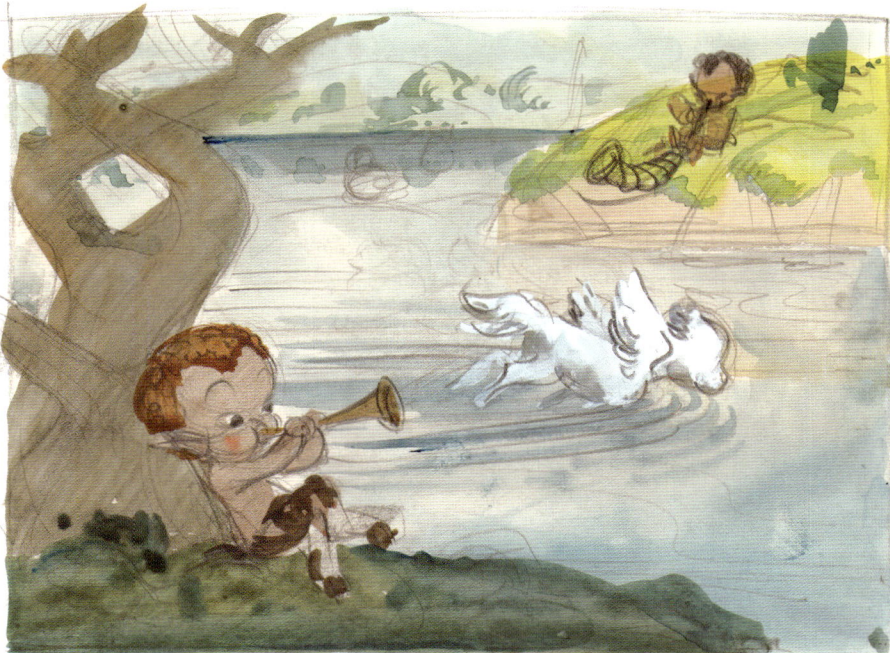
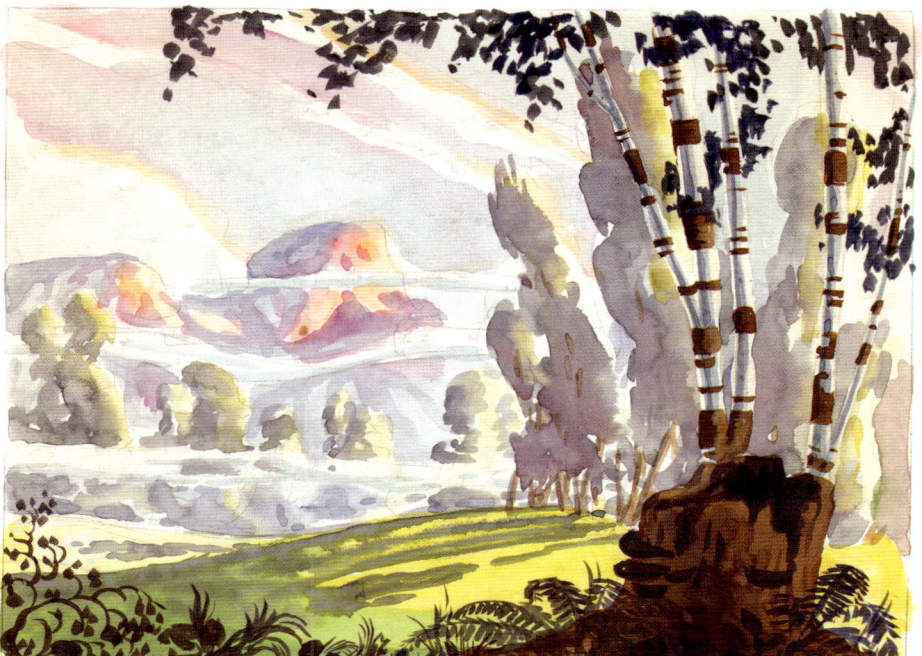

ABOVE: Concept sketches for "The Pastoral Symphony" sequence in *Fantasia*.

MEL SHAW 149

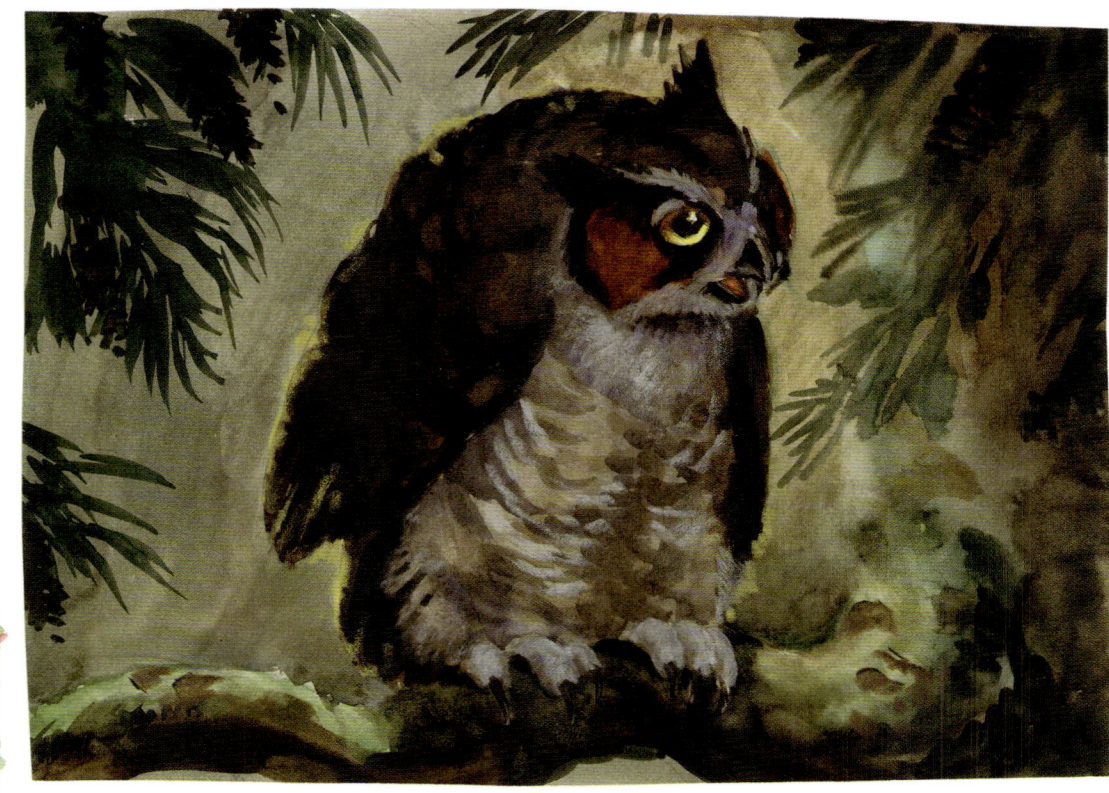
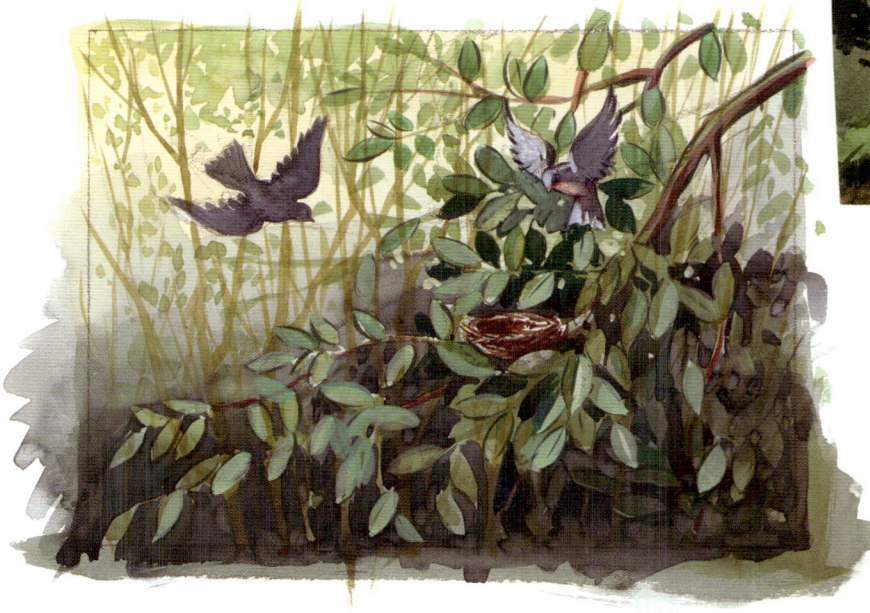

PAGES 150–153: Concept sketches for *Bambi*.

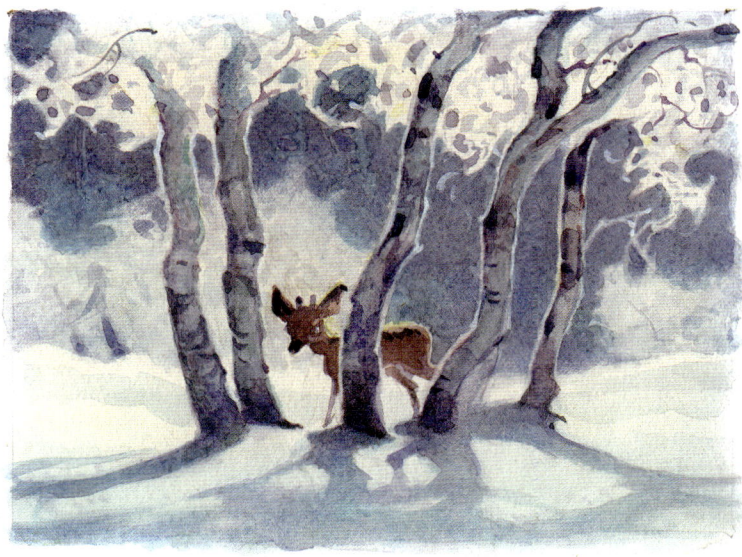
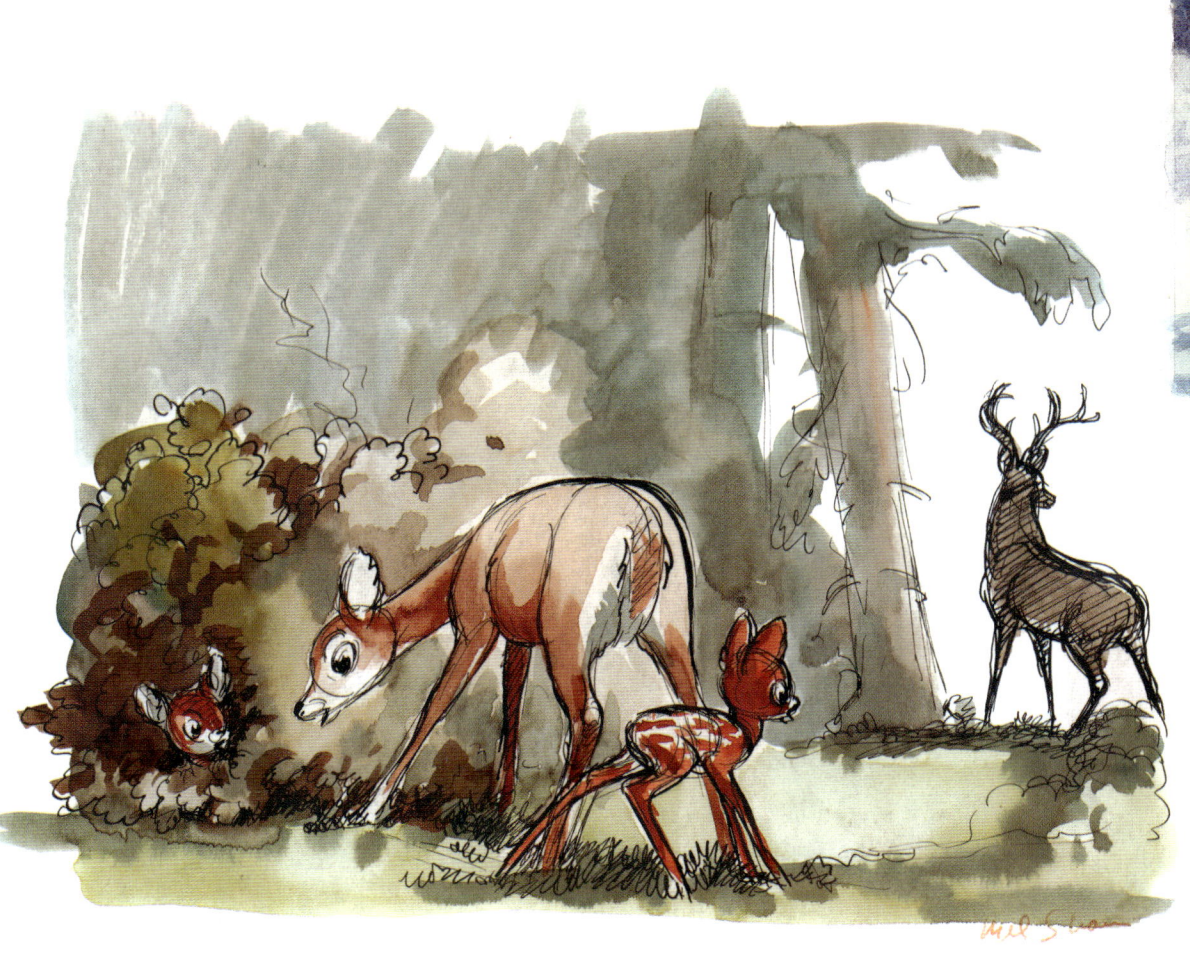

ABOVE LEFT: Courtesy: Rick Shaw and Melissa Couch-Deranleau.

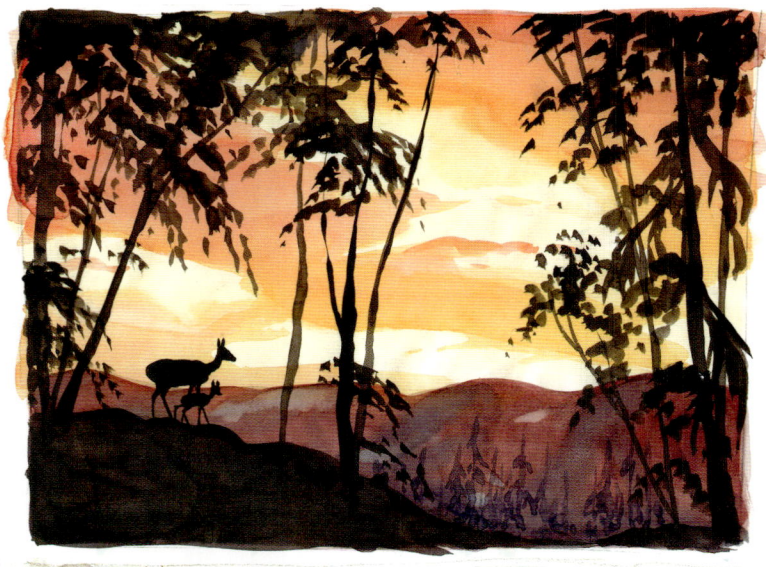
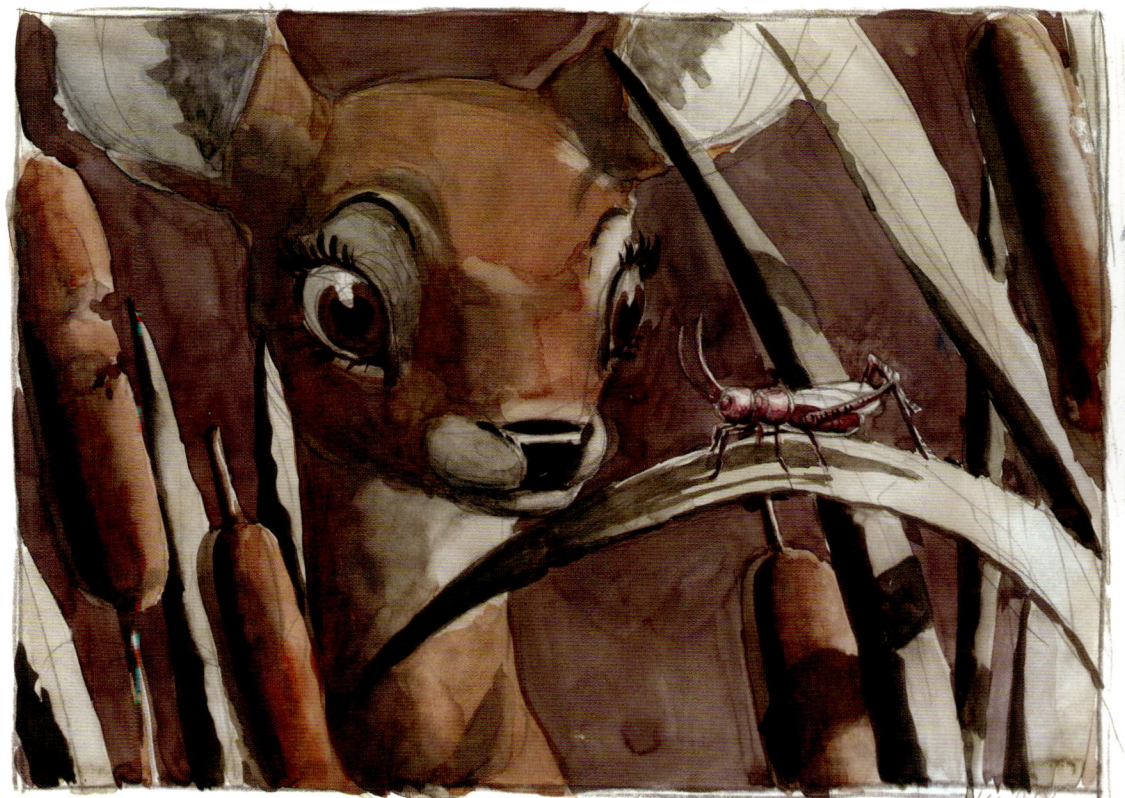
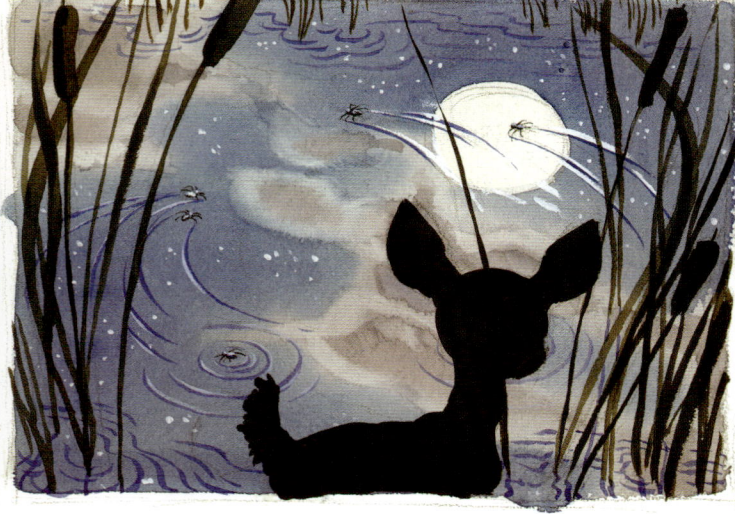

LEFT AND OPPOSITE: Courtesy: Rick Shaw and Melissa Couch-Deranleau.

152 THEY DREW AS THEY PLEASED

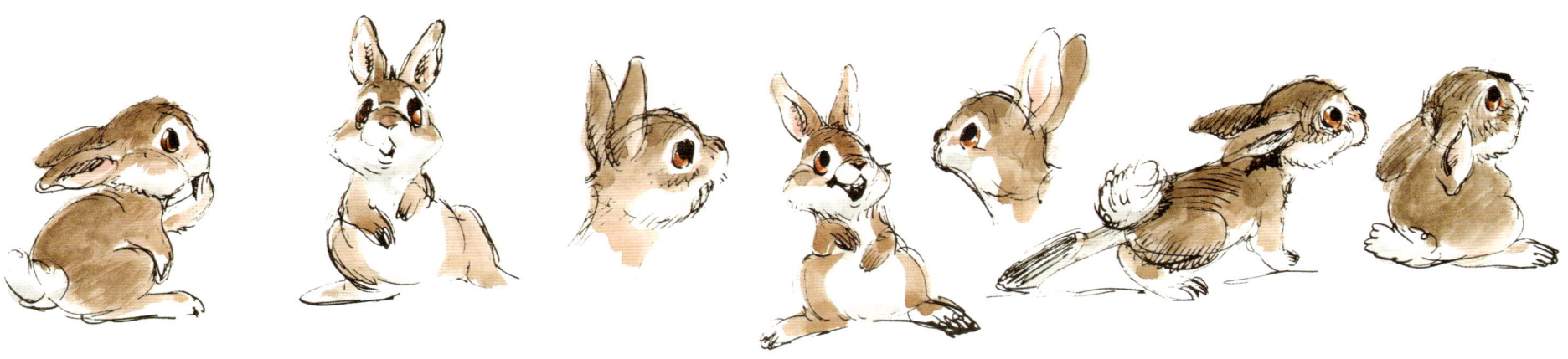
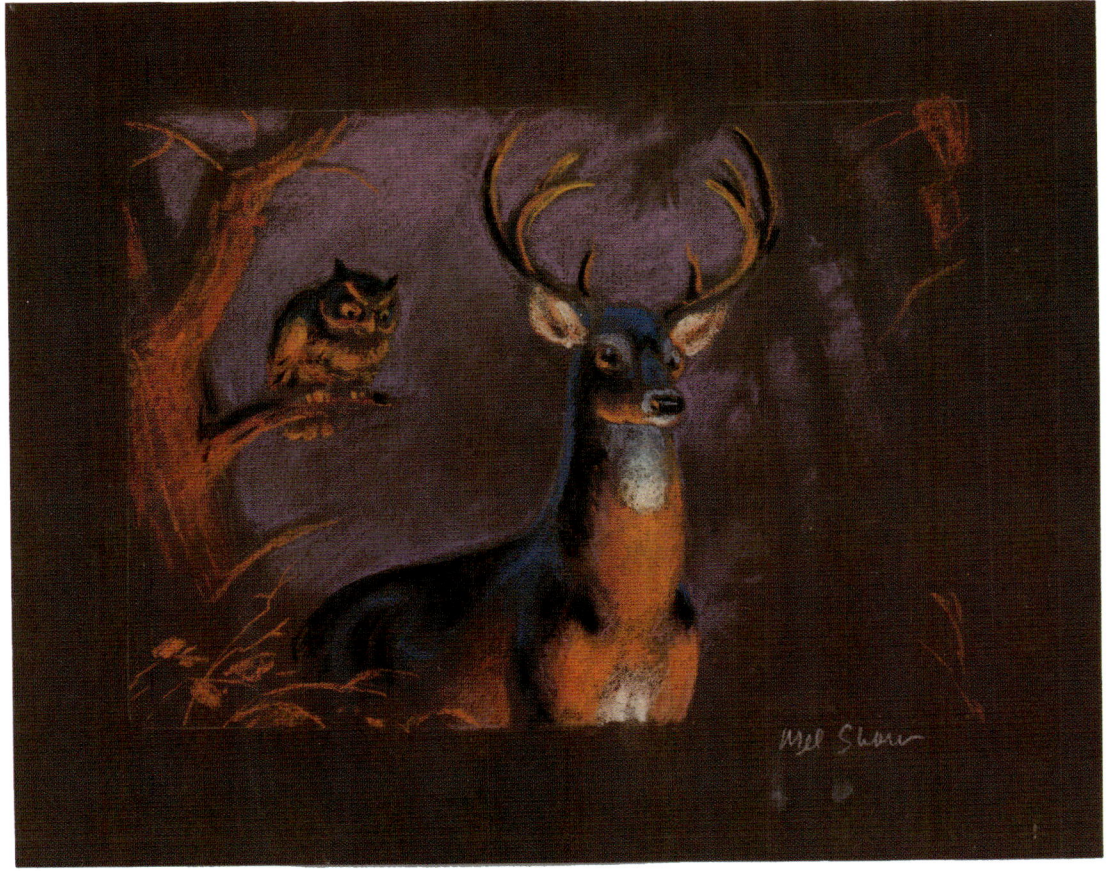
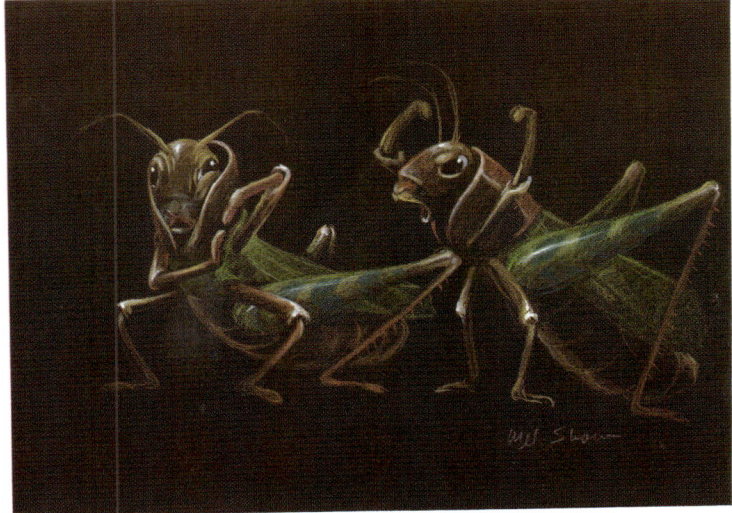

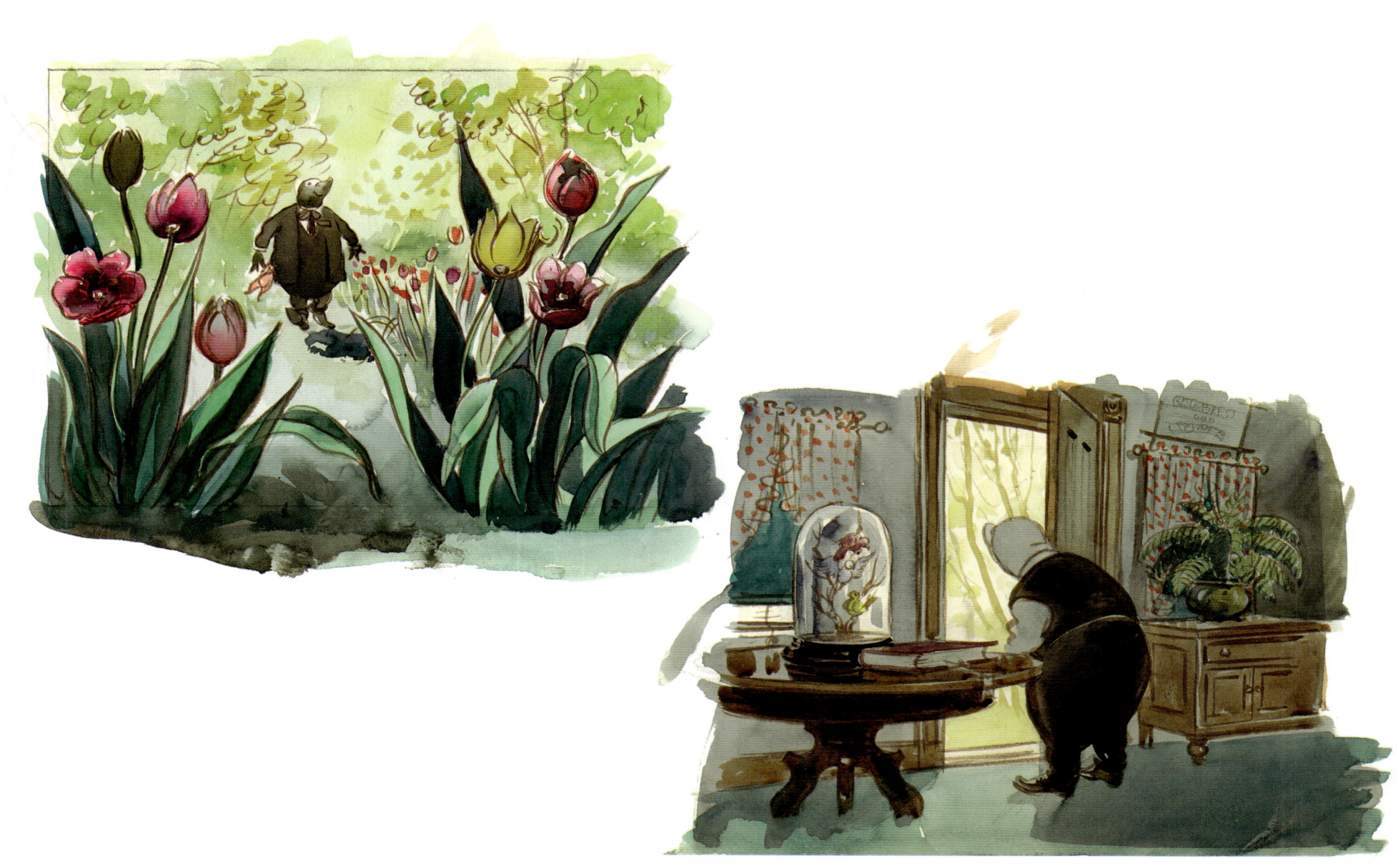

ABOVE AND OPPOSITE: Concept sketches for *The Wind in the Willows* (which became one of the sequences of *The Adventures of Ichabod and Mr. Toad*).

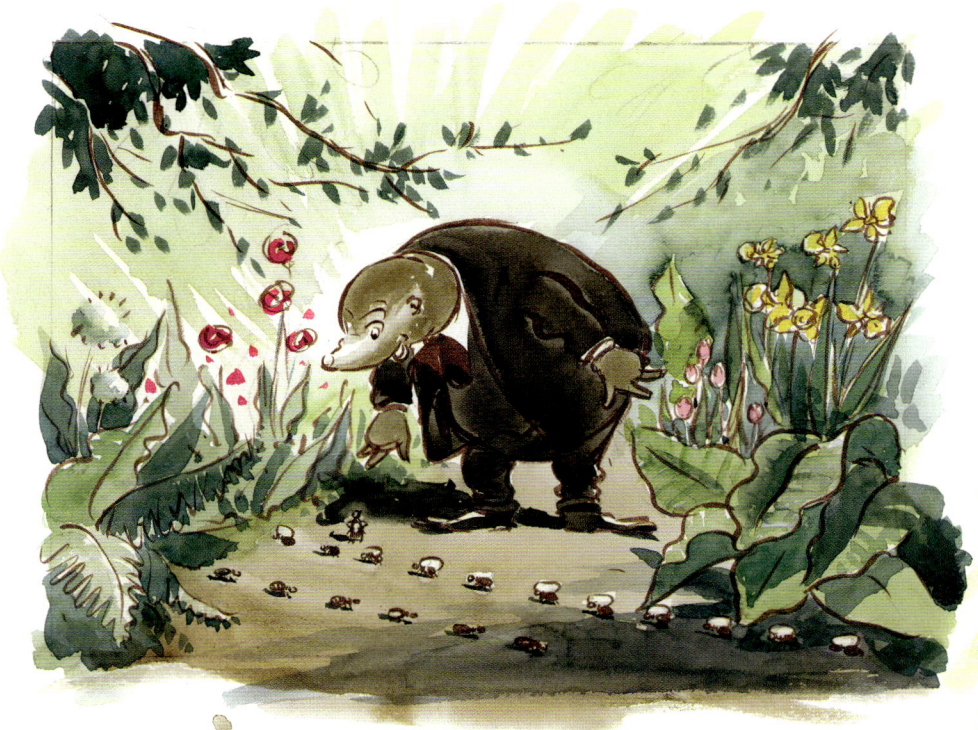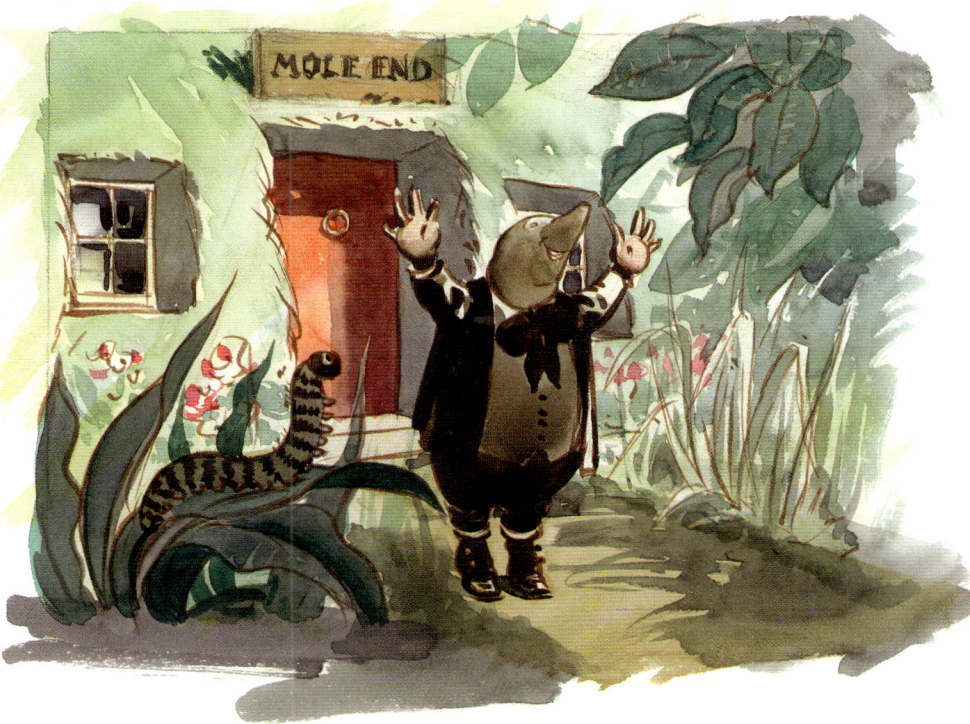

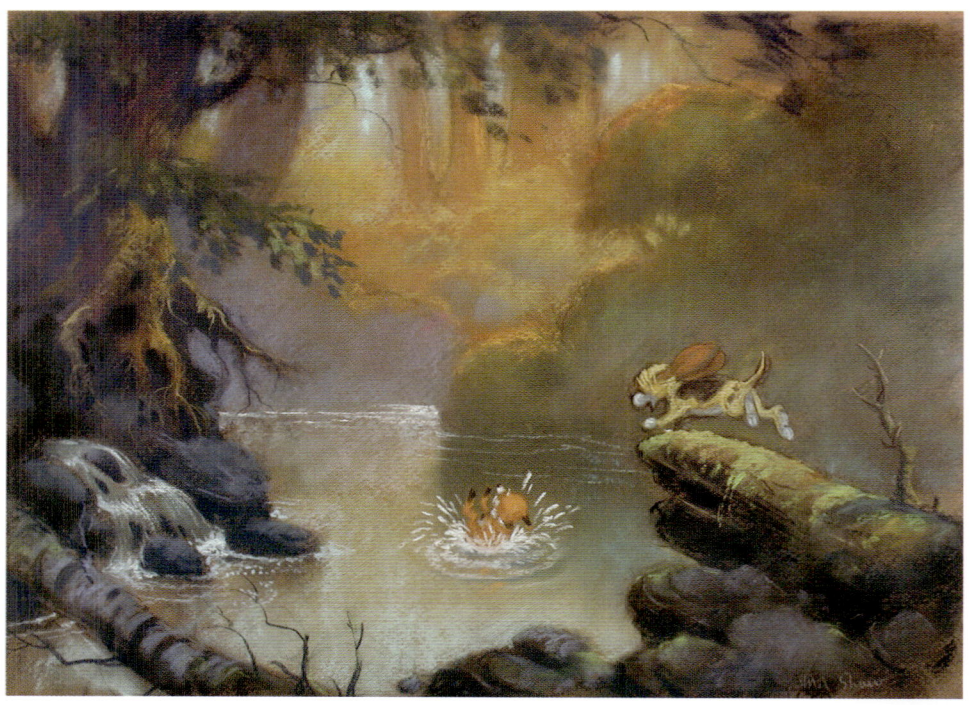

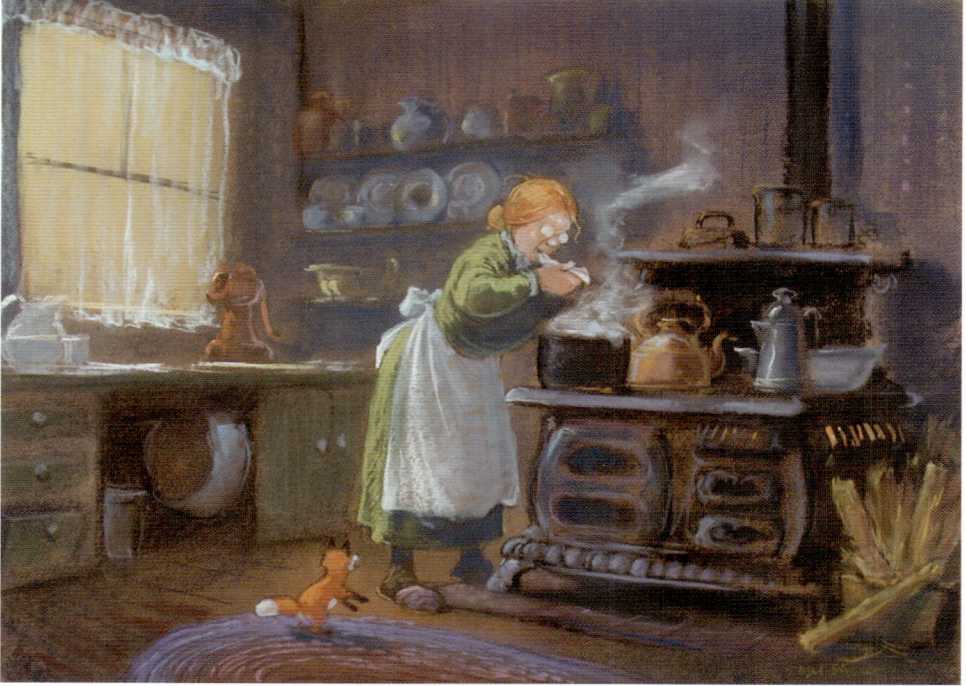

PAGES 156–159: Concept sketches for *The Fox and the Hound*.

156   THEY DREW AS THEY PLEASED

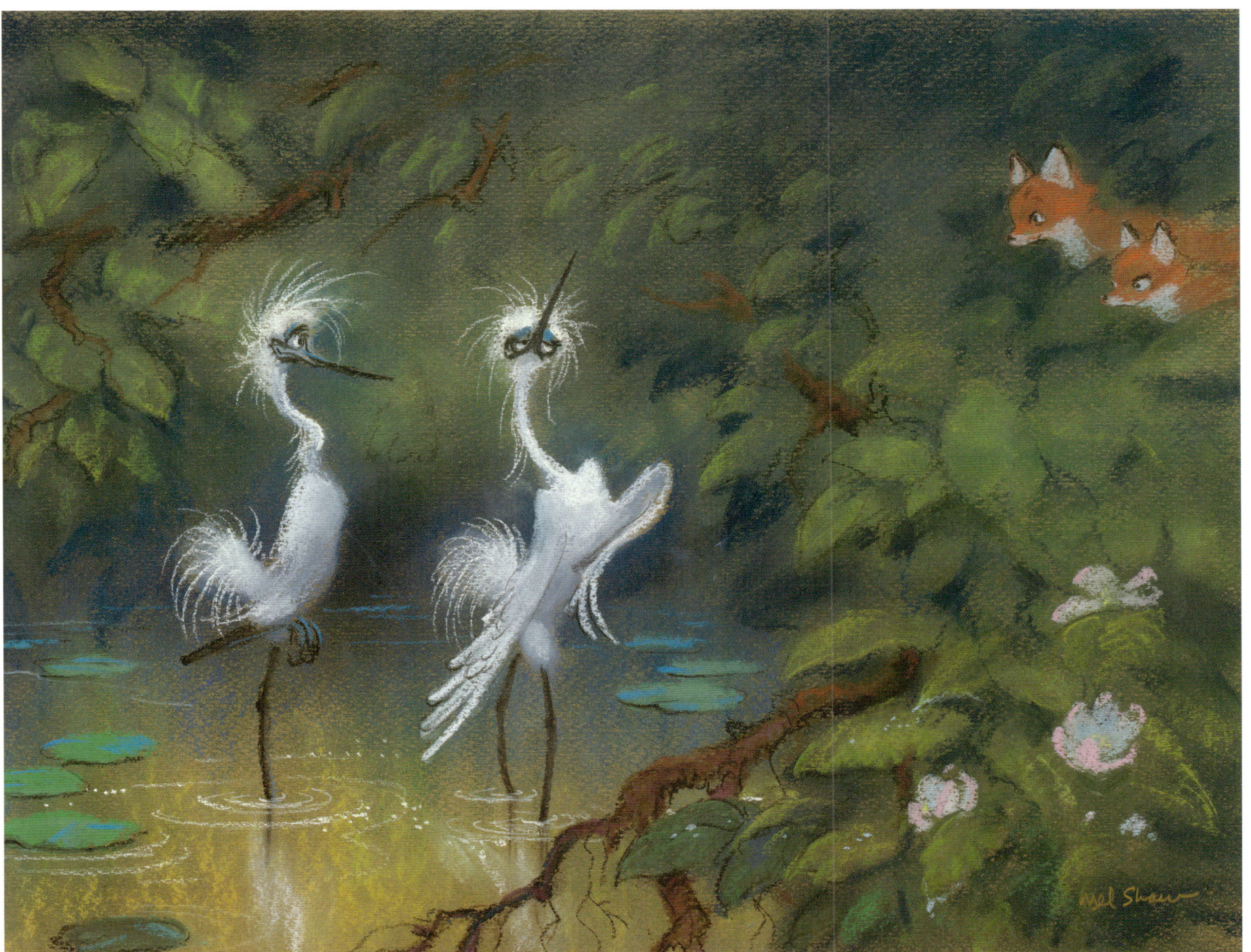

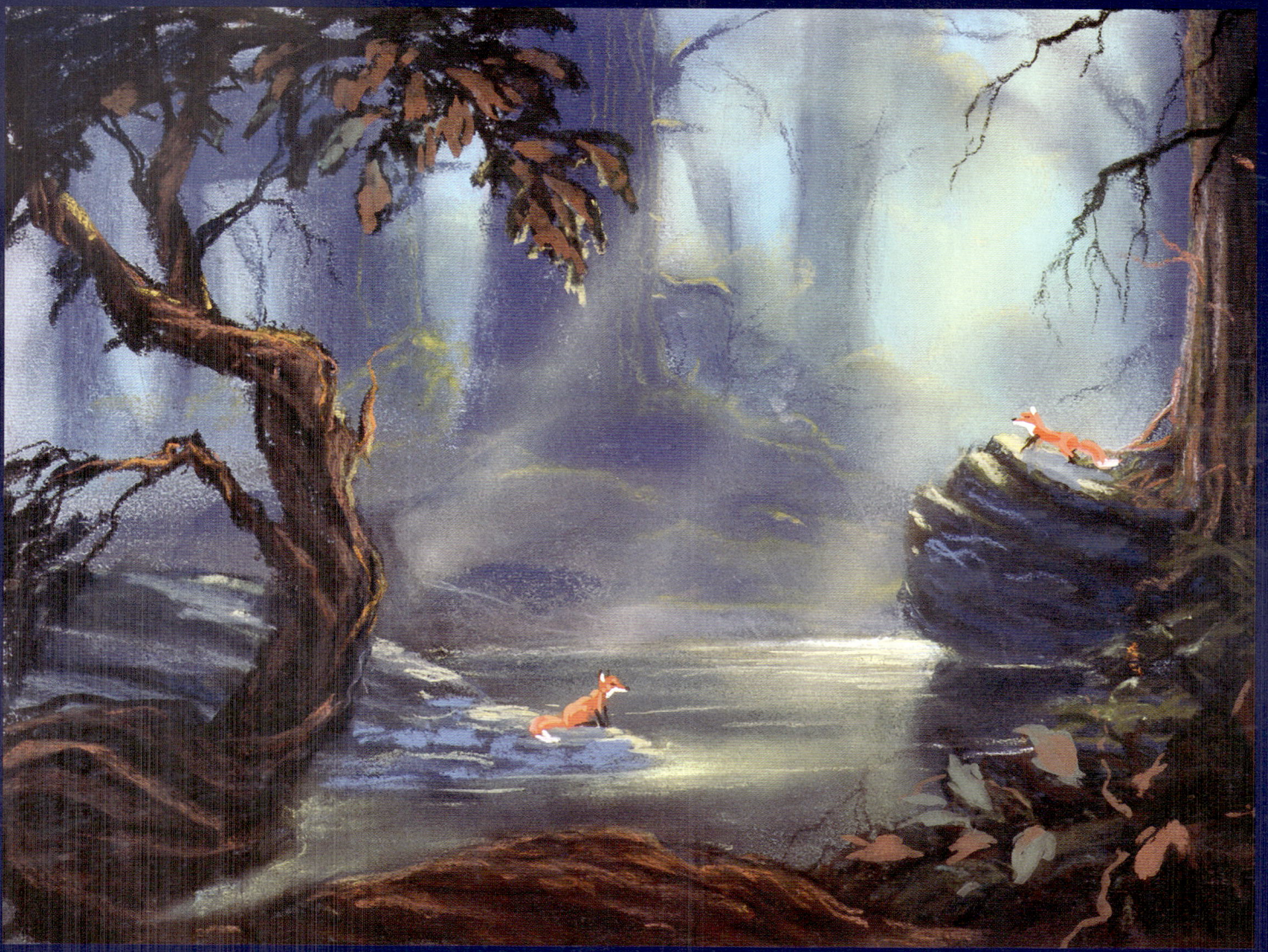

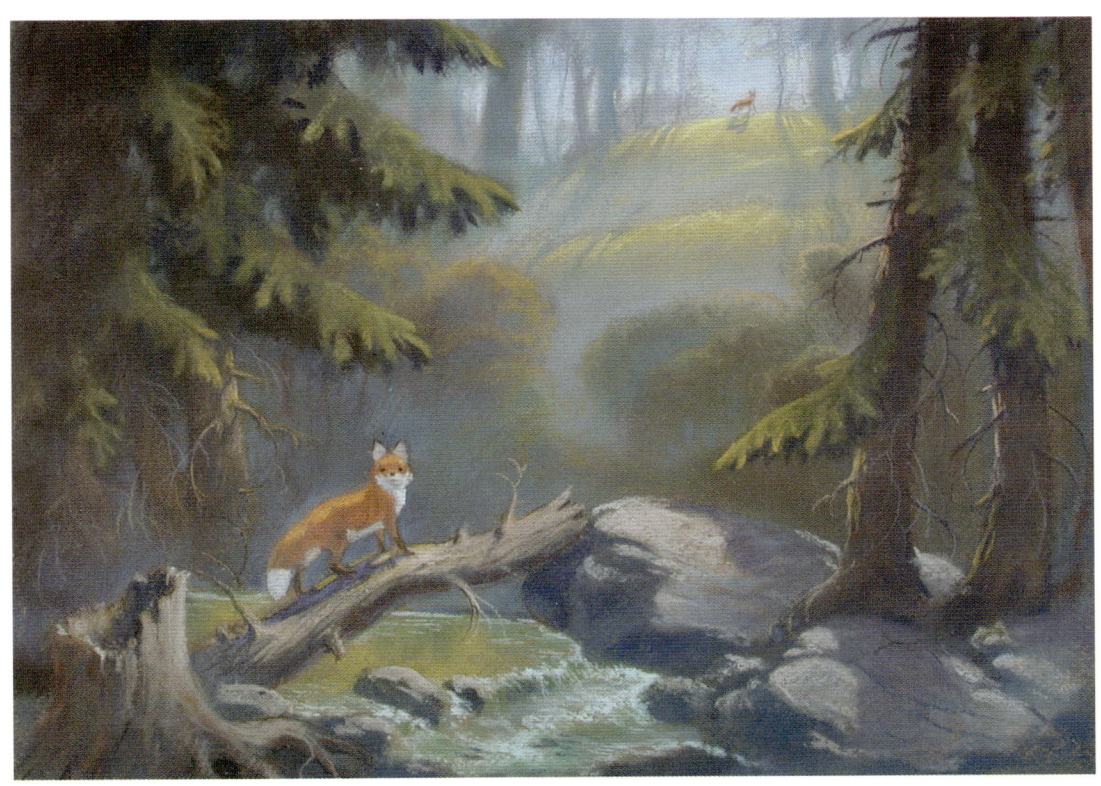
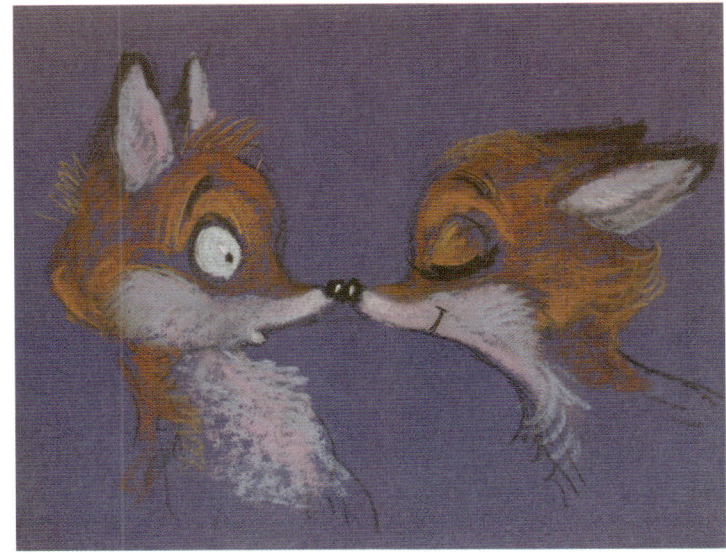
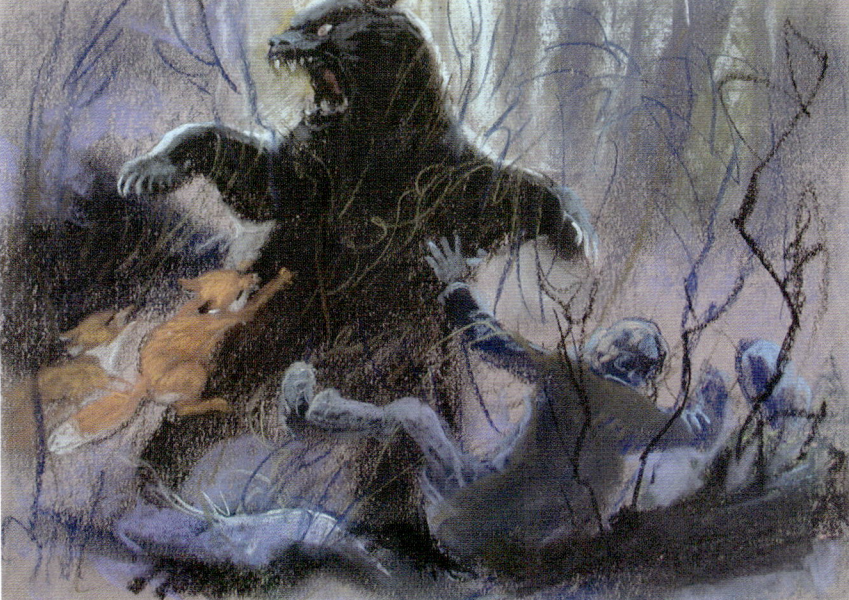

RIGHT: Courtesy: Gretchen Vander Weide.

MEL SHAW

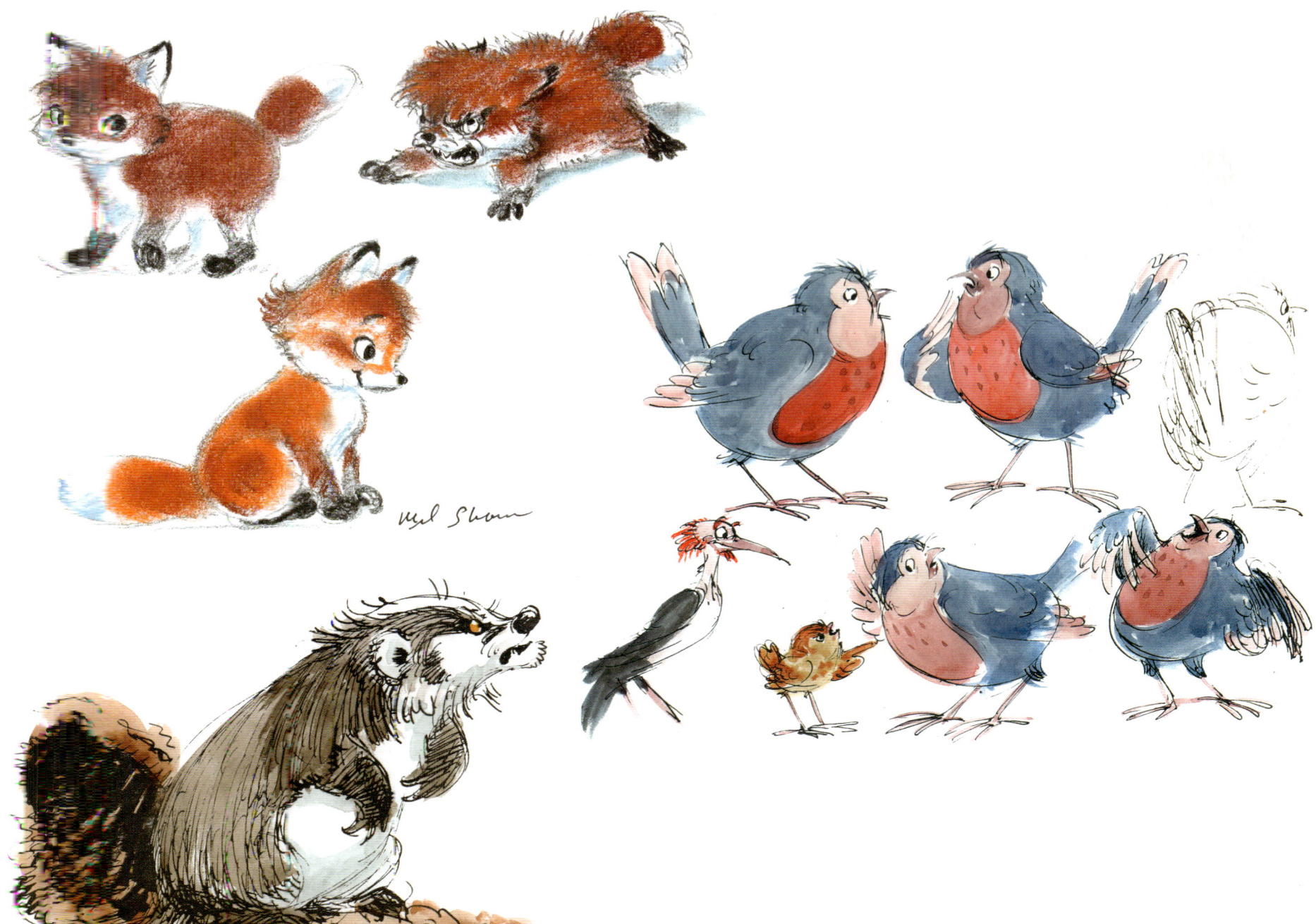

ABOVE: Character designs for *The Fox and the Hound*.

BOTTOM AND RIGHT: Courtesy: Rick Shaw and Melissa Couch-Deranleau.

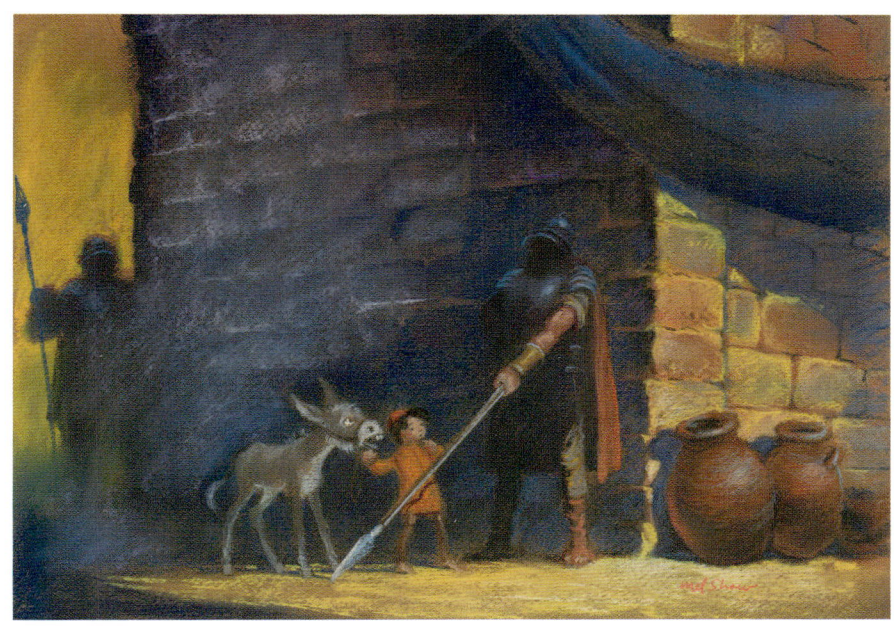

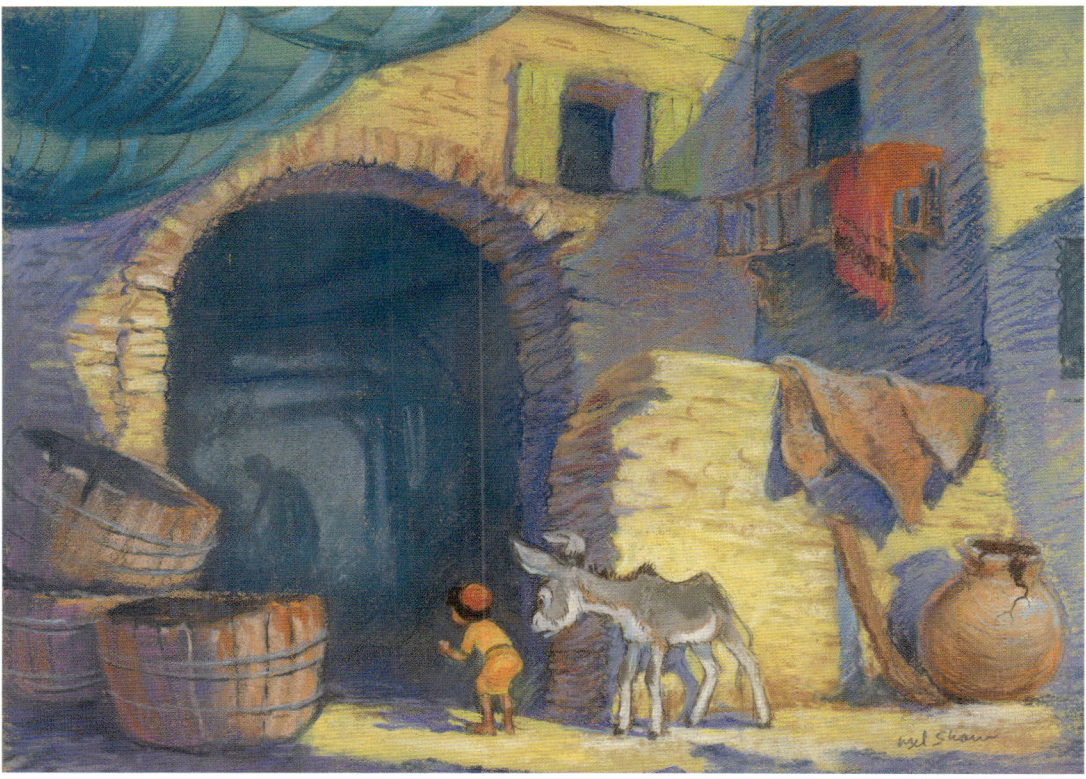

ABOVE AND PAGE 162: Concept sketches for *The Small One*.

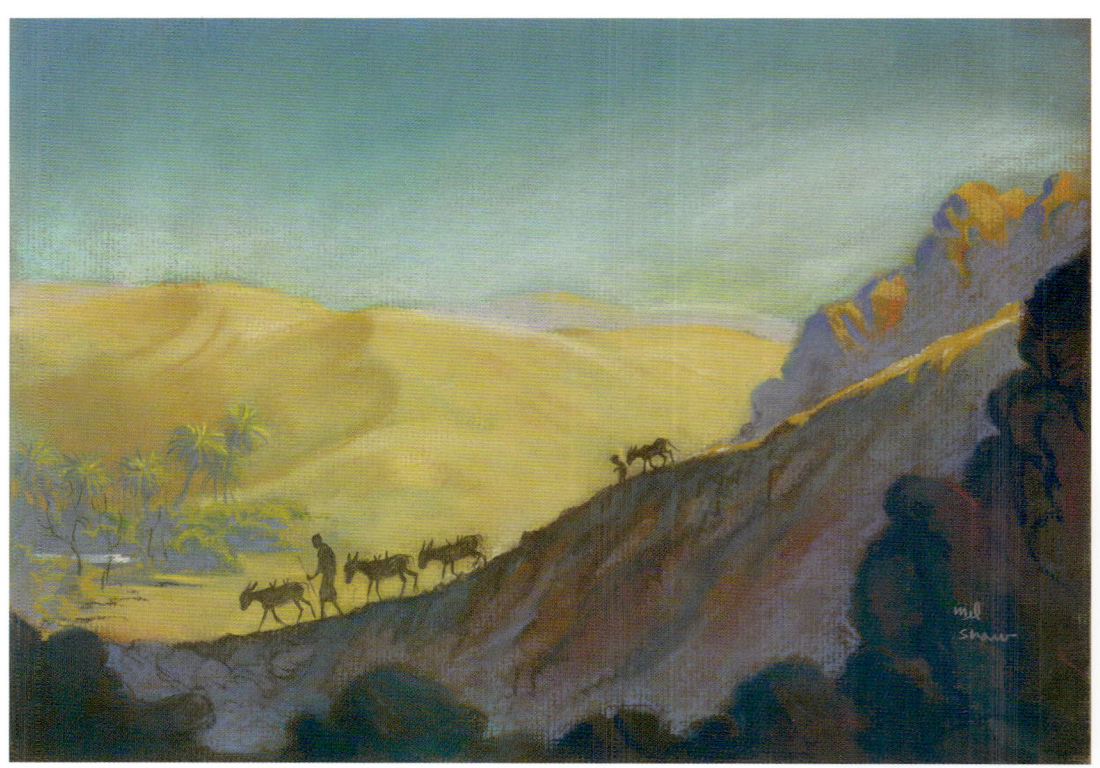
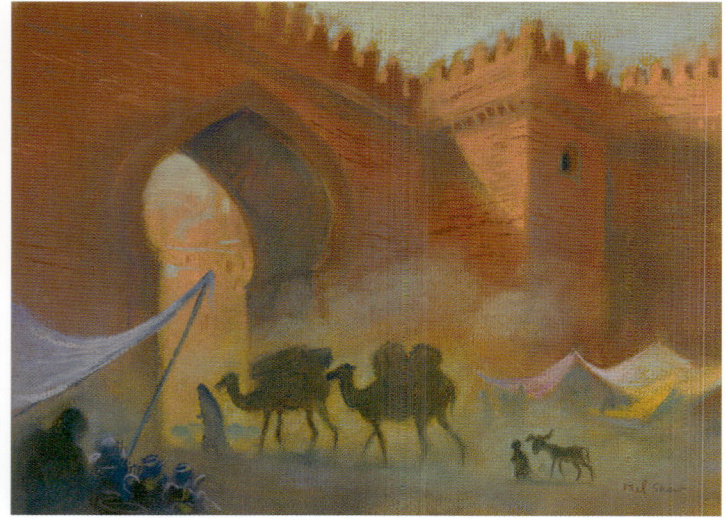
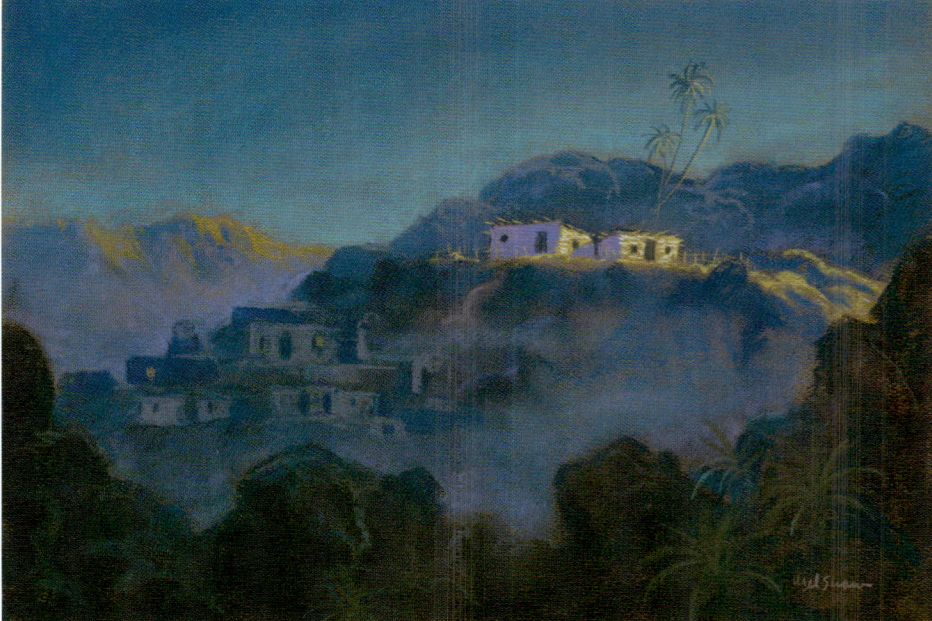

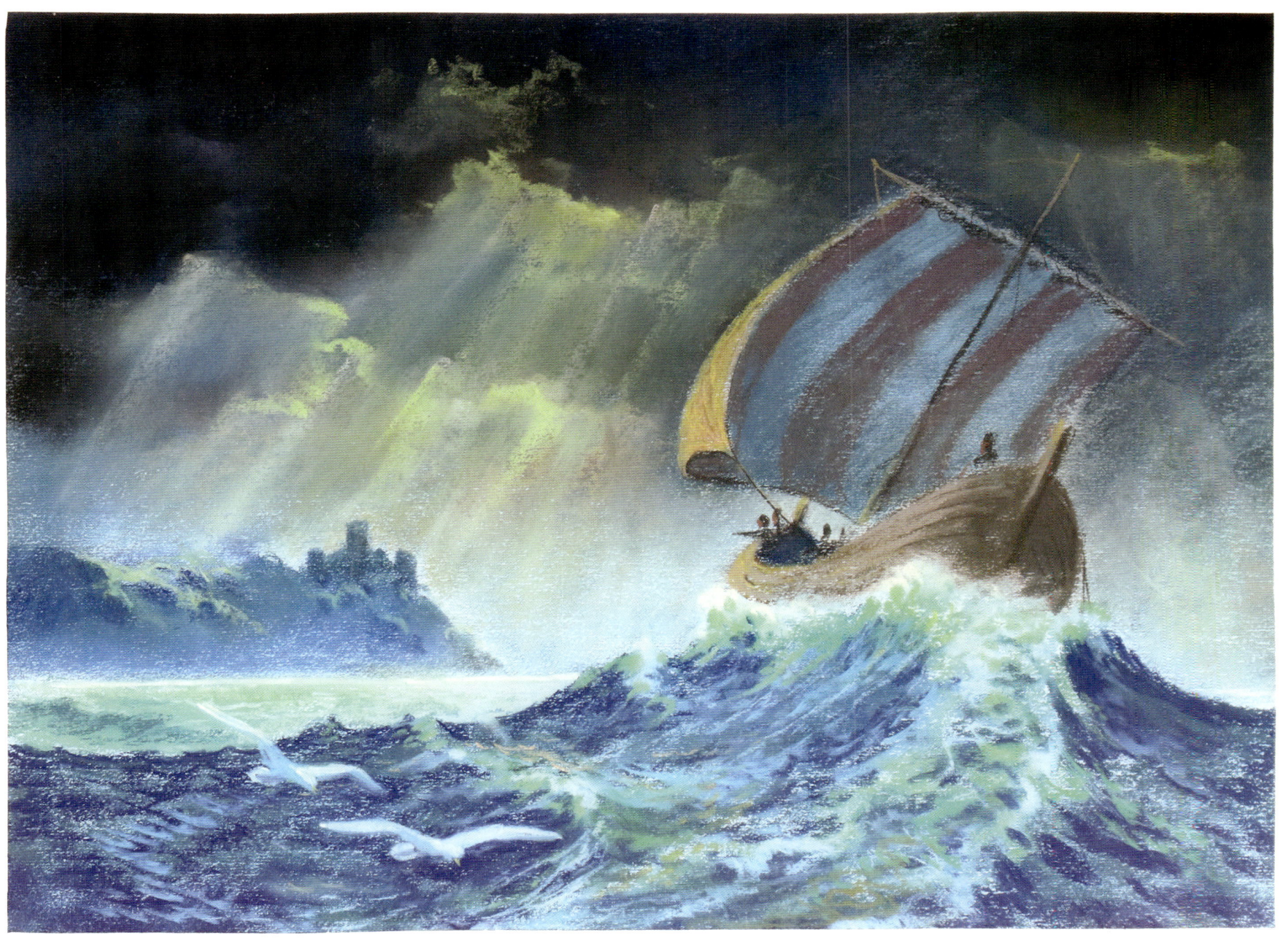

ABOVE: Concept sketch for *The Hero From Otherwhere*.
Courtesy: Rick Shaw and Melissa Couch-Deranleau.

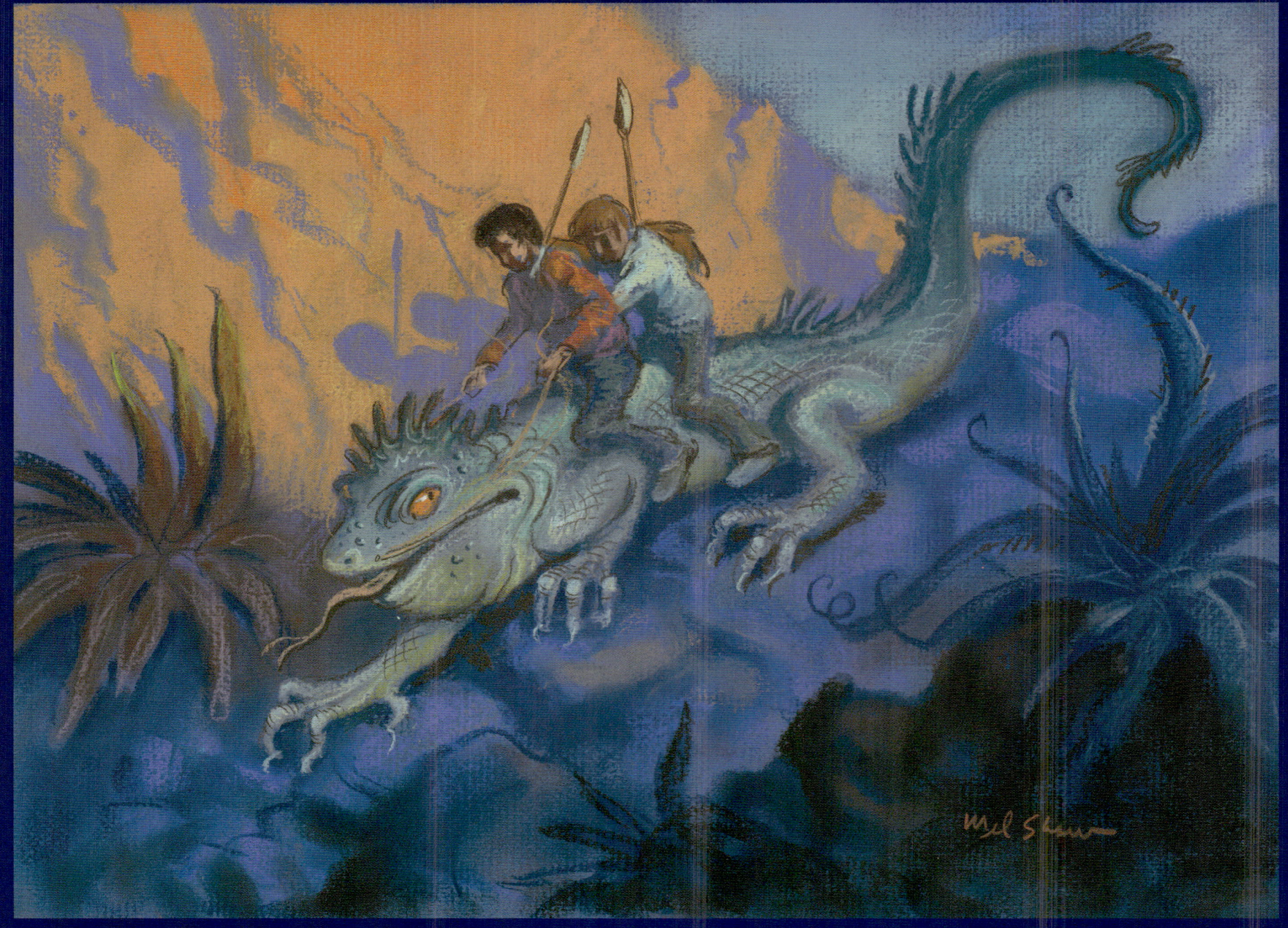

ABOVE AND OPPOSITE: Concept sketches for *The Hero From Otherwhere*.

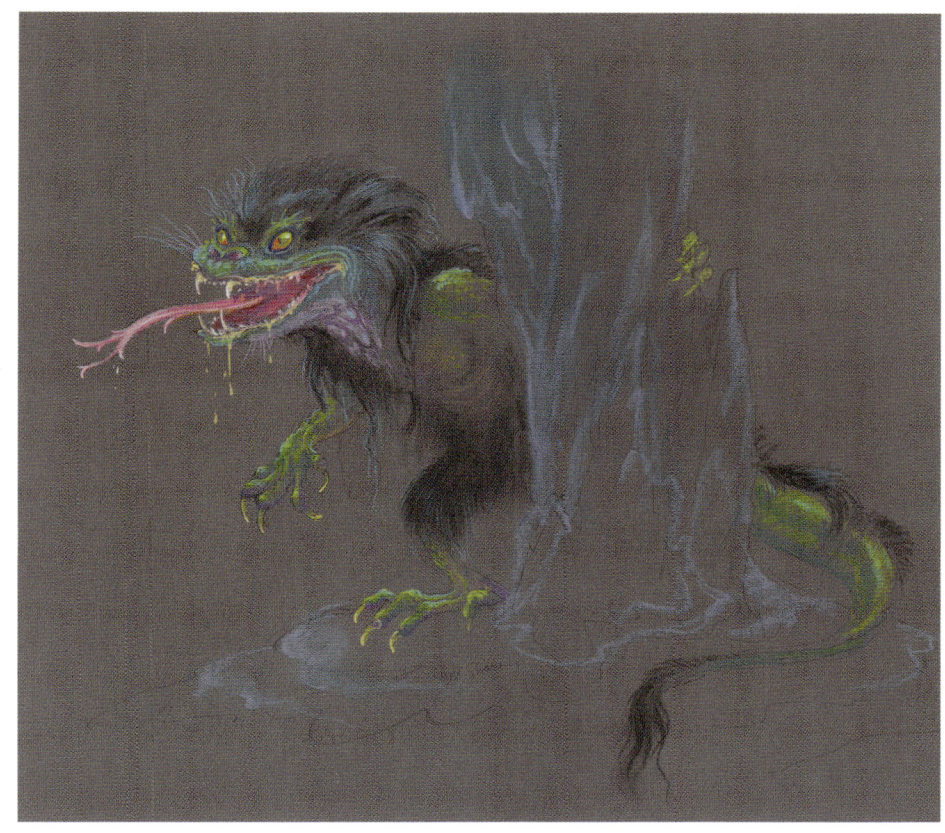
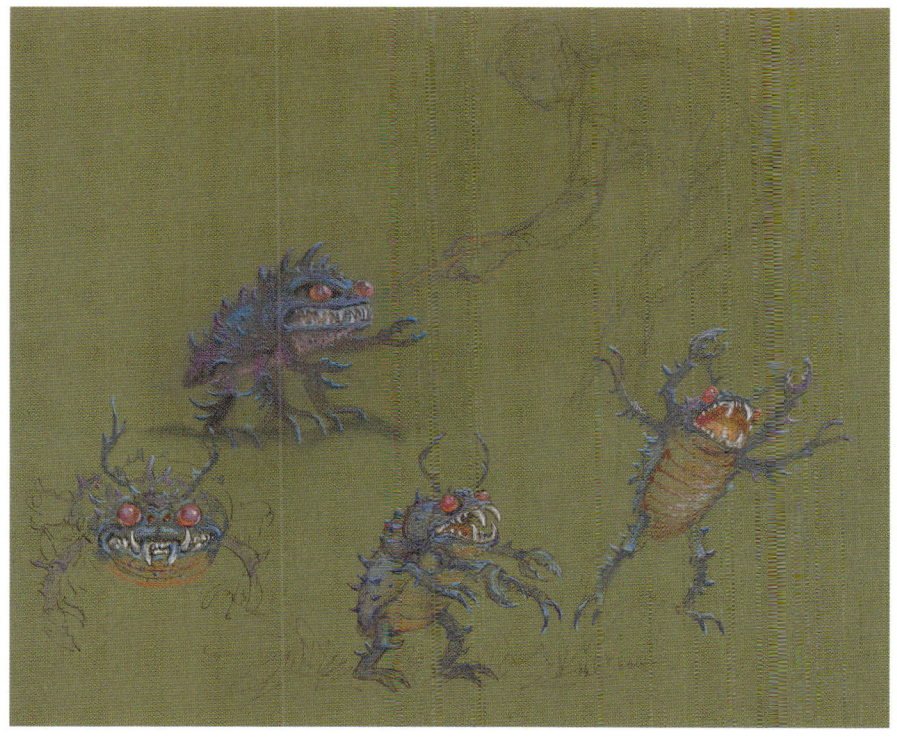
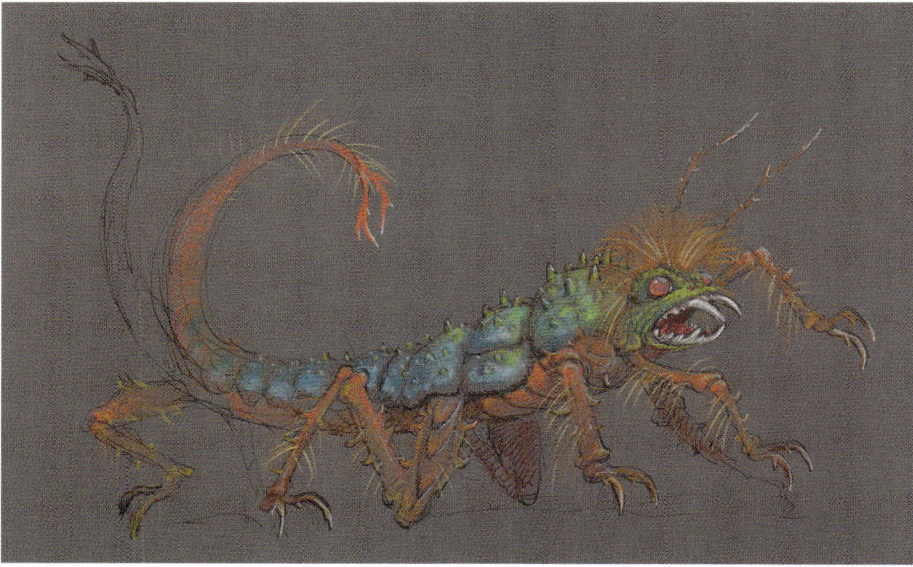

MEL SHAW 165

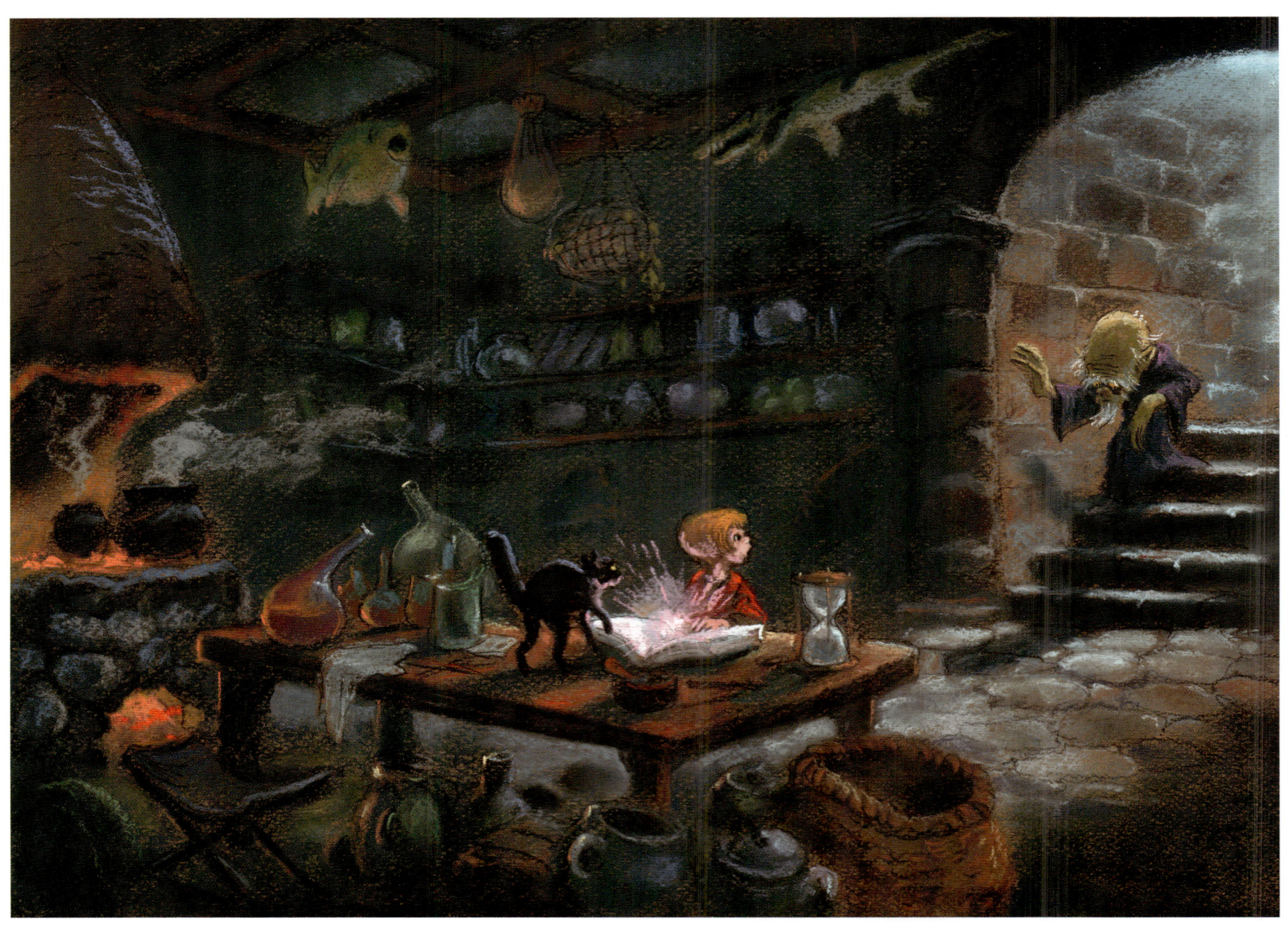

ABOVE: Concept sketch for *The Little Broomstick*.
Courtesy: Bruce Reitherman.

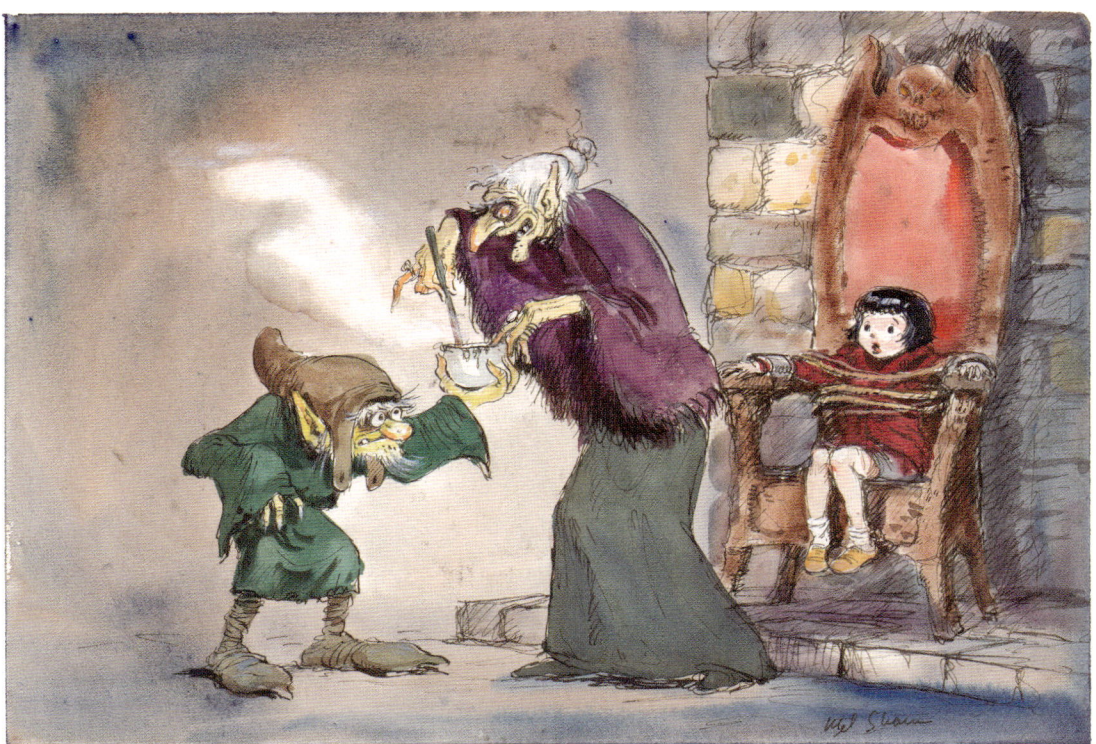
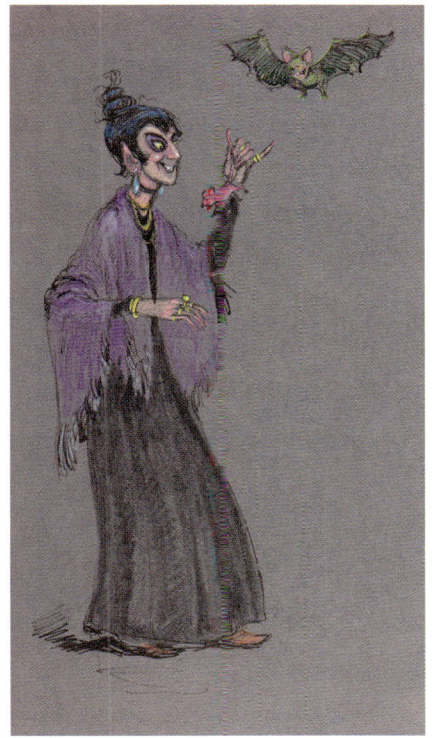
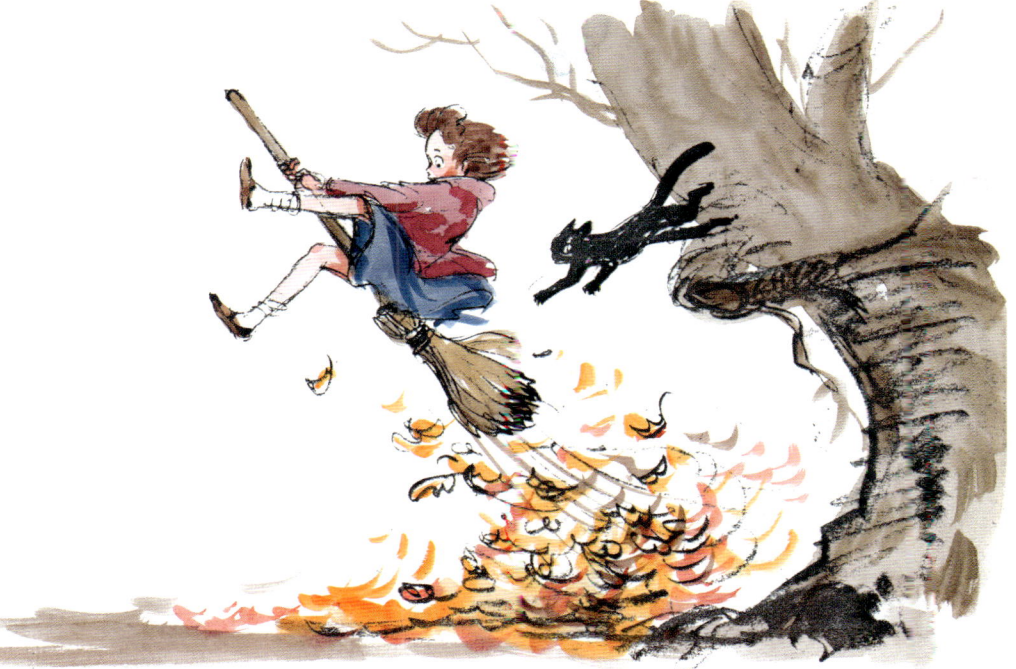

ABOVE AND PAGE 168: Concept sketches for *The Little Broomstick*.

MEL SHAW **167**

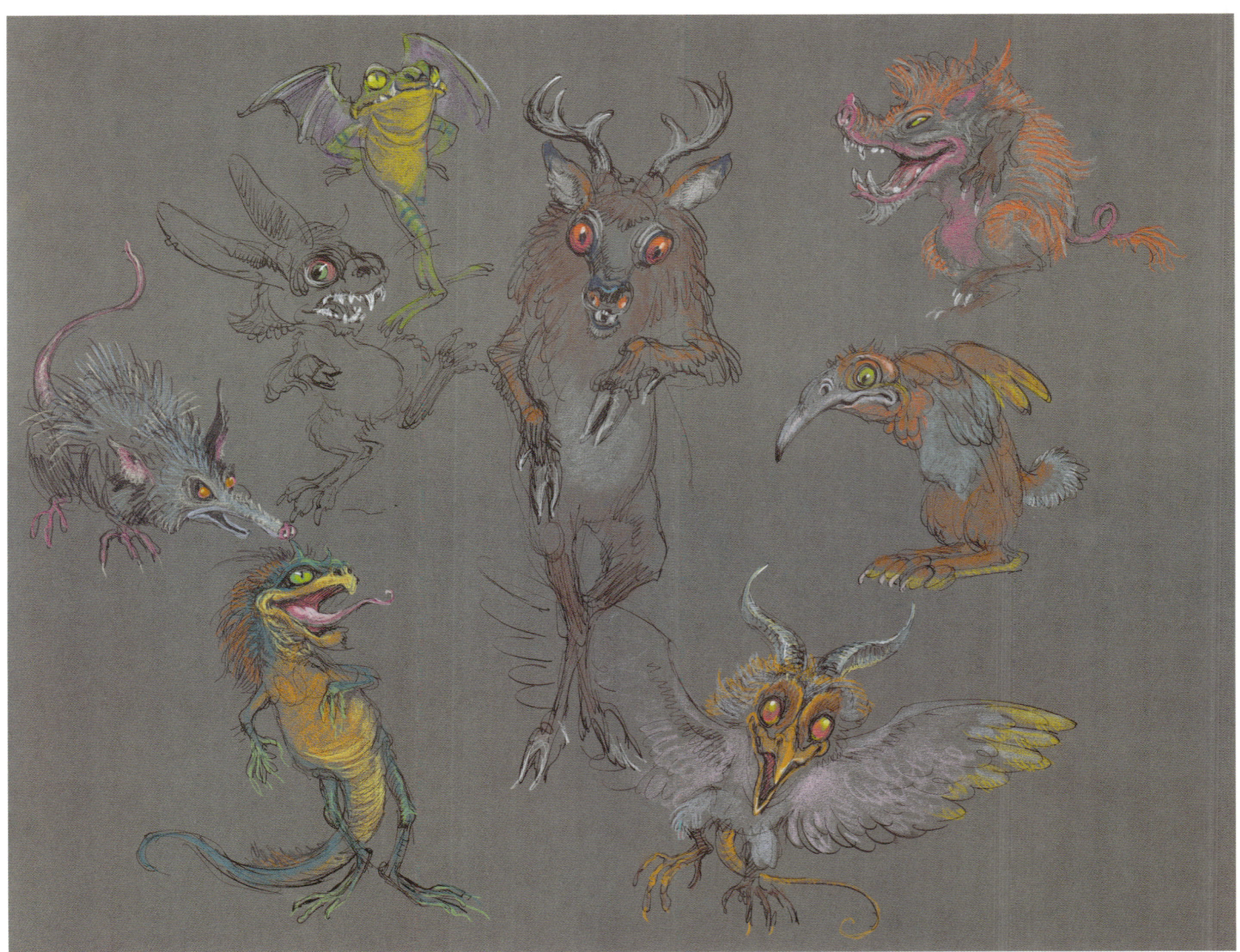

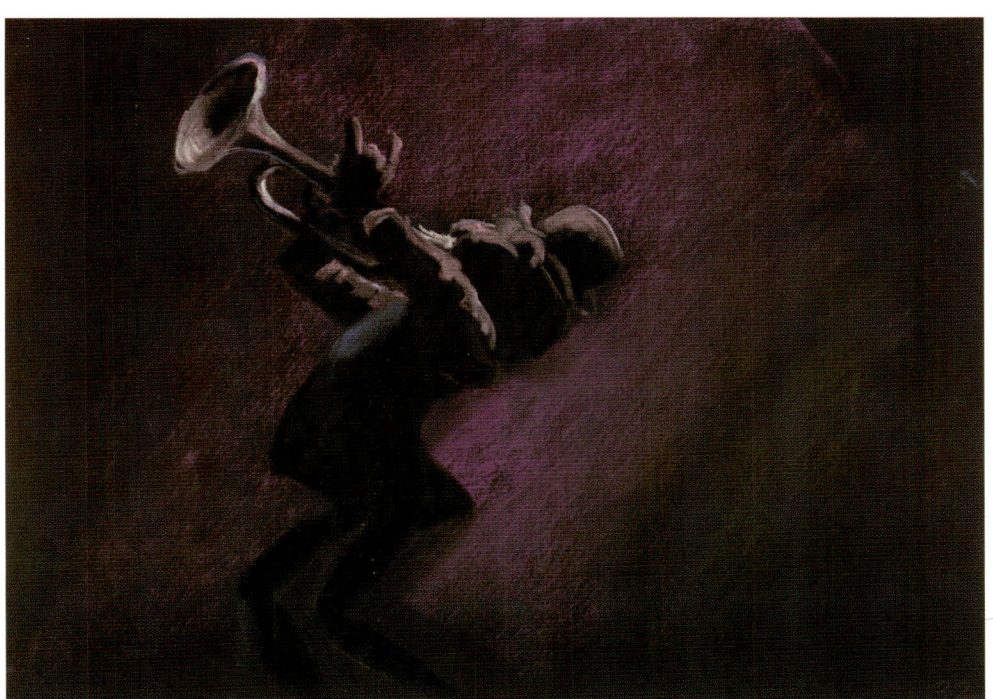
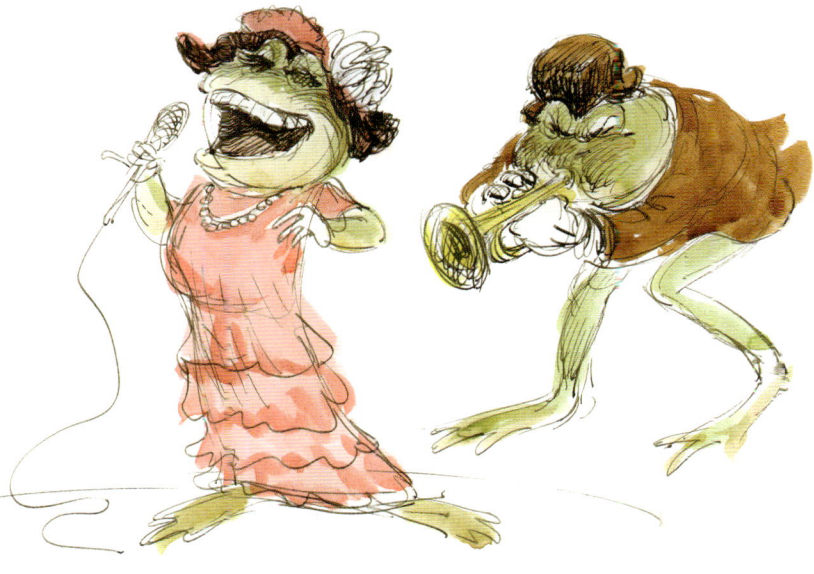
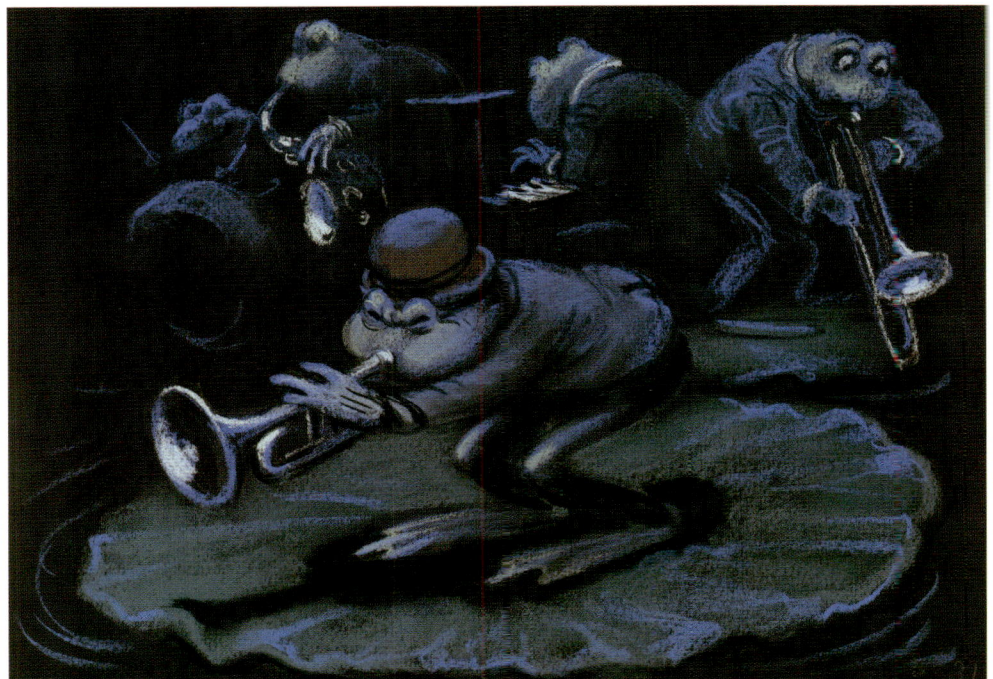

ABOVE: Concept sketches for the Louis Armstrong and Ella Fitzgerald sequence of the proposed feature *Musicana*.

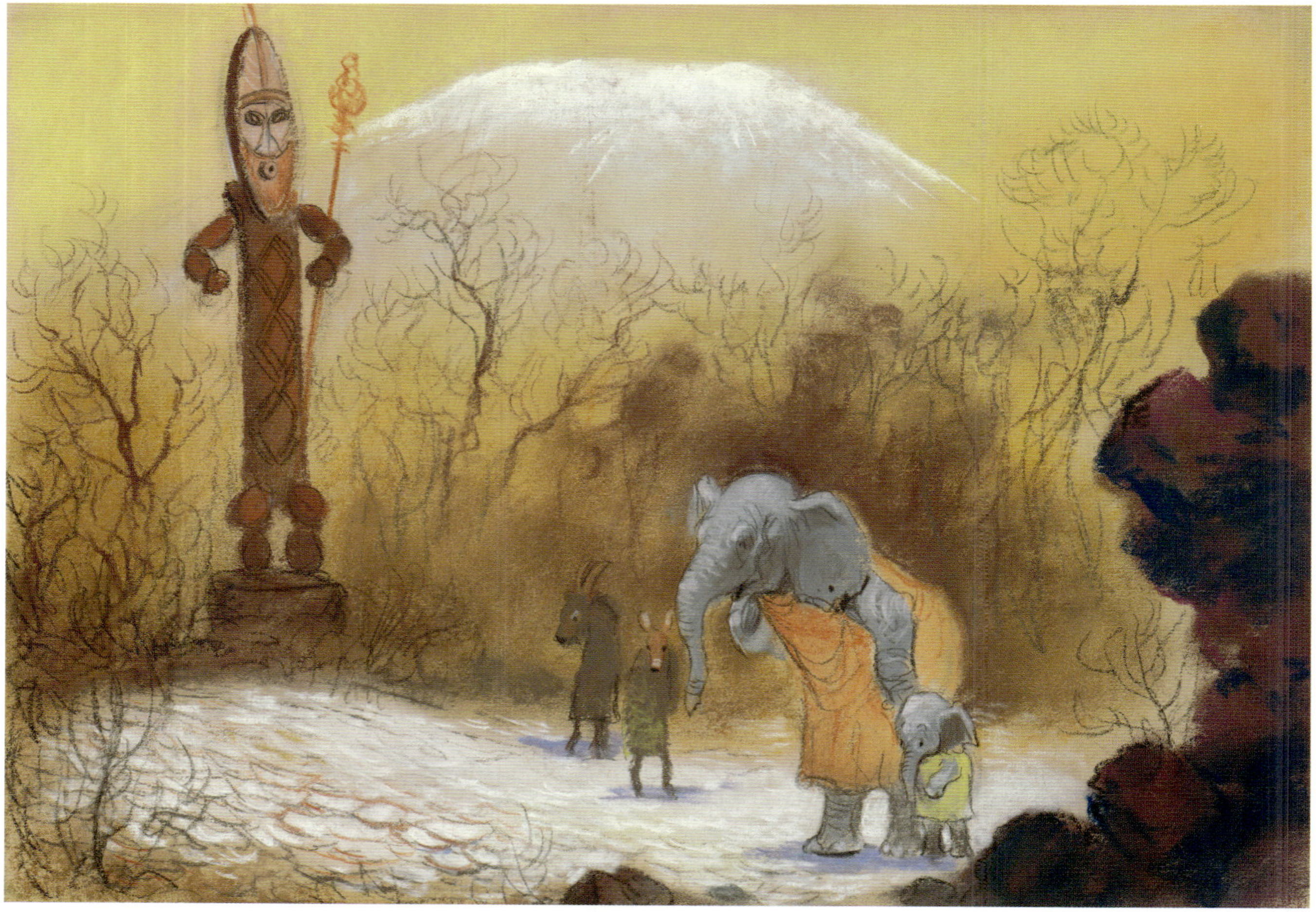

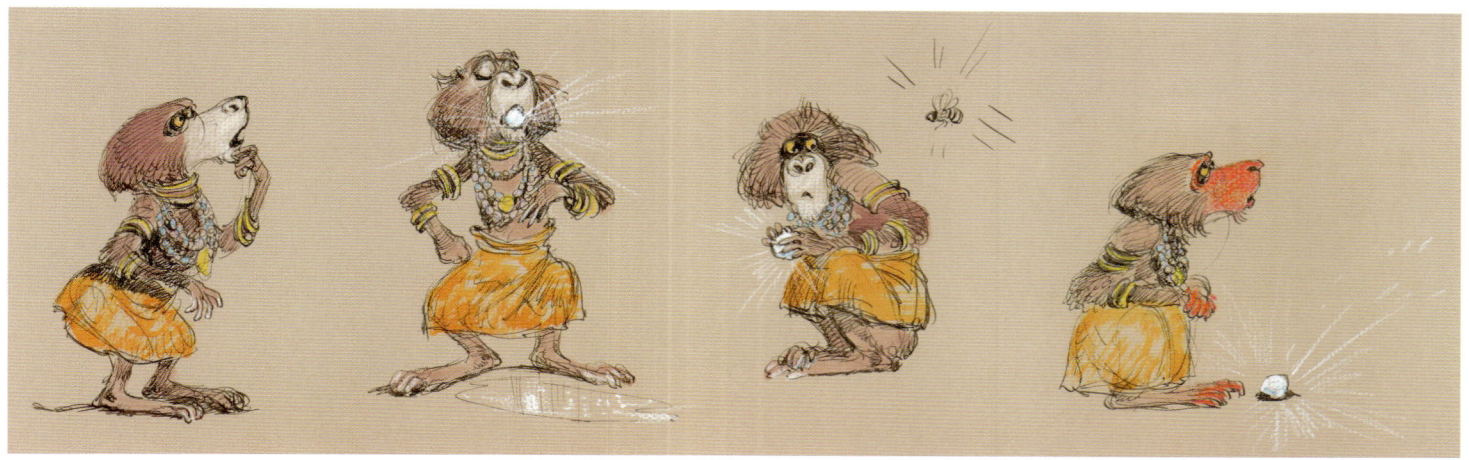

ABOVE AND OPPOSITE: Concept sketches for the rain god sequence of *Musicana*.

170 THEY DREW AS THEY PLEASED

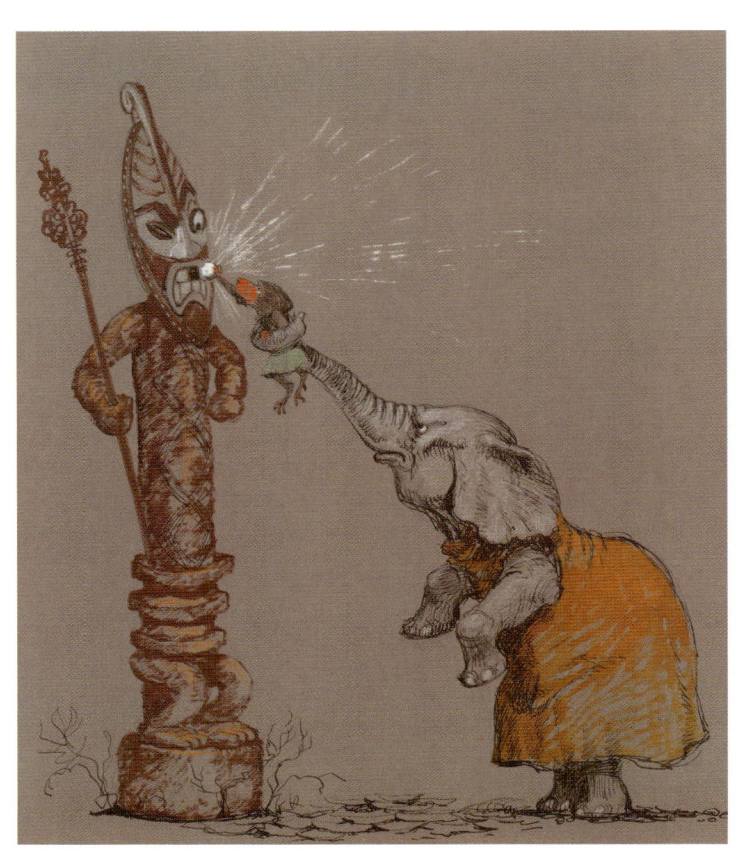

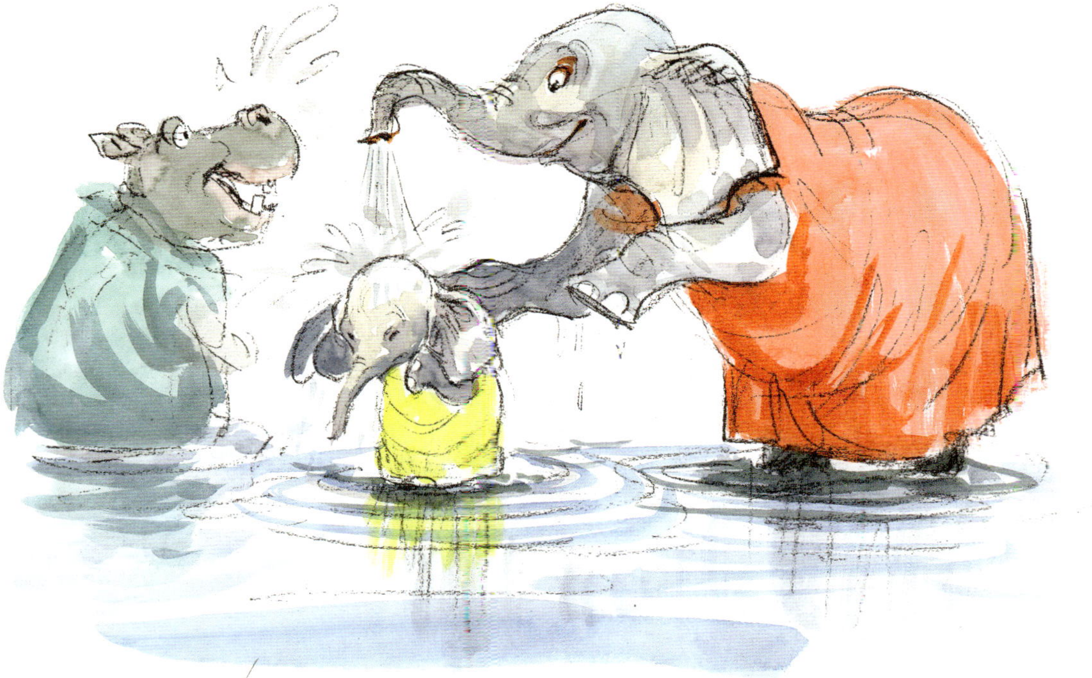

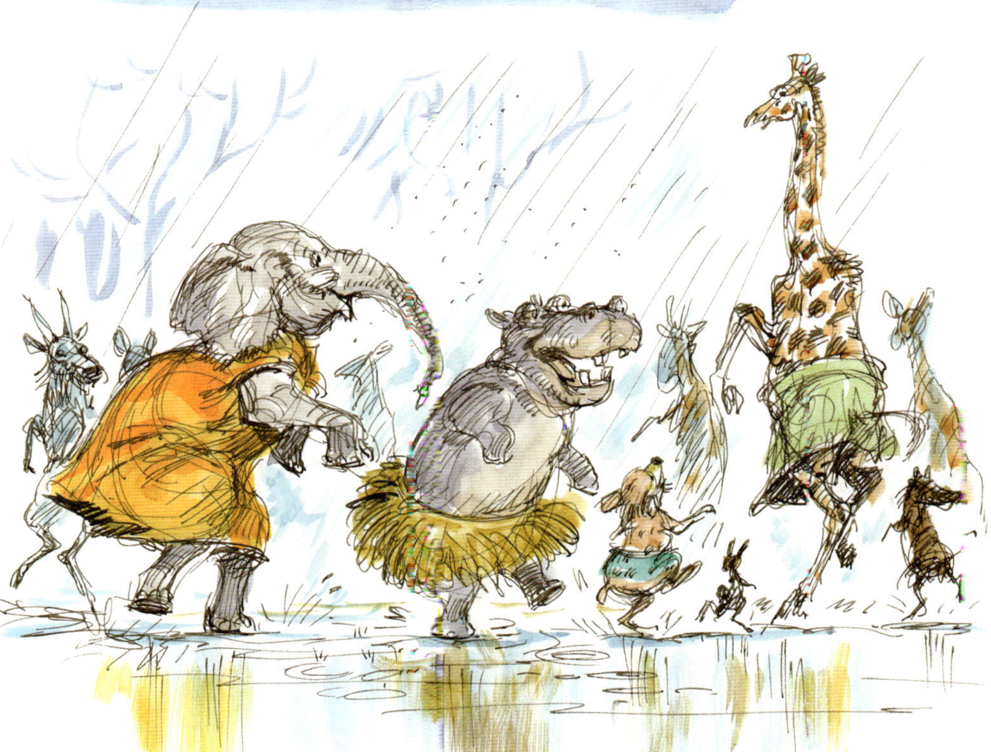

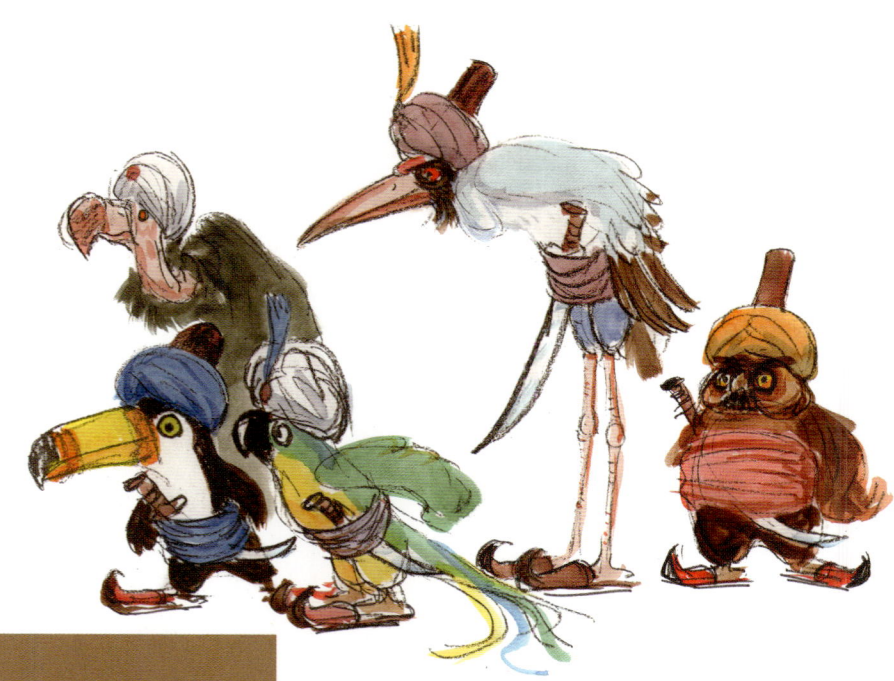

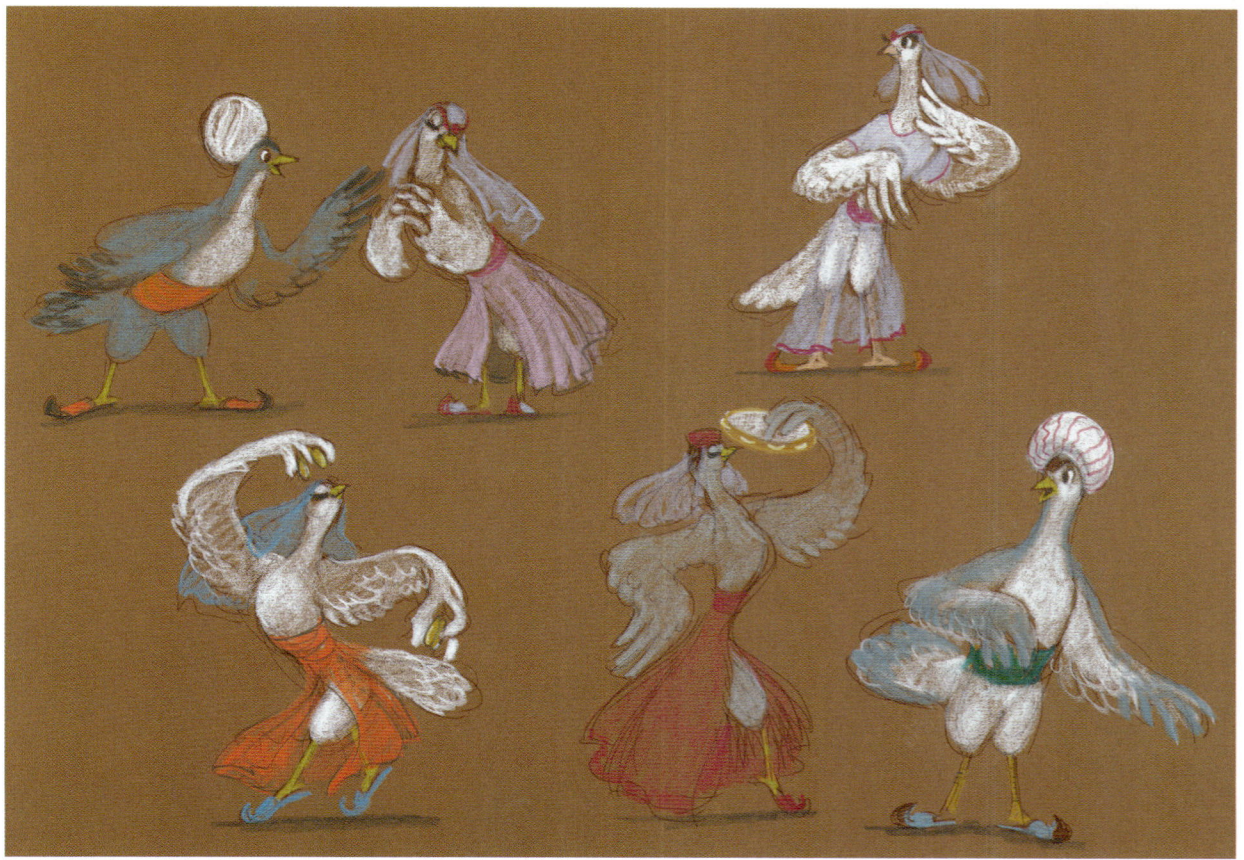

LEFT: Character designs for the Ali Baba with birds sequence of *Musicana*.

TOP: Courtesy: Rick Shaw and Melissa Couch-Deranleau.

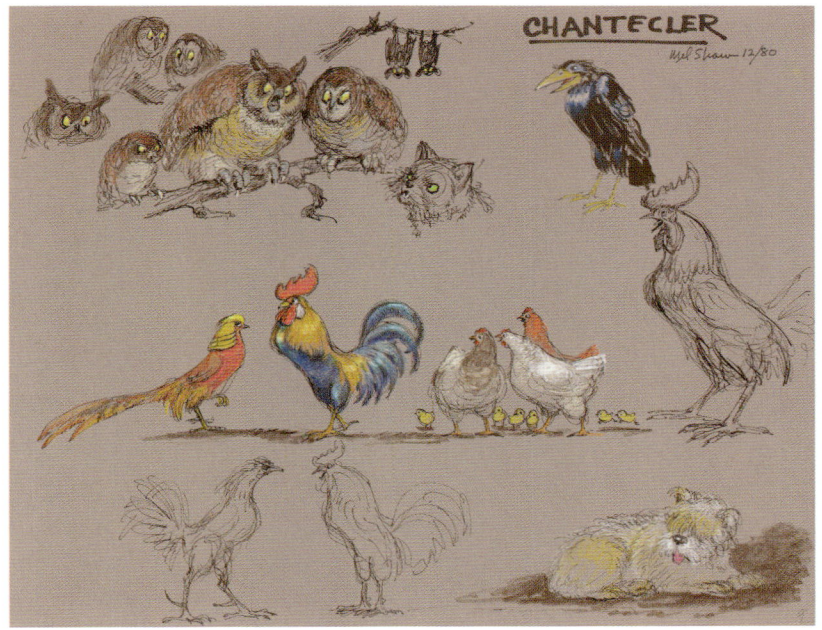
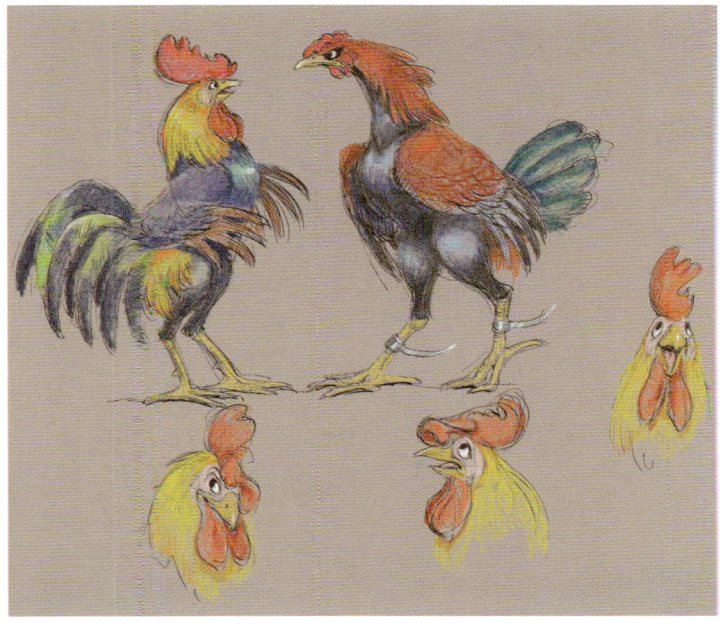
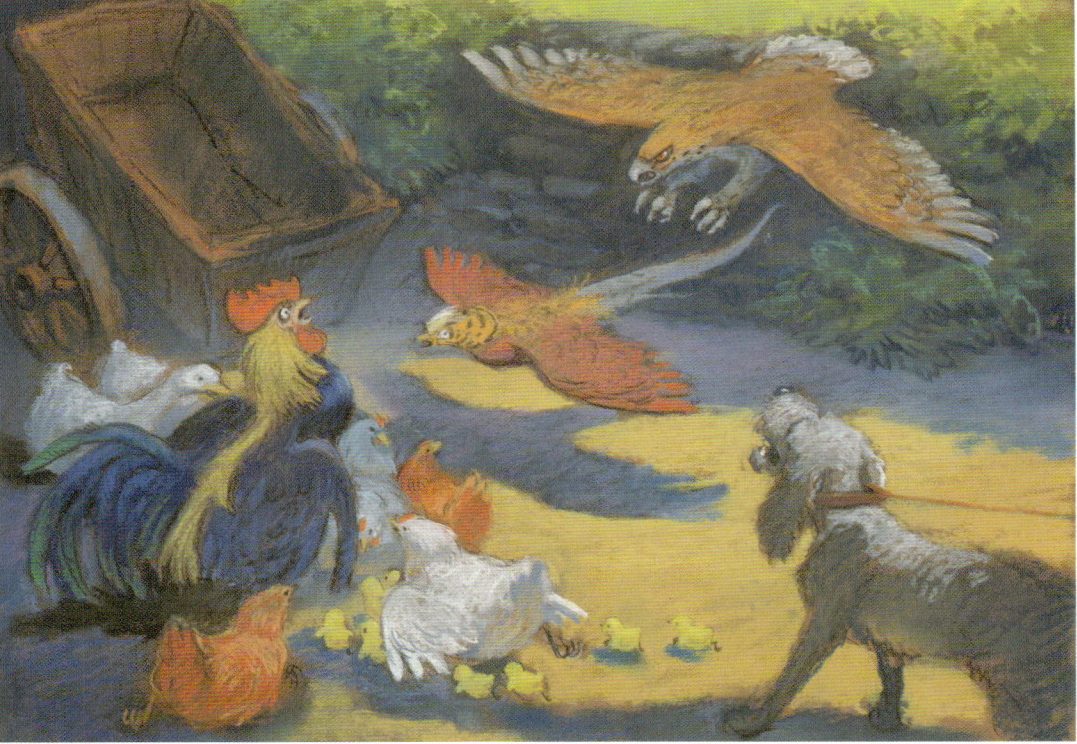

TOP AND RIGHT: Character designs for the abandoned project *Chanticleer*.

LEFT: Concept sketch for the abandoned project *Chanticleer*.

MEL SHAW

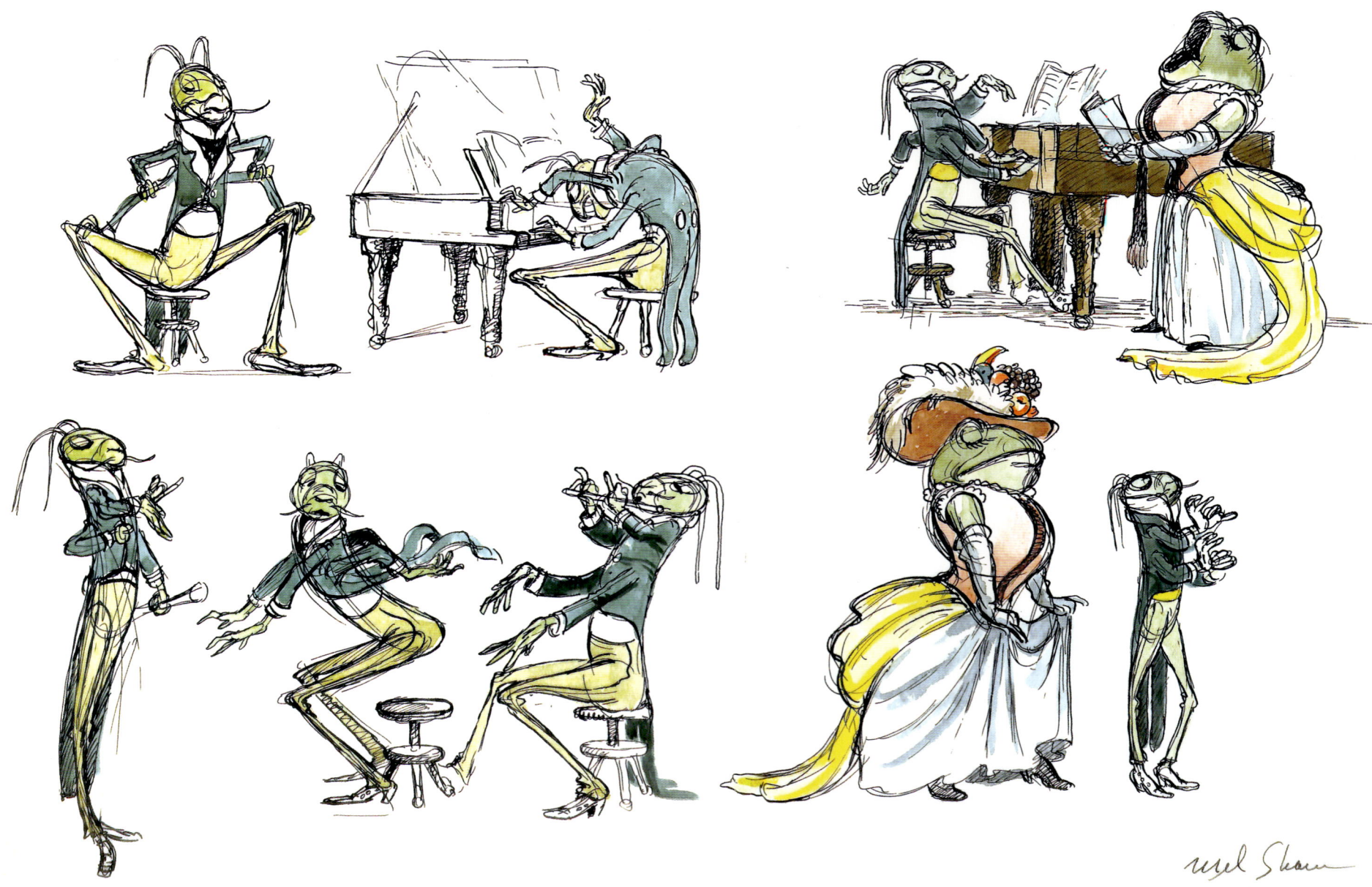

ABOVE: Character designs for some of the incidental characters in the abandoned project *Chanticleer*. Courtesy: Rick Shaw and Melissa Couch-Deranleau.

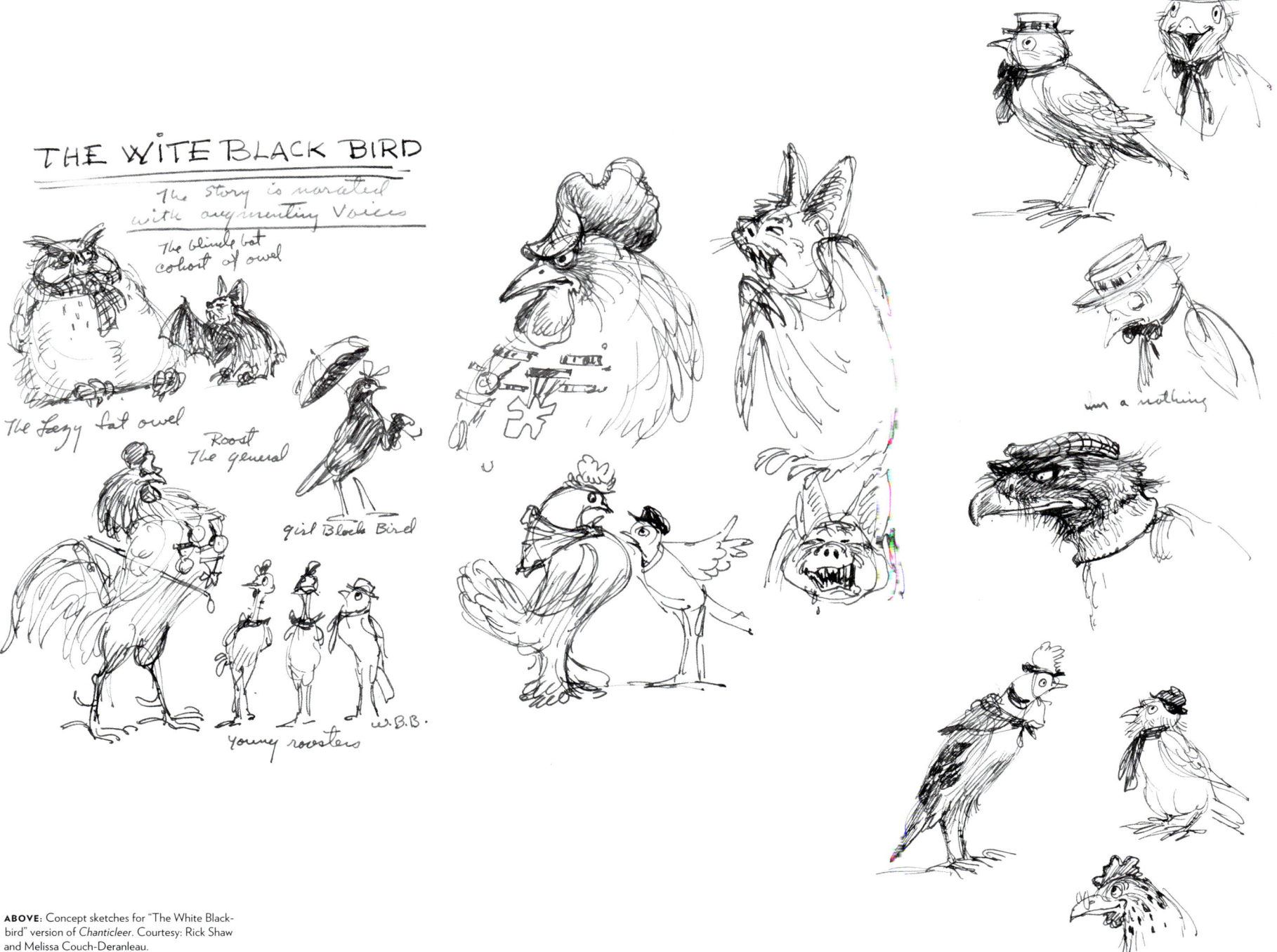

ABOVE: Concept sketches for "The White Blackbird" version of *Chanticleer*. Courtesy: Rick Shaw and Melissa Couch-Deranleau.

MEL SHAW 175

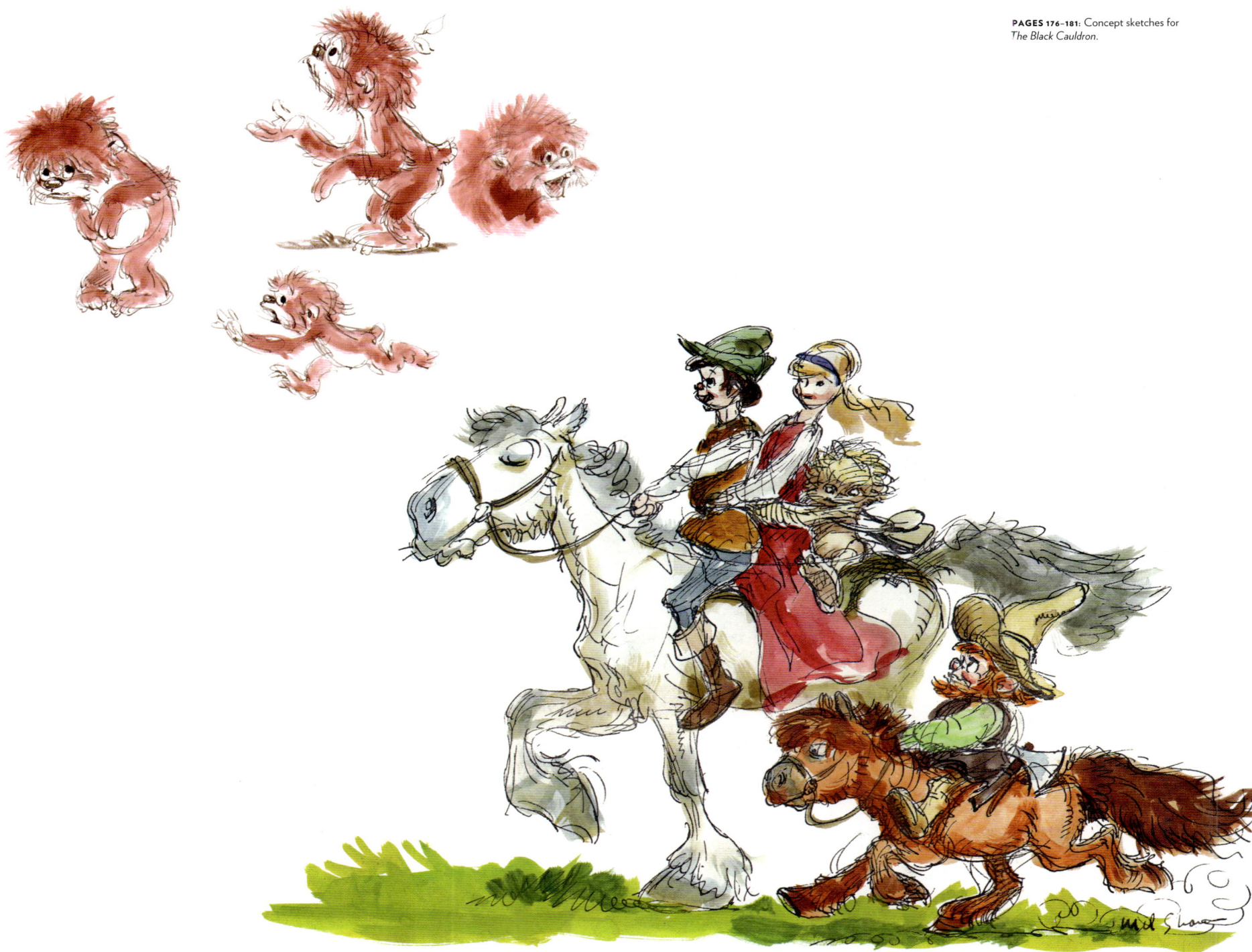

PAGES 176–181: Concept sketches for *The Black Cauldron*.

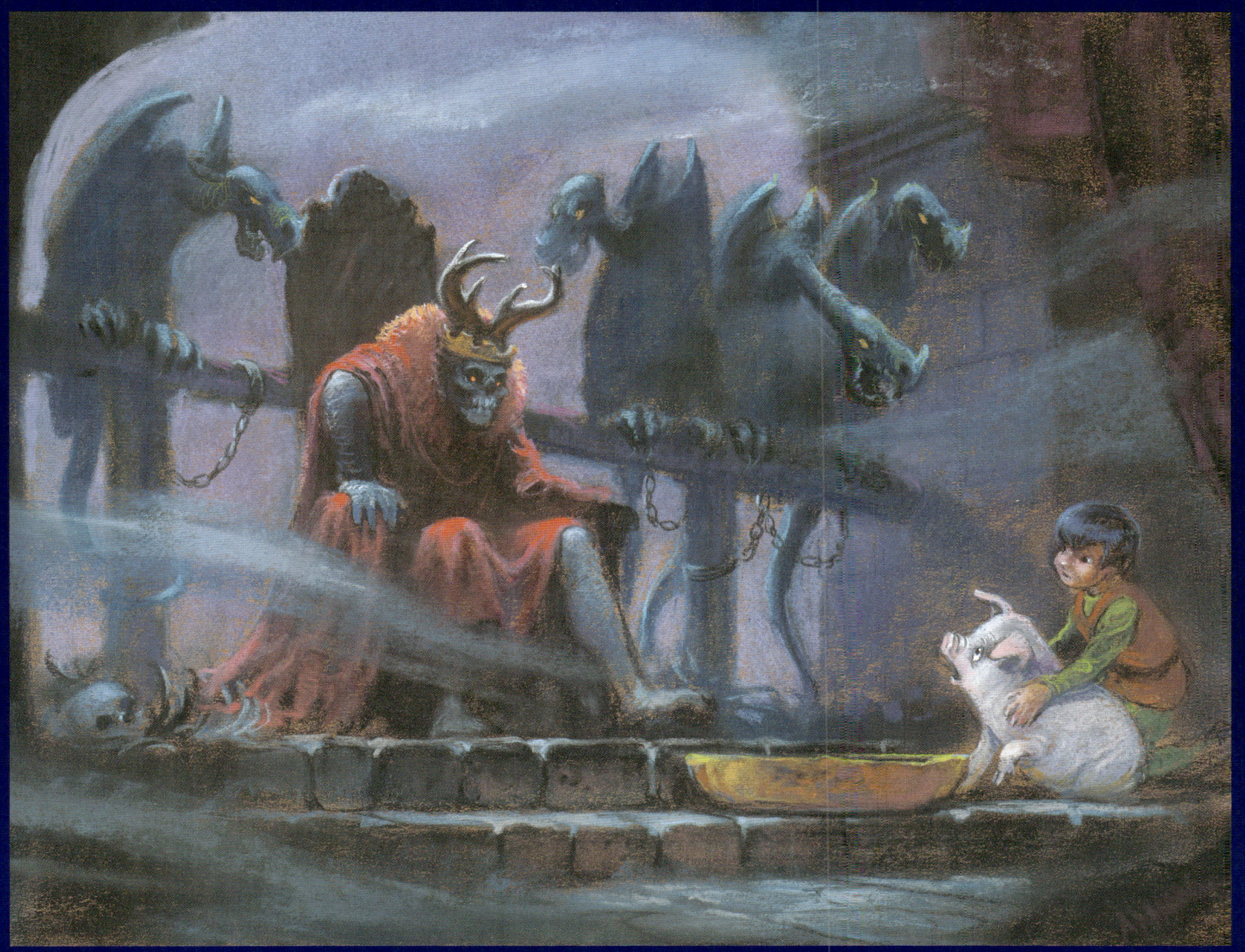

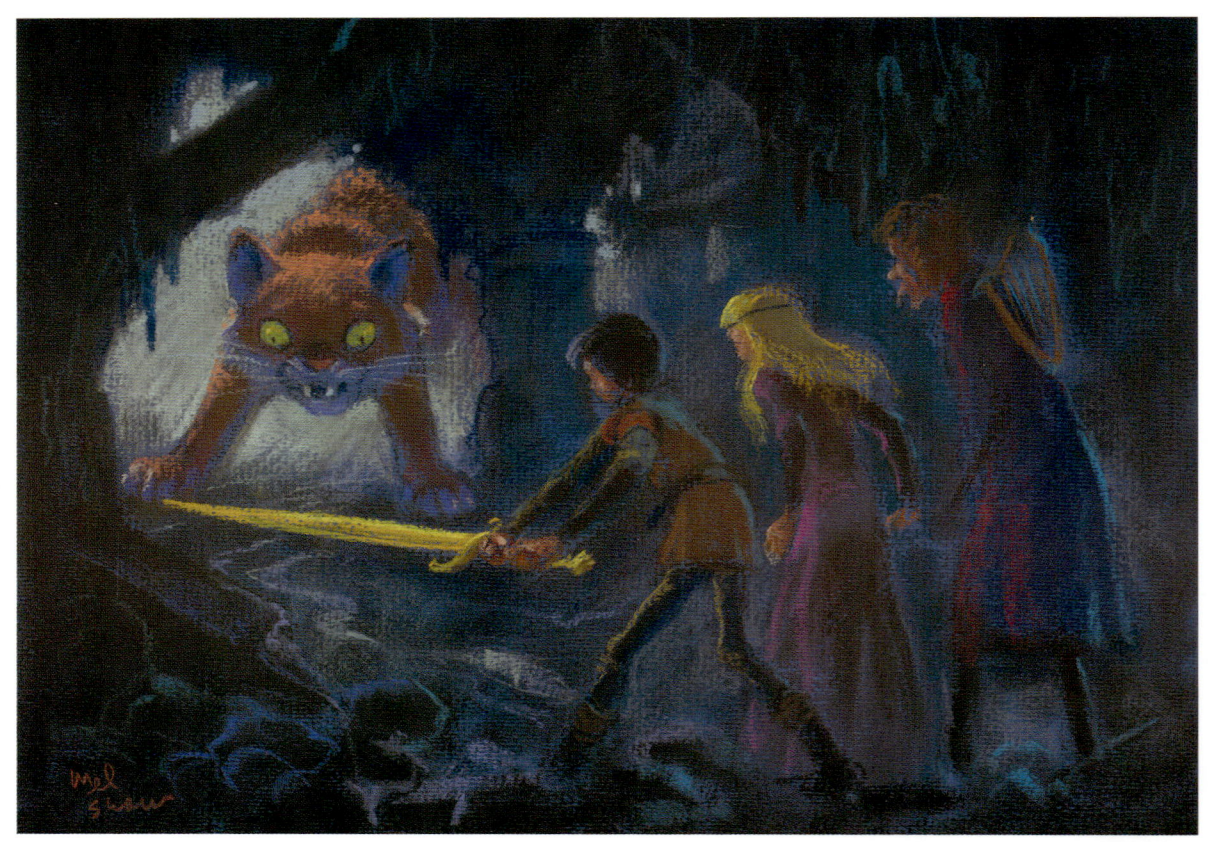
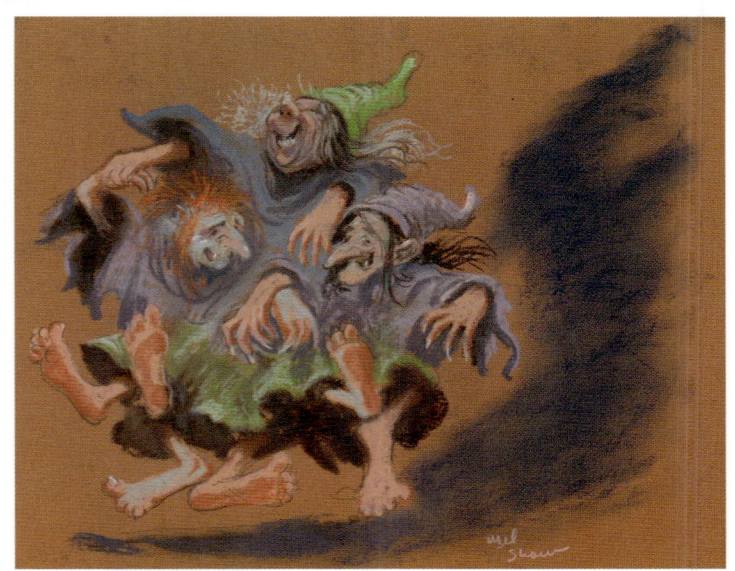

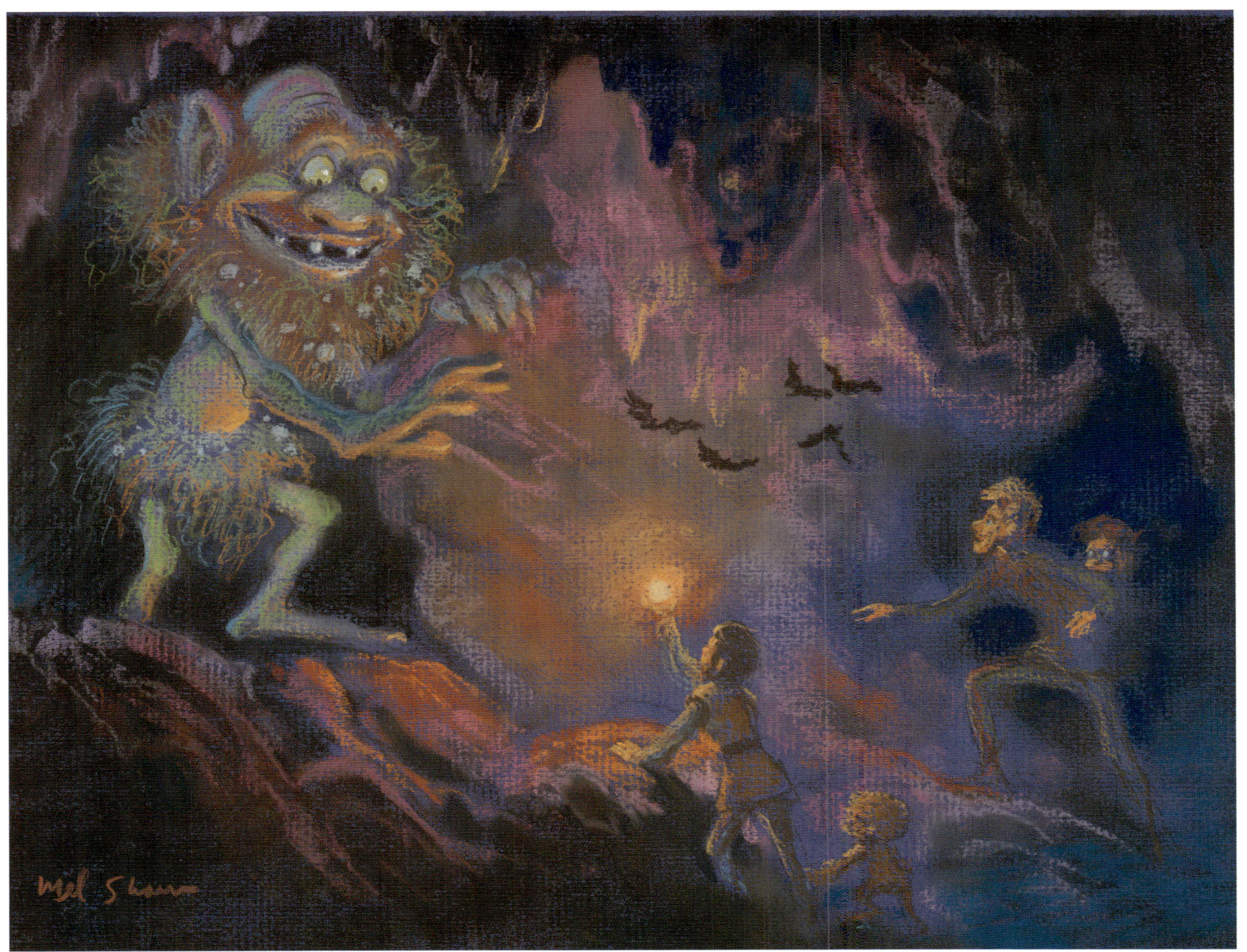

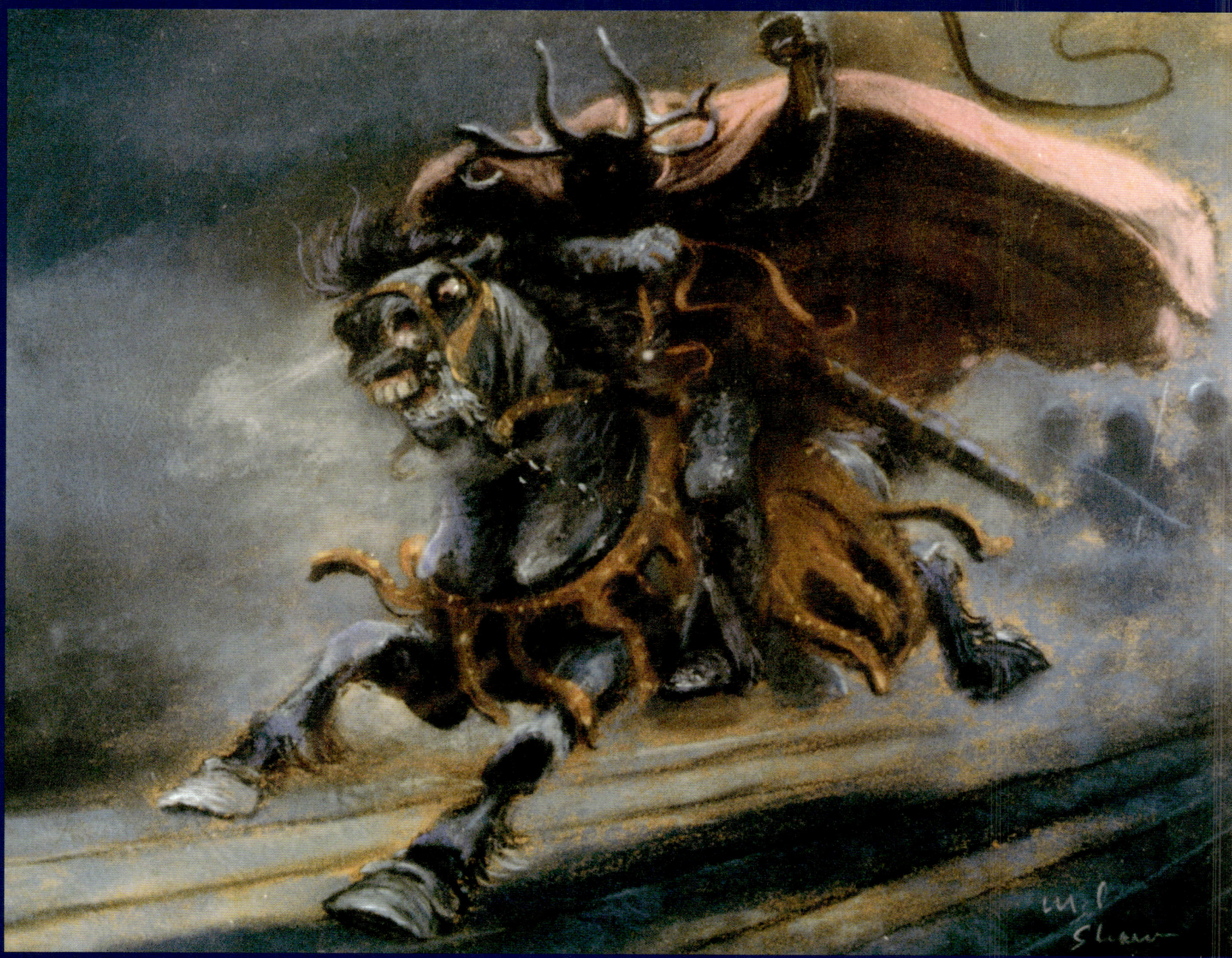

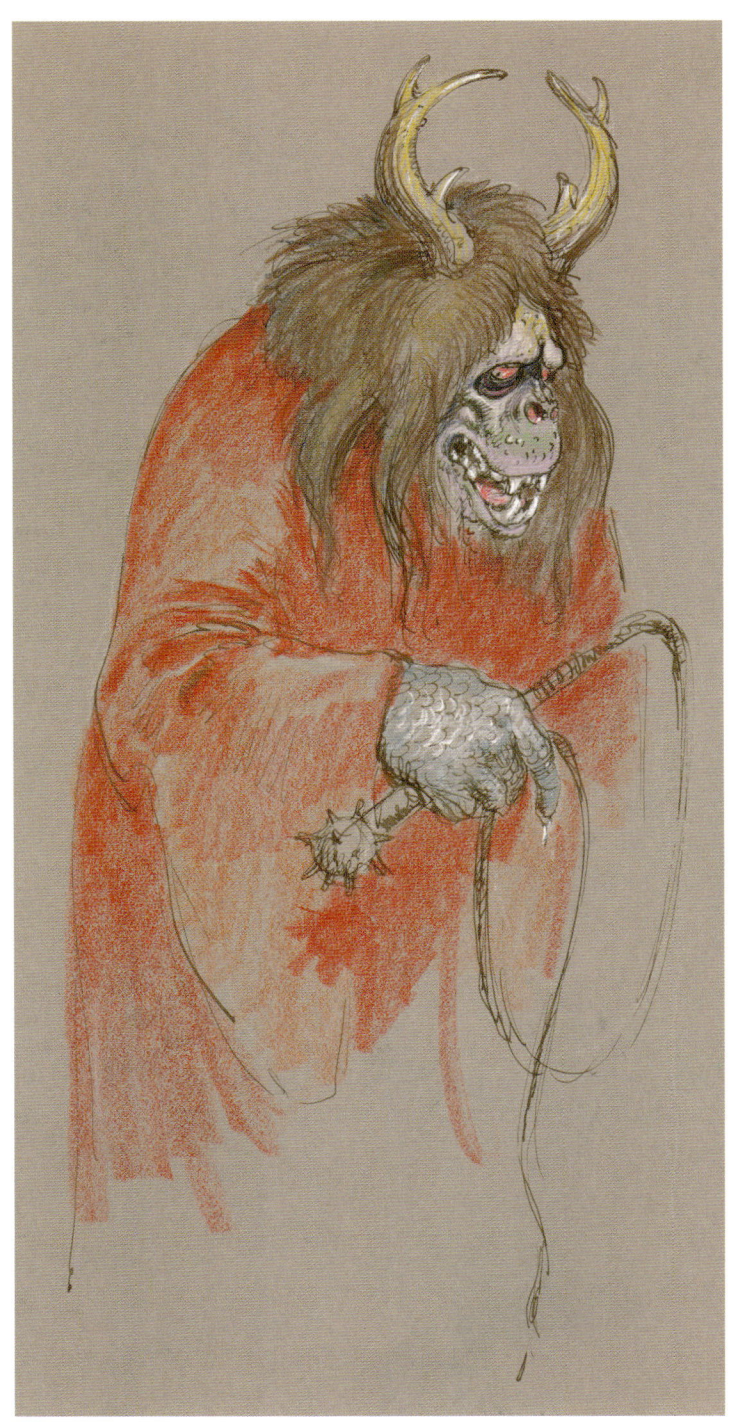
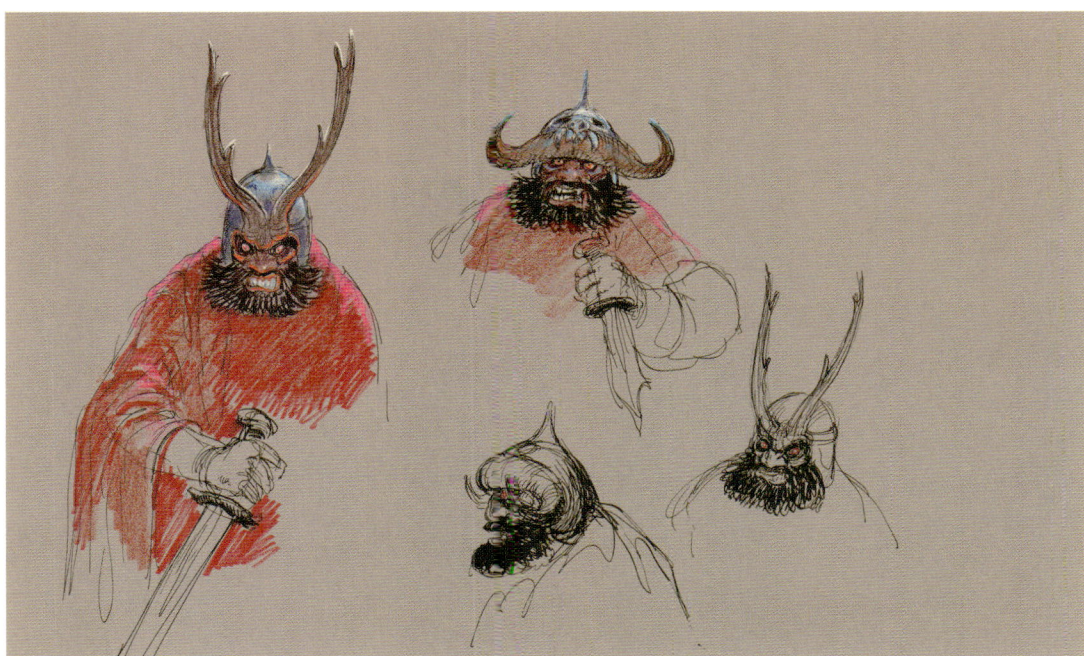
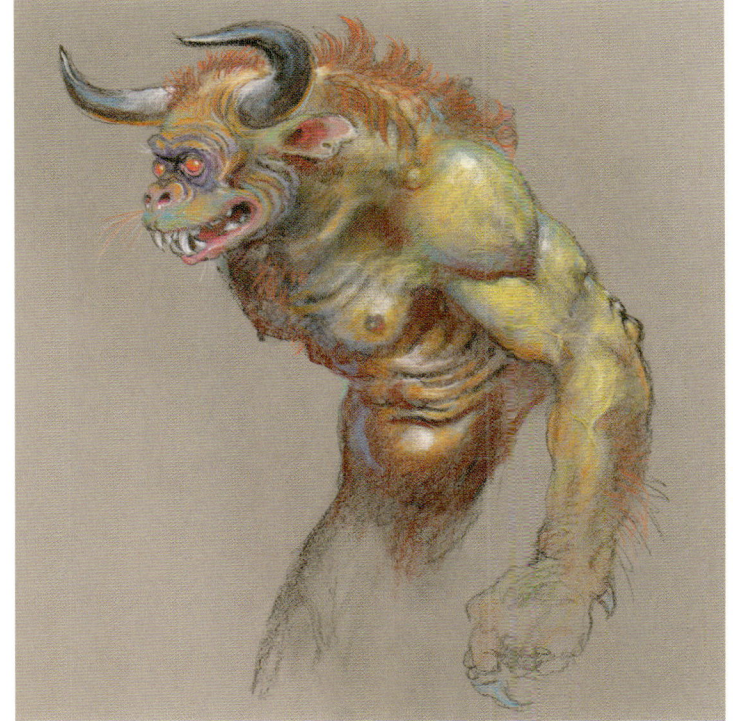

MEL SHAW

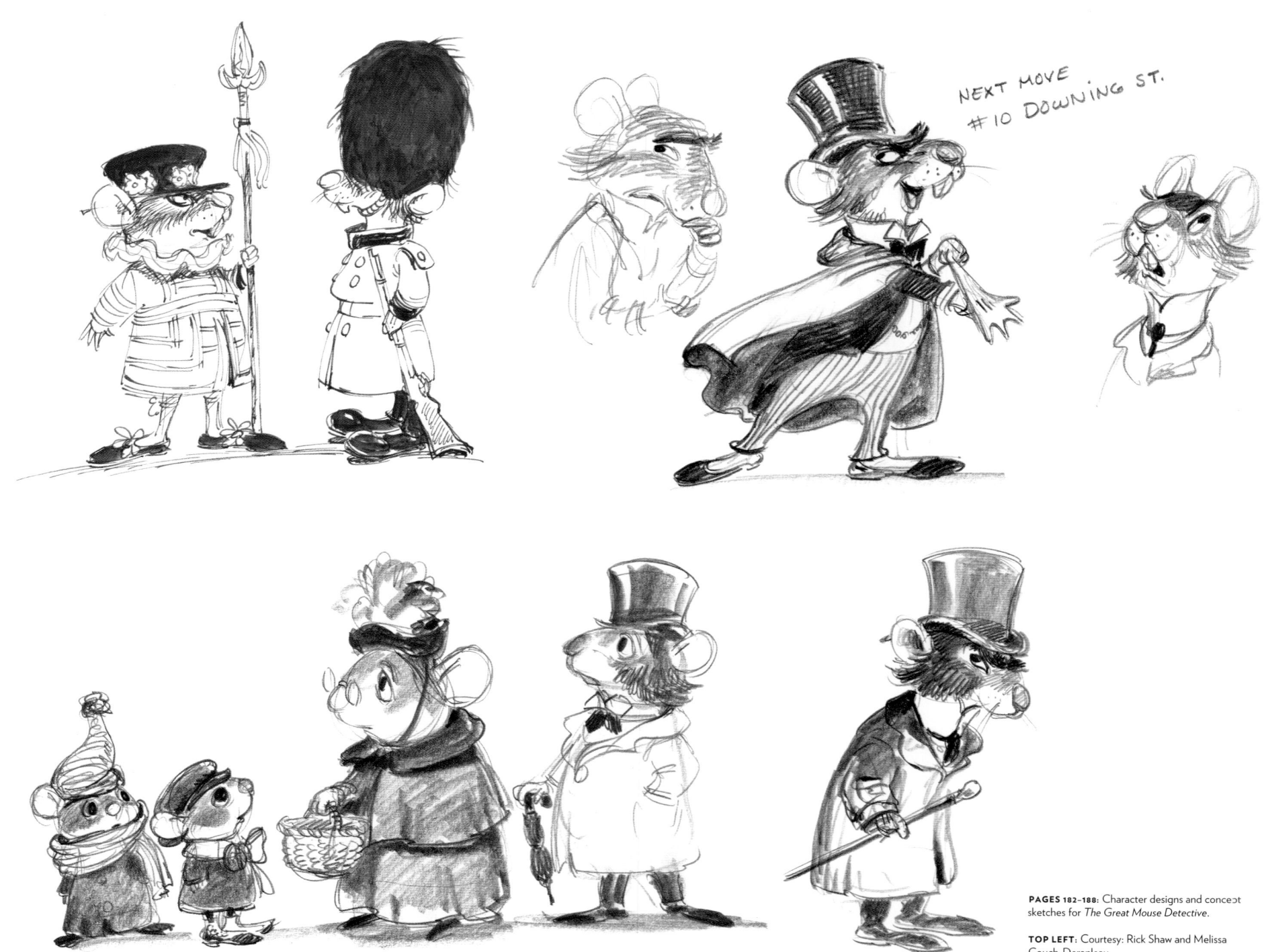

PAGES 182–188: Character designs and concept sketches for *The Great Mouse Detective*.

TOP LEFT: Courtesy: Rick Shaw and Melissa Couch-Deranleau.

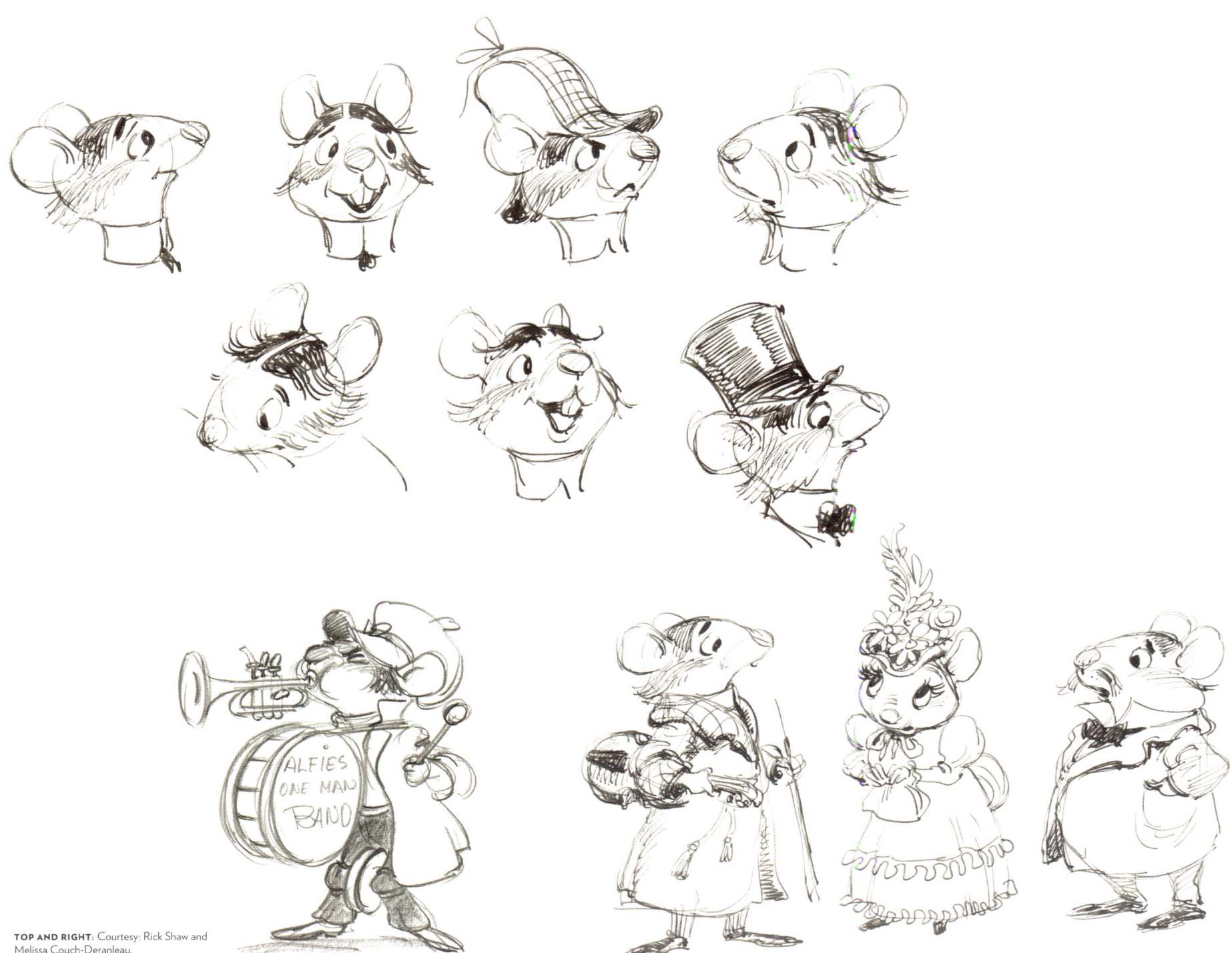

TOP AND RIGHT: Courtesy: Rick Shaw and Melissa Couch-Deranleau.

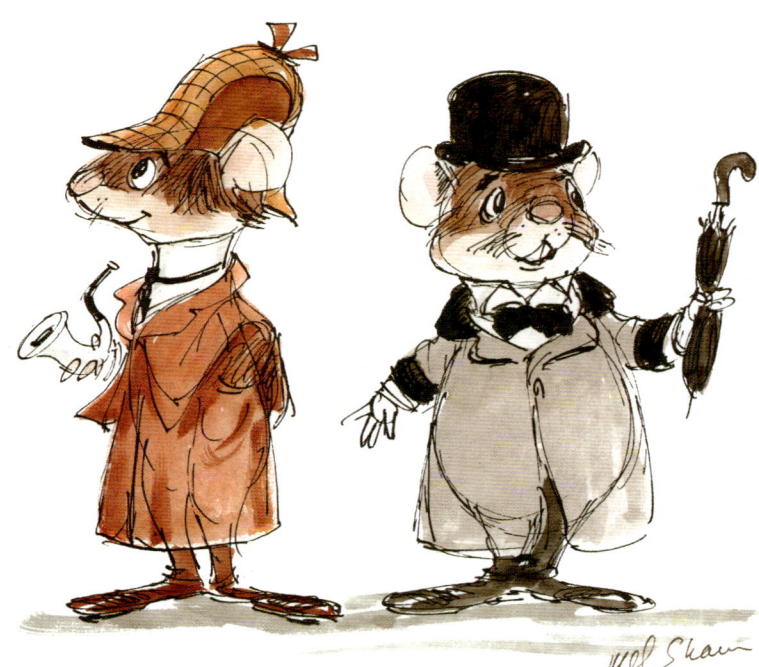
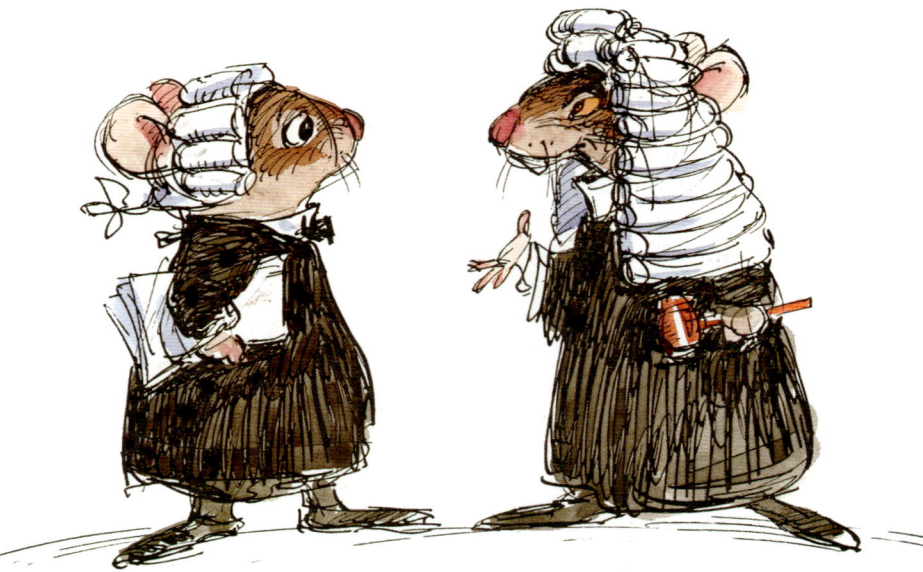
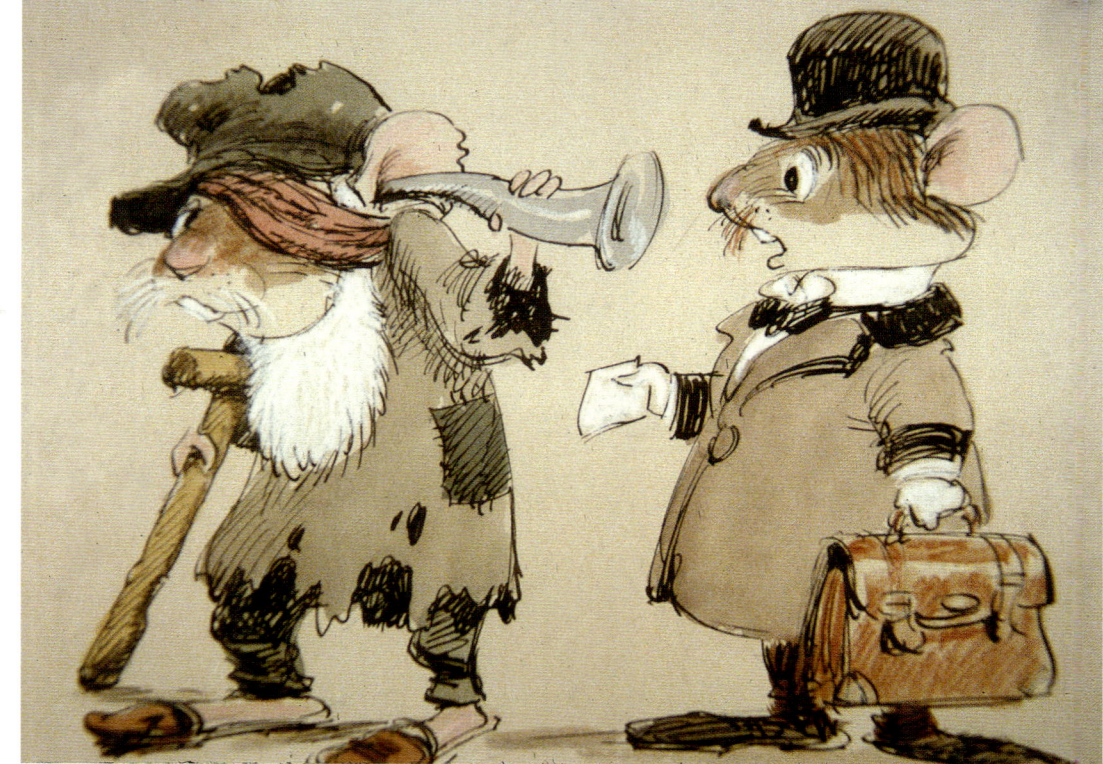

LEFT: Courtesy: Rick Shaw and Melissa Couch-Deranleau.

RIGHT: Courtesy: Burny Mattinson.

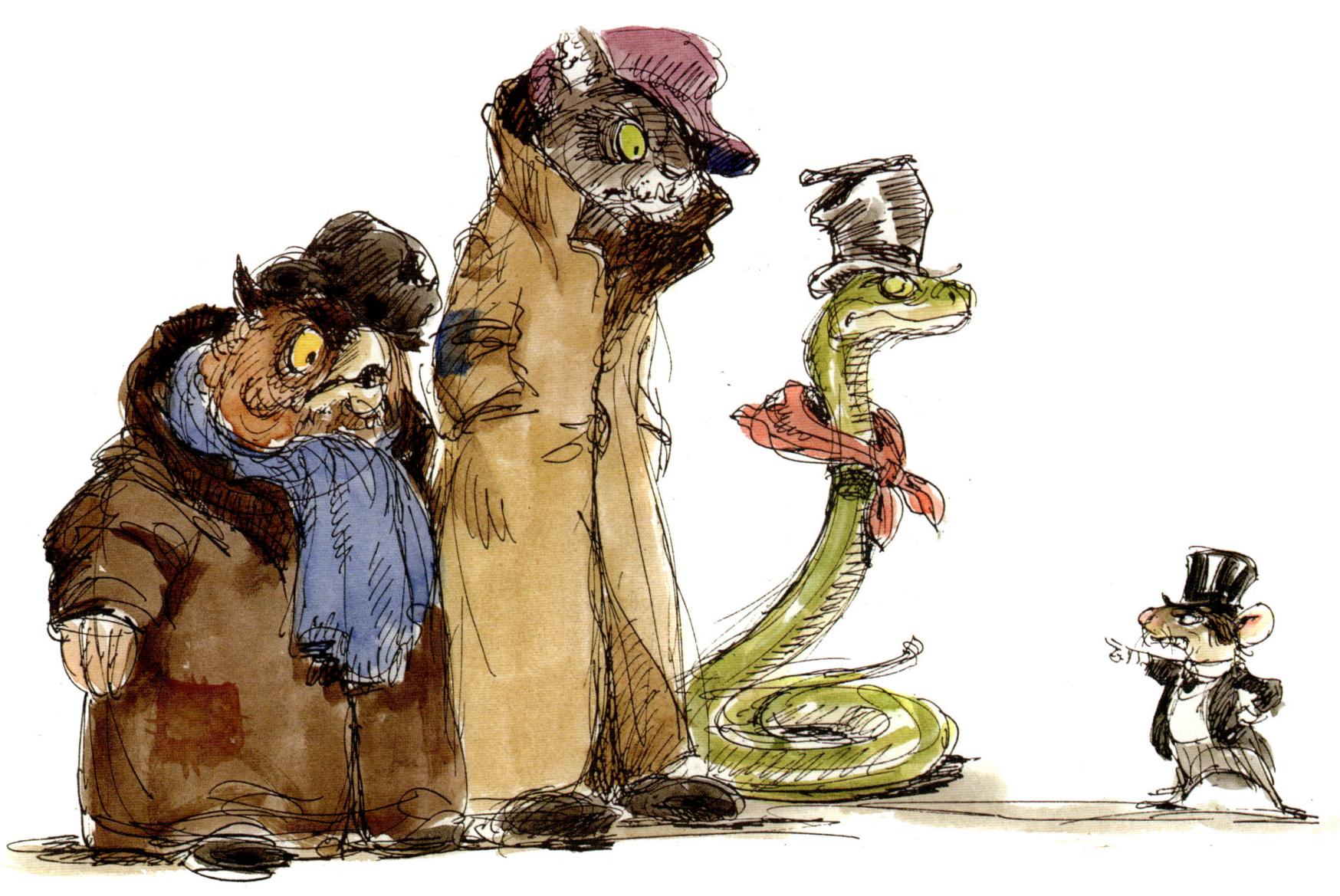

ABOVE: Courtesy: Philippe Cauvin.

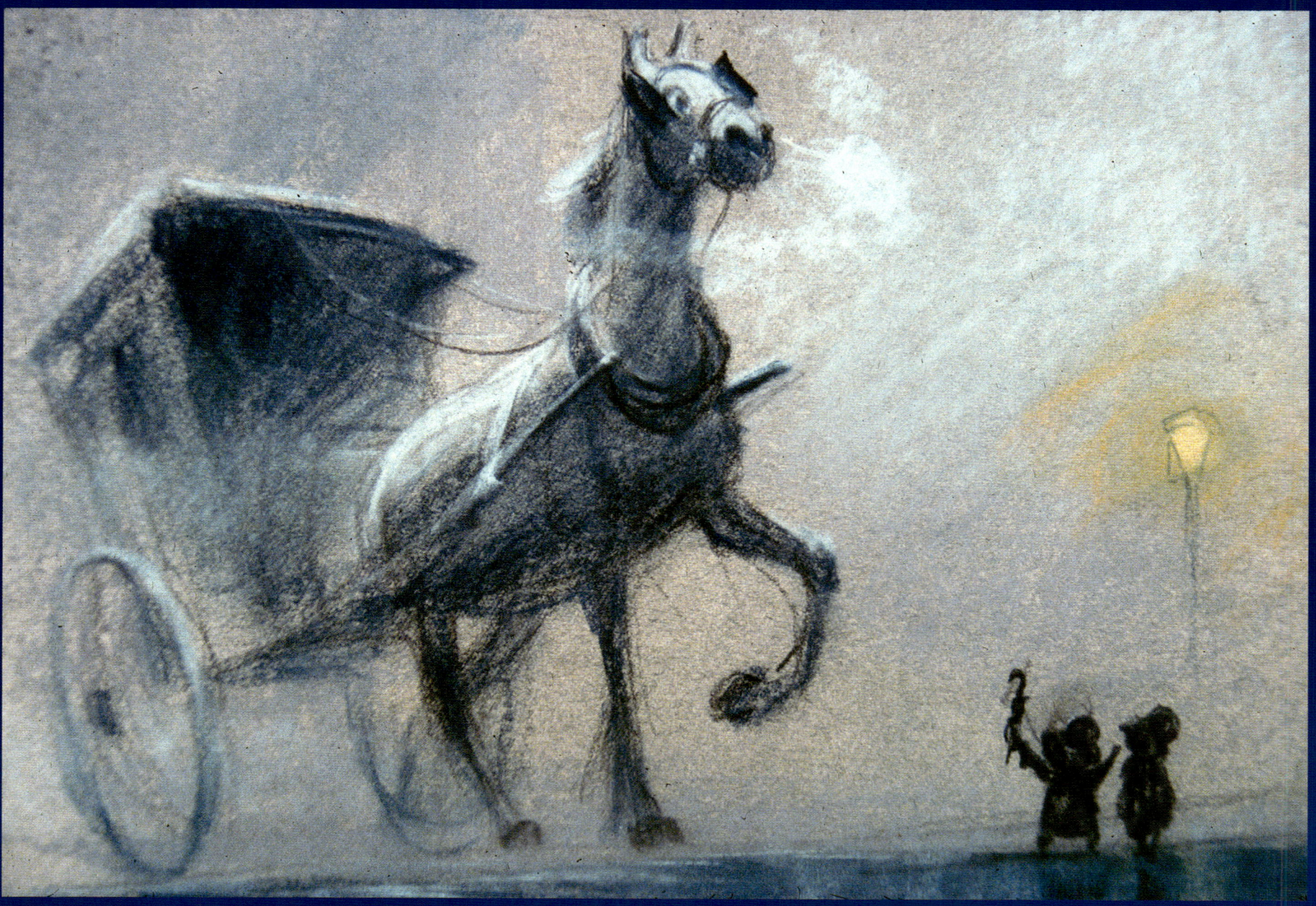

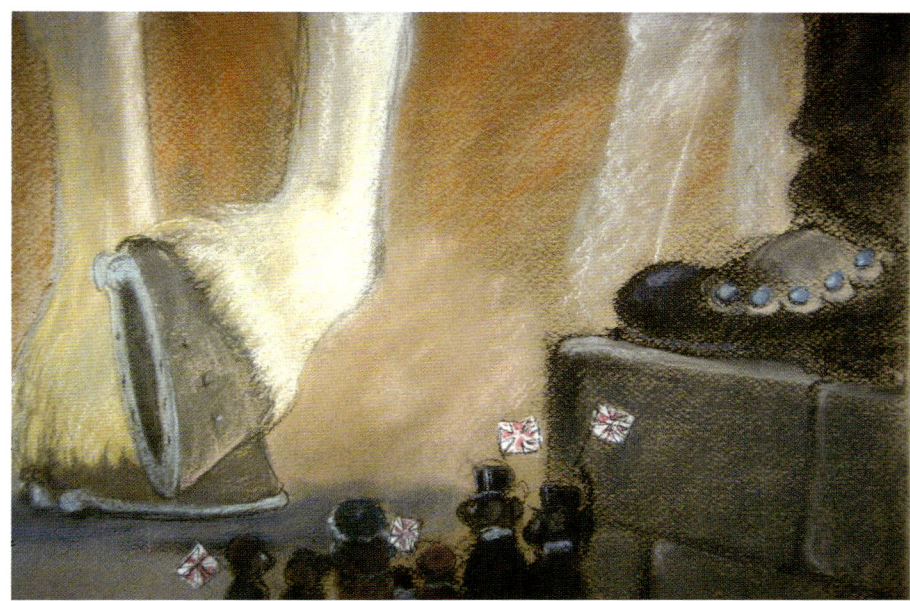
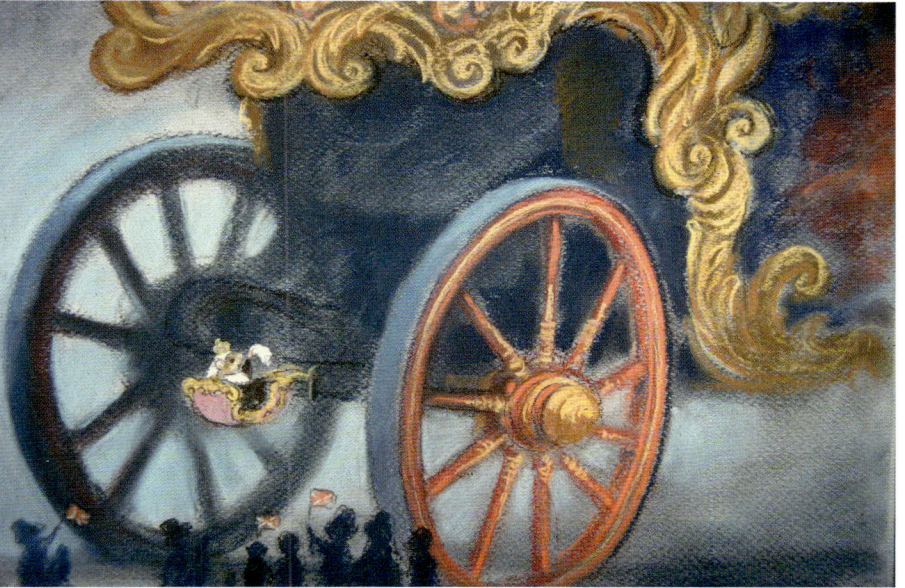
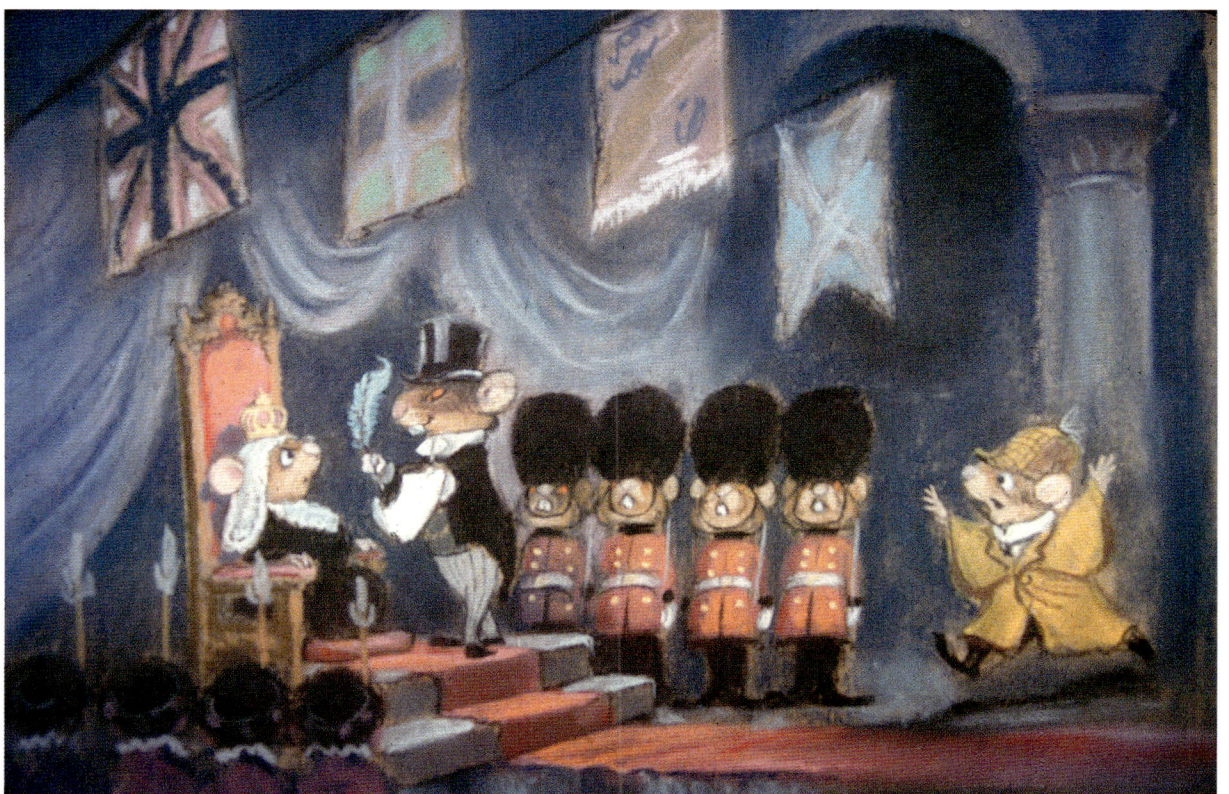

OPPOSITE AND ABOVE: Courtesy: Burny Mattinson.

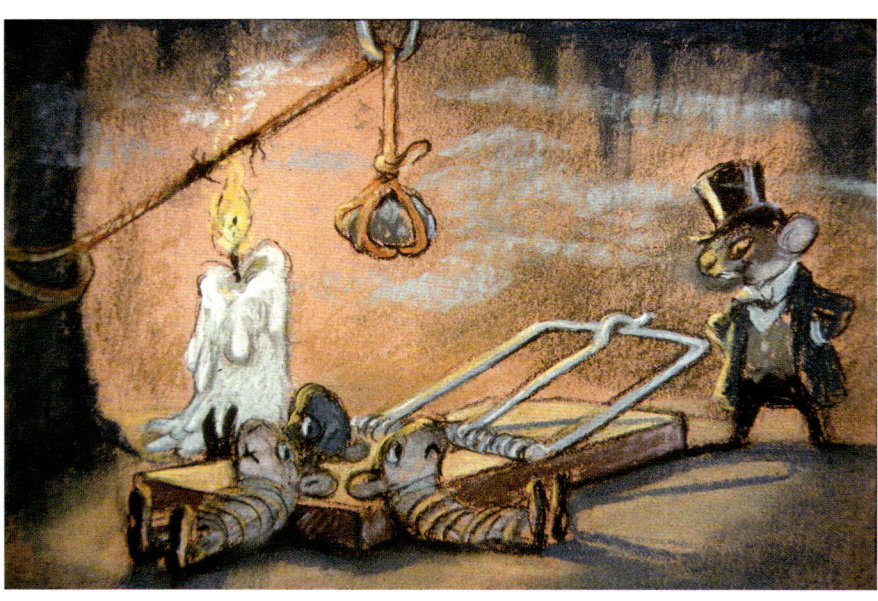

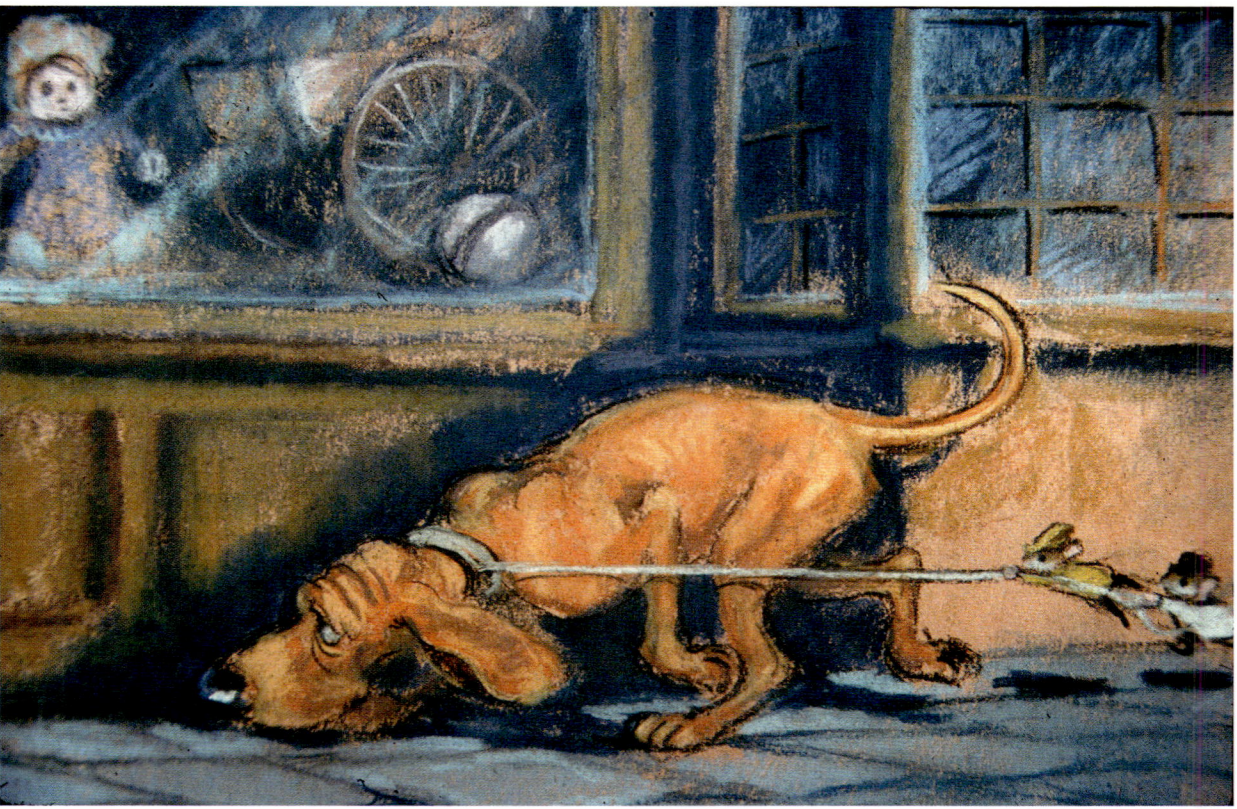

ABOVE: Courtesy: Burny Mattinson.

PAGES 189–194: Character designs and story sketches for *Beauty and the Beast*.

LEFT AND BOTTOM RIGHT: Courtesy: Rick Shaw and Melissa Couch-Deranleau.

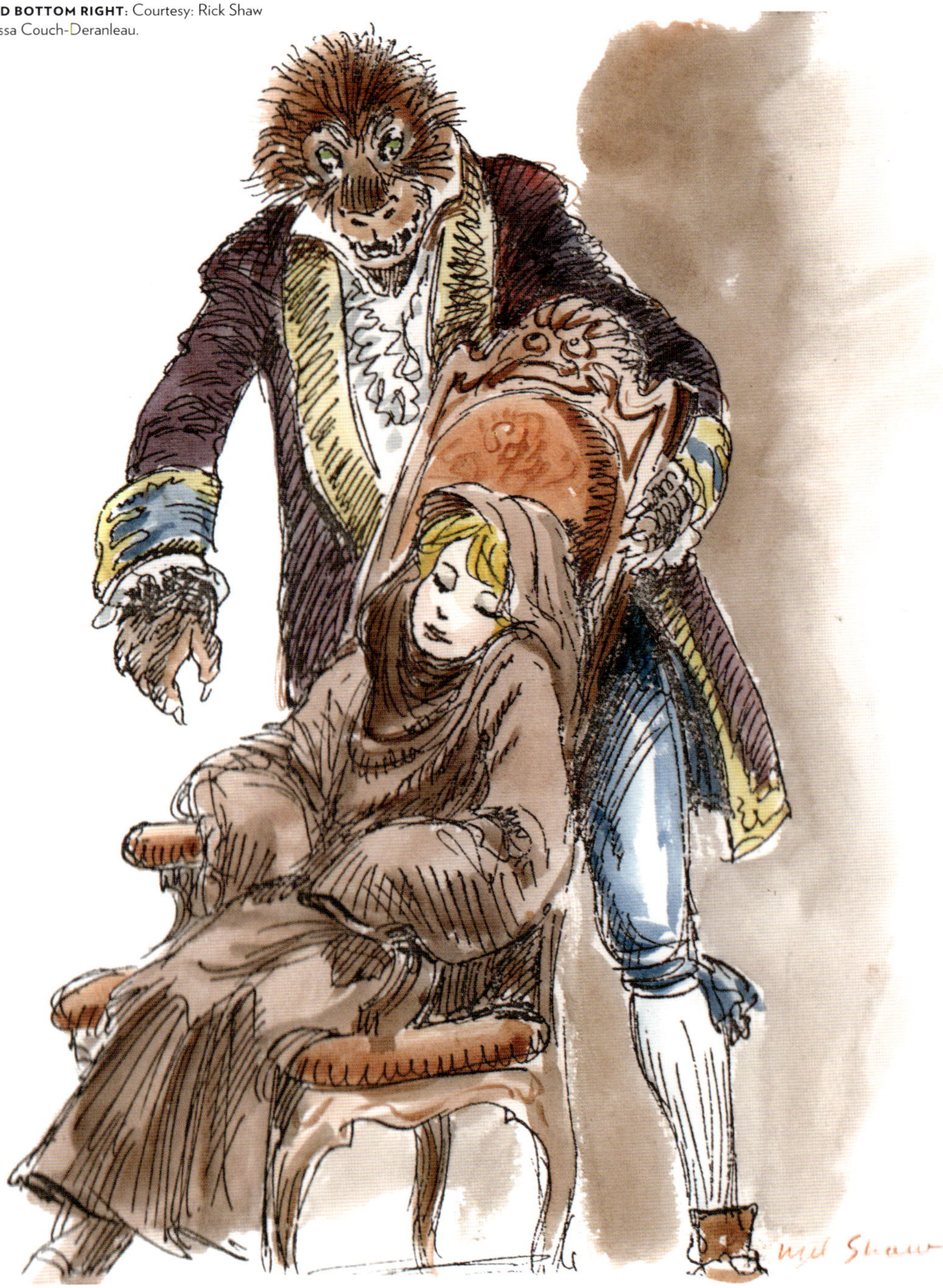

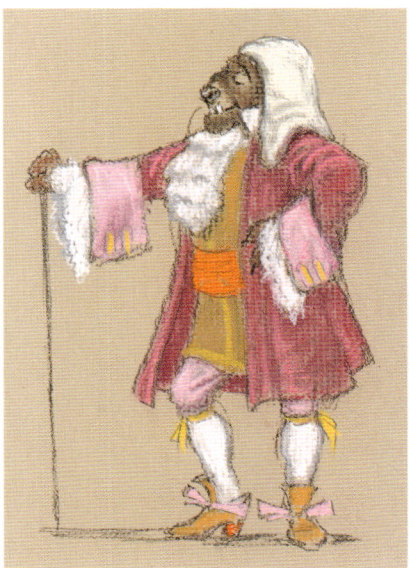

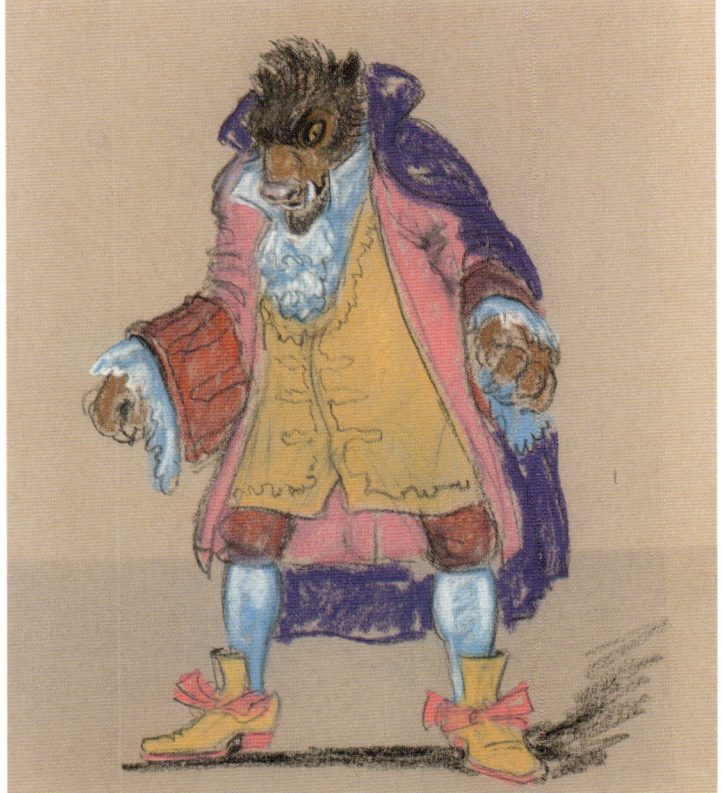

MEL SHAW   189

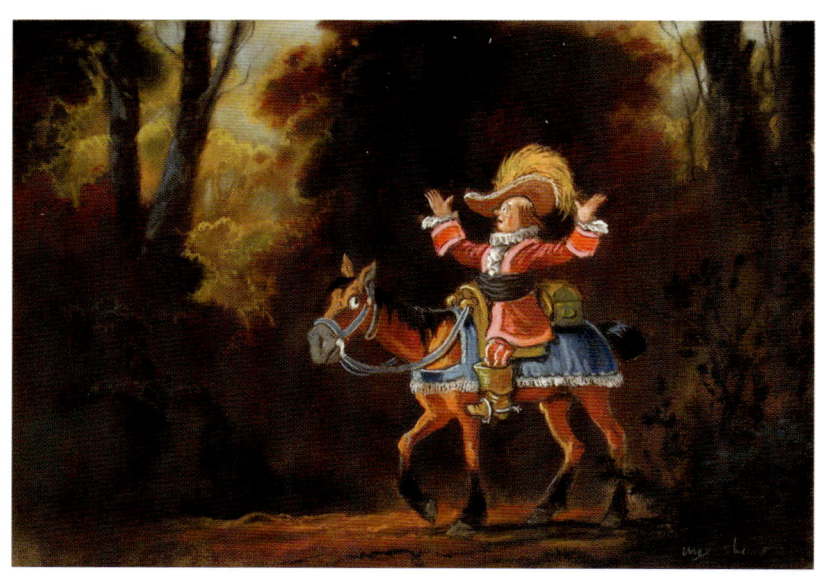
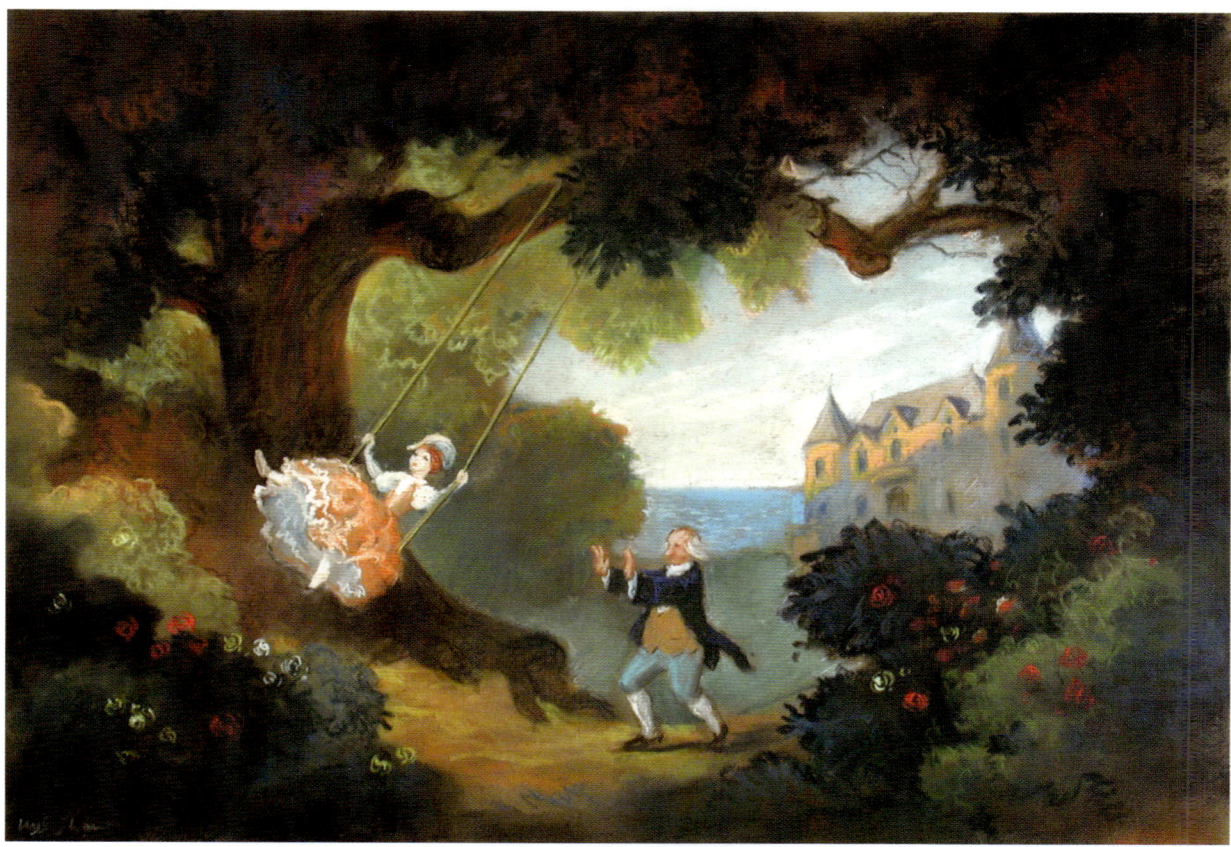

190　THEY DREW AS THEY PLEASED

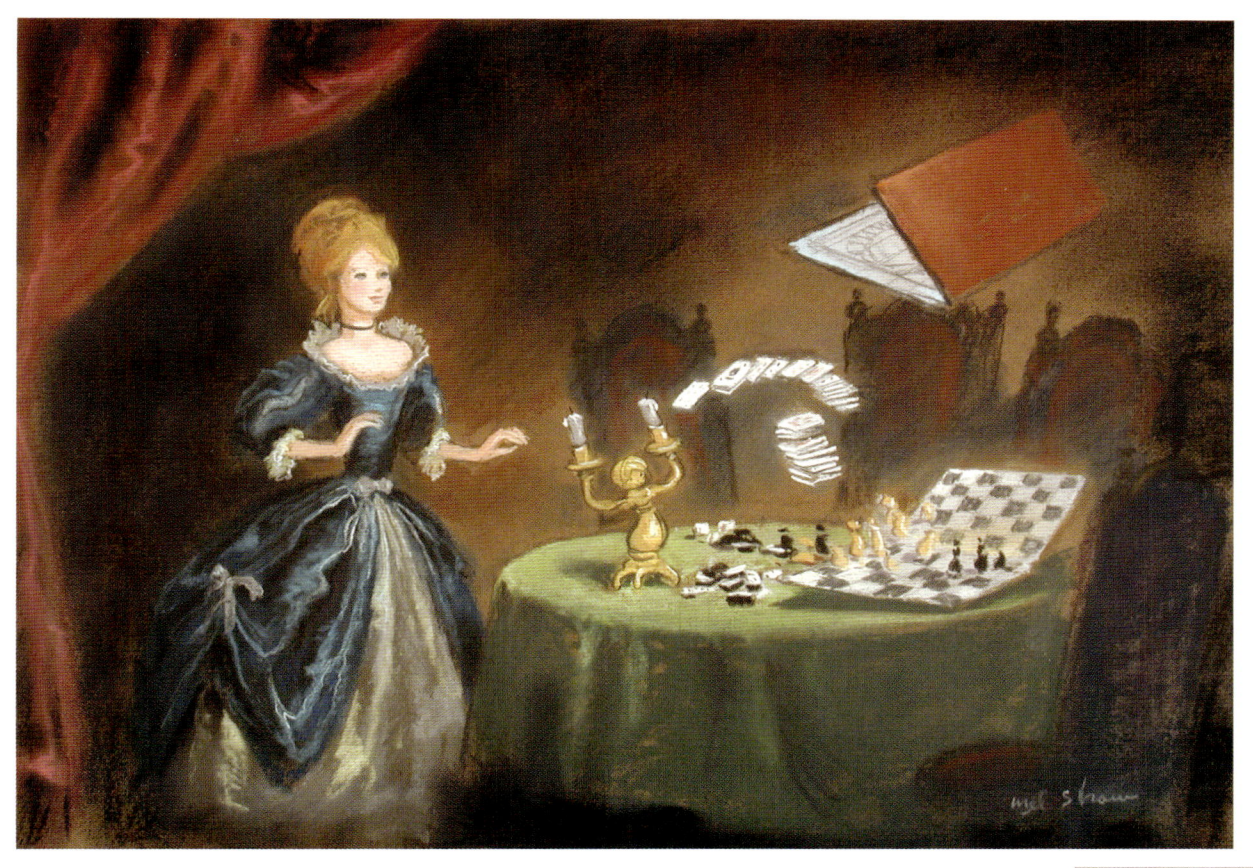
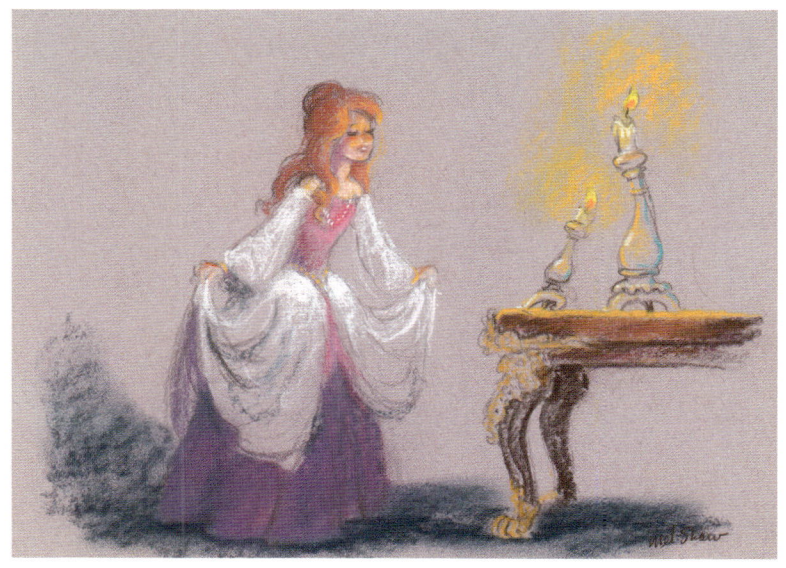

MEL SHAW

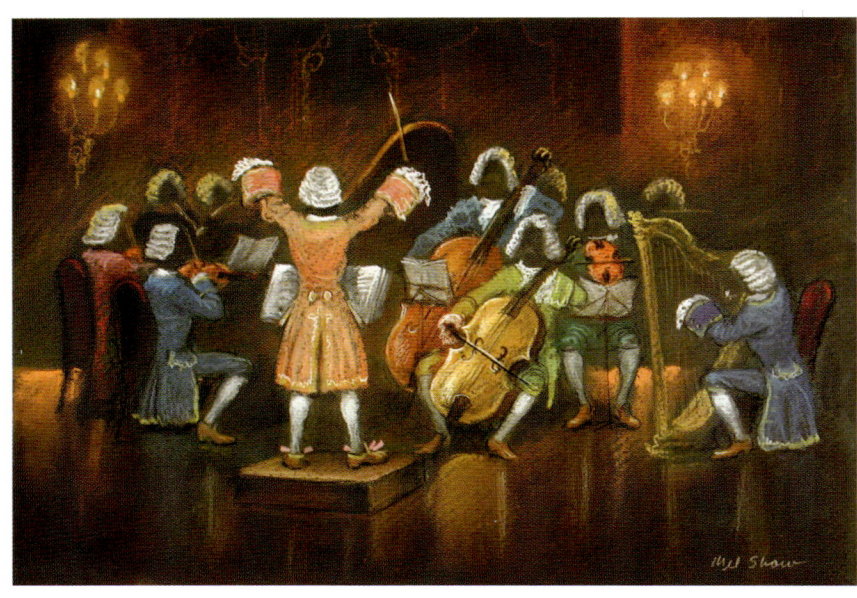
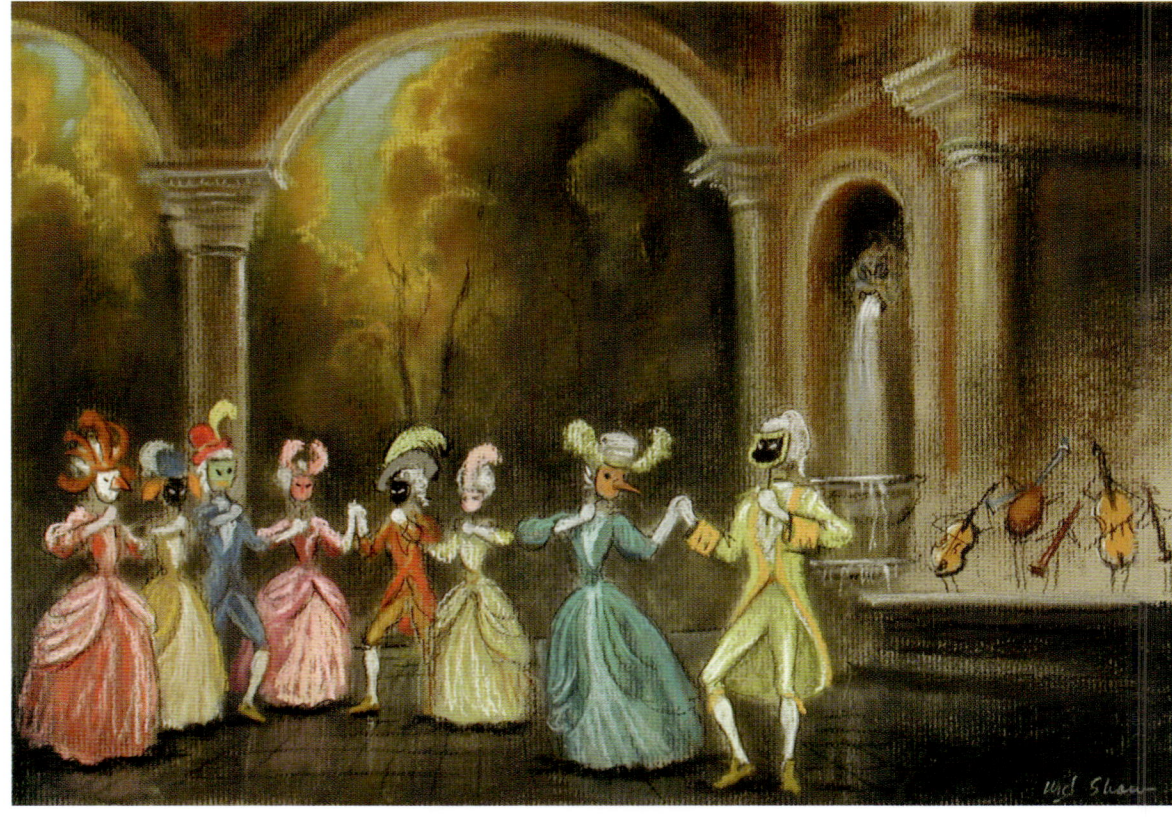

192 THEY DREW AS THEY PLEASED

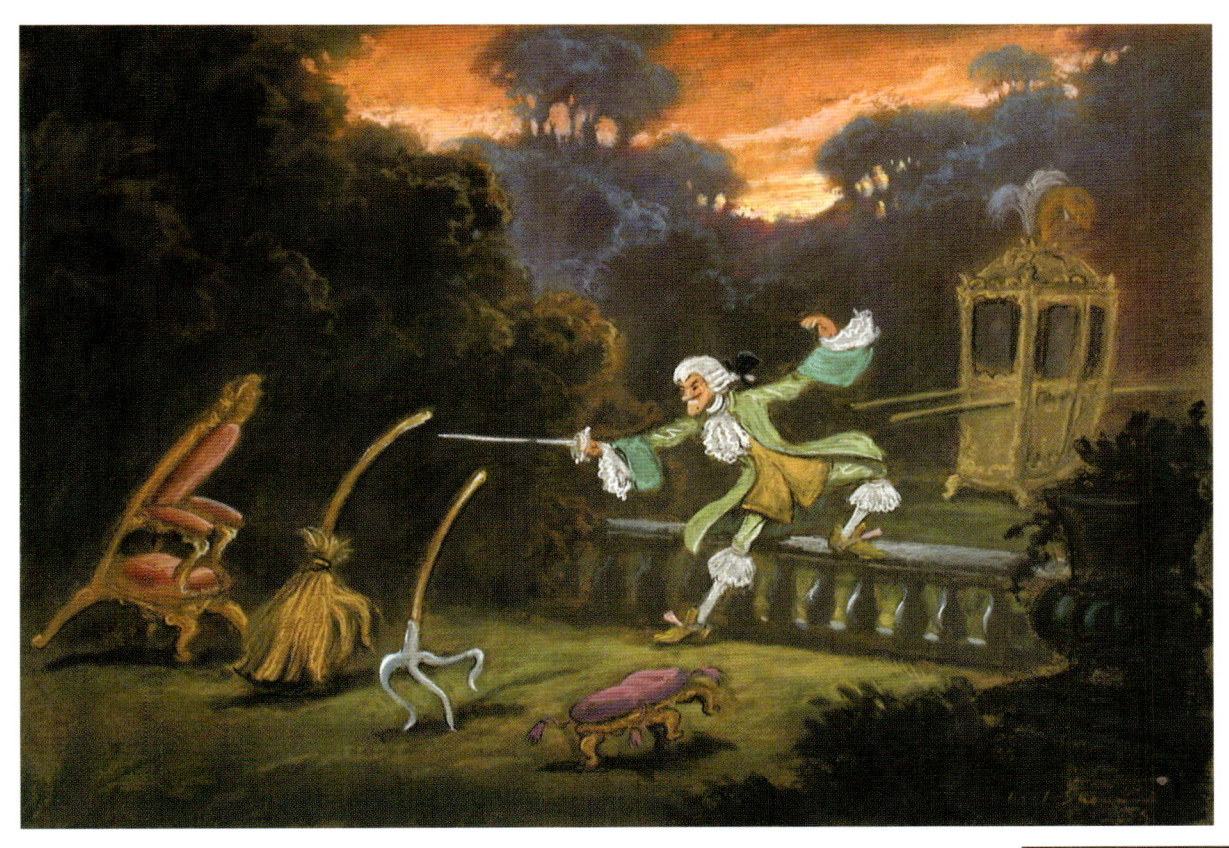
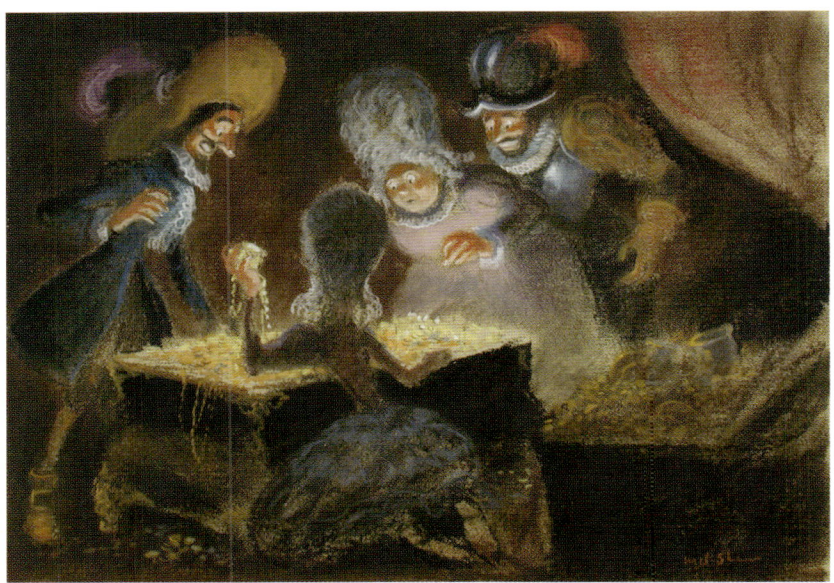

MEL SHAW

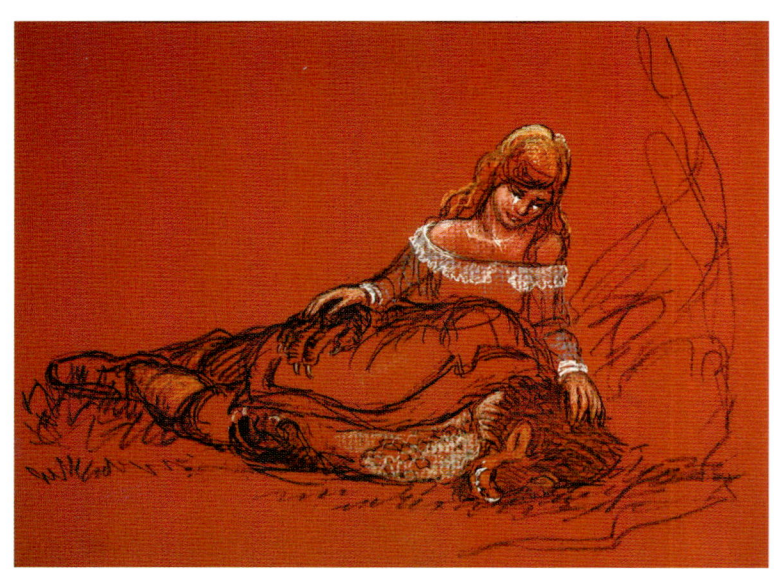

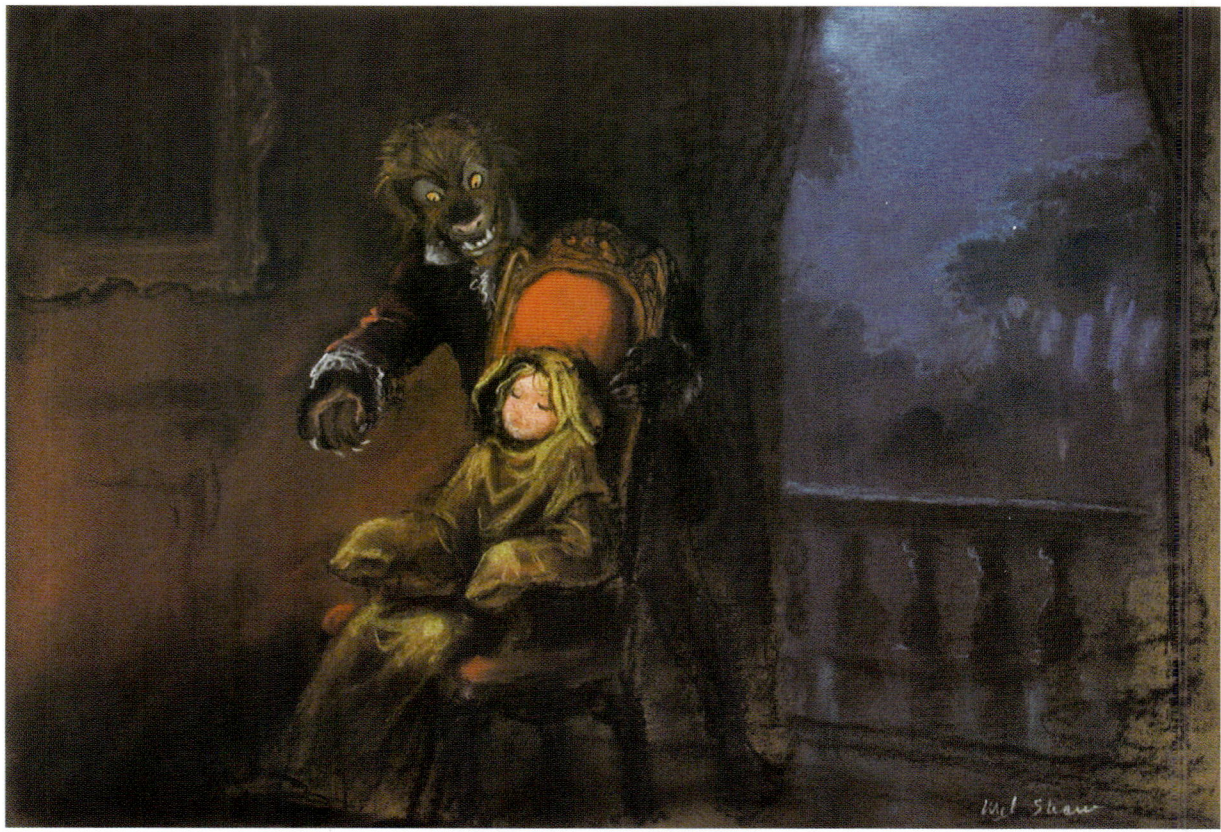

194   THEY DREW AS THEY PLEASED

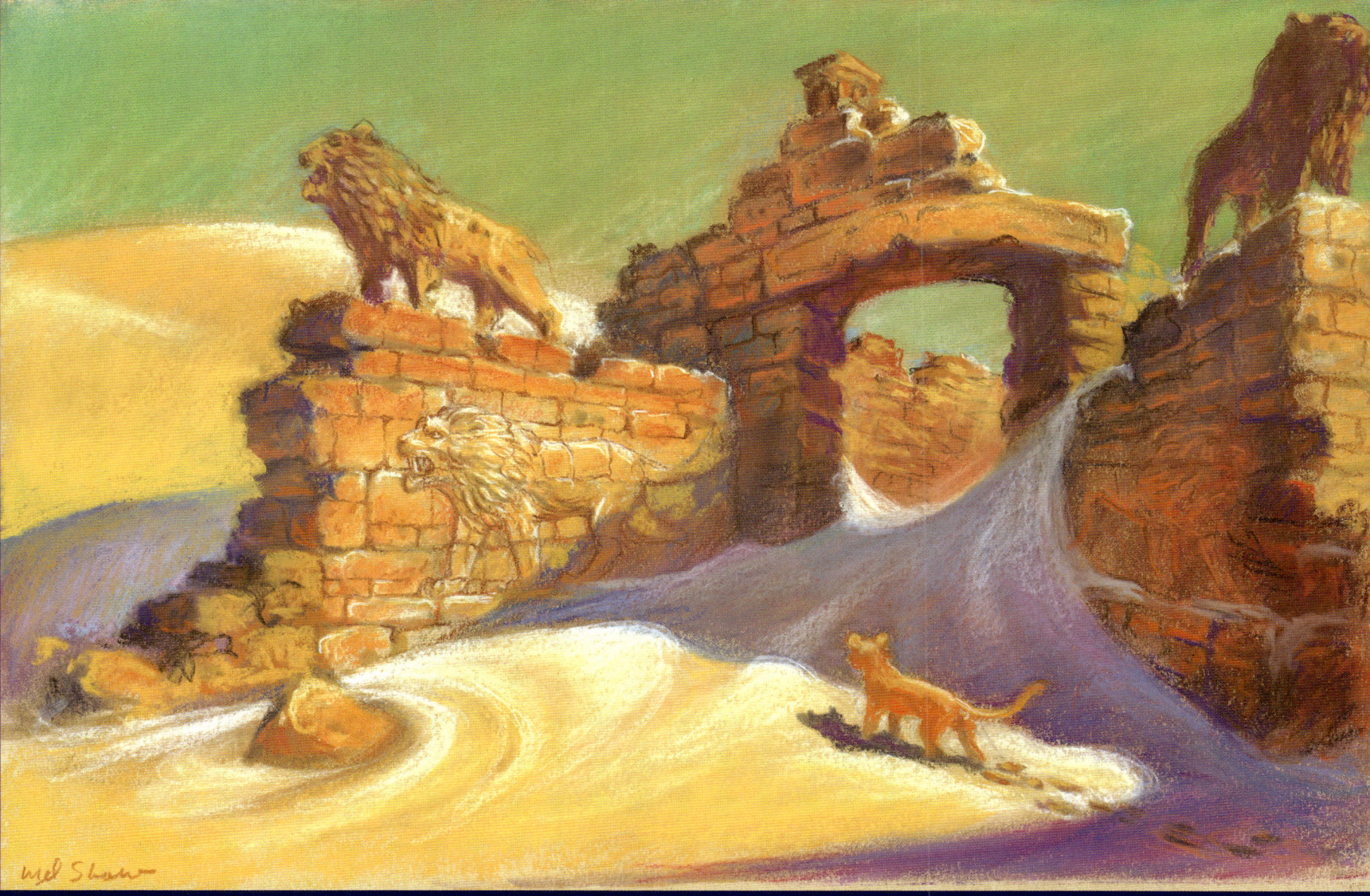

PAGES 195–200: Story sketches for *The Lion King*.

MEL SHAW

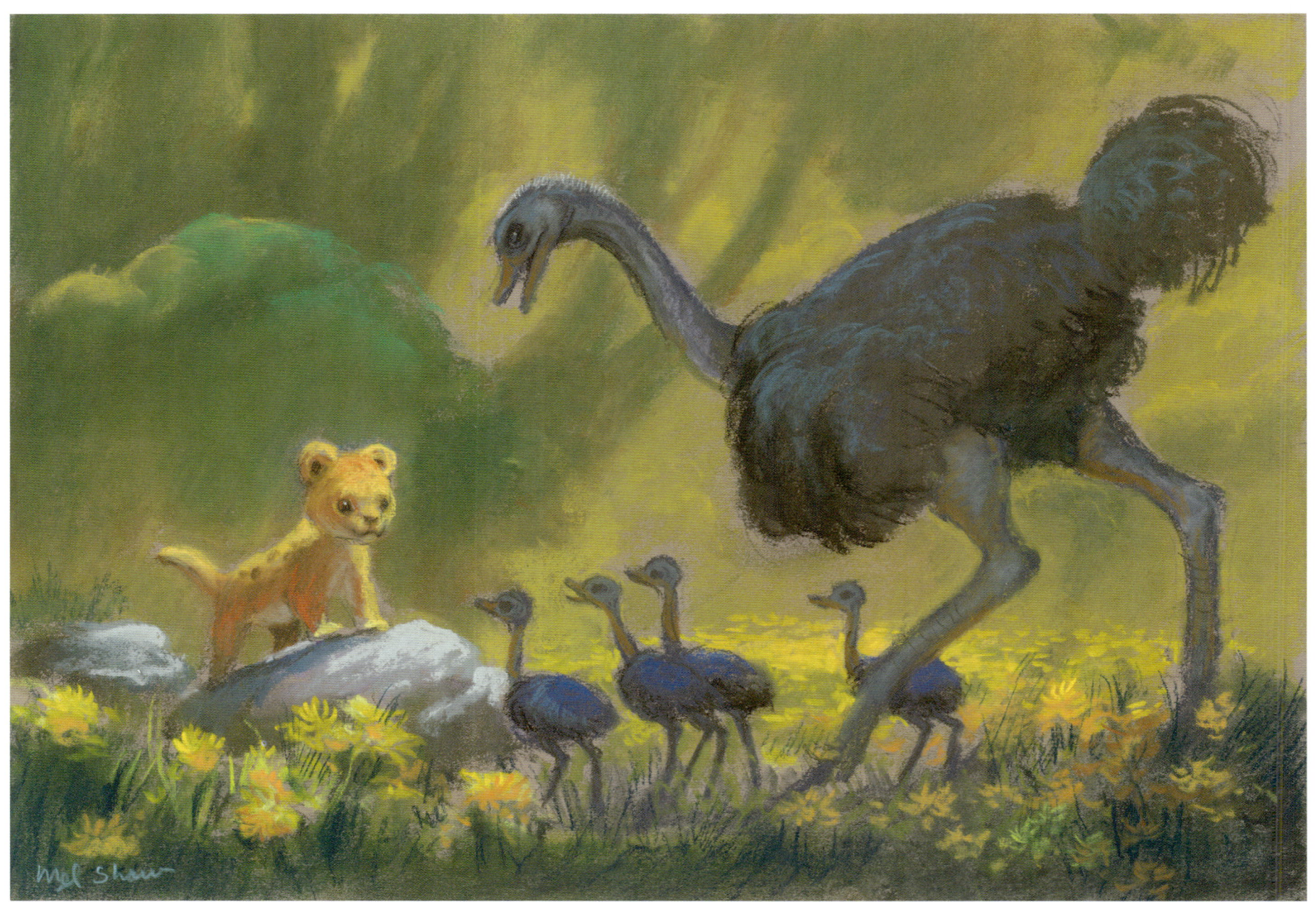

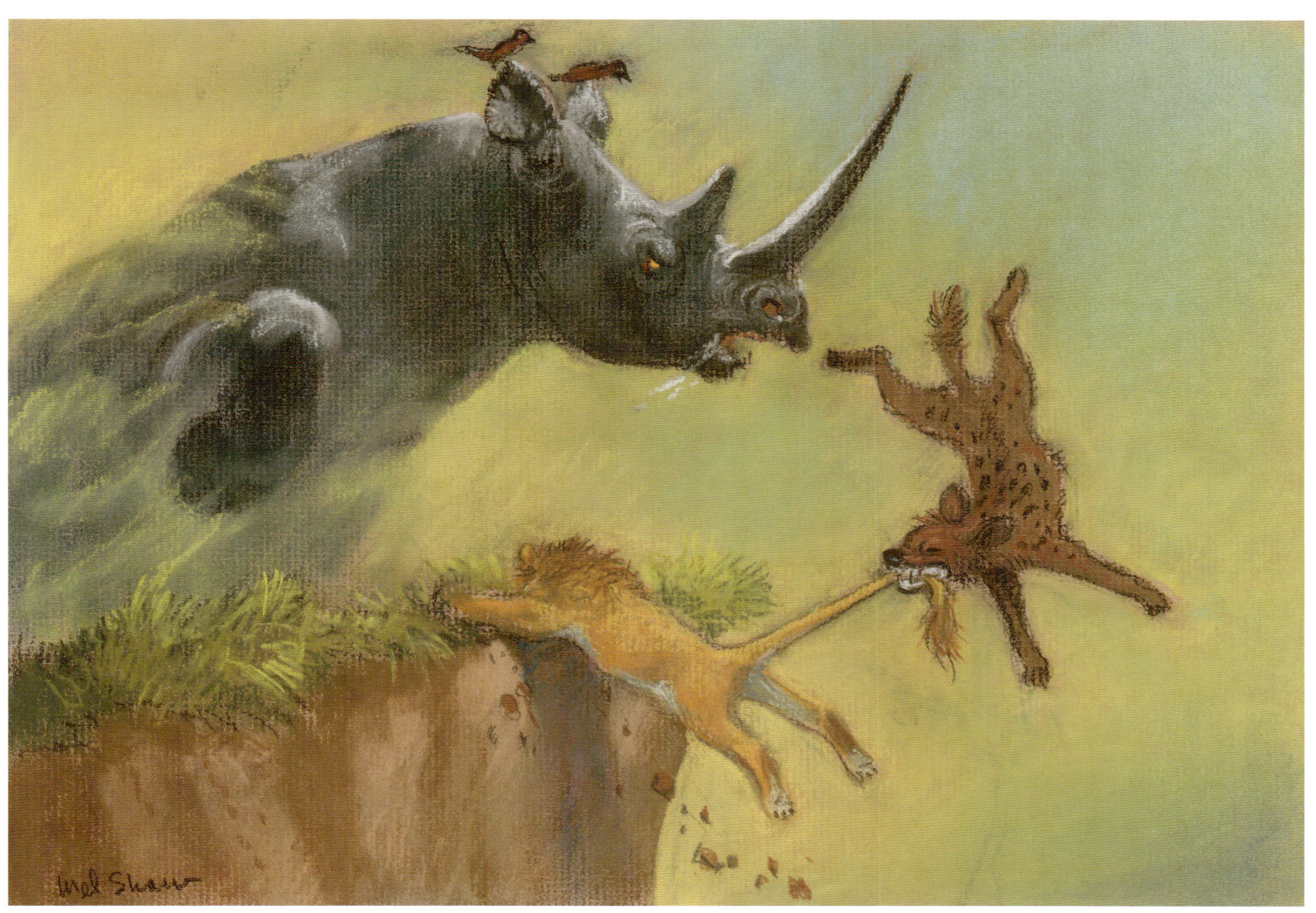

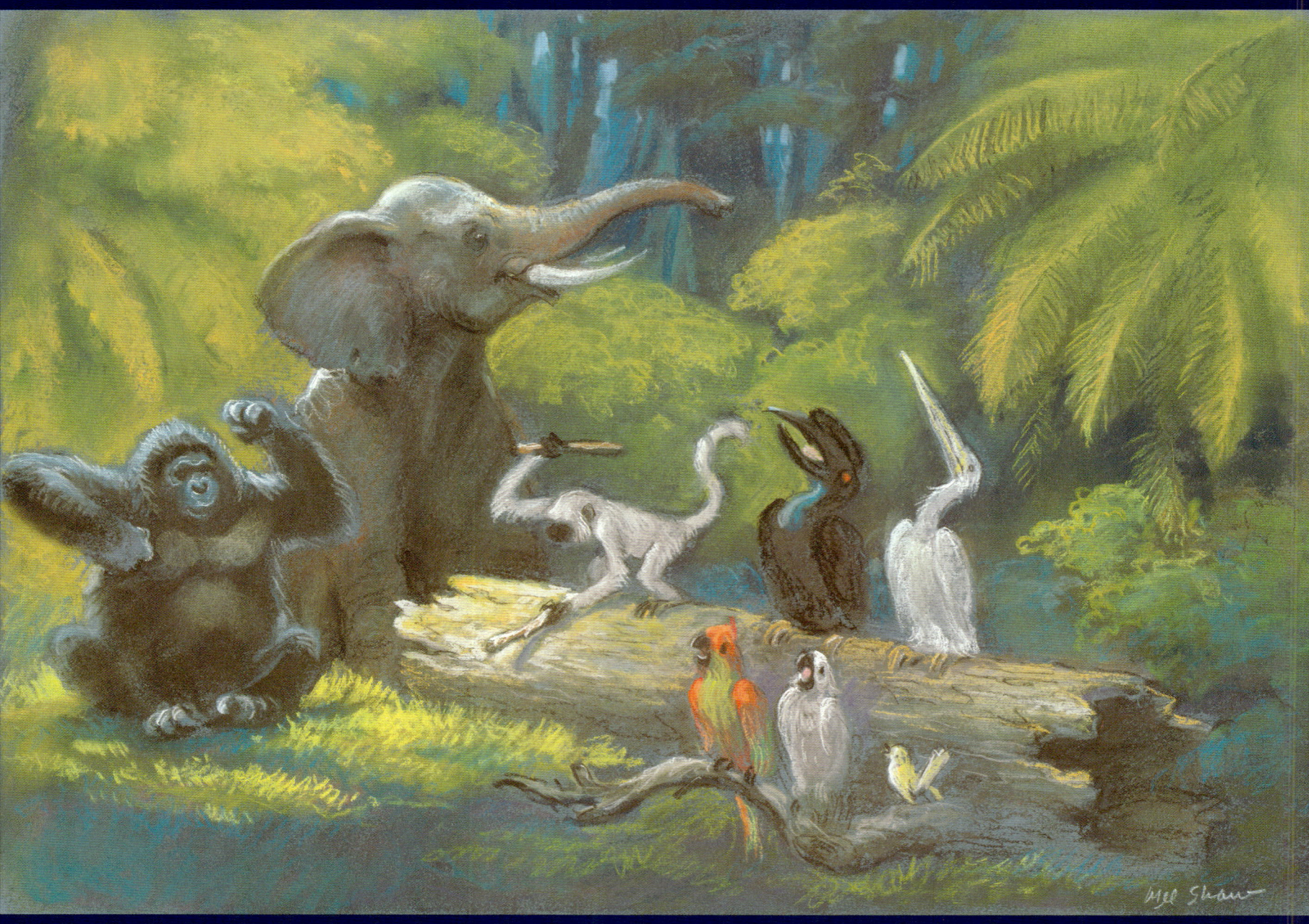

THEY DREW AS THEY PLEASED

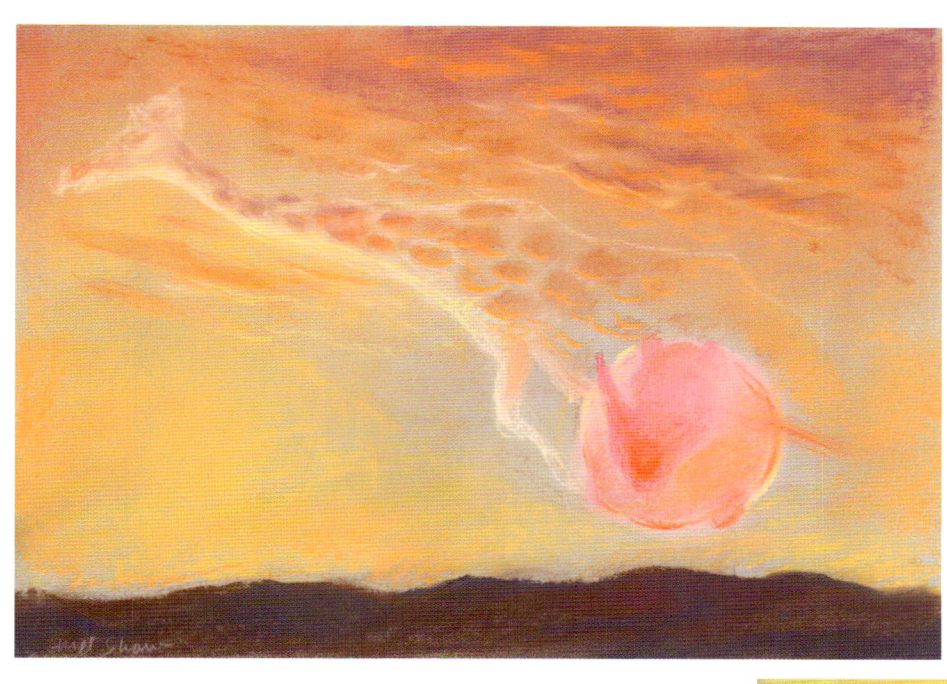
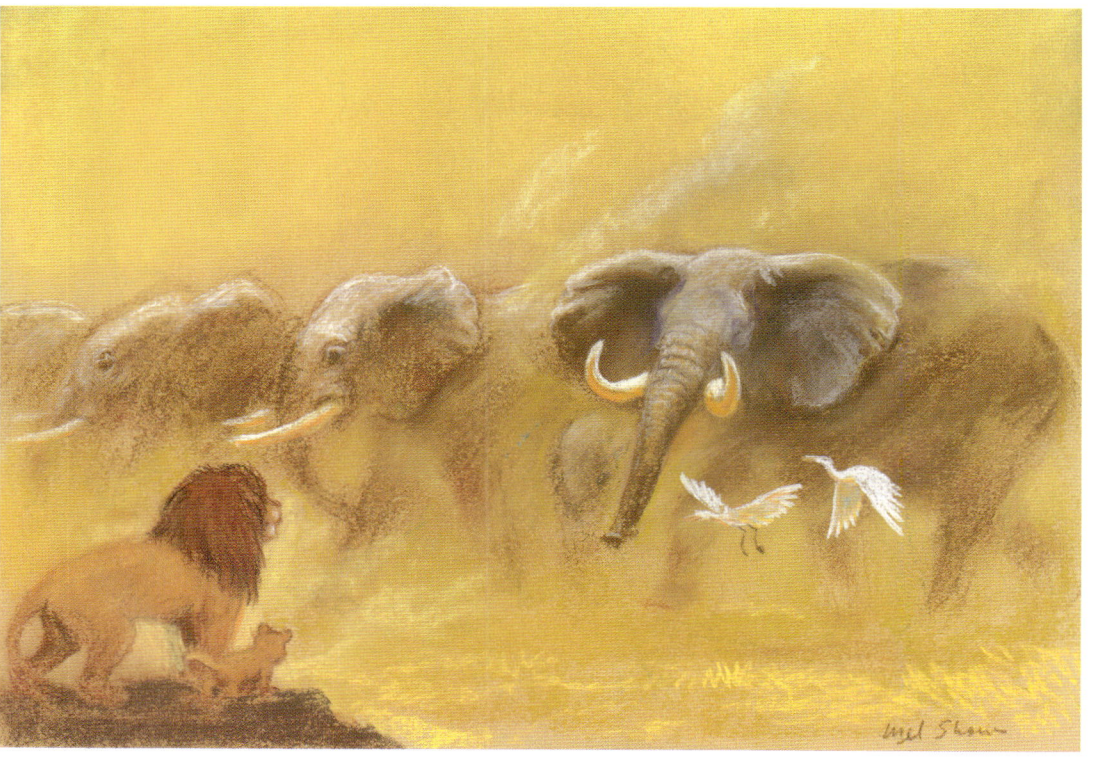

MEL SHAW

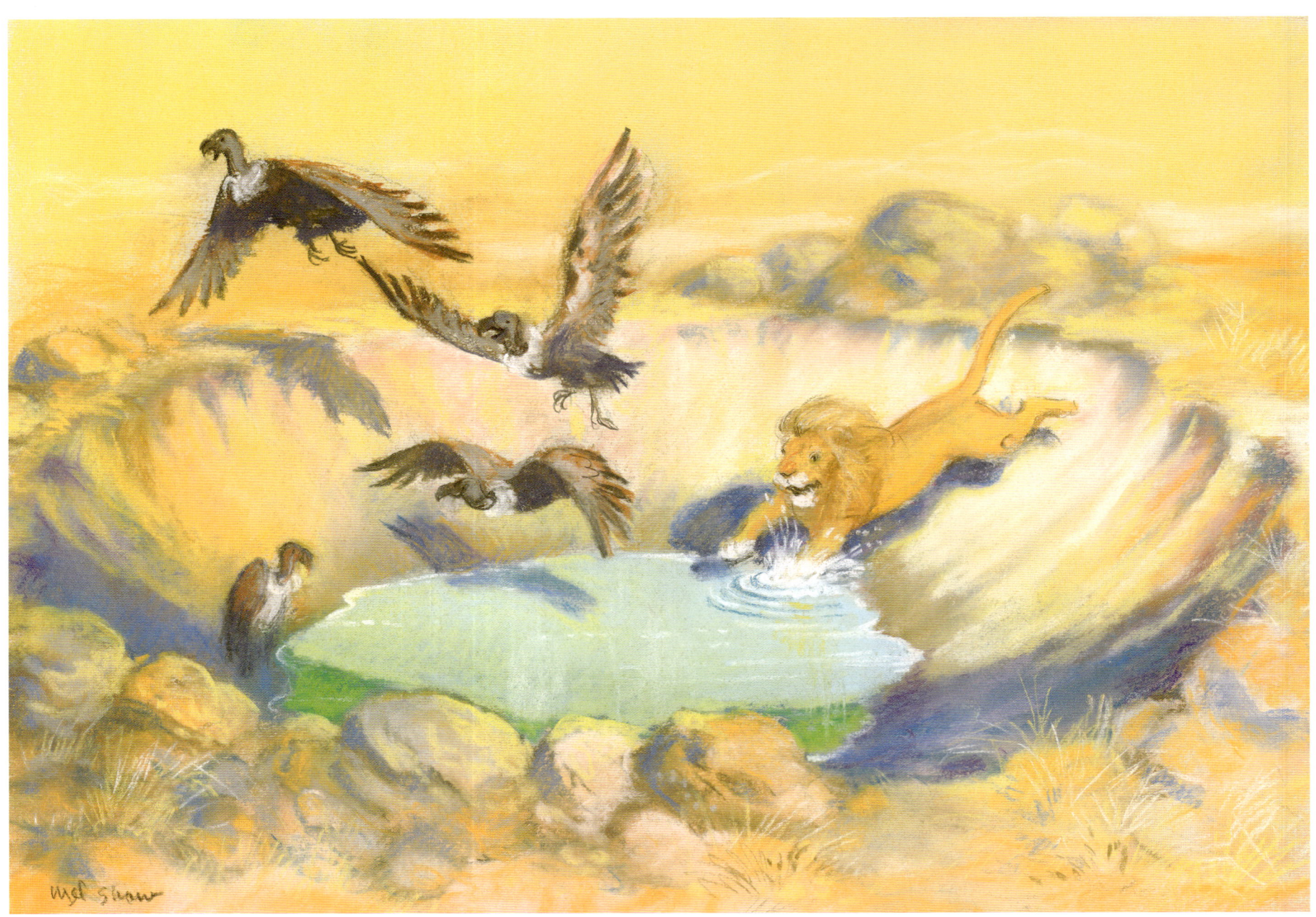

ACKNOWLEDGMENTS

This fifth volume of They Drew as They Pleased *is a dream come true: I always wanted to write a book about Ken Anderson and Mel Shaw; I always wanted to explore the almost uncharted territory of animation at Disney in the 1970s and early 1980s.*

As always, I owe a special debt of gratitude to my wife, Rita, who lived through my bouts of exhilaration, stress, and joy throughout the whole project. And to my good friend and fellow Disney historian, Joe Campana, who hosted me during my weeks of research in Los Angeles, scanned parts of the Mel Shaw collection, provided moral support, and helped in countless other ways. Lucas Seastrom and Jenna Benton also deserve special thanks for having spent days scanning the extensive Ken Anderson collection, as well as Steve and Virginia Reeser, Leslie Smith, and Libby Spatz for scanning the remainder of the Mel Shaw collection.

Good historians stand on the shoulders of their predecessors; this book would not exist without the groundbreaking efforts and the exhaustive research conducted by John Canemaker for his own book *Before the Animation Begins*, and without the interviews that Paul F. Anderson conducted for the book *Jack of All Trades: Conversations with Disney Legend Ken Anderson*.

The families of the artists discussed in this volume were key to locating fascinating treasure troves. This book would not be half of what it is without Judy Amos, Wendy Greer, and Sue Tanner, who allowed me to access the Ken Anderson collection, nor without Melissa Couch-Deranleau and Rick Shaw, who provided access to Mel Shaw's collection. Bob and Bruce Reitherman, Andrea Gessell-Severe, and Eric Tanner also deserve special thanks.

As always, fellow Disney historians Michael Barrier, Bill Cotter, Don Hahn, Jim Hollifield, Hans Perk, J. B. Kaufman, Todd James Pierce, and Paula Sigman-Lowery also contributed in significant ways to the different chapters of the book.

This art book relied heavily on the collections of the Walt Disney Animation Research Library, and its whole staff went the extra mile to unearth rare documents and other unseen treasures. Fox Carney, Doug Engalla, Ann Hansen, Tamara Khalaf, Mary Walsh, and especially Jackie Vasquez were some of the heroes of this venture.

No significant book about Disney history could be written without the critical help of the Walt Disney Archives. I can't thank its whole team enough for all their support. I tested their patience more than once and I am therefore especially grateful to Rebecca Cline and her team, especially Kevin Kern, who spent hours trying to locate obscure memos, and Ed Ovalle, who unearthed several rare documents; Michael Buckhoff from the Photo Library, who helped dig up rare photos of the Disney artists; and Kelsey Williams, who put up with my constant requests for photocopies.

Paul F. Anderson, Emmanuel Bourmalo, Philippe Cauvin, Andreas Deja, Pierre Lambert, Burny Mattinson, David P. Smith, Erika Thorpe, and Gretchen Vander Weide all provided artwork from their own collections, as did Heritage Auctions (thanks to Jim Lentz), Van Eaton Galleries (thanks to Mike Van Eaton and Gabriel Copp), the Walt Disney Family Foundation (thanks to Kirsten Komoroske, Michael Labrie, and Mark Gibson), and Wonderful World of Animation (thanks to Rob Faucette and Debbie Weiss). Various photographs came from the collections of Hans Bacher and Harry Sabin. A million thanks to all of you.

I also owe some very special thanks to Don Bluth, Dave Bossert, Ron Clements, Gena Downey, Sébastien Durand, Robert Fitzpatrick, Mark Fleming, Gary Goldman, Howard Green, Allen Gonzales, Joe Hale, Lisa Janacua, Mindy Johnson, Jim Korkis, Jeremy Marx, David R. Smith, Joseph Smith, and Tad Stones, who all helped in countless ways.

I would like to acknowledge the efforts of my wonderful editor from Chronicle Books, Frank Parisi, the exceptional designer Cat Grishaver, and the Disney Publishing team: Wendy Lefkon, Daniel Saeva, Sara Srisoonthorn, and Krista Wong.

Finally, on page 28 of *The Hidden Art of Disney's Mid-Century Era*, Lee Blair mentions the nickname "Brophy" in one of his letters. Animation historian Michael Barrier emailed me recently to explain that, based on interviews he conducted with Hugh Harman and Rudy Ising; "Brophy" is animator Norm Blackburn.

NOTES

[1] Frank Thomas and Ollie Johnston, interviewed by Michael Barrier, July 13, 1987, in *Walt's People: Vol. 17*, Didier Ghez, ed. (Theme Park Press, 2015).

[2] Woolie Reitherman, interviewed by MICA Productions, ca. 1983, Walt Disney Archives (WDA).

[3] Story meeting on *The Aristocats*, December 28, 1966, WDA.

[4] Frank Thomas and Ollie Johnston, interviewed by Michael Barrier, July 13, 1987, in *Walt's People: Vol. 17*, Didier Ghez, ed. (Theme Park Press, 2015).

[5] Woolie Reitherman, *Ideas and Thoughts Concerning the Future of Animation in the Disney Tradition*, September 9, 1970, courtesy: Bruce Reitherman.

[6] Woolie Reitherman, *Ideas and Thoughts Concerning the Future of Animation in the Disney Tradition*, September 9, 1970, courtesy: Bruce Reitherman.

[7] Memo from Woolie Reitherman to Card Walker, Ron Miller, and Bill Anderson, October 23, 1970, Subject: Ideas and Thoughts Concerning the Future of Animation in the Disney Tradition, courtesy: Bruce Reitherman.

[8] Memo from Don Duckwall to Card Walker, Ron Miller, and Bill Anderson, July 21, 1972, Subject: Animation Talent Development, courtesy: Don Hahn.

[9] Memo from Don Duckwall to Card Walker, Ron Miller, and Bill Anderson, July 21, 1972, Subject: Animation Talent Development, courtesy: Don Hahn. Don Bluth had actually spent one year at the Disney studio from June 18, 1956, to August 23, 1957, then another one from June 12, 1961, to August 17, 1961. He joined the studio again on April 19, 1971. Despite memos from the early 1970s mentioning him as one of the artists who were evaluated as part of the Talent Development Program, it is clear from later interviews that Don never saw himself as part of the program.

[10] Minutes Visual Communications Curriculum Committee, July 10, 1974, courtesy: Wendy Greer.

[11] Transcript of telephone call to Art Babbitt, July 29, 1974, courtesy: Wendy Greer.

[12] Jack Hannah, interviewed by Jim Korkis, July 1978 and May 1981, plus additional conversations until 1994, in *Walt's People: Vol. 1*, Didier Ghez, ed. (Theme Park Press, 2014).

[13] Robert Fitzpatrick, interviewed by Didier Ghez, November 29, 2017, unpublished.

[14] Gary Goldman, interviewed by Didier Ghez, December 2017, unpublished.

[15] Gary Goldman, interviewed by Didier Ghez, December 2017, unpublished.

[16] John Cawley, *The Animated Films of Don Bluth* (Image Pub of New York, 1991).

[17] Dorse A. Lanpher, *Flyin' Chunks and Other Things to Duck: Memoirs of a Life Spent Doodling for Dollars* (iUniverse.com, 2010).

[18] Paul F. Anderson, *Jack of All Trades: Conversations with Disney Legend Ken Anderson* (Theme Park Press, 2017).

[19] *The Books of the Weather Bird Press, Vance Gerry Interviewed by Rebecca Ziegler, 1992*. Oral History Program, University of California, Los Angeles, https://archive.org/details/booksofweatherbi00gerr.

[20] *Ken and Polly also known as Daddy and Mother* by Sue, Judy, and Wendy, July 29, 1984. Unpublished manuscript, courtesy: Wendy Greer.

[21] Ken Anderson, interviewed by Jim Korkis, Spring 1985, in *Walt's People: Vol. 6*, Didier Ghez, ed. (Xlibris, 2008).

[22] Paul F. Anderson, *Jack of All Trades: Conversations with Disney Legend Ken Anderson* (Theme Park Press, 2017); and Ken Anderson, interviewed by MICA Productions, ca. 1983, WDA.

[23] Ken Anderson, interviewed by MICA Productions, ca. 1983, WDA.

[24] Paul F. Anderson, *Jack of All Trades: Conversations with Disney Legend Ken Anderson* (Theme Park Press, 2017).

[25] Paul F. Anderson, *Jack of All Trades: Conversations with Disney Legend Ken Anderson* (Theme Park Press, 2017).

[26] Ken Anderson, interviewed by Dave Smith, September 5, 1975, in *Walt's People: Vol. 9*, Didier Ghez, ed. (Xlibris, 2010).

[27] Paul F. Anderson, *Jack of All Trades: Conversations with Disney Legend Ken Anderson* (Theme Park Press, 2017).

[28] Ken Anderson, interviewed by Dave Smith, September 5, 1975, in *Walt's People: Vol. 9*, Didier Ghez, ed. (Xlibris, 2010); and Ken Anderson, interviewed by David Johnson, 1988, in David Johnson, *Snow White's People: An Oral History of the Disney Film* Snow White and the Seven Dwarfs, Vol. 2, Didier Ghez, ed. (Theme Park Press, 2018).

[29] Stories in Idea Files, December 11, 1939, courtesy: Bruce Reitherman. Around March 1935, Ken had also suggested a few ideas for a proposed Mickey short titled *The Invisible Man*, and on March 7, 1935, he sent an idea for the proposed short *Dog Race*, which read in part: "As in *Broadway Bill*, Pluto could have a mascot in the person of a pet flea. The flea, however, is the bane of Mickey's existence and he is constantly trying to get rid of him with flea powder. Just before the race Mickey tries again and Pluto swallows the flea powder by accident…" (ARL)

[30] Memo from Walt Disney to Ted Sears, October 23, 1935, WDA.

[31] Memo from Walt Disney to Ken Anderson, January 15, 1936, Subject: Re Puppets, WDA. A memo from Walt Disney and Paul Hopkins to the Story Department, dated January 28, 1936, titled "New Story Material," still listed *Marionettes* as a story under consideration: "Not carried as if moved by human means, but more or less humanized." Courtesy: Michael Barrier. In July, 1936, commenting on another puppet-story idea, the head of the Story Department, Ted Sears, explained: "Ken Anderson tried to do a story like that … he and I went through it and wrote up a short outline showing possibilities and Walt, at first glance, turned it down—that is, he put it aside at the time … It was a Mickey and Minnie picture, with both working a puppet show that involved the Duck and Pluto and the Goof and the audience could have been made up of the kids and the orphans; the puppets could have been caricatures of celebrities. We had quite a few amusing things—Minnie suspended on a platform playing the piano and working puppets at the same time … at one point the cartoon characters would be in a heap and the puppet characters would be doing their stuff." Class in Creative Story Writing by Dr. Morkovin, July 5, 1936, Special Speaker: Ted Sears, Topic: Discussion and Criticism of Class Stories, WDA.

[32] Paul F. Anderson, *Jack of All Trades: Conversations with Disney Legend Ken Anderson* (Theme Park Press, 2017).

[33] Ken Anderson, interviewed by David Johnson, 1988, in David Johnson, *Snow White's People: An Oral History of the Disney Film* Snow White and the Seven Dwarfs, Vol. 2, Didier Ghez, ed. (Theme Park Press, 2018); and Ken Anderson, interviewed by Nancy Beiman, 1979, in Nancy Beiman, *Prepare to Board!* (Focal Press, 2007).

[34] Paul F. Anderson, *Jack of All Trades: Conversations with Disney Legend Ken Anderson* (Theme Park Press, 2017).

[35] J. B. Kaufman, *Pinocchio: The Making of the Disney Epic* (Walt Disney Family Foundation Press, 2015).

[36] Ken O'Connor, interviewed by Steve Hulett, April 30, 1978, in *Walt's People: Vol. 6*, Didier Ghez, ed. (Xlibris, 2008).

[37] Paul F. Anderson, *Jack of All Trades: Conversations with Disney Legend Ken Anderson* (Theme Park Press, 2017).

[38] Ken Anderson, interviewed by MICA Productions, ca. 1983, WDA; and Ken Anderson, interviewed by Robin Allan, May 10 1985, unpublished.

[39] Paul F. Anderson, *Jack of All Trades: Conversations with Disney Legend Ken Anderson* (Theme Park Press, 2017).

[40] Ken Anderson, interviewed by Bob Thomas, May 15, 1973, in *Walt's People: Vol. 10*, Didier Ghez, ed. (Theme Park Press, 2017); and Ken Anderson, interviewed by MICA Productions, ca. 1983, WDA.

[41] Ken Anderson, interviewed by MICA Productions, ca. 1983, WDA.

[42] Ken Anderson, interviewed by Dave Smith, September 5, 1975, in *Walt's People: Vol. 9*, Didier Ghez, ed. (Xlibris, 2010).

[43] Ken Anderson, interviewed by MICA Productions, ca. 1983, WDA.

[44] Paul F. Anderson, *Jack of All Trades: Conversations with Disney Legend Ken Anderson* (Theme Park Press, 2017).

[45] Storyboard photostats and scan of original story sketch from *Reynard the Fox* identified as his by Ken Anderson, courtesy: Wendy Greer and Paul F. Anderson.

[46] Story conference, *Reynard the Fox*, February 12, 1938, Animation Research Library (ARL).

47 Jack Kinney, *Reynard the Fox*, outline, January 28, 1947; *Reynard the Fox* treatments by Ferguson, April 17, 1947, and May 1, 1947; and *Treasure Island*, first rough draft, March 4, 1948, ARL.

48 In a recently rediscovered memo from Eyvind Earle to story artist Joe Rinaldi, June 18, 1957, Eyvind explained: "Tom Oreb was chiefly responsible for Briar Rose, the horse, squirrels, rabbits, the first ideas on the 3 fairies, the kings, the princes, and the designing of all the incidental characters in the crowd scenes, and the goons. He helped [me] at the very beginning in the refining of composition within the backgrounds—and the main castle used in the picture is taken from one of the first paintings created by myself and Tom together. A year later—1953—preliminary production was started. Ken Anderson and Don DaGradi came on the picture—their job being mainly that of making story continuity sketches, breaking the story down into exact scenes cuts, timing the music, incorporating the styling into the first rough production layouts, scene planning and the actual staging of each scene," ARL.

49 Ray Aragon, interviewed by Didier Ghez, February 23 and March 5, 2009, in *Walt's People: Vol. 11*, Didier Ghez, ed. (Xlibris, 2011).

50 Memo from Ken Peterson to Walt Disney, November 14, 1956, Subject: *Sleeping Beauty*, WDA.

51 Floyd Norman, interviewed by Celbi Vagner Pegoraro, between March 2005 and June 2006, in *Walt's People: Vol. 4*, Didier Ghez, ed. (Theme Park Press, 2015).

52 Frank Thomas and Ollie Johnston, interviewed by Michael Barrier, October 27, 1976, in *Walt's People: Vol. 17*, Didier Ghez, ed. (Theme Park Press, 2015).

53 Ken Anderson, *Proposed Outline for Oz Feature Cartoon*, February 16, 1959, courtesy: Wendy Greer.

54 David R. Smith, "Walt Disney and *The Rainbow Road to Oz*," in *The Baum Bugle*, Winter 1980–81.

55 Rinaldi and Englander, *Return to Oz*, Rough Outline Prod. 1899, October 4, 1962. Collection of the author. On February 5, 1958, Joe Rinaldi also submitted a document titled "Rough Story Outline for *Dorothy's Return to Oz*," WDA.

56 Ken Anderson, *A Story Outline for Chanticler* [sic], April 10, 1960, courtesy: Wendy Greer.

57 Both *Chanticleer* and *Robin Hood* were mentioned as early as January 9, 1934, in a memo from Roy O. Disney to United Artists listing possible Silly Symphony titles which the studio wanted to see registered for future use, courtesy: Michael Barrier.

58 Story Research Report, *Chantecler*, comments by Ted Sears and Al Perkins, November 27, 1937, ARL.

59 Ken Anderson's drawings of the characters from *Reynard the Fox* were inspired by the illustrations of artist Keith Ward for the book *The Scandalous Adventures of Reynard the Fox* by Harry J. Owens (Alfred A. Knopf, 1945).

60 Marc Davis, interviewed by Jim Korkis, September 1998, in *Walt's People: Vol. 7*, Didier Ghez, ed. (Xlibris, 2009).

61 Memo from Ken Peterson to Ken Anderson, May 11, 1960, Subject: *Chantecler*, ARL.

62 Story Meeting Notes, *Chantecler* #1766—Opening Sequence, August 24, 1960, ARL.

63 Ken Anderson's presentation at The Walt Disney Studios, May 12, 1987, WDA.

64 Ken Anderson, interviewed by Milton Gray, December 14, 1976, unpublished, courtesy: Michael Barrier.

65 Paul F. Anderson, *Jack of All Trades: Conversations with Disney Legend Ken Anderson* (Theme Park Press, 2017).

66 Memo from Ken Peterson to Walt Disney, May 21, 1958, Subject: "Casting," WDA.

67 Paul F. Anderson, *Jack of All Trades: Conversations with Disney Legend Ken Anderson* (Theme Park Press, 2017).

68 Ken Anderson, interviewed by Robin Allan, May 10, 1985, unpublished.

69 Paul F. Anderson, *Jack of All Trades: Conversations with Disney Legend Ken Anderson* (Theme Park Press, 2017).

70 Ken Anderson, interviewed by MICA Productions, ca. 1983, WDA.

71 Paul F. Anderson, *Jack of All Trades: Conversations with Disney Legend Ken Anderson* (Theme Park Press, 2017).

72 Ollie Johnston at CalArts, February 1978, in *Walt's People: Vol. 7*, Didier Ghez, ed. (Xlibris, 2009).

73 Milt Kahl at CalArts, April 2, 1976, in *Walt's People: Vol. 7*, Didier Ghez, ed. (Xlibris, 2009).

74 Ken Anderson, interviewed by MICA Productions, ca. 1983, WDA.

75 *Pooh*, Prod. No. 1059, by Jack Miller, March 8, 1941; and *Conversation with Walt*, May 31, 1966, ARL.

76 Harry Tytle, *One of Walt's Boys* (ASAP Publishing, 1997).

77 *The Aristocats*, story and treatment by Tom Rowe, based on a story by Tom McGowan, undated; and *The AristoCats*, screenplay by Tom Rowe, undated, courtesy: Bruce Reitherman.

78 Ken Anderson, interviewed by Nancy Beiman, 1979, in Nancy Beiman, *Prepare to Board!* (Focal Press, 2007); Ken Anderson, interviewed by Robin Allan, May 10, 1985, unpublished; and Ken Anderson, interviewed by MICA Productions, ca. 1983, WDA.

79 Paul F. Anderson, *Jack of All Trades: Conversations with Disney Legend Ken Anderson* (Theme Park Press, 2017).

80 Frank Thomas and Ollie Johnston, interviewed by Michael Barrier, October 27, 1976, in *Walt's People: Vol. 17*, Didier Ghez, ed. (Theme Park Press, 2015).

81 Story Meeting on *The Aristocats*, December 28, 1966, WDA.

82 *The Aristocats*, Prod. 7192, April 10, 1967, courtesy: Wendy Greer.

83 Ken Anderson, *Robin Hood*, May 1, 1970, unpublished, courtesy: Wendy Greer; and Ken Anderson, interviewed by MICA Productions, ca. 1983, WDA.

84 Ken Anderson, interviewed about the making of *Robin Hood*, interviewer unknown, ca. 1973, courtesy: Bruce Reitherman; and John Culhane's animation seminar featuring Ken Anderson, July 18, 1973, recorded by Edward Summer, courtesy: Renee Russell.

85 Ken Anderson, "Walt Disney Productions' All Cartoon Feature *Robin Hood*," in *The Official Bulletin of IATSE*, Winter 1973–74; and Ken Anderson, interviewed about the making of *Robin Hood*, interviewer unknown, ca. 1973, courtesy: Bruce Reitherman.

86 *Hiawatha* portfolio by Ken Anderson, courtesy: Van Eaton Galleries; and *Hiawatha*, Breakdown by Ed Coffey, May 22, 1969, courtesy: Wendy Greer.

87 Letter from Holling C. Holling to his mother, June 6, 1944, in *Walt's People: Vol. 14*, Didier Ghez, ed. (Theme Park Press, 2014).

88 Charles Solomon, *The Disney That Never Was* (Hyperion, 1995).

89 Memo from Ken Peterson to Ron Miller, July 20, 1971, Subject: "Children of the World," courtesy: Wendy Greer.

90 John Culhane's animation seminar featuring Ken Anderson, July 18, 1973, recorded by Edward Summer, courtesy: Renee Russell.

91 Miscellaneous *Catfish Bend* outlines and treatments from December 23, 1976, to December 8, 1977, courtesy: Wendy Greer; and correspondence with Ben Lucien Burman at Tulane University Special Collections: Ben Lucien and Alice Caddy Burman papers, 1927–1984.

92 Story Conference Notes, *Catfish Bend*, July 31, 1978, ARL.

93 Story Conference Notes, *Catfish Bend*, August 8 and August 23, 1978, ARL.

94 Story Meeting Notes, *Mickey Mouse Feature*, November 21, 1978, present: Woolie Reitherman, Mel Shaw, Phil May, and Cal Howard, courtesy: Bruce Reitherman.

95 *Proposed Mickey Mouse Feature*, November 26, 1979, courtesy: Bruce Reitherman.

96 Frank Thomas, interviewed by Bob Thomas, September 15th, 1976, in *Walt's People: Vol. 10*, Didier Ghez, ed. (Theme Park Press, 2017).

97 *#2503 The Rescuers—Treatment*, January 2, 1963, courtesy: Bruce Reitherman; and photographs of April 1964 *The Rescuers* storyboards, Walt Disney Photo Library.

98 Otto Englander, *Rough Format Suggestion for Animated Feature*, August 21, 1968, WDA.

99 Miscellaneous *The Rescuers* outlines and treatments from January 24, 1972 to February 20, 1973, courtesy: Wendy Greer.

100 Woolie Reitherman, interviewed by MICA Productions, ca. 1983, WDA.

[101] Burny Mattinson, interviewed by Didier Ghez, May 28, 2017, unpublished.

[102] Ken Anderson, interviewed by MICA Productions, ca. 1983, WDA.

[103] Miscellaneous *Scruffy* outlines, treatments, and story meeting notes from October 15, 1971 to April 19, 1974, courtesy: Wendy Greer; and *Characters [for] Scruffy* by Ken Anderson, August 2, 1975, WDA. *Scruffy* was first conceived as a live-action project, according to a memo from A. J. Carothers to Bill Dover, February 21, 1964; a treatment by William Raynor and Myles Wilde, March 12, 1969; and a memo from director Bob Stevenson to Bill Walsh, August 24, 1970. A memo from Woolie Reitherman to Bill Anderson, November 2, 1971, shows that by that date the project had morphed into a proposed animated feature, WDA.

[104] Ken Anderson, interviewed by John Culhane, 1976, in *Walt's People: Vol. 17*, Didier Ghez, ed. (Theme Park Press, 2015).

[105] Memo from Bob Aller to Ken Anderson, February 2, 1976, Subject: *Concept for a Film on Energy*, courtesy: Wendy Greer; and Ken Anderson, interviewed by John Culhane, 1976, in *Walt's People: Vol. 17*, Didier Ghez, ed. (Theme Park Press, 2015).

[106] Max Lark, "For Pete's Sake: The Long Road to *Pete's Dragon*," August 16, 2016, https://d23.com/for-petes-sake-the-long-road-to-petes-dragon/.

[107] Bob Thomas, "Disney Movie Stars Animated Dragon," in *The Bryan Eagle*, December 29, 1977.

[108] Ken Anderson, interviewed by MICA Productions, ca. 1983, WDA.

[109] Tony Baxter, interviewed by Didier Ghez, May 31, 1995, in *Walt's People: Vol. 13*, Didier Ghez, ed. (Theme Park Press, 2013).

[110] Drawings for "*M. S. Wizard*" from the collection of Andreas Deja; and Bill Cotter, *The Wonderful World of Disney Television, A Complete History*, "Appendix N: The Shows that Never Were," unpublished, courtesy: Bill Cotter.

[111] "Dumbo's Circus" and "Gummi Bears" original drawings, Ken Anderson *[Wuzzles]—A Background Suggestion*, September 11, 1984; and Ken Anderson, *Hamster Hamlet—Outline of Story*, October 14, 1986, courtesy: Wendy Greer.

[112] Letter from Joseph B. McHugh (WED) to Ken Anderson, January 22, 1985, courtesy: Wendy Greer.

[113] Don Bluth, "Wizards of the Biz—Ken Anderson," in *Don Bluth's ToonTalk*, January 2001.

[114] Ted Kierscey, interviewed by Didier Ghez, June 1 and June 2, 2001, in *Walt's People: Vol. 16*, Didier Ghez, ed. (Theme Park Press, 2015).

[115] Mel Shaw, *Animator on Horseback* (Theme Park Press, 2016).

[116] Mel Shaw, interviewed by Paul F. Anderson, March 15, 1994, in *Walt's People: Vol. 12*, Didier Ghez, ed. (Xlibris, 2012).

[117] Mel Shaw, *Animator on Horseback* (Theme Park Press, 2016).

[118] Mel Shaw, interviewed by Michael Barrier, October 11, 1988, unpublished.

[119] Mel Shaw, *Animator on Horseback* (Theme Park Press, 2016).

[120] Mel Shaw, interviewed by Michael Barrier, October 11, 1988, unpublished.

[121] Mel Shaw, interviewed by Michael Barrier, October 11, 1988, unpublished; and Mel Shaw, interviewed by Paul F. Anderson, March 15, 1994, in *Walt's People: Vol. 12*, Didier Ghez, ed. (Xlibris, 2012).

[122] Mel Shaw, interviewed by Paul F. Anderson, March 15, 1994, in *Walt's People: Vol. 12*, Didier Ghez, ed. (Xlibris, 2012).

[123] Mel Shaw, interviewed by Paul F. Anderson, March 15, 1994, in *Walt's People: Vol. 12*, Didier Ghez, ed. (Xlibris, 2012).

[124] J. B. Kaufman and Russell Merritt, *Walt Disney's Silly Symphonies: A Companion to the Classic Cartoon Series* (Disney Editions, 2016).

[125] Mel Shaw's personnel record, courtesy: Michael Barrier.

[126] *Donald Munchausen*, Preliminary Outline No. 36, Story No. M-582P, April 15, 1938; and story meeting notes, April 7, 1938, ARL.

[127] In his 1938 Daily Reports, on February 3, executive Bill Garity shows the head of the Story Research Department, John Rose, preparing to stock up on records, which seems like a clear indication that things were evolving toward the idea of a feature, WDA; and according to Disney historian J. B. Kaufman, in *The Sorcerer's Apprentice* scene instruction sheet that was issued to Marvin Woodward for scene 92, on March 21, 1938, we read: "The exact manner of ending our scene will depend on the decision as to how the various pictures in the Concert Feature are to be connected."

[128] Bob Carr, "Music Titles—Complete, Combined List," October 19, 1940, collection of the author.

[129] According to Michael Barrier, "Disney's Standard Daily Journal, 1938, shows a 'Dance of the Fauns' meeting on 25 April, an 'Afternoon of the Faun' meeting on 9 June, and an entry on May 24 that read 'Perce-Schwartzman [Mel Shaw]—Faun,'" email from Michael Barrier to Didier Ghez, July 12, 2017; Leigh Harline working with Mel Shaw on "Cydalise Suite": Mel Shaw, interviewed by Paul F. Anderson, March 15, 1994, in *Walt's People: Vol. 12*, Didier Ghez, ed. (Xlibris, 2012).

[130] Mel Shaw, *Animator on Horseback* (Theme Park Press, 2016). In a letter to animation historian Michael Barrier, dated April 13, 1989, Mel explained: "When I made my storyboard for the 'Flight of the Bumblebee' I did it in full color (watercolor). At that time there was no *Fantasia*. It was a classic music short. After my 1st meeting with Walt we discussed the possibilities of doing a full concert program including this subject as one segment . . ." Courtesy: Michael Barrier.

[131] Memo from Bill Garity to Those Concerned, June 20, 1938, Subject: New Method of Presenting Story Sketches, collection of the author.

[132] Bill Garity Daily Report, 1938, WDA.

[133] Michael Barrier, *Hollywood Cartoons—American Animation in Its Golden Age* (Oxford University Press, 1999); and memo from Alma Fenter to Herb Lamb, January 6, 1939, Subject: Concert Feature, WDA.

[134] The first known story meeting notes document from *Bambi* in which Mel Shaw is listed as attending is dated September 15, 1938, WDA.

[135] Mel Shaw, *Animator on Horseback* (Theme Park Press, 2016).

[136] Mel Shaw, *Animator on Horseback* (Theme Park Press, 2016).

[137] Mel Shaw, *Animator on Horseback* (Theme Park Press, 2016).

[138] Mel Shaw, interviewed by Paul F. Anderson, March 15, 1994, in *Walt's People: Vol. 12*, Didier Ghez, ed. (Xlibris, 2012).

[139] Mel Shaw, interviewed by Paul F. Anderson, March 15, 1994, in *Walt's People: Vol. 12*, Didier Ghez, ed. (Xlibris, 2012). According to Walt Disney's desk diary, Mel Shaw was already attending story meetings on *Wind in the Willows* as early as September 23, 1940, courtesy: Michael Barrier.

[140] Mel Shaw, *Animator on Horseback* (Theme Park Press, 2016).

[141] *Report of Stories in Progress*, ca. 1943, in Ralph Parker folder, WD Corresp. Inter Office, 1938–1944, N-Q, WDA.

[142] Mel Shaw, *Animator on Horseback* (Theme Park Press, 2016).

[143] Neal Gabler, *Walt Disney—The Triumph of the American Imagination* (Knopf, 2006).

[144] Mel Shaw, interviewed by Paul F. Anderson, March 15, 1994, in *Walt's People: Vol. 12*, Didier Ghez, ed. (Xlibris, 2012).

[145] Mel Shaw, interviewed by Paul F. Anderson, March 15, 1994, in *Walt's People: Vol. 12*, Didier Ghez, ed. (Xlibris, 2012).

[146] Mel Shaw, interviewed by Paul F. Anderson, March 15, 1994, in *Walt's People: Vol. 12*, Didier Ghez, ed. (Xlibris, 2012).

[147] Mel Shaw, interviewed by Paul F. Anderson, March 15, 1994, in *Walt's People: Vol. 12*, Didier Ghez, ed. (Xlibris, 2012).

[148] Mel Shaw, *Animator on Horseback* (Theme Park Press, 2016).

[149] Mel Shaw, interviewed by Paul F. Anderson, March 15, 1994, in *Walt's People: Vol. 12*, Didier Ghez, ed. (Xlibris, 2012). Around the same time, in 1973, at the request of Disney producer Harry Tytle, Mel Shaw developed some storyboards for a live-action feature-length remake of *The Country Cousin* known as *The Tale of Two Mice* (later renamed *The Tale of a Mouse*). The unlikely project never made it to the screen. For more information about *The Tale of a Mouse* (illustrated with a large amount of pastels by Mel Shaw), check Russell Schroeder, *Disney's Lost Chords 2* (Voigt Publications, 2008).

[150] John Culhane, "Man on the Move: Ron Miller," 1978, unpublished, courtesy: Hind Culhane.

151 Mel Shaw, interviewed by Paul F. Anderson, March 15, 1994, in *Walt's People: Vol. 12*, Didier Ghez, ed. (Xlibris, 2012); and Mel Shaw, *The Fox and the Hounds* [sic], rough outline, August 6, 1974, courtesy: Bruce Reitherman.

152 Mel Shaw, *Animator on Horseback* (Theme Park Press, 2016). According to an undated press release titled *The Small One—Production Information* (WDA): "*The Small One*, written by Charles Tazewell, was first published in 1974 and quickly became a favorite Christmas story . . . In 1960, rights to the book were bought by Walt Disney, but the property was never developed. Then, in 1973, Disney story artist Pete Young rediscovered the book in the studio library and fell in love with it. He worked nearly a year, on his own time at home, to develop a story line suitable for an animated film."

153 Burny Mattinson, interviewed by Didier Ghez, May 28, 2017, unpublished.

154 Memo from Don Duckwall to Ron Miller, October 17, 1975, Subject: Long Range Animation Schedule, courtesy: Don Hahn.

155 Memo from Chris Vogler to Charlie Fink, June 24, 1987, Subject: *The Little Broomstick*, ARL.

156 Mike Peraza, interviewed by Didier Ghez, January 23, 2013, in *Walt's People: Vol. 15*, Didier Ghez, ed. (Theme Park Press, 2014).

157 According to a memo from Chris Vogler to Charlie Fink, June 24, 1987, summarizing the efforts to develop the property, the first character sketches and outline were presented on January 17, 1979, and the last video slide presentation took place on June 27, 1980. Five years later, on June 25, 1985, artist Tad Stones submitted a treatment for *The Nethermoon Rose* adapted from *The Little Broomstick* and "Little Broomstick," Screening for the Animation Department, April 9, 1979, WDA.

158 Burny Mattinson, interviewed by Didier Ghez, September 2 and 11, 2008, in *Walt's People: Vol. 12*, Didier Ghez, ed. (Xlibris, 2012). Astonishingly, the title *Musicana* already appeared in a list of title ideas drafted by story artist Joe Grant in the mid-1940s for the movie which became *Make Mine Music*. "Sketchbook Titles," undated memo, courtesy: Jennifer Grant Castrup.

159 James A. Johnson, *Neo Fantasia*, October 24, 1969, courtesy: Bruce Reitherman.

160 *Musicana*, Prod. #0216, October 20, 1980.

161 Meeting with Woolie and Mel, June 25, 1980, courtesy: Bruce Reitherman.

162 Mel Shaw, *Chantecler—Notes and Simplified Outline*, February 11, 1981, ARL; and *The White Blackbird*, sketches and outline, undated, courtesy: Rick Shaw and Melissa Couch-Deranleau.

163 *Basil of Baker Street*, Character Ideas, May 18, 1981, courtesy: Rick Shaw and Melissa Couch-Deranleau; and *Basil of Baker Street*, Story Meeting Notes, June 16, 1981, ARL.

164 *The Books of the Weather Bird Press, Vance Gerry Interviewed by Rebecca Ziegler*, 1992, Oral History Program, University of California, Los Angeles.

165 Mel Shaw, *Animator on Horseback* (Theme Park Press, 2016).

166 Hans Bacher, interviewed by Didier Ghez, March 12, 2017, unpublished.

167 Mel Shaw, *Animator on Horseback* (Theme Park Press, 2016).

168 Mel Shaw, *Animator on Horseback* (Theme Park Press, 2016).

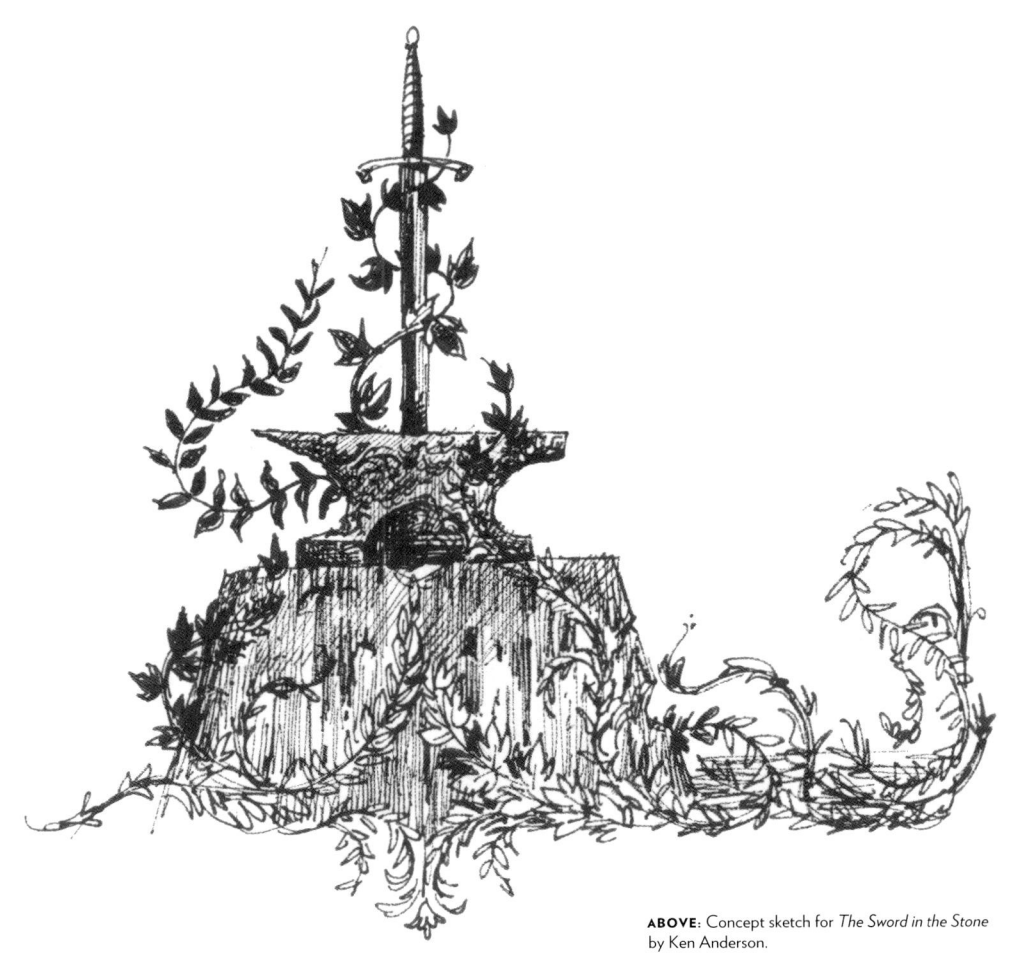

ABOVE: Concept sketch for *The Sword in the Stone* by Ken Anderson.

INDEX

Page numbers in italics indicate images.

A

Adams, John Quincy, 24
The Adventures of Ichabod and Mr. Toad, 134, *135*, *154–55*
Alexander, Lloyd, 138
Algar, Jimmy, 27
Alguire, Danny, 13
Alice in Wonderland, *134*
Allen, Bob, 137
Allen-Shaw Associates, 137
Andersen, Hans Christian, 141
Anderson, Bill, 14, 44, 46
Anderson, Ken
   birth and childhood of, 24
   education of, 25
   at Disney, 10, 12, 14, 16, 19, 24, 25–44, 46–49, 51–54
   death of, 54
   caricature of, *16*
   personality of, 35–36, 54
   photographs of, *27*, *33*, *36*, *40*, *44*, *46*, *48*
   work of, *2*, *6*, *9*, *11*, *15*, *17*, *18*, *23*, *25*, *26*, *31*, *32*, *34–35*, *38*, *41*, *42*, *43*, *45*, *47*, *49*, *50*, *53*, *54–123*, *205*, *208*
Anderson, Luther, 24
Anderson, Polly, 25
Anderson, Roberta, 24
Anderson, Ruth, 24
Anthony Adverse, 29
Aragon, Ray, 34–35
The Aristocats, 4, 6, 10, 13, 14, *15*, 23, 24, 43–44, 46, *82–89*
Armstrong, Louis, 141, 169
Art Students League, 127, 128
Aurora Productions, 19

B

Babbitt, Art, 16
Bacher, Hans, 146
Baer, Dale, 14
Bain, Sarah, 24
Bambi, 4, *5*, 33, 37, 128, *133*, 134, 135, *150–53*
Bambi's Children, *133*, 135
Barker, Tim, *21*
Barks, Carl, 131
Basil of Baker Street, 143
Baum, L. Frank, 36
Baxter, Tony, 53
Beauty and the Beast, 146–47, *148*, *189–94*
Bedknobs and Broomsticks, *90–91*
Beiman, Nancy, 17, *21*
Berman, Ted, 140
Bird, Brad, 17, *21*, 48
The Black Cauldron, 10, 20, 48, 51, 138, 139, 140, 145, *176–81*
Blair, Lee, 42
Blair, Mary, 32
Blank, Dorothy Ann, 34
Bluth, Don, 14, 19, *20*, 54
Böcklin, Arnold, 30
Burman, Ben Lucien, *48*

C

California Institute of the Arts (CalArts), 16–17, 19, 20, 21
Canfield, Myrt, *20*
Carroll, Lewis, 134
Cartwright, Randy, *20*, 48
Catfish Bend, 48, *49*, 51, 52, *112–15*, *144–45*
Cedeno, Mike, *21*
Chanticleer, 36–37, *38*, 39, *60–61*, 143, *173–75*
Chouinard Art Institute, 16
The Chronicles of Prydain, 138
Cinderella, 33, *56–57*
Clark, Les, 130
Clements, Ron, *20*, 143
Clemmons, Larry, 12, 44, *46*, 47, 49, 51
Cook, Lorna Pomeroy, *20*
Couch, Chuck, 131
Couffer, Jack, 54
Courtland, Jerome, 52
Culhane, John, 51, 138
Cutting, Jack, 31

D

DaGradi, Don, 34–35, 44
Davis, Marc, 16, 36, 38, 39, 40, 51, *134*
de Musset, Alfred, 143
Disney, Roy, 27, 135–36
Disney, Walt, 24
   art liked by, 27, 29, 31–32, 132
   death of, 10, 44
   decisions made by, 13, 14, 16, 26–27, 29, 33, 36, 40–41, 42, 130–31, 132–33, 135, 137
   quotations from, 26, 28–29, 30, 38, 39, 42, 132, 134
   technology and, 27
The Disney Channel, 54
Disneyland (theme park), 33, 40, 41, 53–54
"Disneyland" (TV show), 36, 52, 137
Disney's Adventures of the Gummi Bears, 54, 122, 123
Donald Munchausen, *130*, 131
Don Quixote, 134
Drake, George, 25, 26, 28
Dukas, Paul, 131
Dumbo, 134
Dumbo's Circus, 54

E

Eisner, Michael, 20, 146
Engel, Jules, 16, 17
Englander, Otto, 34, 36, 43, 46, 49
EPCOT, 51, 54

F

Fallberg, Carl, 133, *134*
Fantasia, 30, 31, 131–32, 135, 140–41, *149*
Ferguson, Norm, 34
Field, S. S., 52
Finch, Christopher, 10
Fitzgerald, Ella, 141, 169
Fitzpatrick, Robert, 16–17
Foster, Bob, 14
The Fox and the Hound, 20, 48, 138, *139*, 140, 146, *156–60*
Frost, A. B., 135

G

Gallico, Paul, 51
Garbo, Greta, 25
Garity, Bill, 27, 132
Gaskill, Andy, *20*
Gerry, Vance, 23, 24, 44, 143
Gessell, Andrea, 10
The Goddess of Spring, 26
Goldman, Gary, 14, 19, *20*
Gollub, Moe, 135
Gombert, Ed, *20*
Gonzales, Allan, 14
Grahame, Kenneth, 134
Grant, Joe, 29, 34
The Great Mouse Detective, *143*, 146, *182–88*
Griffith, Don, 12
Guedel, Heidi, *20*
Guimard, Hector, 30

H

Hahn, Don, 8–9, 146, 148
Haley, Alex, 54
Hamster Hamlet, 54
Hand, Dave, 131, 132, 133
Hannah, Jack, 16, 26
Harline, Leigh, 131
Harman, Hugh, 129, 131, 133, 136
Harman-Ising, 129–31, 133
Harris, Joel Chandler, 135
Haskett, Dan, *20*
Hellmich, Fred, 14
The Hero from Otherwhere, 139, *163–65*
Hiawatha, 47
Hibler, Winston, 44
Holling, Holling C., 47
Hoover, Herbert, 24
Huemer, Dick, 37
Hugh Harman Productions, 136
Hulett, Steve, 48
Hurrell, Phyllis, 39

I

The Invisible Man, 25
Ising, Rudy, 129, 131, 133
Ising, Sid, 129
Iwerks, Ub, 39

J

Jackson, Wilfred, 29, 32
Jenkins, Dorothy, 128
Johnson, Jimmy, 141
Johnston, Ollie, 12, 14, 20, 26, 36, 40, 42, 44, *46*, 49, 138, 140
Juliano, Emily, *20*
The Jungle Book, 11, 12, 13, 24, 42, 43, 44, *46*, 73–81

K

Kahl, Milt, 12, 14, 26, 39, 40, 41, 42, *46*, 51, 138
Kamen, Kay, 137
Katzenberg, Jeffrey, 20, 146, 148
Keane, Glen, *20*
Kelsey, Dick, 47
Kierscey, Ted, 127
King Arthur, 136
Kinney, Jack, 34
Kroyer, Bill, *20*

L

La Gatta, John, 25
Langley, Noel, 52
Lanzisero, Joe, *21*
Lark, Max, 52
Larson, Eric, 12, 14, 16, *20*
Lasseter, John, 17, *21*
Lefler, Doug, *21*
The Lion King, *147*, 148, *195–200*
The Little Broomstick, 140, *166–68*
The Little Mermaid, 11
The Little Prince, 136
London, Jack, 24
The Look of Things, 137
Los Angeles Conservatory of Music, 16
Lounsbery, John, 10, 12, 14

Lucas, Dick, 44
Luske, Ham, 30, *39*

M

Mackendrick, Alexander "Sandy," 16
Majolie, Bianca, 34, 37
Make Mine Music, 33
Marmorstein, Malcolm, 52
Mattinson, Burny, 14, 51, 125, 138, 140
McGowan, Tom, 43
Meador, Josh, 141
Merbabies, *128–29*, 131
MGM, 25, 36, 54, 130, 133
Michener, Dave, 14, *46*, 48
Mickey's Polo Team, 26
Miller, Diane Disney, 10, 137
Miller, Jack, 42
Miller, Ron, 10, 14, 48, 49, 51, 52, 137, 138, 140, 143
Miller, Seton I., 52
Milne, A. A., 42
Morey, Larry, 134
Morris, Bruce, *21*
Musicana, *13*, *140–41*, 142–43, *169–72*
Musker, John, 17, *21*, 143

N

Nielsen, Kay, 142
Norman, Floyd, 35

O

O'Connor, Ken, *21*, 30
One Hundred and One Dalmatians, 12, 39–40, 41, 51
Orff, Carl, 138
Otis Art Institute, 128
Oz, 36

P

Pacific Title, 129
The Painted Veil, 25
Pearce, Perce, 131, 133
Peet, Bill, 33, 36, *39*, 41
Penguin Island, 37

Peraza, Mike, 140
Peregoy, Walt, 40
Peri, Don, 10
Perkins, Al, 37, 38
Peter Pan, *34*, *58–59*
Peterson, Ken, 38, 40
Pete's Dragon, 19, 52, *53*, *122*
Pierné, Gabriel, 131
Pinocchio, 27, *28–29*, 30
Pomeroy, John, 19, *20*
Powell, Mel, 16

R

The Rainbow Road to Oz, 37
Rees, Jerry, 17, *21*
Rees, Terry, *21*
Reitherman, Wolfgang "Woolie," 12, *13*, 14, 19, 20, *39*, 44, *46*, 47, 48, 49, 127, 138, 139, 140, 141, 143
The Rescuers, *9*, 10, 13, *18*, 19, 24, 49, *50*, 51, *116–21*, 127, *138*
Return to Oz, 36
Reynard the Fox, *34–35*, 37, 46
Richard Purdum Productions, 146
Rimsky-Korsakov, Nikolai, 131, 141
Rinaldi, Joe, 36, 49
Robin Hood, *2*, 4, 10, *11*, 13, 14, *45*, 46, *47*, 49, *92–108*, 208
Roosevelt, Theodore, 24
Rostand, Edmond, 36, 143
Rowe, Tom, 43
Ryman, Herb, 54

S

Sabin, Harry, *21*
Salten, Felix, 135
Saludos Amigos, 31
Sanders, George, 42
Schlesinger, Leon, 129
Schwartzman, Lillian and Theodore, 127
Scott, Retta, *126*, 127
Scruffy, 51, *109–11*
Searle, Ronald, 40
Sears, Ted, 28, 37, 38

Selick, Henry, 20, *21*
Sharp, Margery, 49
Shaw, Evan K., 137
Shaw, Mel
  birth and childhood of, 127–28
  education of, 128
  early career of, 129–31
  at Disney, 10, 14, 48, 127, 131–36, 137–43, 146–48
  other ventures of, 136–37
  death of, 148
  autobiography of, 10, 127
  caricature of, *134*
  name change of, 127
  photographs of, *126*, *139*, *145*, *148*
  work of, *5*, *13*, *16*, *20*, *128–29*, *130*, *132*, *133*, *134*, *135*, *136*, *140*, *141*, *143*, *144–45*, *147*, *148–200*
Shaw Associates, 137
Sibelius, Jean, 141
Sleeping Beauty, 14, 24, *34–36*, 39
The Small One, 139, *161–62*
Smith, David R., 36
Snow White and the Seven Dwarfs, 26, 27, 28, 29–30, *55*, 131
Song of the South, *32*, 33, 34, 46, *136*
The Sorcerer's Apprentice, 131
Stallings, George, 135
Stevens, Art, 140
Stewart, Jim, 19
Stewart, Mary, 140
Sumac, Yma, 141
The Sword in the Stone, 39, 40, *41*, 42, *62–67*, 205

T

Terrazas, Ernie, 31
Thomas, Bob, 52, 138
Thomas, Frank, 12, 13, 14, 20, 26, 40, *46*, 49, 139, 140
Thompson, Brett, *21*
The Three Caballeros, *31*, 32
Three Little Wolves, 26
Three Orphan Kittens, 26, 28
Toland, Gregg, 32

Tracy, Don, 14
Treasure Island, 34
Tytle, Harry, 43, 137

U
The Ugly Dachshund, 42
Uncle Remus, 135–36
United Artists, 32

V
Van Citters, Darrell, 17, *21*

W
Walker, Card, 14, 46, 49
Walsh, Bill, 44
Walt Disney Imagineering, 53
Way, Ethel, 24
Webb, Kaye, 40
WED Enterprises, 53, 54
Welles, Orson, 136
Wells, Frank, 20, 146
Welsh, William P., 30
The White Blackbird, 143
Williams, Jay, 139
Williams, Roy, 133
Wind in the Willows, 134, *135*, 154–55
Winnie the Pooh, 42, 43, 68–72
Wizards, 54, *122*
Wonderful World of Disney magazine, 17, 42
Wong, Tyrus, 128
Woollcott, Alexander, 133
The Wuzzles, 54

Y
Young, Cy, 27
Young, Pete, 14

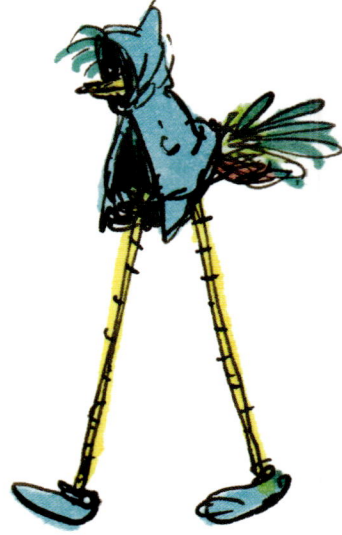

ABOVE: Character design for *Robin Hood* by Ken Anderson.